# CAREER OPPORTUNITIES IN LAW ENFORCEMENT, SECURITY, AND PROTECTIVE SERVICES

## SECOND EDITION

Susan Echaore-McDavid

Checkmark Books®
*An imprint of Facts On File, Inc.*

**Career Opportunities in Law Enforcement, Security, and Protective Services, Second Edition**

Copyright © 2006 by Susan Echaore-McDavid

Checkmark Books
An imprint of Facts On File, Inc.
132 West 31st Street
New York NY 10001

**Library of Congress Cataloging-in-Publication Data**

Echaore-McDavid, Susan.
    Career opportunities in law enforcement, security, and protective services/Susan Echaore-McDavid.—2nd ed.
        p. cm.
    Includes bibliographical references and index.
    ISBN 0-8160-6070-3 (hc: alk. paper)—ISBN 0-8160-6071-1 (pbk.)
    1. Law enforcement—Vocational guidance—United States. 2. Police—Vocational guidance—United States.
    3. Private security services—Vocational guidance—United States. 4. Safety engineers—Vocational guidance—
    United States. I. Title.
    HV8143.E34 2005
    363.2'023'73—dc22                                                2005040520

Checkmark Books are available at special discounts when purchased in bulk quantities for businesses, associations, institutions, or sales promotions. Please call our Special Sales Department in New York at (212) 967-8800 or (800) 322-8755.

You can find Facts On File on the World Wide Web at http://www.factsonfile.com

Cover design by Cathy Rincon

Printed in the United States of America

VB Hermitage 10 9 8 7 6 5 4 3 2 1

This book is printed on acid-free paper.

*To Richard McDavid and to Frances D. Echaore—*
*two wonderful people who give me much inspiration, joy, and love!*

# CONTENTS

# ACKNOWLEDGMENTS

I could not have completed this second edition of *Career Opportunities in Law Enforcement, Security, and Protective Services* without the help of many people and organizations. In particular, I would like to thank the following people who helped me with various occupations for this edition: Michael Drapkin, National Treasury Employees Union; John Firman, Director of Research, International Association of Chiefs of Police; Lieutenant William Kitzerow, Traffic Services Section, Fairfax Police Department, Fairfax, Virginia; John Murray, National Park Service Ranger; Donald P. Sims, Special Agent in Charge, U.S. Environmental Protection Agency, Criminal Investigation Division, Portland Area Office; and Stephanie Wallace, Surveillance Manager, American Casino and Entertainment Properties, LLC, Las Vegas, Nevada.

I would also like to say thanks to Richard McDavid, my patient and generous husband, for checking my grammar and convoluted sentence structures before the words headed over to the wonderful folks at Facts On File, Inc. Thank you, Sarah Fogarty and Vanessa Nittoli, and especially my many thanks and appreciation to my editor James Chambers.

And once again, I want to thank the following people and organizations who helped me learn about the various occupations in this book while I was writing the first edition.

American Academy of Forensic Sciences; American Industrial Hygiene Association; American Society for Industrial Security; Charlottesville-Albemarle Rescue Squad, Inc.

Sgt. Jack Adkins, Bomb Squad Commander, Big Ben Bomb Squad, Tallahassee Police Department; Alex Arends, Crime Prevention Association of Michigan; David Arndt, Education Assistant, International Association of Fire Fighters; Patrick Barker, WALMART Investigation Task Force; Jon Berryhill, Berryhill Computer Forensics.

Jeanne Choy-Allen, Special Agent, Drug Enforcement Administration; Diane L. Cowan, Certified Legal Investigator; Jamey Crandall, Personnel Administrator, Nebraska Game and Parks; Leroy Dal Porto, Special-Agent-in-Charge, San Francisco Field Office, Secret Service; Joseph N. Dassaro, VP, Local 1613-San Diego, National Border Patrol Council; Dr. Edmund R. Donoghue, Chief Medical Examiner of Cook County, Illinois; Jerry Elder, VP, Airline Dispatchers Federation.

Rodney Eldridge, Loss Prevention Training Specialist, TJ Maxx; Tammy Empson, American Public Works Association; Janet Fox, Special Agent, Federal Bureau of Investigation; Amy Geffen, Director of Professional Development, Risk and Insurance Management Society; Ed German, Special Agent, United States Army Criminal Investigation Laboratory.

Robert Heard, President, California Association of Polygraph Examiners; Lt. Tom Honan, Charleston County Sheriff's Office, South Carolina; Morgan Hurley, Technical Director, Society of Fire Protection Engineers; Rhonda A. Jackson, Building Officials and Code Administrators International; M. E. Kabay, Ph.D., CISSP, Director of Education, ICSA, Inc.; Ken Kerle, Managing Editor, American Jail Association; Jim King, International Association of Personal Protection Agents; Chris Krall, CIRSA, Inc.; Robert E. Kramer, Investigator, Cedar Falls Police Department, Iowa; Mike Lane, Corporate Investigative Services; Donald C. Lhotka, CSP (Ret.), American Society of Safety Engineers.

Sgt. Steve Lindley, Anderson County Sheriff's Office, South Carolina; Ning Ludovico, U.S. Postal Inspection Service; Doug McDavid, Consultant, IBM Global Services; Mary McKendree, Manager, Assessment and Continuing Education, American Society of Clinical Pathologists; Gary Martin, North American Wildlife Enforcement Officers Association; Sgt. Jonathan B. Mills, Calistoga Police Department, California; Ron Morris, President, Sheffield School of Aeronautics; Jeff Obrecht, Information Officer, Services Division, Wyoming Game and Fish Department; Captain Ken R. Pence, Metro Nashville Police.

Detective Carl Rackley and Bubba, Cedar Park Police Department, Williamson County, Texas; Joseph Remigio, Special Agent, Deputy U.S. Marshal; Selwyn Russell, SIGMOD, Association for Computing Machinery; Glenn Sanders, Illinois Conservation Police; WCO John G. Smith, Pennsylvania Game Commission; Anthony W. Stoll, Master Indiana Conservation Officer, Indiana Conservation Officers Organization, VP.

Ralph Thomas, Director, National Association of Investigative Specialists, Inc.; Jim Watson, National Secretary, North American Police Work Dog Association; Emily Will, Questioned Documents Expert; Steve Wolin, Society of Fire Protection Engineers; Dawn Wright, Air Traffic Controller, Otis ANGB (Air National Guard Base), Massachusetts; Sgt. Brian Wunderlich, Douglas Co. Sheriff's Office, Castle Rock, Colorado.

# HOW TO USE THIS BOOK

In *Career Opportunities in Law Enforcement, Security, and Protective Services,* you will learn about 86 occupations in the areas of law enforcement, forensics, corrections, security, emergency services, code enforcement, and safety. Perhaps after reading some, or all, of the job profiles, you will find your future career.

Protective service jobs are often portrayed in the movies, TV shows, books, and media as exciting, intriguing, and yes, even dangerous. But how much of what you see or read is fictitious, and how much is real? What is a job—as a police officer, for example—really like? What requirements do you need to be eligible for a job? What are your chances of getting a job? What kind of career can you have? Those are some of the questions that are answered in this book.

## Sources of Information

The information for *Career Opportunities in Law Enforcement, Security, and Protective Services* comes from many different sources. They include:

- books about the different professions
- professional textbooks, handbooks, and manuals
- articles from general newspapers and magazines as well as professional and trade periodicals
- brochures, pamphlets, and other written materials from professional associations, federal agencies, firms, academic programs and other organizations
- questionnaires answered by professional individuals as well as organizations
- interviews with professionals
- Web sites of law enforcement agencies, fire departments, federal agencies, professional associations, security firms, and other organizations.

## How This Book Is Organized

*Career Opportunities in Law Enforcement, Security, and Protective Services* is especially designed to be accessible to the reader. The 86 jobs are divided into 12 sections. A section may have between five to 16 job profiles, and the profiles are usually between two to three pages long. Each profile follows the same format so that you can read the job profiles or sections in any order you prefer.

The first two sections of the book describe police and criminal investigator jobs that can be found in local, state, and federal law enforcement agencies.

The third section describes forensic opportunities, while section four covers different types of private investigators. Section five details various public safety occupations, including a few in emergency medical services.

In section six, some jobs in physical security are discussed, followed by section seven, which presents profiles about several occupations that involve aviation safety and security. Section eight covers some occupations in the computer security field.

Section nine discusses several occupations in corrections, whereas sections 10 and 11 detail such occupations as compliance inspectors and code enforcers. Finally, in section 12, you will find a few profiles about occupations that address safety and security issues and measures in the workplace.

## The Job Profiles

Each job profile gives you basic information about one of 86 protective service careers. Each entry starts with *Career Profile,* a summary of a job's major duties, salary, job outlook, and promotion possibilities. In addition, this section provides a brief description of requirements that are needed to be eligible for a job. *Career Ladder* is a visual presentation of a typical career path, showing what positions lead to and stem from the job being profiled.

The rest of the job profile is a narrative description that is divided into the following parts:

- *Position Description* details a job's major responsibilities and working conditions; with some positions, duties may vary depending on the type of employers.
- *Salaries* presents a general idea of the kind of wages that workers may earn.
- *Employment Prospects* describes employers and the job outlook for today as well as for the future.
- *Advancement Prospects* discusses promotional opportunities, and whenever possible, alternative career paths.
- *Education and Training* describes educational and training prerequisistes needed to apply for a job, as well as training programs that recruits must successfully complete.
- *Special Requirements* lists any professional license, certification, or registration that may be required.
- *Experience, Skills, and Personality Traits* generally covers the job requirements needed for entry-level positions. It also discusses some employability skills that employers desire in candidates. In addition, this section describes

some personality traits that successful professionals have in common.

- *Unions and Associations* provides the names of some professional associations and other organizations that professionals are eligible to join.
- *Tips for Entry* presents advice for finding jobs; suggestions for enhancing your employability and chances for promotions; and ways to find out more information on the Internet.

## The Appendixes

At the end of the book are six appendixes that provide additional information about the various professions described in *Career Opportunities in Law Enforcement, Security, and Protective Services.*

You can learn about resources for academic programs, technical training, and professional certification programs for various occupations. You can also find contact information for professional associations, state private investigator licensing agencies, and federal agencies. In addition, you can read about resources on the World Wide Web that may give you further information about various occupations in this book. Furthermore, a glossary—which defines some of the words used in this book—and a bibliography are included at the back of the book.

## The Constantly Changing World Wide Web

Resources on the Internet are provided throughout the book so that you can learn more on your own about the occupations that interest you. All the Web sites were accessible as the book was being written. Keep in mind that Web site owners sometimes change Web addresses or remove their sites completely. Many Web sites are continually being updated, thus a Web page to which you are referred may no longer be available. If you come across a URL that no longer works, you may still be able to find the new Web address by entering the name of the organization, individual, Web site, or Web page into a search engine.

## This Book Is Yours

*Career Opportunities in Law Enforcement, Security, and Protective Services* is your reference book. Use it to read about jobs you have often wondered about. Use it to learn about protective services that you never knew existed. Use it to start your search for the career of your dreams.

Good luck!

# INTRODUCTION

Think of jobs you would find in protective services. What are some of them?

More than likely, you thought of Police Officer, FBI Special Agent, and perhaps, Correctional Officer, Security Guard, and Firefighter. Those are jobs we most commonly think of as protective service occupations—and ones that will be described in this book.

There are many other types of protective service occupations, however. You can find protective service professionals working in both the public and private sectors. Many enforce laws, codes, standards, rules, or regulations as part of their jobs. Some conduct investigations into criminal activities, workplace accidents, or other matters. Other professionals develop or manage security or safety plans. Others guard individuals, property, premises, or other assets. Still other professionals provide rescue services in emergency situations; or monitor events, security procedures, or other types of situations to make sure everything is safe and secure. They perform many other duties and tasks that vary from job to job; but essentially all protective service professionals do this: in some manner, they provide for the safety and security of people, communities, organizations, businesses, and companies.

*Career Opportunities in Law Enforcement, Security, and Protective Services* covers 86 occupations in a variety of areas, including law enforcement, criminal investigations, forensic investigations, private investigations, physical security, security management, computer security, corrections, fire protection, emergency services, code enforcement, and safety. Many of the occupations that will be described are ones that we don't normally consider. For example, the following are also protective service jobs, which will be described in this book too: Police Detective, Crime Prevention Specialist, Crime Scene Technician, Polygraph Examiner, Financial Investigator, Locksmith, Fire Protection Engineer, Security Consultant, Bailiff, Probation Officer, Emergency Medical Technician, Food Safety Inspector, Environmental Health Officer, Plan Reviewer, Plumbing Inspector, Industrial Hygienist, and Air Traffic Controller.

## What's New in the Second Edition

Several new job profiles have been added to the second edition of *Career Opportunities in Law Enforcement, Security, and Protective Services*. In addition, all the original profiles have been updated with information about salaries, employment prospects, job requirements, and job duties. Furthermore, contact information and Web site addresses have been updated in the appendixes.

## Professional Characteristics

Those who enter the various protective service fields usually have high ethical and moral standards along with strong commitments to protect the general welfare of people and businesses. They generally are leaders who have positive attitudes and enjoy helping people. Typically they are reliable, self-motivated individuals who can work with little or no supervision, yet have the ability to work well with others. Protective service professionals are analytical, flexible, and can manage multiple tasks and issues. Most are faced with making decisions that may affect the safety and well-being of their lives and/or others. Furthermore, protective service professionals willingly take on the stress that comes with enforcing laws or regulations, inspecting sites for violations, monitoring potential problems, helping people in trouble, issuing citations for violations, taking criminals into custody, or any of the other more dangerous duties that they perform.

Those who choose to work in protective service fields are brave souls.

## Job Outlook

In general, job opportunities continue to be strong and favorable for qualified personnel in the protective services due to increased concern about crime and public safety as well as the need for compliance with governmental laws and regulations. In addition, the terrorist events of September 11, 2001, in the United States have contributed to the demand for stronger security measures.

Job growth varies with the different occupations in protective services. For example, the U.S. Bureau of Labor Statistics (an agency within the U.S. Department of Labor) reports that employment through 2012 is expected to grow:

- between 21 and 35 percent for police, detectives, correctional officers, security guards, gaming surveillance officers, private investigators, emergency medical technicians, and computer support specialists (which includes computer security specialists)
- between 10 and 20 percent for forensic science technicians, insurance investigators, probation officers, air traffic controllers, and occupational health and safety specialists

Many job openings will also be created as workers advance to higher positions, transfer to other occupations, retire, or leave the workforce for various reasons. Opportunities for federal government positions, such as air traffic controller, are also expected to increase in the next few years due to the large number of federal employees who will become eligible for retirement.

Keep in mind that employers generally create new jobs as their needs grow and expand and as long as funding is available. However, when the economy is in a downturn, employers hire fewer employees and sometimes lay off workers.

## Job Requirements

Minimum education and experience requirements vary with the different jobs as well as with the different employers. Professionals in the various protective service fields encourage young people to get life experiences and college educations before applying. In fact, to stay competitive with other job seekers and to enhance chances for promotions, college education is necessary.

As you read the different job descriptions in this book, you may notice that certain employability skills—communication, reading, writing, teamwork, and people skills—are emphasized again and again. Those skills are highly important to success in protective service careers. In addition, learning basic computer skills would be to your advantage as most, if not all, professionals use computers for routine tasks, such as report writing, record keeping, and searching databases.

## The Selection Process

Years ago, to get a job you merely had to complete a job application and pass one or more job interviews. Usually, you learned whether you got a job in a day or two, or within one or two weeks. These days, the selection process is more complex and can be rather long. In addition to job applications and oral interviews, applicants may also need to pass job-related aptitude and skills tests; medical examinations; screenings for drug use; psychological reviews, and polygraph examinations. Most employers also complete background investigations that may include looking into current and past employment, financial, criminal, driving, and other relevant records.

For law enforcement positions, particularly with federal agencies, the selection process can take several months, and sometimes up to a year. Individuals who pass an agency's selection process are usually placed on an eligibility list. As positions or training sessions become available, the agency then recruits individuals from its eligibility list.

## Using the Internet

The Internet has become a valuable tool for career development and job hunting. Hundreds of law enforcement agencies, fire departments, federal agencies, professional associations, private companies, and professionals have Web sites on the Internet that allow you to learn about their different departments, services, and activities. Many Web sites also list career information and job opportunities; some even let you apply for jobs on-line.

Many Web sites also provide a Web page of links that can point readers to other relevant Web sites on the Internet. Some Web sites allow you to download job applications, job descriptions, brochures, tables, and even work manuals to your computer for you to read at your leisure when you're off the Internet.

In addition, you can find articles on the Internet about issues, techniques, and other matters written by professionals in the different fields. You can learn about prospective employers, and find their names, addresses, and phone numbers. Furthermore, you can network with professionals throughout the country by way of the Internet, as many Web sites provide names with their e-mail addresses whom you can contact for further information.

## One Final Note

Keep in mind that *Career Opportunities in Law Enforcement, Security, and Protective Services* introduces you to 86 protective service occupations. The references mentioned throughout the book and in the appendixes can help you further research careers in which you are interested. In addition, you can learn whether an occupation is right for you by:

- reading professional journals, magazines, and other periodicals
- reading books about the profession
- visiting relevant Web sites on the Internet
- talking with professionals
- attending professional conferences or meetings
- taking courses related to the profession
- volunteering, if possible, in an actual workplace (for example, a police department if you are interested in going into law enforcement or security work)
- obtaining internships in related businesses, agencies, or other organizations
- obtaining part-time or seasonal entry-level positions such as security guards, store detectives, lifeguards, or park rangers

If you are in high school, check out high school clubs and youth groups that promote your interests. For example, if you are interested in the law enforcement field, find out if a local law enforcement agency sponsors an Explorer unit. Law enforcement Explorers are allowed to participate in various activities, such as "ride alongs" with patrol officers.

Should you decide to pursue a career in protective services you'll find that you already have some knowledge of the field, possibly some experience, and perhaps the beginning of a valuable network with professionals who can help you with the next steps—getting further education, training, and work.

Good luck!

# POLICE WORK

# POLICE OFFICER

## CAREER PROFILE

**Duties:** Enforce laws; preserve peace; protect life and property; investigate crime; apprehend lawbreakers; provide community service

**Alternate Title(s):** Patrol Officer

**Salary Range:** $27,000 to $68,000

**Employment Prospects:** Good

**Advancement Prospects:** Excellent

**Prerequisites:**

**Education or Training**—High school diploma; police academy training, field training

**Experience**—No experience necessary

**Special Skills and Personality Traits**—Problem-solving, observational, teamwork, communication, interpersonal, writing, math, computer, and self-management skills; be mature, levelheaded, honest, intelligent, cooperative, courteous, and dependable

**Licensure/Certification**—Police officer certification; driver's license

## CAREER LADDER

```
┌────────────────────────────────────┐
│      Special Assignments,          │
│ Police Detective, or Police Sergeant│
└────────────────────────────────────┘

┌────────────────────────────────────┐
│          Police Officer            │
└────────────────────────────────────┘

┌────────────────────────────────────┐
│      Police Officer Trainee        │
└────────────────────────────────────┘
```

## Position Description

Police Officers work for city or municipal police departments. Their job is to enforce laws; preserve peace; protect life and property; investigate crime; apprehend lawbreakers; and provide community service. The basic unit of all police departments is the uniformed Police Officer who performs patrol duty within the jurisdiction of the police department. These officers are assigned beats, or areas, in which they patrol regularly to make sure that people and businesses are safe. Working alone or with partners, most Police Officers patrol their beat in police cars or on foot, keeping in contact with their headquarters by two-way radios. Some officers perform patrol duty on bicycles, on horses, or in boats.

Police Officers must be familiar with the daily routines of people and businesses on their beats. As they do their rounds, they watch for suspicious activities, investigate potential trouble and, if necessary, call their headquarters for assistance. Police Officers have the authority to stop people and question them about their actions. In addition, they have the power to arrest people who are committing crimes or are suspected of committing crimes. They may also arrest people who are public nuisances, such as drunk persons who are bothering others.

Police Officers also enforce traffic laws on their beats. For instance, they look for motorists who drive over speed limits or run through red traffic lights and stop signs. Violators stopped by an officer are either issued warnings or citations.

As part of their rounds, Police Officers must also be alert to public hazards such as fallen electrical wires, missing traffic signs, potholes, and spilled chemicals. They report such hazards to the proper authorities; and, if necessary, block off streets and direct traffic around the danger. When an accident, fire, or other emergency occurs, Police Officers must take immediate control of the scene. They make sure people are safe and unharmed, provide first aid, and summon emergency medical help. In addition, they block off the scene from traffic and crowds.

Throughout their work shift, Police Officers receive dispatches from headquarters to investigate trouble or provide immediate help to individuals and businesses. For example, a Police Officer might be called on to respond to the following situations: a patient is missing from a nursing home; a person is attempting to commit suicide; a fight has broken out at a shopping center; traffic lights are out at an intersection; a resident complains about noisy neighbors; a grocery store is being robbed; people are living in an abandoned building.

Police Officers keep a daily field notebook on their activities as well as complete accurate accidents and incidents report. Report-writing is an essential duty for all Police Officers as their reports are permanent public records that can be used as evidence in trials.

Police Officers fulfill other duties as they are needed. For example, they might:

- escort citizens
- guard visiting dignitaries
- guard prisoners
- direct traffic around parades, fairs, and other special events
- assist in crowd control at public demonstrations
- operate radar equipment to catch speeding violators
- investigate serious traffic accidents
- assist in criminal investigations, such as doing surveillance or undercover work
- collect and process evidence at crime scenes
- testify at court trials
- present crime prevention workshops
- perform office duty

Occasionally, Police Officers work on assignments with law enforcement officers from other local, state, or federal agencies.

After serving two to three years of patrol duty, Police Officers can apply for positions on special details, such as the bike patrol unit, bomb squad, SWAT unit, crime prevention unit, or traffic enforcement unit. Officers perform special detail duties in addition to their regular duties.

Police Officers work a rotating shift that includes nights, weekends, and holidays. They are on call 24 hours a day, every day of the year.

## Salaries

Earnings for Police Officers vary, depending on such factors as their rank, experience, education, and geographical location. According to the November 2003 *Occupational Employment Statistics* survey by the U.S. Bureau of Labor Statistics (BLS), the estimated annual salary for most police patrol officers ranged between $26,510 and $68,160.

## Employment Prospects

According to the U.S. Bureau of Justice Statistics, 440,920 full-time, sworn police officers were employed in the United States in 2000.

Most openings will be created to replace officers who retire, resign, or are promoted to higher positions. The creation of additional positions in a police department will depend on its budget. Applicants can expect to face a long and highly competitive selection process for any police job.

## Advancement Prospects

Police Officers can develop satisfying and diverse law enforcement careers. Throughout their careers, they can apply for any number of special units within their police force.

In addition, Police Officers might choose to pursue a career in police investigations. They usually become eligible to take the competitive detective exam in their department after completing two or three years of patrol duty. Officers interested in supervisory or administrative duties can seek promotions as sergeants, lieutenants, and captains. They must have additional experience and education as well as pass competitive exams and reviews.

Police Officers may retire with a pension after serving 20 to 25 years on the force. Many officers retire while still in their 40s and 50s and pursue a second career in law enforcement or another field that interests them.

## Education and Training

Applicants must have a high school diploma or general equivalency diploma. Many departments also require applicants to have a minimum number of college credits with courses in police science or other related study. Some police departments require applicants to have either an associate's or bachelor's degree.

Police Officer trainees generally complete 12 to 14 weeks of training at a police academy where they study law, investigative procedures, self-defense, use of firearms, and other basic law enforcement skills. After their academy training, trainees are assigned to patrol duty under the supervision of field-training officers.

Throughout their careers, Police Officers enroll in educational programs, training seminars, conference workshops, and so on to increase their knowledge and update their skills.

## Special Requirements

All Police Officers must hold a current POST (Peace Officer Standard and Training) certificate, which is earned upon completion of basic training at a police academy. In addition, Police Officers must possess a valid driver's license.

## Experience, Skills, and Personality Traits

No law enforcement experience is necessary to apply for a trainee position. Applicants must be U.S. citizens and have no criminal records. They must meet certain vision, weight, and height requirements. Age, residency, and other specific qualifications vary from department to department. In addition, applicants should be in good physical condition.

To perform their job effectively, Police Officers must have excellent problem-solving, observational, and teamwork skills. They also need strong communication and interpersonal skills, as they must be able to work well with people of different backgrounds. Having adequate writing, math, and computer skills is also important. Additionally, Police Officers need exceptional self-management skills, such as the ability to work independently, handle stressful situations, prioritize tasks, and understand and follow directions.

Being mature, levelheaded, honest, intelligent, cooperative, courteous, and dependable are some personality traits that successful Police Officers share.

### Unions and Associations

Police Officers are usually members of a union that represents them in contract negotiations with their employers. The union seeks to get the best contract terms in regard to pay, benefits, and working conditions. It also handles any grievances that officers may have against their employers.

Many Police Officers belong to professional associations to take advantage of networking opportunities, educational programs, and other professional services and resources. Some national and international societies that serve the general interests of Police Officers are the American Federation of Police and Concerned Citizens, Fraternal Order of Police, International Association of Women Police, and National Black Police Association.

Additionally, Police Officers can join professional associations that serve the interests of special police units. For example, Police Officers performing bike patrol duties might join the Law Enforcement Bike Association, while officers serving in police aviation units might belong to the Airborne Law Enforcement Association.

(For contact information for all of the above organizations, see Appendix IV.)

### Tips for Entry

1. Gain experience by doing volunteer work with a police department. Many agencies have a Police Reserves program, which trains volunteers to assist Police Officers with some of their duties.
2. Earn an associate's or bachelor's degree in police science or other related field as more and more police departments are making a college degree a requirement.
3. Call a police department or city personnel office to learn about current and upcoming job openings.
4. According to the BLS, opportunities are generally better with police departments that offer lower salaries or that serve communities where the crime level is high.
5. You can learn more about police work on the Internet. Many police departments have Web sites that provide general agency information as well as job opportunity listings. To find out if a particular police department has a presence on the Internet, enter its name into a search engine.

# CAMPUS POLICE OFFICER

---

## CAREER PROFILE

**Duties:** Maintain peace and order on a college or university campus; enforce governmental laws and regulations as well as institutional policies and rules; perform police, traffic, crime prevention, and other duties

**Alternate Title(s):** Campus Public Safety Officer

**Salary Range:** $27,000 to $68,000

**Employment Prospects:** Good

**Advancement Prospects:** Excellent

**Prerequisites:**

**Education or Training**—High school diploma; police academy training

**Experience**—Previous law enforcement or security experience in an educational setting preferred

**Special Skills and Personality Traits**—Self-management, communication, writing, interpersonal, teamwork, and decision-making skills; be calm, composed, friendly, cooperative, tactful, honest, ethical, and organized

**Licensure/Certification**—Police officer certification; driver's license; firearms certification may be required

## CAREER LADDER

```
+-------------------------------------------+
|   Campus Police Officer (Journeyman)      |
+-------------------------------------------+

+-------------------------------------------+
|        Campus Police Officer              |
+-------------------------------------------+

+-------------------------------------------+
|      Campus Police Officer Recruit        |
+-------------------------------------------+
```

---

## Position Description

Campus Police Officers are members of police departments that are dedicated to serving two-year colleges, four-year colleges, and universities. These agencies are responsible for the protection of all life and property on academic campuses. Many campus police departments use community-based policing to ensure the safety and cooperation of the entire campus. This approach involves developing and maintaining a positive relationship with students, faculty, and staff.

As commissioned law enforcement officers, Campus Police Officers maintain peace and order on college and university campuses. They make sure that students, faculty, employees, and visitors have a safe and secure environment in which to study, work, and live. Their job involves the enforcement of federal, state, and local laws and regulations on academic campuses. In addition, they make sure that institutional policies and rules are being upheld.

Campus Police Officers have the power to perform general police duties, such as deterring and preventing unlawful behavior, issuing citations, serving warrants, apprehending offenders, making arrests, preserving crime scenes, investigating crimes, conducting surveillance, and testifying in court. Many Campus Police Officers have the authority to carry and use firearms to perform their duties.

Campus Police Officers are assigned areas, or beats, on campus to patrol, which they conduct on foot, on bicycles, or in marked vehicles. They patrol buildings, grounds, and facilities, and keep an eye out for criminal and suspicious activity as well as for violations of laws, regulations, policies, and rules. They also watch for unusual conditions as well as for signs of fire and safety hazards. As part of their police duty, these law enforcement officers respond to a wide range of requests for service from students, faculty, and others on campus. The requests may be about criminal or noncriminal matters. For example, a Campus Police Officer might check out a report of vandalism in the student union, a complaint of loud music in a dormitory, or a call for medical emergency assistance in a classroom.

Traffic duty is another area in which Campus Police Officers are involved. Their tasks include enforcing traffic laws and regulations, directing traffic, issuing traffic citations, investigating traffic accidents, and so on. In addition, Campus Police Officers provide directions and help operators of disabled motor vehicles.

Another major area of concern for Campus Police Officers is crime prevention. On most, if not all campuses, officers provide escort service for anyone who is afraid to walk alone on campus during certain hours, particularly after dark. Many Campus Police Officers are also involved in the development and implementation of education programs for students, faculty, and staff. Some officers are responsible for making presentations on such topics as alcohol abuse, drugs, crime prevention, sexual assault, and traffic safety.

Campus Police Officers perform various other duties, depending on their level of responsibility. For example, they might:

- screen visitors for firearms and other contraband
- provide security at games, receptions, and other special events
- mediate disputes between individuals or groups
- coordinate medical emergency situations
- train and supervise noncommissioned or student personnel
- assist other law enforcement agencies as needed
- raise and lower flags on campus

An essential aspect of their job is writing accurate and detailed reports of their activities. For example, Campus Police Officers are responsible for completing daily logs, incident reports, and investigative reports. These officers also maintain records and files about incidents, criminal records, lost and found items, and so on.

Campus Police Officers operate various types of equipment on their job. These include two-way radios, public address systems, emergency medical equipment, riot control equipment, and office machines. Their job also requires them to sit, stand, walk, run, and climb for long periods of time. When necessary, they lift, carry, or drag heavy objects or people. On occasion they must handle people who are upset, disturbed, angry, or hostile.

Campus Police Officers work a 40-hour week. Many of them work rotating shifts, which include nights, weekends, and holidays. They put in overtime hours whenever their work requires it.

## Salaries

Earnings for Campus Police Officers vary, depending on such factors as their rank, job duties, education, experience, and geographical location. Some employers provide additional compensation for working overtime or certain shifts, as well as for performing certain duties. According to the November 2003 *Occupational Employment Statistics* sur-

vey by the U.S. Bureau of Labor Statistics, the estimated annual salary for most police patrol officers ranged between $26,510 and $68,160.

## Employment Prospects

Some campus police departments are part of academic institutions, while others are divisions of local or state police agencies. Typically, larger campuses employ a greater number of police officers than smaller campuses. In general, opportunities become available as officers retire or transfer to other occupations. An agency generally creates additional positions as their needs grow, as long as funding is available.

## Advancement Prospects

Campus Police Officers can develop a satisfying and diverse law enforcement career, according to their interests and ambitions. As they gain experience and training, they can rise through the ranks as detectives, sergeants, lieutenants, and so on up to police chief.

Some officers use their campus police experience as a stepping-stone for a career with other law enforcement agencies at the local, state, or federal level.

## Education and Training

Minimally, applicants must possess a high school diploma or general equivalency diploma. Some employers prefer to hire applicants who have completed some college work.

Recruits generally receive several weeks of training at a police academy. They study such topics as criminal procedure law, the role of campus law enforcement, crisis intervention, defensive tactics, and diversity. If their position requires them to be armed, recruits then complete training on the use of firearms.

## Special Requirements

Employers generally require that candidates possess the POST (peace officer standard and training) certificate, which is earned upon completion of basic training at a police academy. Candidates must also have a valid driver's license. For armed positions, candidates must be able to qualify for firearms certification.

## Experience, Skills, and Personality Traits

Many employers prefer to hire individuals with previous law enforcement or security experience. Experience in an educational setting is desirable. Many employers allow candidates to substitute a college degree in law enforcement, criminal justice, or another related field for one or more years of experience. Some employers may hire individuals without work experience if they have recently completed or are about to complete training at a police academy.

In general, applicants must be U.S. citizens. Some employers may hire permanent residents if they are in the process of completing their naturalization process. Applicants must meet a minimum age requirement, which varies with the different employers. They must also be in good physical condition and of high moral character.

Campus Police Officers must have excellent self-management skills, which includes the ability to work independently, follow and understand instructions, handle stressful situations, and prioritize and organize tasks. Their job also requires that they have strong communication, writing, interpersonal, teamwork, and decision-making skills. Being calm, composed, friendly, cooperative, tactful, honest, ethical, and organized are some personality traits that successful Campus Police Officers share.

## Unions and Associations

Campus Police Officers can join local, state, or national professional associations to take advantage of networking opportunities, education programs, and other professional resources and services. The International Association of Campus Law Enforcement Administrators specifically serves the interests of campus law enforcement staff members. (For contact information, see Appendix IV.)

Many Campus Police Officers are members of a union, which represents them in negotiations and grievance processes.

## Tips for Entry

1. Gain experience by joining the student security patrol on your college campus, if such a program is offered.
2. Many campus police departments hire noncommissioned officers to perform security and other nonpolice duties on campus. You might apply for such a position to get an idea if campus police work may be a career that interests you.
3. For information about job vacancies and application procedures, contact the human resources department at academic institutions where you would like to work.
4. Many campus police departments have a Web site, which often includes job recruitment information. To find the Web site for the organization that interests you, enter its name into a search engine.

# POLICE DETECTIVE

## CAREER PROFILE

**Duties:** Investigate criminal cases; apprehend criminals; testify in court

**Alternate Title(s):** Police Investigator, Police Inspector

**Salary Range:** $32,000 to $84,000

**Employment Prospects:** Good

**Advancement Prospects:** Excellent

**Prerequisites:**

**Education or Training**—Academic study and field training

**Experience**—One to five years of police duty

**Special Skills and Personality Traits**—Communication, interpersonal, teamwork, writing, interviewing, critical-thinking, and problem-solving skills; be curious, open-minded, fair, unbiased, patient, confident, logical, perceptive, and well organized

## CAREER LADDER

```
┌─────────────────────────┐
│     Police Sergeant     │
└─────────────────────────┘

┌─────────────────────────┐
│     Police Detective    │
└─────────────────────────┘

┌─────────────────────────┐
│      Police Officer     │
└─────────────────────────┘
```

## Position Description

Police Detectives are plainclothes police officers who conduct criminal investigations. They are responsible for identifying suspects as well as finding proof that links them to crimes in order to arrest and prosecute them in court. Robbery, burglary, vandalism, theft, assault, murder, suicide, stalking, domestic violence, fraud, forgery, arson, vice, narcotics, gangs, and terrorism are some of the many types of crime that Police Detectives may investigate.

Police Detectives usually begin each case by gathering information to help them decide upon an effective plan of investigation. They carefully examine a crime scene, writing thorough notes as well as drawing well-detailed sketches. (Some Police Detectives also photograph the crime scene.) They search for physical evidence including bullets, weapons, tools of entry, bloodstains, fibers, hair, and fingerprints. Police Detectives might collect and process the physical evidence or direct other officers in performing these tasks. Police Detectives interview victims, witnesses, suspects, and other people who may have knowledge of the crime in question. In addition, they assess crime lab reports, medical examiner reports, and other pertinent police reports. They review written statements of interviews conducted by themselves or other officers.

Police Detectives develop leads on suspects, conduct more interviews, gather additional facts, and examine police records for possible suspects. When suspects are identified, Police Detectives then must prove that the suspects had the motives, means, and opportunity to commit the crimes. Police Detectives look for evidence that links the suspects to the victims, physical evidence, or the crime scene. They reread reports and records. They may interview additional witnesses and often return to talk with persons they have previously interviewed. In addition, Police Detectives may do surveillance or stakeouts on suspects, and with the proper warrants, they might search suspects' property. Once sufficient evidence is gathered, Police Detectives arrest suspects or order their arrest.

With every case, Police Detectives keep accurate and proper documentation of their activities, as their reports may be used in court trials. Police Detectives obtain signed written statements from witnesses, victims, and suspects. They keep well-detailed field notes and progress reports. They prepare comprehensive summaries that include all documentary, testimonial, and physical evidence. Police Detectives may assist prosecutors in preparing for court trials. If necessary, Police Detectives gather more facts to strengthen a case, and in some cases, testify in court about their findings.

Depending on the size and need of a police department, Police Detectives might specialize in one or more types of criminal cases. They might handle cases alone, with a partner, or as part of a crime investigation unit. A case may take several days, weeks, months, or years to solve. Some cases remain unsolved.

Occasionally, Police Detectives work on assignments with law enforcement officers from other local, state, or federal agencies.

Some Police Detectives volunteer for positions in special details, such as the bomb squad, SWAT unit, or aviation unit. They perform special detail duties in addition to their investigation duties.

Detectives are assigned an eight-hour shift but put in many hours of overtime to solve their cases. They are on call 24 hours a day, seven days a week.

## Salaries

Earnings for Police Detectives vary, depending on such factors as their rank, education, experience, and geographical location. According to the November 2003 *Occupational Employment Statistics* survey by the U.S. Bureau of Labor Statistics (BLS), the estimated annual salary for most Police Detectives ranged between $31,760 and $84,060.

## Employment Prospects

The BLS reports that an estimated 85,670 detectives and criminal investigators were employed by local law enforcement agencies, as of November 2003. Qualified Detective candidates often outnumber the positions that open up in a department. Most openings will be created to replace Police Detectives who retire, resign, or who are promoted to higher positions. The creation of additional positions within any police department depends on its budget.

Opportunities are usually better with large police departments or police departments in metropolitan areas.

## Advancement Prospects

Those interested in supervisory or administrative duties can seek promotions as sergeants, lieutenants, and captains. They must have additional experience and education as well as pass competitive exams and reviews.

Other career paths for Police Detectives are found in state and federal law enforcement agencies in such positions as special agents and other investigative specialists. Police Detectives might also consider working in the private sector as private investigators.

Police Detectives may retire with a pension after 20 to 25 years of service on the force. Some Detectives retire while still in their 40s or 50s and pursue a second career in law enforcement or another field that interests them.

## Education and Training

Newly hired Police Detectives complete a probation period in which they receive field training as well as academic investigative training at a police academy, college, or their police department. Those who go into specialized investigative areas, such as arson and homicide, receive additional training.

## Experience, Skills, and Personality Traits

Requirements vary with the different police departments. In many agencies, police officers must have one to five years of experience performing patrol duty before they are eligible to apply for the detective exam. Upon passing this competitive exam, candidates are placed on an eligibility list according to their scores. They are offered a detective position as one becomes available.

Because they must work and deal with many people of different backgrounds, Police Detectives need exceptional communication, interpersonal, and teamwork skills. In addition, they should have strong writing, interviewing, critical-thinking, and problem-solving skills.

Being curious, open-minded, fair, unbiased, patient, confident, logical, perceptive, and well-organized are some personality traits that Police Detectives have in common.

## Unions and Associations

Many Police Detectives join different professional organizations for the opportunity to network with peers and to obtain training, continuing education, current research, and other professional services and support. Most continue their membership with the unions and police organizations that they joined as police officers. In addition, Detectives might join professional groups such as the International Homicide Investigators Association, International Narcotics Interdiction Association, and International Association of Crime Analysts. For contact information, see Appendix IV.

## Tips for Entry

1. Take criminal justice, law, computer science, logic, forensic science, and other classes that can enhance and improve investigative skills and knowledge.
2. Keep up with new and improved forensic techniques.
3. Contact a police department's criminal divisions commander or personnel office to find out the specific qualifications for a Police Detective.
4. You can read about the criminal investigation units of some police departments on the Internet. Enter the keywords *police criminal investigation units* into a search engine to get a list of Web sites.

# POLICE CHIEF
# (MUNICIPAL POLICE DEPARTMENT)

## CAREER PROFILE

**Duties:** Oversee his or her agency's law enforcement and administrative operations; develop, implement, and evaluate and agency's goals, policies, programs, and budgets; provide direction and guidance to police and civilian staffs

**Alternate Title(s):** Chief of Police

**Salary Range:** $56,000 to $150,000

**Employment Prospects:** Fair

**Advancement Prospects:** Fair

**Prerequisites:**

**Education or Training**—Bachelor's degree generally required; law enforcement management training program

**Experience**—Usually 10 or more years of experience in police work; several years of supervisory and managerial experience

**Special Skills and Personality Traits**—Leadership, team-building, interpersonal, problem-solving, organizational, self-management, communication, writing, public speaking, and public relations skills; be accessible, friendly, ethical, trustworthy, decisive, analytical, flexible, innovative, creative, and inspirational

**Licensure/Certification**—Police officer certification

## CAREER LADDER

```
┌─────────────────────────────┐
│     Police Chief of a       │
│  Large Police Department    │
└─────────────────────────────┘

┌─────────────────────────────┐
│        Police Chief         │
└─────────────────────────────┘

┌─────────────────────────────┐
│    Assistant Police Chief   │
└─────────────────────────────┘
```

## Position Description

Police Chiefs are the chief executive officers of police departments. Municipal Police Chiefs oversee agencies that serve towns and cities throughout the United States. Police departments vary in size, from agencies in small towns with a handful of personnel to organizations in metropolitan cities with thousands of employees. Police Chiefs are held accountable for the delivery of efficient and effective law enforcement and public safety services to their municipalities. They are also responsible for the conduct of their police force and the public image of their departments.

Police Chiefs are in charge of the overall administration of their agencies. They oversee the direction, management, and coordination of the law enforcement operations (patrol services, criminal investigations, technical services, and so on) as well as the administrative operations (such as human resources, finance, and public relations). Whether in charge of small or large police departments, Police Chiefs make sure that the different areas of their operations are running smoothly each day. Police Chiefs may handle some or all of the different areas directly or direct and supervise departmental managers.

Police Chiefs have the authority to formulate and implement objectives, policies, procedures, strategies, and programs that would best fulfill the missions and goals for their agencies. Police Chiefs also have the responsibility of planning and administering budgets, which may run in the millions of dollars. They make sure that they have sufficient funds each year to cover the expenses of manpower, equipment, materials, programs, and other needs.

Police Chiefs are also responsible for ensuring that their organizations are in compliance with all required local, state, and federal laws and regulations, such as those relating to employment and labor. In addition, Police Chiefs ensure that their agencies follow the organizational policies and rules set by their municipal governments.

As the top-ranking officer of their departments, Police Chiefs have the primary responsibility to provide leadership to all commissioned officers, civilian employees, and volunteers. Hence, Police Chiefs oversee the supervision, direction, and training of all personnel. Depending on the size of their departments, chiefs of police may be directly or indirectly involved with the selection and hiring of employees, assigning work, evaluating the job performance of staff, disciplining employees, developing training programs, and so on.

Police Chiefs perform a wide range of tasks that varies each day. For example, they:

- evaluate current policies to determine if changes are needed
- make recommendations regarding grievances filed by police officers
- review reports of investigations concerning police misconduct
- direct studies of public safety needs for the community
- oversee the grant writing for funds to create or maintain special units (such as bike patrols and bomb squads) and crime prevention programs
- prepare required forms and reports about police department activities
- meet with departmental managers
- make status and budget reports to the city council
- participate in collective bargaining negotiations with the police union
- release information to the news media
- represent the police department at state and national conferences
- keep up-to-date with new laws and regulations, court decisions, and developments in police administration

Police Chiefs are expected to maintain positive relationships with the public, city officials, businesses, local government agencies, community organizations, and others. Many Police Chiefs serve on local committees and boards, as well as participate in social, educational, and other community events. In addition, Police Chiefs develop working relationships with other public safety departments (such as fire departments). Furthermore, they form cooperative relationships with other local, state, and federal enforcement agencies, such as the sheriff's office, special jurisdiction police agencies (such as an airport police department), the state police department, the FBI, the Drug Enforcement Agency, and the U.S. Customs and Border Patrol.

Although their job is primarily administrative, Police Chiefs perform law enforcement duties—patrol work, traffic enforcement, criminal investigations, tactical support—as needed. In small police departments, many Police Chiefs perform police duties on a daily basis.

Municipal Police Chiefs are appointed to their position by city mayors or city managers, to whom they are directly responsible. In some municipalities, Police Chiefs are offered renewable contracts for limited terms. Some Police Chiefs are required to live within the jurisdiction that they serve.

Police Chiefs put in long hours each day, including weekends. Their job sometimes requires them to travel to other cities and states to attend professional meetings and conferences. Police Chiefs are on call 24 hours a day.

## Salaries

Earnings for Police Chiefs vary, depending upon various factors, such as their experience, the size of their police agency, and their geographical location. Police chiefs of departments in major cities typically earn the highest wages in the United States.

An expert in the field estimates that the annual salary for Police Chiefs generally ranges from $20,000 to $150,000. According to the November 2003 *Occupational Employment Statistics* survey by the U.S. Bureau of Labor Statistics, most chief executives (which includes Police Chiefs) earned an estimated annual salary that ranged between $55,760 and $145,600.

## Employment Prospects

In addition to municipal police departments, Police Chiefs are employed by special jurisdiction police agencies, such as park, university, airport, and public transit system police departments. According to the U.S. Bureau of Justice Statistics, there were 12,666 local police agencies and 1,376 special jurisdiction agencies in the United States in 2000.

In general, job openings become available when Police Chiefs retire or transfer to other positions. Well-qualified candidates with demonstrated success as administrators should be able to obtain the type of position they seek.

Police Chiefs can also seek employment as administrators with other law enforcement agencies, including sheriff's offices, state police departments, and federal agencies.

## Advancement Prospects

Although they hold the top-ranking position in police departments, many Police Chiefs continue to develop their careers according to their interests and ambitions. Some Police Chiefs pursue advancement by seeking positions with agencies that offer greater challenges, higher pay, or serve larger municipalities.

Other career paths available for Police Chiefs include becoming politicians, consultants, professors, or administrative managers with governmental, private sector, and nonprofit organizations.

## Education and Training

Employers generally require that Police Chiefs possess a bachelor's degree in law enforcement, criminal justice, criminology, sociology, or a related field from an accredited college or university. Having an advanced degree in criminal justice, public administration, law enforcement management, business, or a related field is desirable. Many employers prefer that candidates have completed an advanced law enforcement training program offered by a recognized institution such as the FBI National Academy.

## Special Requirements

Police Chiefs must possess current police officer certification, which has been granted in the state in which they work. Employers typically give a new Police Chief who has come from another state sufficient time in which to obtain this certification.

## Experience, Skills, and Personality Traits

Police Chiefs typically work up through the ranks from patrol officer to captain to deputy chief of police. They have gained broad and extensive experience in both police and administrative operations.

Qualifications vary with the different agencies. Many agencies prefer that applicants have between 10 and 15 years of law enforcement experience, which includes several years of supervisory and administrative experience. In addition, employers prefer candidates to have experience working in the type and size of the police department that they would be overseeing. Candidates should also have knowledge about the issues that concern the community which they would be serving.

To perform their work effectively, Police Chiefs must have exceptional leadership, team-building, interpersonal, problem-solving, organizational, and self-management skills. Their job also requires that they have excellent communication, writing, public speaking, and public relations skills. Being accessible, friendly, ethical, trustworthy, decisive, analytical, flexible, innovative, creative, and inspirational are some personality traits that successful Police Chiefs share.

## Unions and Associations

Many Police Chiefs belong to professional associations to take advantage of networking opportunities, training programs, and other professional services and resources. Along with state and regional associations, Police Chiefs can join such national societies as the International Association of Chiefs of Police, the National Organization of Black Law Enforcement Executives, and the National Association of Women Law Enforcement Executives.

## Tips for Entry

1. In high school, you can begin developing your leadership, interpersonal, communication, and other basic skills needed to become a successful Police Chief. For example, you might participate in student government, athletics, or other student activities.
2. Early in your career as a police officer, seek a mentorship with an administrator whom you respect and trust and from whom you would like to learn.
3. Many municipalities use executive recruiters to search for the most qualified applicants for a Police Chief position.
4. You can learn more about the world of Police Chiefs on the Internet. You might start by visiting the International Association of Chiefs of Police Web site: http://www.theiacp.org.

# DEPUTY SHERIFF

## CAREER PROFILE

**Duties:** Perform patrol duty; conduct investigations; act as officers of local courts; perform jail duty

**Alternate Title(s):** None

**Salary Range:** $27,000 to $84,000

**Employment Prospects:** Fair

**Advancement Prospects:** Good

**Prerequisites:**

**Education or Training**—High school diploma; academy training, field training

**Experience**—One to two years of law enforcement experience preferred

**Special Skills and Personality Traits**—Problem-solving, memory, observational, writing, interpersonal, and communication skills; be self-motivated, dependable, ethical, trustworthy, fair, and tolerant

## CAREER LADDER

```
┌─────────────────────────────────┐
│     Deputy Sheriff Sergeant      │
└─────────────────────────────────┘

┌─────────────────────────────────┐
│         Deputy Sheriff           │
└─────────────────────────────────┘

┌─────────────────────────────────┐
│      Deputy Sheriff Trainee      │
└─────────────────────────────────┘
```

## Position Description

Deputy Sheriffs are uniformed law enforcement officers who represent county governments, and enforce county and state laws and ordinances. As members of a sheriff's office, Deputy Sheriffs might perform a variety of assignments in a number of areas—patrol, criminal investigations, court security, and jail (or corrections). Their jurisdiction covers all the cities, rural areas, and unincorporated cities and towns within the county. But they mostly focus on rural and unincorporated areas and cities without a municipal police department.

Driving marked sheriff's vehicles, Deputy Sheriffs perform patrol duty within their assigned areas. They usually work alone, using two-way radios to keep in contact with their headquarters. While making their rounds, Deputy Sheriffs investigate suspicious activities, report public hazards, enforce traffic laws, and provide community service. They respond to dispatches to investigate trouble or provide immediate assistance. They issue warnings and citations to violators and arrest lawbreakers.

A Deputy Sheriff's investigative duties differ in every sheriff's department. In small departments, Deputy Sheriffs generally conduct complete criminal investigations. In larger departments, they usually perform crime scene investigations only. They might also assist in joint investigations with federal, state, and local law enforcement officers.

As officers of the court, Deputy Sheriffs serve and execute subpoenas, court orders, summonses, and other court documents. They may also collect fees, such as property taxes, that citizens owe the county. During trials, Deputy Sheriffs provide court security by patrolling the grounds, keeping order in the courtrooms, and guarding the jury and judge. They also guard the inmates who are on trial and escort them between jail and the courtroom.

Some sheriff's departments are in charge of local jails. In those departments, Deputy Sheriffs may be assigned to perform various duties. They may book inmates and take custody of their possessions, supervise or guard inmates, and even transport inmates to hospitals, courts, and other locations. They also may maintain records such as fingerprint files.

Deputy Sheriffs are responsible for keeping accurate, detailed field logs on all of their activities as well as writing reports. Their logs and reports are permanent public records and can be submitted as evidence in court trials.

Deputy Sheriffs perform other duties as they are required. They might:

- testify in court
- do surveillance and undercover work
- collect and process physical evidence

- teach crime prevention workshops to the public or other government agencies
- teach classes on dangerous drugs, crime scene investigations, and other departmental functions to other staff members
- perform office duty

On occasion, Deputy Sheriffs work on assignments with law enforcement officers from other local, state, or federal agencies.

After serving a minimum number of years of patrol duty, Deputy Sheriffs in most agencies can apply for assignments in special details such as the canine patrol, the marine patrol, or the crime scene investigation unit. They perform special detail duties in addition to their regular duties.

Deputy Sheriffs work rotating shifts that include nights, weekends, and holidays. They are on call 24 hours a day, every day of the year.

## Salaries

Earnings for Deputy Sheriffs vary, depending on such factors as their rank, education, experience, and geographical location. According to the November 2003 *Occupational Employment Statistics* survey by the U.S. Bureau of Labor Statistics, the estimated annual salary for most patrol officers ranged from $26,510 to $68,160; and for most detectives and criminal investigators, $31,760 to $84,060.

## Employment Prospects

According to the U.S. Bureau of Justice Statistics, 164,711 full-time sworn officers were employed by 3,070 sheriff's offices in the United States in 2000. The competition for Deputy Sheriff positions is high. Most positions become available as Deputies retire, resign, or are promoted to higher offices.

## Advancement Prospects

Supervisory and managerial positions are available in sheriff's departments. Deputy Sheriffs can rise through the ranks of sergeant, lieutenant, captain, chief deputy, and assistant sheriff. In most counties, the sheriff is elected by the voters.

In many agencies, Deputy Sheriffs may retire with a pension after 20 to 25 years of service. Many Deputy Sheriffs retire while still in their 40s and 50s and pursue a second career in law enforcement or another field that interests them.

## Education and Training

Sheriff's departments require a high school diploma or general equivalency diploma. Some departments require an associate's degree or a minimum of 60 credits in police science or other related study from an accredited college.

Most departments require Deputy Sheriff trainees to complete 12 to 14 weeks of training at a law enforcement academy. The trainees study such subjects as law, local and state ordinances, court proceedings, investigative procedures, self-defense, use of firearms, and jail security. After their academy training, trainees perform routine duties under the supervision of field training officers.

## Experience, Skills, and Personality Traits

Many sheriff's departments prefer applicants to have one to two years of law enforcement experience.

An applicant needs to be a U.S. citizen and must have no criminal record. He or she must meet certain age, residency, vision, weight, and height requirements, which varies among agencies. In addition, the applicant must be in good physical condition.

To perform well at their job, Deputy Sheriffs must have effective problem-solving, memory, observational, and writing skills. In addition, they need strong interpersonal and communication skills because they must be able to handle people from different backgrounds on a daily basis.

Being self-motivated, dependable, ethical, trustworthy, fair, and tolerant are some personality traits that successful Deputy Sheriffs share.

## Unions and Associations

Deputy Sheriffs are usually members of a union that represents them in contract negotiations with their employers. The union seeks to get the best contract terms in regard to pay, benefits, and working conditions. It also handles any grievances that officers may have against their employers.

Many Deputy Sheriffs join professional associations to take advantage of networking opportunities, education programs, and other professional resources and services. Two national societies that serve the interests of Deputy Sheriffs are the National Sheriffs' Association, and the American Deputy Sheriffs' Association. (For contact information, see Appendix IV.)

Additionally, Deputy Sheriffs can join other professional associations that serve their particular interests in such areas as canine duty, bomb squad detail, or crime scene investigations.

## Tips for Entry

1. Become a Deputy Sheriff volunteer to get valuable law enforcement experience within the sheriff's department.
2. Contact a sheriff's office or county personnel office to learn about job announcements.
3. Obtain military experience, college training, or work experience in law enforcement or related fields to enhance your chances of finding law enforcement jobs.
4. Many sheriff's departments have Web sites on the Internet, giving information about their organization as well as job opportunities. Enter the keywords *sheriff's department* into a search engine to get a list of Web sites.

# STATE TROOPER

## CAREER PROFILE

**Duties:** Enforce criminal and traffic laws; preserve peace; protect life and property; apprehend lawbreakers; provide community service

**Alternate Title(s):** Highway Patrol Officer

**Salary Range:** $27,000 to $84,000

**Employment Prospects:** Good

**Advancement Prospects:** Good

**Prerequisites:**

**Education or Training**—High school diploma; academy training; field training

**Experience**—No law enforcement experience is needed

**Special Skills and Personality Traits**—Interpersonal, communication, reading, writing, observational, problem-solving, and self-management skills; be trustworthy, honest, responsible, and dedicated

## CAREER LADDER

```
┌─────────────────────────────┐
│   State Trooper Sergeant     │
└─────────────────────────────┘

┌─────────────────────────────┐
│       State Trooper          │
└─────────────────────────────┘

┌─────────────────────────────┐
│    State Trooper Trainee     │
└─────────────────────────────┘
```

## Position Description

State Troopers are law enforcement officers for state police departments. They are responsible for enforcing criminal and traffic laws, preserving the peace, protecting lives and property, apprehending lawbreakers, and providing community service. In some states, the state police department is known as the highway patrol department. Some states have two separate divisions for police enforcement and traffic enforcement.

State Troopers are uniformed officers who patrol their assigned area in marked state police cars. They work alone, communicating with their headquarters on two-way radios. Their major responsibilities are enforcing traffic laws and managing traffic on a state's freeways, highways, turnpikes, roads, and streets. They monitor the traffic in all types of weather. They issue warnings or citations to motorists who are breaking speed limits or other traffic laws as well as motorists who are endangering lives by tailgating, weaving through traffic, or other reckless driving. If necessary, State Troopers arrest violators and escort them to headquarters for detainment.

When automobile accidents or other emergency situations occur, State Troopers take command of the scene. They make sure people are safe and unharmed. They provide first aid and summon ambulances, tow trucks, and other appropriate assistance. They block off the scene and direct traffic around it.

As part of their traffic duty, State Troopers also help motorists. They might give motorists directions to their destinations as well as information about nearby restaurants, gas stations, and lodging. They might make calls to tow truck companies for motorists with car trouble.

State Troopers perform patrol duties in rural and unincorporated areas that do not have a police department or sheriff's department. They safeguard buildings and property, investigate suspicious activities, report public hazards, enforce traffic laws, provide community service, interrogate suspects, and arrest lawbreakers. In addition, State Troopers respond to dispatches from headquarters to investigate trouble or provide immediate assistance.

Many State Troopers take turns performing station duty. They do routine desk work, such as preparing reports or correspondence and making entries into station records. They send and receive radio messages. They answer questions from the public about road conditions, weather conditions, directions, or other subjects.

State Troopers are also assigned special duties from time to time. For example, they might:

- manage traffic during parades and special events
- escort visiting dignitaries, military convoys, and funeral processions on highways and freeways
- patrol areas that were devastated by fires, bombings, floods, earthquakes, or other man-made or natural disasters
- check weights of commercial vehicles
- present workshops on highway safety, crime prevention, and other topics to the public
- conduct drivers' examinations
- perform desk duty
- conduct auto theft investigations
- execute search and arrest warrants

Upon completing their probation period, they usually can request a transfer to other parts of a state. They are also eligible to apply for special units such as canine patrol, motorcycle patrol, air support detail, and auto theft investigations.

State Troopers are on call 24 hours a day, seven days a week. They work rotating shifts that include nights, weekends, and holidays.

## Salaries

Earnings for State Troopers vary, depending on such factors as their rank, education, and experience. According to the November 2003 *Occupational Employment Statistics* survey by the U.S. Bureau of Labor Statistics, the estimated annual salary for most patrol officers ranged from $26,510 to $68,160; and for most detectives and criminal investigators, $31,760 to $84,060.

## Employment Prospects

According to the U.S. Bureau of Justice Statistics, 56,348 full-time, sworn officers were employed in 49 state police or highway patrol agencies in 2000. (Hawaii is the only state without a state police department, but it does have a state department of public safety.)

Most opportunities become available as officers retire, resign, or are promoted to higher positions. The competition for State Trooper positions is high in most states because of the attractive salaries and benefit packages that are offered for this occupation.

## Advancement Prospects

Opportunities for supervisory and management positions are available. State Troopers can become sergeants, lieutenants, captains, and majors. Promotions are based on job performance and education, and in some states, high scores on competitive exams.

State Troopers may retire with a pension after 20 to 25 years of service. Many State Troopers retire while still in their 40s or 50s and pursue a second career in law enforcement or another field that interests them.

## Education and Training

State police departments require a high school diploma or a general equivalency diploma. Some departments require an associate's degree or a minimum of 60 credits in police science, law, or other related field from an accredited college.

State Trooper trainees complete several months of law enforcement academy training. The curriculum includes basic law, motor vehicle codes, vehicle patrol, investigation skills, use of firearms, advanced driving skills, first aid, and self defense. After their academy training, trainees perform routine duties under the supervision of field training officers or senior officers.

## Experience, Skills, and Personality Traits

Previous law enforcement experience is not necessary for anyone to apply for a trainee position. Applicants, however, must be U.S. citizens and meet a certain age requirement. In addition, they need to be in excellent physical condition.

State Troopers need good interpersonal and communication skills for the job along with good reading, writing, observational, and problem-solving skills. In addition, they need self-management skills—such as the ability to get to work on time, follow directions, take initiative, work safely, and stay calm while working under pressure.

Being trustworthy, honest, responsible, and dedicated are some personality traits that successful State Troopers share.

## Unions and Associations

Most, if not all, State Troopers belong to a union that represents them in contract negotiations with their employers. The union seeks to get the best contract terms in regard to pay, benefits, and working conditions. It also handles any grievances that officers may have against their employers.

Many State Troopers belong to state, regional, and national professional associations, such as the Fraternal Order of Police and the National Troopers' Coalition, that serve the general interests of law enforcement officers. Additionally, State Troopers can join various other societies that serve their particular interests in such areas as bomb squad detail or crime scene investigations. By joining professional associations, State Troopers can take advantage of networking opportunities, educational programs, and other professional services and resources.

## Tips for Entry

1. Obtain some law enforcement experience, such as volunteer work with a police department, to enhance your chances in the highly competitive selection process for State Trooper positions.

2. Find out if your state has a State Trooper cadet program for high school graduates. Cadets are paid to perform civilian duties. When they reach the appropriate age, they may apply for available State Trooper trainee positions.

3. Many state police departments have Web sites on the Internet, giving information about their organization as well as job opportunities. Enter the keywords *state police department* or *state highway patrol* into a search engine to get a list of Web sites.

# CONSERVATION OFFICER

## CAREER PROFILE

**Duties:** Enforce state game and fishing laws; perform patrol duty; promote wildlife preservation; teach hunting and boating safety workshops

**Alternate Title(s):** Fish and Wildlife Officer, Game Warden, Conservation Police Officer

**Salary Range:** $28,000 to $70,000

**Employment Prospects:** Limited

**Advancement Prospects:** Fair

**Prerequisites:**

**Education or Training**—Requirements differ with each state; academy training, field training

**Experience**—Law enforcement experience or natural resource conservation experience is desirable

**Special Skills and Personality Traits**—Interpersonal, communication, writing, public speaking, organizational, teamwork, and self-management skills; be independent, self-motivated, disciplined, ethical, trustworthy, and friendly

## CAREER LADDER

```
┌─────────────────────────────────────┐
│  Supervising Conservation Officer     │
└─────────────────────────────────────┘

┌─────────────────────────────────────┐
│       Conservation Officer            │
└─────────────────────────────────────┘

┌─────────────────────────────────────┐
│    Conservation Officer Trainee       │
└─────────────────────────────────────┘
```

## Position Description

Conservation Officers work for state wildlife or natural resource conservation departments. They are responsible for law enforcement and public safety of state-owned parks, recreation areas, fish and wildlife areas, and other state properties. They are commissioned as law enforcement officers, but most Conservation Officers are allowed to make felony arrests only in emergency situations. Many Conservation Officers enforce boating laws and regulations. Some Conservation Officers also enforce state environmental laws and regulations. Others may enforce certain federal wildlife laws and regulations.

Conservation Officers are uniformed officers. They are required to live within their assigned area, which may cover several counties. They perform patrol duty alone, working in all kinds of weather and terrain. They patrol by foot, four-wheel-drive trucks, motorboats, canoes, and any other type of vehicle that gets them where they need to go.

As part of their patrol duty, they might:

• issue hunting licenses
• check hunting and fishing licenses
• issue warnings or citations for violations
• investigate reports of illegal hunting and fishing
• inspect game farms and other commercial operations
• arrest lawbreakers
• respond to public complaints about deer, wildcats, and other wildlife that come into urban areas

Another major duty is educating the public about wildlife preservation as well as hunting and boating safety. Conservation Officers give workshops and presentations to schools, sports clubs, and other civic groups on topics such as the safe use of firearms and wildlife conservation.

Many Conservation Officers are also involved in game management and conservation. For example, Conservation Officers might participate in tracking and monitoring the health of local wildlife populations, or they might assist in the development of plans to control a particular game species.

Conservation Officers perform other duties as required. They may prepare incident reports for use in court as well as testify in trials. They may assist in putting out forest fires, or participate in search and rescue operations for missing persons. They also may assist other law enforcement agents with criminal investigations.

Accurate report-writing is essential to the job. They keep a daily log of their activities, wildlife observations, and arrest information. In addition, they complete all necessary reports as well as required forms.

Many officers work out of their homes. They are on call 24 hours a day, seven days a week.

## Salaries

Earnings for Conservation Officers vary, depending on such factors as their experience, job responsibilities, years of service, and employer. According to the November 2003 *Occupational Employment Statistics* survey by the U.S. Bureau of Labor Statistics (BLS), the estimated annual salary for most fish and game wardens ranged from $27,540 to $70,010.

Most Conservation Officers receive compensation for overtime hours as well as a uniform allowance. Officers who work from their homes may receive a monthly allowance for office expenses.

## Employment Prospects

All 50 states have a fish and game department. It may be known as the fish and wildlife department, natural resources division, conservation police, or other names.

Job opportunities for Conservation Officers are limited. According to the BLS, an estimated 7,010 fish and game wardens were employed in the United States, as of November 2003. Positions usually become available when Conservation Officers have retired, resigned, or been promoted. The competition for jobs is tough. For example, a department might receive hundreds of applications for a few openings.

## Advancement Prospects

Promotions in rank are based on experience, job performance, and competitive examination scores. However promotional opportunities for supervisory and management positions are limited.

Conservation Officers might pursue other career paths. With further experience and education, they can become training officers, special wildlife investigators, canine handlers, resource specialists, and forensic examiners.

## Education and Training

Education requirements vary with the different agencies. Some agencies require only a high school diploma or general equivalency diploma. Other agencies require an associate's or a bachelor's degree—preferably in natural resources conservation, biological sciences, criminal justice, or another related field.

Trainees complete one to six months of police academy training by studying a basic wildlife law enforcement curriculum. After their academy training, trainees are assigned to field training officers and begin performing routine patrol duty. Trainees serve a probation period, which varies from department to department. Upon passing their probation, they officially become Conservation Officers.

Most Conservation Officers continue throughout their careers to do independent study, enroll in training and educational programs, and network with peers to enhance their job performance.

## Experience, Skills, and Personality Traits

Many departments choose candidates who have some experience and knowledge in law enforcement and natural resource conservation.

Because they must deal with people from different backgrounds, Conservation Officers need effective interpersonal and communication skills for their work. Their job also requires that they have strong writing, public speaking, organizational, teamwork, and self-management skills. Being independent, self-motivated, disciplined, ethical, trustworthy, and friendly are some personality traits that successful Conservation Officers share.

## Unions and Associations

Many Conservation Officers belong to a union that represents them in contract negotiations with their employer. Many Conservation Officers also belong to regional or national professional associations, such as the North American Wildlife Enforcement Officers Association, to take advantage of networking opportunities, educational programs, and other professional services and resources. For contact information, see Appendix IV.

## Tips for Entry

1. Talk with conservation officers and professional associations to find out about job opportunities.
2. Obtain field experience with fish and wildlife agencies by volunteering, getting an internship, or doing seasonal work.
3. Earn a college degree in natural resources, police science, or other related field to improve your chances of being hired.
4. Many fish and wildlife agencies post job vacancy information at their Web site. To find a particular agency's Web site, enter its name into a search engine.
5. Learn more about Conservation Officers on the Internet. Two Web sites you might visit are the North American Wildlife Enforcement Officers Association, http://www.naweoa.org, and the Federal Wildlife Officers Association, http://www.fwoa.org.

# DEPUTY U.S. MARSHAL

## CAREER PROFILE

**Duties:** Fugitive investigations; personal and witness security; asset seizure; court security; prisoner transportation and custody

**Alternate Title(s):** None

**Salary Range:** $25,000 to $59,000

**Employment Prospects:** Limited

**Advancement Prospects:** Good

**Prerequisites:**

**Education or Training—**Bachelor's degree; Deputy U.S. Marshal's training program

**Experience—**Three years of work experience if one has no college degree

**Special Skills and Personality Traits—**Interpersonal, communication, writing, problem-solving, and self-management skills; be tactful, courteous, trustworthy, honest, and dedicated

## CAREER LADDER

```
┌─────────────────────────────────┐
│     Specialist or Supervisory    │
│        Deputy U.S. Marshal       │
└─────────────────────────────────┘

┌─────────────────────────────────┐
│         Deputy U.S. Marshal      │
└─────────────────────────────────┘

┌─────────────────────────────────┐
│     Deputy U.S. Marshal Trainee  │
└─────────────────────────────────┘
```

## Position Description

Deputy U.S. Marshals work for the United States Marshals Service, a law enforcement agency affiliated with the Department of Justice. These federal law enforcement agents have two major roles: they provide protective services for the federal government, and they act as officers of the federal courts.

Throughout their careers, Deputy U.S. Marshals are assigned to perform various duties. One duty is conducting fugitive investigations. These cases involve prisoners who have escaped from federal prison as well as parolees (of federal prisons) who have violated their parole, probation, or other conditions of release. Some cases involve tracking fugitives from other countries who may be in the United States.

Another duty is providing personal and witness security. Deputy U.S. Marshals protect important federal witnesses who will testify in serious cases such as those involving organized crime or terrorism. The Deputy U.S. Marshals move witnesses and their families to safe locations; and, if necessary, provide changes of identity for them.

Deputy U.S. Marshals also perform the duty of asset seizure. In federal drug and criminal cases, they seize all proceeds made from the sale of illegal drugs or other criminal activity. They are responsible for managing and disposing of millions of dollars of assets and forfeited properties such as cash, jewelry, vehicles, banks, hotels, and retail businesses.

As officers of the federal courts, Deputy U.S. Marshals provide court security. They guard federal judges and juries. They plan for and set up security systems in federal court buildings for important court cases. In addition, they serve court summonses and complaints.

The transport of federal prisoners is another major duty. Deputy U.S. Marshals are responsible for delivering federal prisoners to prisons, courts, hospitals, and other institutions. They are also responsible for escorting foreign fugitives back to the appropriate nations.

Some Deputy U.S. Marshals serve on special operations missions in addition to their regular duties. They provide law enforcement and security support in emergency situations where federal law has been violated or federal property is in danger. These officers are on call 24 hours a day.

Deputy U.S. Marshals have a 40-hour week but often put in longer and irregular hours to perform their duties. These federal law enforcement officers are required to retire upon reaching the age of 57.

## Salaries
Earnings for Deputy U.S. Marshals vary, depending on such factors as their education, experience, pay level, and geographical location. Salaries are generally higher for those who live in metropolitan areas, where the cost of living is high.

Entry-level Deputy U.S. Marshals earn a salary that begins at either the GS-5 or GS-7 level. (GS stands for General Schedule, the pay schedule for most federal employees.) These law enforcement officers can progress up to the GS-11 level. In 2005, the annual basic pay for GS-5 to GS-11 levels ranged from $24,677 to $58,811.

## Employment Prospects
The headquarters for the U.S. Marshals Service is in Washington, D.C. The agency has 94 district offices, which are located throughout the United States as well as in Puerto Rico, U.S. Virgin Islands, Guam, and North Mariana Islands.

Job openings usually become available as Deputy U.S. Marshals retire or transfer to other positions. Applicants may apply during open recruitment drives. In 2005, the U.S. Marshals Service limited their hiring selection to individuals who were:

- former military personnel
- college students participating in the cooperative education program that the agency sponsors
- eligible candidates who had passed the Deputy U.S. Marshals exam and were already listed on its register of eligible candidates

## Advancement Prospects
Deputy U.S. Marshals must complete three years of service at their first assigned field office before they can request a transfer to another field office. After three years, they also become eligible to apply for special key operations duty.

After serving several years, Deputy U.S. Marshals are eligible to become supervisors, academy instructors, and specialists (such as court security inspectors).

## Education and Training
For the GS-5 grade, applicants need at least a bachelor's degree with a 3.0 GPA or higher in their majors. For the GS-7 grade, applicants must have completed graduate work in law, police science, or other field related to law enforcement.

Deputy U.S. Marshal trainees complete an intensive 10-week training program at the U.S. Marshals Service Training School in Glynco, Georgia. They receive basic training in such areas as firearms, defensive tactics, physical conditioning, courtroom evidence and procedure, court security, search and seizure, and surveillance.

Upon graduation, trainees are assigned to a field office in the United States. They begin performing routine duties under the supervision of a field-training officer.

## Experience, Skills, and Personality Traits
To enter at the GS-5 level, applicants must have a minimum of three years of paid or nonpaid work experience if they do not have a bachelor's degree. Previous jobs should demonstrate their leadership ability to be Deputy U.S. Marshals. For example, applicants may have worked in law enforcement, security, classroom training, management, or sales.

All applicants must be U.S. citizens. Additionally, they must be between the ages of 21 and 36 at the time of their appointment as Deputy U.S. Marshals.

Deputy U.S. Marshals must have excellent interpersonal and communication skills, because they must meet and deal with people of different backgrounds. In addition, they need strong writing, problem-solving, and self-management skills (such as the ability to handle stressful situations, follow directions, prioritize tasks, and work independently). Being tactful, courteous, trustworthy, honest, and dedicated are some personality traits that successful Deputy U.S. Marshals share.

## Unions and Associations
Deputy U.S. Marshals might belong to the Federal Law Enforcement Officers Association, a professional organization for all federal law enforcement agents. This group offers professional support, services, and networking opportunities. For contact information, see Appendix IV.

## Tips for Entry
1. College students might apply for the U.S. Marshals Service Centralized Student Career Experience Program, a college work-study program.
2. Being fluent in one or more foreign languages is highly desirable.
3. For current recruitment information, contact a U.S. Marshals Service field office. You might find a listing in your local telephone book under *U.S. Government.* You can also write to: U.S. Marshals Service, Human Resources Division—Law Enforcement Recruiting, Washington, DC 20530-1000.
4. To learn more about the U.S. Marshals Service, visit its Web site on the Internet: http://www.usmarshals.gov.

# FBI SPECIAL AGENT

## CAREER PROFILE

**Duties:** Enforce more than 260 federal laws; conduct criminal investigations

**Alternate Title(s):** None

**Salary Range:** $41,000 to $84,000

**Employment Prospects:** Limited

**Advancement Prospects:** Good

**Prerequisites:**

**Education or Training**—Bachelor's degree; academy training, field training

**Experience**—Three years of work experience

**Special Skills and Personality Traits**—Teamwork, interpersonal, communication, research, writing, computer, analytical, and problem-solving skills; be dedicated, ethical, trustworthy, reliable, and discreet

## CAREER LADDER

```
┌─────────────────────────────────┐
│     Senior FBI Special Agent     │
└─────────────────────────────────┘

┌─────────────────────────────────┐
│        FBI Special Agent         │
└─────────────────────────────────┘

┌─────────────────────────────────┐
│     FBI Special Agent Trainee    │
└─────────────────────────────────┘
```

## Position Description

The Federal Bureau of Investigation (FBI), a part of the U.S. Department of Justice, is the primary investigative arm of the federal government. Special Agents are responsible for conducting investigations in more than 200 types of federal crime. Their criminal investigations are divided into the following categories: civil rights violations, counterterrorism (such as espionage), foreign counterintelligence, organized crime/drugs, violent crimes and major offenders, and financial crime. In addition, FBI Special Agents conduct background investigations of federal applicants, appointees, and candidates.

With every case, FBI Special Agents analyze the charges and determine the laws that have been violated. They identify the issues that must be addressed and determine the types of evidence they must find. Their primary activity is gathering accurate information to link suspects to their crimes. When they have sufficient evidence in a case, they present it to a U.S. Attorney or Department of Justice official who decides what action should be taken. If suspects are prosecuted, the Special Agents must prepare to testify in court about their findings.

Due to the nature of their investigations, FBI Special Agents have the authority to gather confidential information about persons, businesses, and groups. With the proper court documents, Special Agents collect credit reports, bank statements, police records, personnel files, medical records, business correspondence, and other confidential files.

Along with gathering paper information, FBI Special Agents interview witnesses, victims, and any person who they believe can help them with their cases. They interrogate possible suspects and develop informants. They may also perform surveillance and undercover work.

FBI Special Agents carry firearms, but have limited powers to arrest criminals. They may only arrest persons who are committing federal offenses in their presence. If Special Agents have reasonable grounds to believe that someone is committing a felony, they may arrest that person.

FBI Special Agents also work with other law enforcement agencies in joint investigations and in formal task forces. For example, FBI Special Agents and local and state authorities might work together on a kidnapping case.

Throughout their career with the FBI, Special Agents undergo a background check every few years to maintain their security clearance status. In addition, they must pass random drug tests. FBI Special Agents are required to retire upon reaching the age of 57.

FBI Special Agents can be reassigned to any FBI office in the United States and throughout the world at any time in their career. They are on call 24 hours a day.

## Salaries

Earnings for FBI Special Agents vary, depending on such factors as their experience, pay level, and geographical location.

Entry-level agents earn a salary at the GS-10 level. (GS stands for General Schedule, the pay schedule for most federal employees.) FBI Special Agents can advance to the GS-13 level in field nonsupervisory assignments. In 2005, the annual basic pay for GS-10 to GS-13 levels ranged from $41,175 to $83,819. FBI Special Agents who live in metropolitan areas, such as San Francisco and New York, typically earn higher salaries.

## Employment Prospects

As of June 2003, 11,633 Special Agents were employed by the FBI. They are stationed in FBI offices throughout the United States as well as in liaison posts around the world.

Most openings become available when Special Agents retire, resign, or are promoted to higher positions. The creation of additional Special Agent positions depends on legislation passed by Congress.

## Advancement Prospects

FBI Special Agents can advance to supervisory and administrative positions. After serving several years, they may become Senior Special Agents, who head investigation teams. They also qualify for additional training for special assignments.

## Education and Training

Applicants must have a bachelor's degree, preferably in law, accounting, computer science, criminal justice, or other area in which the FBI can use expertise and knowledge.

FBI recruits complete 16 weeks of intensive training at the FBI Academy in Quantico, Virginia. Courses include law, counterterrorism, organized crime, informant development, forensic science, computer skills, firearm skills, ethics, behavioral science, physical training, and defensive tactics.

Upon graduation from the academy, new Special Agents are assigned to a field office, working under the supervision of a field training officer. They also attend in-service seminars to build their knowledge and skills.

## Experience, Skills, and Personality Traits

Applicants need three years of work experience that shows they are capable of performing as FBI Special Agents. The FBI prefers applicants with backgrounds in law enforcement, law, and accounting as well as those with expertise in language, computers, or the sciences.

To perform their job effectively, FBI Special Agents need strong teamwork, interpersonal, and communication skills. Having excellent research, writing, computer, analytical, and problem-solving skills are also essential. Being dedicated, ethical, trustworthy, reliable, and discreet are some personality traits that successful FBI Special Agents share.

## Unions and Associations

FBI Special Agents might belong to the Federal Law Enforcement Officers Association and the Federal Criminal Investigators Association. They offer networking opportunities as well as professional resources and services. For contact information, see Appendix IV.

## Tips for Entry

1. Learn how to use computers, as computer skills are rapidly becoming essential in law enforcement careers.
2. The FBI hires its personnel directly. Special Agent recruitment is done through the FBI's field offices. For current information, contact an FBI field office. You might find a listing in your local telephone book under *U.S. Government.*
3. The use of illegal drugs or a conviction for a felony or a major misdemeanor can disqualify you from applying for an FBI Special Agent position.
4. To learn more information about an FBI Special Agent career, visit the FBI's employment Web page: http:// www.fbijobs.com.
5. To learn more about the FBI, visit its Web site on the Internet. Its URL is http://www.fbi.gov.

# DEA SPECIAL AGENT

## CAREER PROFILE

**Duties:** Enforce federal drug laws and regulations; conduct criminal investigations

**Alternate Title(s):** None

**Salary Range:** $31,000 to $70,000

**Employment Prospects:** Good

**Advancement Prospects:** Good

**Prerequisites:**

**Education or Training**—Bachelor's degree; academy training, field training

**Experience**—One year of relevant work experience

**Special Skills and Personality Traits**—Interpersonal, teamwork, communication, and problem-solving skills; be responsible, compassionate, honest, ethical, intuitive, calm, and self-motivated

## CAREER LADDER

```
┌─────────────────────────────────┐
│     Senior DEA Special Agent     │
└─────────────────────────────────┘

┌─────────────────────────────────┐
│        DEA Special Agent         │
└─────────────────────────────────┘

┌─────────────────────────────────┐
│     DEA Special Agent Trainee    │
└─────────────────────────────────┘
```

## Position Description

Special Agents of the Drug Enforcement Administration (DEA) investigate major violators of federal drug laws and regulations. They conduct investigations on individuals and groups who are suspected of growing, manufacturing, or distributing controlled substances in the United States. They gather sufficient proof to link suspects to their crimes in order for federal attorneys to prosecute the suspects in court.

DEA investigations are complex and dangerous. Some are joint investigations with other law enforcement agencies. As part of their investigative duties, DEA Special Agents analyze the charges and the appropriate laws that are violated. They identify principal suspects and the issues that must be addressed. They identify the types of evidence they must find, such as the assets earned from drug trafficking.

Gathering information is their primary activity. Special Agents conduct interviews and interrogations. They collect and process evidence. They develop confidential sources. In addition, they may perform surveillance and undercover work, sometimes becoming part of the drug world.

DEA Special Agents prepare necessary affidavits for search warrants and execute search warrants. They confiscate illegal narcotics and drug-making equipment and supplies. They also confiscate drug money, vehicles, jewelry, property, and any other profits that suspects made from sell-ing drugs. DEA Special Agents have limited arresting powers, however, and they may only arrest persons who are committing a federal offense in their presence. If Special Agents have reasonable grounds to believe that someone is committing a felony, they may arrest that person.

As part of their duties, DEA Special Agents keep accurate and proper documentation on their cases. They write clear, highly detailed technical reports that can lead to the conviction of criminals. In addition, Special Agents give sworn testimony in court trials.

DEA Special Agents travel frequently in their work, often at short notice. At any time in their career, they may be reassigned to any DEA post in the United States or in foreign countries. These federal law enforcement officers are required to retire upon reaching the age of 57.

## Salaries

Earnings for DEA Special Agents vary, depending on such factors as their education, experience, pay level, and geographical location. Entry-level DEA Special Agents usually earn a salary starting at the GS-7 or GS-9 level, depending on their qualifications. (GS stands for General Schedule, the pay schedule for most federal employees.) Journey agents can progress to the GS-12 level. In 2005, the annual basic pay for the GS-7 to GS-12 levels ranged from $30,567 to $70,484.

Agents who live in metropolitan areas, such as Chicago or New York, typically receive higher pay.

## Employment Prospects

Special Agents serve in DEA offices throughout the United States and the world. In 2003, Congress allotted funding for 4,680 DEA Special Agents. Job opportunities generally become available as agents retire, are promoted, or transfer to other occupations. Additional positions are created to meet growing needs as long as funding is available.

## Advancement Prospects

Throughout their careers, DEA Special Agents can advance to supervisory and administrative positions. After serving five to seven years, they may be promoted to Senior Special Agents. In addition, they are eligible to apply for overseas assignments.

## Education and Training

The DEA seeks candidates who hold a bachelor's degree with a cumulative grade point average of 2.95 or better. Having a degree in criminal justice, police science, finance, accounting, economics, computer science, or electrical engineering is desirable.

DEA Special Agent trainees complete 16 weeks of specialized training at the FBI Academy in Quantico, Virginia. The program includes academic, tactical, practical, firearms, and legal instruction. Upon completion of their training program, new DEA Special Agents are assigned to a field office, working under the supervision of field training officers.

## Experience, Skills, and Personality Traits

Applicants must be U.S. citizens, and they must be no younger than 21 and no older than 36 at their time of appointment. Additionally, applicants must have at least one year of experience conducting criminal investigations or related investigative experience. Having a military officer background, pilot skills, maritime experience, technical skills, mechanical skills, or accounting experience may also qualify applicants. Fluency in Spanish, Russian, Hebrew, Arabic, Nigerian, Chinese, or Japanese is also desirable.

To perform their work effectively, DEA Special Agents need excellent interpersonal, teamwork, communication, and problem-solving skills. Being responsible, compassionate, honest, ethical, intuitive, calm, and self-motivated are some personality traits that successful DEA Special Agents share.

## Unions and Associations

DEA Special Agents might belong to the Federal Law Enforcement Officers Association and the Federal Criminal Investigators Association. They might also join the National Drug Enforcement Officers Association. These organizations provide opportunities for networking as well as offer professional support and services. For contact information, see Appendix IV.

## Tips for Entry

1. Computer skills and a foreign language fluency are two areas that can enhance your chances for a law enforcement position.
2. A willingness to relocate may enhance your employability.
3. Call 1-800-DEA-4288 for the latest information about Special Agent openings or contact a DEA field office. You might find a listing in your local telephone book under *U.S. Government.* You can also write to: Special Agent Recruitment, DEA, 700 Army Navy Drive, Arlington, VA 22202.
4. To learn more about DEA, visit its Web site on the Internet: http://www.dea.gov.

# SECRET SERVICE SPECIAL AGENT

## CAREER PROFILE

**Duties:** Protect U.S. president and other officials; investigate counterfeiting and financial crime

**Alternate Title(s):** None

**Salary Range:** $25,000 to $70,000

**Employment Prospects:** Limited

**Advancement Prospects:** Good

**Prerequisites:**

**Education or Training**—Bachelor's degree (without experience); academy training, field training

**Experience**—Three years of law enforcement or criminal investigation experience (without a college degree)

**Special Skills and Personality Traits**—Teamwork, interpersonal, problem-solving, writing, and communication skills; be honest, trustworthy, and responsible

## CAREER LADDER

```
┌─────────────────────────────────────────┐
│   Senior Secret Service Special Agent     │
└─────────────────────────────────────────┘

┌─────────────────────────────────────────┐
│      Secret Service Special Agent         │
└─────────────────────────────────────────┘

┌─────────────────────────────────────────┐
│   Secret Service Special Agent Trainee    │
└─────────────────────────────────────────┘
```

## Position Description

Secret Service Special Agents are law enforcement officers with the U.S. Secret Service, an agency in the U.S. Department of Homeland Security. Before 2003, the Secret Service was part of the U.S. Department of the Treasury. Secret Service Special Agents are charged with two major responsibilities. The more familiar duty is that of protecting the U.S. president and other important officials. The other duty is conducting criminal investigations.

As part of the protective detail, Secret Service Special Agents protect the president, vice president, and their immediate families. They protect former presidents, their spouses, and their children who are sixteen or younger. In the last few months of a presidential campaign, Special Agents protect all major presidential and vice presidential candidates and their spouses. In addition, they protect heads of foreign countries or governments who visit the United States. Also, official U.S. representatives on special missions to foreign countries are protected by the Secret Service Special Agents.

The U.S. Secret Service refers to an individual that it protects as a *protectee*. When a protectee plans to visit a city or other locale, Secret Service Special Agents organize and arrange security measures as well as gather information about individuals and groups who may be threats or risks to

their protectee. Secret Service Special Agents also plan travel itineraries and arrange the modes of transportation.

Secret Service Special Agents on advance teams inspect the locations that their protectees will visit. There they create security perimeters and determine what equipment and staff is needed to safeguard their protectee. They also make necessary arrangements with local authorities for security measures such as police escorts or special police patrols. In addition, they investigate threats made against their protectees.

As part of the investigative detail, Secret Service Special Agents have the authority to investigate:

- threats against protectees
- counterfeiting of U.S. currency
- forgery, theft, and trafficking of government identification, government checks, bonds, and other financial certificates
- major financial crime, such as credit card fraud, identity fraud, computer fraud, telecommunications fraud, and automatic teller machine fraud

Special Agents are responsible for gathering information for a case and presenting it to a U.S. Attorney or other appropriate official who decides what action should be taken. If suspects are prosecuted, the Secret Service Special Agents may testify in court about their findings.

Secret Service Special Agents carry firearms, but have limited powers to arrest criminals. They may only arrest persons who are committing a federal offense in their presence. If Special Agents have sufficient facts to believe that someone is committing a felony, they can arrest that person.

They work a regular 40-hour week but put in many long, irregular hours of overtime. Throughout their careers, Secret Service Special Agents may be reassigned to any Secret Service office in the United States or in other countries. These federal law enforcement officers are required to retire upon reaching the age of 57.

## Salaries

Earnings for Secret Service Agents vary, depending on such factors as their experience, pay level, and geographical location. Entry-level agents earn a salary at the GS-5, GS-7, or GS-9 level, depending on their qualifications. (GS stands for General Schedule, the pay schedule for most federal employees.) Secret Service Special Agents can advance to the GS-12 level in field nonsupervisory assignments. In 2005, the annual basic pay for GS-5 to GS-12 levels ranged from $24,677 to $70,484.

Agents who live in metropolitan areas, where the cost of living is high, receive additional compensation.

## Employment Prospects

The U.S. Secret Service has over 125 field offices throughout the United States and in some foreign countries. It employs about 2,100 Special Agents.

The agency is always interested in qualified applicants, but job opportunities are limited. The attrition rate is low, and most openings become available when Secret Service Special Agents retire, resign, or are promoted to higher positions.

## Advancement Prospects

Throughout their careers, Secret Service Special Agents are rotated in tours of duty to gain knowledge, skills, and experience in all areas. Those with the desire and ability to assume supervisory and administrative responsibilities compete for available positions. Upon reaching the GS-12 grade, they may be promoted to Senior Secret Service Special Agent.

## Education and Training

A bachelor's degree, without relevant work experience, qualifies an applicant at the GS-5 level. An additional year of graduate work in law enforcement, criminal justice, or other related field qualifies an applicant at the GS-7 level.

Secret Service Special Agent trainees undergo 11 weeks of criminal investigative training at the Federal Law Enforce-ment Training Center in Glynco, Georgia, or Artesia, New Mexico. This is followed by another 11 weeks of training at the Secret Service Training Academy in Beltsville, Maryland. They learn specific Secret Service policies, procedures, and basic knowledge. In addition, they receive firearms training, control tactics, water survival skills, and physical fitness training. Upon completion of academy training, they are assigned to a field office, and under the supervision of a field-training officer, begin performing routine tasks.

## Experience, Skills, and Personality Traits

Applicants who have no college degree can qualify at the GS-5 grade with three years of criminal investigative or law enforcement work experience. Applicants with a bachelor's degree and one year of criminal investigative or law enforcement experience can qualify at the GS-7 level.

To perform their job effectively, Secret Service Special Agents must have superior teamwork and interpersonal skills. In addition, they need strong problem-solving, writing, and communication skills. Being honest, trustworthy, and responsible are some personality traits that successful Secret Service Special Agents share.

## Unions and Associations

Secret Service Special Agents might join the Federal Law Enforcement Officers Association, a professional organization that offers networking opportunities as well as professional services and resources. For contact information, see Appendix IV.

## Tips for Entry

1. The U.S. Secret Service offers internship and work experience programs to college students, in which they can explore career options within the agency. Opportunities are available at the agency's headquarters in Washington, D.C., as well as in field offices throughout the United States. Contact a field office for specific information.
2. Proficiency in a foreign language may enhance your employability.
3. Applicants must be U.S. citizens who are at least 21 years old and no older than 36 years upon their appointment to a special agent position. In addition, they must be in excellent physical condition.
4. To apply for a Special Agent position, contact a Secret Service field office. You might find a listing in your local telephone book under *U.S. Government.* You can also contact the U.S. Secret Service Personnel Division at 245 Murray Drive, Building 410, Washington, DC 20223 or call (202) 406-5800.
5. To learn more about the U.S. Secret Service, visit its Web site: http://www.secretservice.gov.

# BORDER PATROL AGENT

## CAREER PROFILE

**Duties:** Detect and prevent undocumented aliens from entering the United States; detect and prevent drug smuggling into the United States

**Alternate Title(s):** None

**Salary Range:** $25,000 to $40,000

**Employment Prospects:** Good

**Advancement Prospects:** Good

**Prerequisites:**

**Educations or Training**—Bachelor's degree (without work experience); academy training, field training

**Experience**—one year general work experience (without college degree)

**Special Skills and Personality Traits**—Interpersonal, communication, teamwork, problem-solving, and decision-making skills; be independent, dedicated, loyal, calm, and composed

## CAREER LADDER

```
┌─────────────────────────────────┐
│   Senior Border Patrol Agent     │
└─────────────────────────────────┘

┌─────────────────────────────────┐
│      Border Patrol Agent          │
└─────────────────────────────────┘

┌─────────────────────────────────┐
│     Border Patrol Trainee         │
└─────────────────────────────────┘
```

## Position Description

Border Patrol Agents are uniformed law enforcement officers who work for the Customs and Border Protection division of the U.S. Department of Homeland Security. They are responsible for protecting the U.S. borders along Mexico and Canada as well as the coastal waters surrounding the Florida Peninsula and Puerto Rico. Their primary mission is to detect and apprehend undocumented aliens from entering the United States illegally. In addition, Border Patrol Agents play a role in uncovering and preventing the smuggling of drugs along the U.S. borders and the U.S. land points of entry, particularly along the southwest border.

Line watch is the basic activity for Border Patrol Agents. As part of their job, Border Patrol Agents carry firearms and operate a variety of vehicles including four-wheel all-terrain vehicles.

Their work can be dangerous and hard. They usually work alone in remote areas, such as deserts and mountains, without any backup. They often work at night, in bad weather, and on rough terrain. They might perform surveillance from a hidden position; respond to electronic sensor alarms and use infrared scopes; or follow tracks, marks, and other physical evidence. In addition, they may be involved in high-speed chases and armed encounters.

Border Patrol Agents are also assigned to checkpoint stations along the borders where they complete traffic and transportation checks. Some Border Patrol Agents are assigned to interior stations such as in Dallas, San Francisco, and New York. They observe traffic on highways and roads, keeping a watch for vehicles that may be smuggling illegal aliens. The Border Patrol Agents also patrol cities and agricultural areas for illegal aliens who may be living there. In addition, they check ranches and farms for illegal aliens who may be working there.

Border Patrol Agents are assigned a rotating shift, but they often work overtime. It is not unusual for Border Patrol Agents to be involved in operations that keep them away from home for more than a month at a time.

Border Patrol Agents are expected to speak Spanish fluently. Many of them learn the language during their academy training. Generally, new Border Patrol Agents are assigned to a duty station along the southwestern border with Mexico. Upon being promoted to a journeyman level, Border Patrol Agents are eligible to apply for duty with the canine, horse, bike patrol, or other special units. These federal law enforcement officers are required to retire upon reaching the age of 57.

## Salaries

Earnings for Border Patrol Agents vary, depending on such factors as their experience, pay level, and geographical location. New Border Patrol Agents earn a salary at the GS-5 or GS-7 level, depending on their qualifications. (GS stands for General Schedule, the pay schedule for most federal employees.) In 2005, the annual basic pay for GS-5 to GS-7 levels ranged from $24,677 to $39,738.

Agents who live in metropolitan areas, where the cost of living is high, receive additional compensation.

## Employment Prospects

Job opportunities vary each year, depending on the needs of the U.S. Border Patrol. Openings usually become available as Border Patrol Agents retire, transfer to other positions, or resign from their post.

From time to time, Congress passes legislation for additional Border Patrol Agents. But applicants can expect to face a long and highly competitive selection process.

## Advancement Prospects

After passing their probation period, Border Patrol Agents may apply for special units such as horse patrol, bike patrol, canine detail, and tactical detail. Those who pursue supervisory and administrative positions can seek such promotions as supervisory border patrol agents and patrol agents-in-charge.

Many Border Patrol Agents go on to work with other law enforcement agencies such as police departments, sheriff's departments, the Federal Bureau of Investigation, Drug Enforcement Administration, and U.S. Secret Service.

## Education and Training

Applicants without any work experience can qualify at the GS-5 grade with a bachelor's degree. They can qualify at the GS-7 grade if they have completed one year of graduate work in law, police science, criminal justice, or another related field.

Border Patrol trainees complete more than five months of training at the Border Patrol Academy in Charleston, South Carolina. Among the subjects they study are immigration law, criminal law, behavioral science, border patrol operations, use of firearms, and Spanish.

Upon graduation from the academy, trainees are assigned to a post on or near the Mexican border. They perform patrol duties under the supervision of a field training officer. They must pass a series of Spanish tests during their probationary period to continue working with the Border Patrol.

## Experience, Skills, and Personality Traits

Applicants who have no college degrees can qualify at the GS-5 grade with one year of general work experience. They can qualify at the GS-7 grade with one year of law enforcement experience. In addition, applicants must be U.S. citizens and must be younger than age 37 at the time of their appointment as a Border Agent.

The Border Patrol looks for applicants who are fluent in Spanish or have the ability to learn the language. It chooses applicants who show they have the stamina and strength to perform duties under harsh environmental conditions.

To perform their work effectively, Border Patrol Agents need strong interpersonal, communication, teamwork, problem-solving, and decision-making skills. Being independent, dedicated, loyal, calm, and composed are some personality traits that Border Patrol Agents have in common.

## Unions and Associations

Border Patrol Agents are members of the National Border Patrol Council, a union that represents them in contract negotiations for pay, benefits, and working conditions. It also handles any grievances that officers may have against their employers. In addition, Border Patrol Agents can join the Federal Law Enforcement Officers Association, which provides networking opportunities as well as various professional services and resources. (For contact information for the above organizations, see Appendix IV.)

## Tips for Entry

1. Take Spanish classes in high school and college to improve your chances of getting a Border Patrol job.
2. The entrance examination for the U.S. Border Patrol covers three areas—an assessment of your past experiences as well as your competency in logical reasoning and the Spanish language. If you do not speak Spanish, you will take an exam that tests your ability to learn Spanish.
3. The application process generally averages five months. Make sure you have filled in your job application completely. The agency will return your application if information is missing.
4. The U.S. Border Patrol provides recruiting information on its Web site, http://www.usborderpatrol.gov. Check it regularly. You can also complete an online job application when openings are available.

# CUSTOMS AND BORDER PROTECTION (CBP) OFFICER

## CAREER PROFILE

**Duties:** Prevent the entry of terrorists, instruments of terror, illegal drugs, contraband, and illegal aliens into the United States; process travelers and conveyances; enforce immigration, customs, and agricultural laws and regulations

**Alternate Title(s):** None

**Salary Range:** $25,000 to $59,000

**Employment Prospects:** Fair

**Advancement Prospects:** Fair

**Prerequisites:**

**Education or Training**—Bachelor's degree, if one has no qualifying work experience; CBP Officer training program

**Experience**—Three years of general experience, if one has no college degree

**Special Skills and Personality Traits**—Communication, writing, problem-solving, interpersonal, and self-management skills; be competent, responsible, fair, trustworthy, and composed

## CAREER LADDER

```
CBP Officer (Journeyman)
```

```
CBP Officer
```

```
CBP Officer Trainee
```

## Position Description

U.S. Customs and Border Protection (CBP) Officers serve at U.S. ports of entry, performing law enforcement and security duties. They monitor and inspect travelers and conveyances (ships, aircraft, and vehicles) as they enter or depart from the United States. In their role as inspectors, CBP Officers fulfill the primary mission of their agency, as well as that of the U.S. Department of Homeland Security (DHS): to prevent terrorists and terrorist weapons from entering the United States. CBP Officers also bar the entry of illegal drugs, contraband, and illegal aliens.

The CBP Officer occupation was created in March 2003 by the CBP, which is a division of the DHS. Traditionally, travelers dealt with three different inspectors at each U.S. port of entry. Their passports, visas, and other identification papers were checked by immigration inspectors. Travelers' baggage and packages were looked at by agricultural inspectors to ensure forbidden plants or animals were not

being brought into the country. Travelers also declared the value of any items they had purchased in foreign countries and paid the required taxes (or duties) to the customs inspectors. These inspectors also inspected baggage, packages, and cargo for arms, stolen property, illegal drugs, and other contraband that had been smuggled into the United States.

Today, the CBP Officers are cross-trained to perform the various duties in customs and immigration inspections at all U.S. ports of entry. Their authority involves the enforcement of federal laws and regulations regarding immigration, revenue and trade, agriculture, and the seizure of contraband. CBP agricultural specialists assist CBP Officers in examining baggage and cargo to ensure that individuals and businesses are in compliance with the laws and regulations governing agricultural imports.

CBP Officers work at more than 300 U.S. ports of entry. Most of them are stationed at airports and seaports, as well as at land ports along the U.S. international borders. Some officers are assigned to work in Guam, Puerto Rico, or other U.S. territories. As armed and uniformed law enforcement officers, CBP Officers have the power to make arrests of individuals who are breaking the laws which the officers enforce. For example, CBP Officers may arrest individuals who are entering the U.S. illegally or who are smuggling contraband. On occasion, CBP Officers work closely with border patrol agents and other law enforcement officers.

CBP Officers are generally assigned to process either travelers or cargo. They keep their eyes open for potential terrorists and terrorist weapons. They make sure that imports and exports are in compliance with laws and international trade agreements. CBP Officers also help to ensure that weapons, narcotics, hazardous waste, and other dangerous or illegal items are not being brought into the country.

Some CBP Officers operate sophisticated machines, such as gamma X-ray machines, to inspect baggage and cargo. Depending on their station, they may be required to speak a foreign language. For example, CBP Officers who work in Miami, Puerto Rico, and along the southwestern U.S. border are expected to be proficient in reading, writing, and speaking Spanish.

The job CBP Officers do is physically demanding. For instance, their tasks may require them to run, climb, or lift heavy objects. At some stations, CBP Officers work outside in all types of weather, including rain, cold, heat, and humidity. Other officers work in confined areas.

CBP Officers work a 40-hour week but often put in additional hours to complete their tasks. They may be required to work nights, weekends, and holidays. They sometimes travel to perform their job or to participate in training programs.

## Salaries

Earnings vary for CBP Officers, depending on such factors as their experience, education, pay level, work schedule, and geographical location. CBP Officers typically earn higher salaries in metropolitan areas such as Los Angeles and New York.

Entry-level officers earn a salary at either the GS-5 or GS-7 level on the federal pay schedule known as the general schedule (GS). CBP Officers can advance to the GS-11 level. In 2005, the annual basic pay for levels GS-5 to GS-11 ranged from $24,677 to $58,811.

## Employment Prospects

CBP converted about 18,000 customs, immigration, and agriculture inspector jobs to CBP Officer and agriculture specialist positions.

Opportunities generally become available to replace CBP Officers who transfer to other occupations, retire, or advance to higher positions. The creation of additional positions depends on the agency's needs and the availability of federal funds.

## Advancement Prospects

Entry-level CBP Officers receive a two-year appointment. If they perform their job satisfactorily, at the end of this period, they become permanent employees. CBP Officers can advance to a journeyman level of GS-11 on the federal pay schedule. At this level, they become eligible to apply for special assignments—to become canine handlers, trainers, or members of the enforcement and special response teams. Those officers with administrative and managerial ambitions can apply for such positions with the CBP, as well as with the Department of Homeland Security.

## Education and Training

Applicants must possess a bachelor's degree (in any field) to qualify at the GS-5 level if they do not have the required work experience. Having a combination of college study and work experience may be acceptable. To qualify at the GS-7 level, applicants must meet specific academic achievements as an undergraduate or possess a master's or higher degree (in any field).

New CBP Officers must complete a comprehensive two-year training program. It includes 12 weeks of basic training at the Federal Law Enforcement Training Center in Glynco, Georgia. This is followed by extensive training in the field, which includes classroom study, computer-based training, and on-the-job training under the supervision of experienced officers.

Non-Spanish-speaking recruits who are required to learn the language must successfully complete a five-week-long Spanish immersion class.

## Experience, Skills, and Personality Traits

Applicants must be U.S. citizens. To qualify at the GS-5 level, applicants without a bachelor's degree must have three years of general work experience that demonstrates their ability to learn and apply new information as well as meet and handle people. To qualify at the GS-7 level, applicants must have one year of specialized experience. Such experience can be acquired by working in immigration, customs, or a related inspection unit at a U.S. port of entry.

To perform their work effectively, CBP Officers need strong communication, writing, and problem-solving skills. They must also have excellent interpersonal skills, as they will deal with people from different backgrounds. In addition, CBP Officers should have good self-management skills, which includes the ability to get to work on time, follow directions, take initiative, work independently, and work well under pressure.

Being competent, responsible, fair, trustworthy, and composed are some personality traits that successful CBP Officers share.

**Unions and Associations**

CBP Officers may join a union to represent them in contract negotiations regarding pay, benefits, and working conditions. A union can also handle any grievances that officers may have against their employer.

**Tips for Entry**

1. Applicants must possess a valid driver's license at the time of their appointment.
2. Proficiency in Spanish or another language that the CBP requires may enhance your employability.
3. Maintain a clean personal record. The CBP conducts an extensive background investigation that covers the past several years of a person's life. The investigation checks for arrests, convictions, job terminations, financial debts, the use of alcohol and illegal drugs, and other such activities. Having problems in any of these areas can disqualify a person for a CBP Officer position.
4. It generally takes at least eight months to complete the job selection process for a CBP Officer position. Applicants who have successfully passed this process are placed on a list of eligible candidates. The CBP will offer positions to candidates as they become available.
5. To learn more about the CBP and CBP Officers, visit the CBP Web site, http://www.cbp.gov.

# U.S. COAST GUARD BOARDING TEAM PERSONNEL

## CAREER PROFILE

**Duties:** Enforce all federal laws in U.S. coastal waters and on the high seas; board vessels to inspect, examine, and search for possible federal violations; perform particular boarding team duties

**Alternate Title(s):** Boarding Officer, Assistant Boarding Officer, Boarding Team Member

**Salary Range:** Varies for enlistees and commissioned officers

**Employment Prospects:** Fair

**Advancement Prospects:** Good

**Prerequisites:**

**Education or Training**—Training program for either boarding officer or boarding team member

**Experience**—No law enforcement experience required

**Special Skills and Personality Traits**—Interpersonal, teamwork, communication, and self-management skills; be mature, diplomatic, ethical, respectful, and dedicated

## CAREER LADDER

```
┌─────────────────────────────────────────┐
│     LEDET Boarding Team Personnel         │
└─────────────────────────────────────────┘

┌─────────────────────────────────────────┐
│        Cutter or Station Boarding         │
│             Team Personnel                │
└─────────────────────────────────────────┘

┌─────────────────────────────────────────┐
│                Trainees                   │
└─────────────────────────────────────────┘
```

## Position Description

The U.S. Coast Guard is one of the five U.S. Armed Forces. While the U.S. Army, Air Force, Navy, and Marines are part of the U.S. Department of Defense, the Coast Guard is under the helm of the U.S. Department of Homeland Security. Hence the Coast Guard not only plays a military role, but also provides the country with valuable seagoing services. One of these major responsibilities is to be the primary federal agency that performs maritime law enforcement.

The Coast Guard enforces all federal laws in the areas of:

- boating safety for recreational, commercial, cargo, and other vessels
- living marine resources, including marine mammals, endangered species, and fisheries
- interdiction (or interception) of illegal drugs being smuggled into the United States
- interdiction of undocumented migrants who are attempting to illegally enter into the United States, a U.S. territory, or a U.S. possession
- crime, including violent acts and terrorism

Coast Guard personnel known as boarding teams have the authority to go aboard vessels that are suspected of violating federal laws. The vessels may be sailing in waters under U.S. jurisdiction or in the high seas. They may be owned by Americans or foreigners.

Coast Guard Boarding Team Personnel are uniformed federal law enforcement officers. They have the authority to make inquiries of vessel captains and crews. They also can examine, inspect, and search vessels as well as cargo, crew, and passengers. In addition, Boarding Team Personnel can seize contraband, drugs, and other illegal items. All Boarding Team Personnel are authorized to carry firearms in the performance of their duties and can make arrests accordingly.

A Coast Guard boarding team consists of a boarding officer (BO), who is charge of the team, and boarding team members (BTMs). Some boarding teams also have an assistant boarding officer.

When teams are to board a vessel, they are generally sent from their unit, which is either a cutter or a shore station. A team may consist of a BO and one BTM or several BTMs depending on the nature of the boarding.

The BO is responsible for directing the boarding and supervising the actions of the BTMs. While the BO meets with the vessel owner or captain and goes over documents and identification, the BTMs check the vessel for violations and criminal activity.

On occasion, boarding teams work with local, state, or other federal agencies. For example, a boarding team might work with U.S. Customs and Border Protection agents to interdict a vessel suspected of smuggling undocumented migrants into the United States.

Commissioned officers as well as enlistees can join their unit's boarding team. (All boat stations and cutters that conduct law enforcement have boarding teams.) Hence boatswain's mates, mechanics, and cooks may work together with ensigns and lieutenants.

It is not uncommon for a BO to hold a lesser rank than some of the BTMs under his or her command. For example, a boarding officer might be a boatswain's mate with a petty officer first-class ranking, while two of the boarding team members could be commissioned officers. When performing boarding duty, all BTMs who rank higher than the BO must obey his or her orders.

Conducting vessel boardings is the secondary job for all Boarding Team Personnel. When they are not performing those duties, they resume the duties of their primary job as commissioned officers, boatswain's mates, machinery technicians, food technicians, and so on.

## Salaries

Coast Guard Personnel earn pay based on their rank, pay grade, and number of years in service. They do not receive additional pay for performing boarding duties.

In 2005, the basic monthly pay scale for these Coast Guard personnel (on active duty) ranged as follows:

- seaman (E-3): $1,456.20 to $1,641.00
- petty officer (E-4 to E-9): $1,612.80 to $5,231.70
- warrant officer (W-1 to W-5): $2,290.20 to $6,121.20
- commissioned officer (O-1 to O-6): $2,343.60 to $8,575.50

Coast Guard personnel also receive various benefits such as a housing allowance and free medical care.

## Employment Prospects

Coast Guard units—cutters and boat stations—that conduct law enforcement missions all have boarding teams. The number of Boarding Team Personnel varies at each unit, depending on the needs of a unit. Most opportunities at a unit become available to replace Boarding Team Personnel who have been reassigned to other duties or posts, as well as those who have retired or resigned from service.

## Advancement Prospects

Enlistees and commissioned officers can develop a Coast Guard career according to their interests and ambitions. For example, enlisted personnel can take advantage of programs to become commissioned officers. Both enlistees and officers are promoted in rank and pay grade as they gain experience and demonstrate satisfactory job performance.

Individuals who perform boarding duty may advance from boarding team member to assistant boarding officer to boarding officer, as long as they hold the appropriate ranks. For example, to be appointed as a boarding officer, one must be a commissioned officer, a warrant officer, or a petty officer with an E-4 ranking or higher.

Various advanced law enforcement opportunities are available for experienced Boarding Team Personnel. For example, they may apply for positions on tactical law enforcement teams, known as Law Enforcement Detachments (LEDETs), which conduct boardings while they are assigned to sail on U.S. Navy ships. Warrant officers and petty officers may qualify for such positions as port security specialist or special agent with the Coast Guard Investigative Service.

Upon retiring from or completing their duty with the Coast Guard, some Boarding Team Personnel have continued to pursue law enforcement careers as civilians. Many have become police officers, criminal investigators, and compliance inspectors with local, state, and federal agencies. Some have entered the private security field, to work as private investigators and security specialists.

## Education and Training

To become part of a boarding team, individuals must first successfully complete a training program where they learn the basic skills and knowledge to perform their jobs. Boarding team members participate in a two-week program, while boarding officers attend a monthlong maritime law enforcement school.

Boarding Team Personnel take part in regularly scheduled practice exercises to maintain and hone their skills. As they are assigned to new types of missions (such as drug interdiction or fisheries enforcement), Boarding Team Personnel complete appropriate training programs, sponsored by the Coast Guard and other agencies.

## Experience, Skills, and Personality Traits

No law enforcement experience is required, but officers and enlistees must meet basic qualifications before they can apply for boarding team positions. Individuals must meet certain physical fitness qualifications. They must also pass a firearms test and other exams which test an individual's ability to make judgments concerning the use of force.

Commissioned officers, warrant officers, and petty officers are eligible for any position on a boarding team. Seamen at an E-3 level may qualify for a boarding team member position.

To perform their work effectively, Boarding Team Personnel must have strong interpersonal, teamwork, and communication skills. They must also possess excellent self-management skills, such as the ability to follow directions, handle stressful situations, organize their tasks, and work independently. Being mature, diplomatic, ethical, respectful, and dedicated are some personality traits that successful Boarding Team Personnel have in common.

## Unions and Associations

Coast Guard personnel are eligible to join the Fleet Reserve Association. This is a professional military association that serves the particular interests of the Coast Guard as well as Navy and Marine Corps personnel. The association's mission is to represent its members' concerns regarding pay, health care, and benefits before Congress and other federal agencies. For contact information, see Appendix IV.

## Tips for Entry

1. Visit a Coast Guard station or cutter to get an idea of what it would be like to be part of the Coast Guard.
2. To learn about qualifications and job options available for enlistees and commissioned officers, talk with a local Coast Guard recruiter. To find the phone number of the nearest recruiter, look under *recruiting* or *U.S. Coast Guard* in the U.S. government section of your telephone book. You can also call (800) 438-8724 or visit the Coast Guard Web site at http://www.uscg.mil.
3. Although an enlistee with any rating can perform law enforcement duties, certain ratings, such as boatswain's mate, machinery technician, and gunner mate, have greater chances of being assigned to boarding teams. Talk with a recruiter as well as Boarding Team Personnel for advice about ratings if you plan on joining as an enlistee.
4. To improve your chances of getting a position on a boarding team, obtain an assignment with a unit that conducts law enforcement.
5. To learn about the Coast Guard, visit its Web site at http://www.uscg.mil.

# EPA SPECIAL AGENT
# (CRIMINAL INVESTIGATION DIVISION)

## CAREER PROFILE

**Duties:** Conduct criminal investigations on individuals or groups suspected of violating federal or state environmental laws and regulations

**Alternate Title(s):** Criminal Investigator

**Salary Range:** $25,000 to $84,000

**Employment Prospects:** Poor

**Advancement Prospects:** Fair

**Prerequisites:**

**Education or Training**—Bachelor's degree; criminal investigations training program

**Experience**—Three years of progressively responsible work experience in administrative, professional, technical, law enforcement, or other areas

**Special Skills and Personality Traits**—Writing, communication, analytical, organizational, problem-solving, interpersonal, and teamwork skills; be dedicated, persistent, unbiased, ethical, resourceful, versatile, and tactful

## CAREER LADDER

```
+-------------------------------------+
|    Senior or Lead Special Agent     |
+-------------------------------------+

+-------------------------------------+
|    Special Agent (Journey-level)    |
+-------------------------------------+

+-------------------------------------+
|     Special Agent (Entry-level)     |
+-------------------------------------+
```

## Position Description

The U.S. Environmental Protection Agency (EPA) is an independent federal agency which has a mission to protect human health and the environment through the enforcement of federal and state environmental laws and regulations. Special Agents in the EPA's criminal investigation division are responsible for the investigations of major violations of environmental laws and regulations. For example, Special Agents would investigate environmental criminal cases that involve individuals or groups:

- tampering with a drinking water supply—for example, dumping poisons into a reservoir
- discharging pollutants illegally into a river, lake, ocean, or other body of water in the United States
- causing oil spills that significantly damage beaches, waterways, or wetlands
- disposing hazardous waste illegally, such as in sewers or storm drains
- discarding hazardous waste in a manner that causes deaths or serious injuries

- handling hazardous substances, such as asbestos and pesticides, in violation of environmental laws and regulations
- importing or smuggling regulated or restricted chemicals, such as CFC refrigerants, into the United States
- committing mail or wire fraud in connection with environmental criminal activities
- committing data fraud, such as submitting false environmental data to the EPA

Like other federal criminal investigators, the EPA Special Agent's job is to identify and apprehend violators as well as help prosecutors convict them. Suspects may be individuals or organizations, such as businesses, manufacturers, academic institutions, and governments.

The primary activity of the EPA Special Agents is to gather accurate and precise information that links suspects to their crimes. The Special Agents plan their investigations carefully, while analyzing the charges and the appropriate laws that are violated. They then begin to collect and process evidence. They review pertinent documents, reports, and records. They interview suspects, victims, witnesses, subject matter experts, and others who may be able to help them with their investigations. EPA Special Agents may develop informants, or confidential sources, who work closely with suspects or their organizations. They may also conduct surveillance or undercover work if necessary. Their investigations may take several days, weeks, months, or years to complete, depending on the complexity and sensitivity of the cases.

EPA Special Agents keep accurate and proper documentation about their cases. They write clear, detailed technical reports that can lead to the conviction of criminals. When they have sufficient evidence in a case, Special Agents turn their findings over to a U.S. Attorney (or to a state official if it is a state matter) who decides what action should be taken. On occasion, the Special Agents are called upon to give sworn testimony about their findings at depositions and trials.

As federal law enforcement officers, EPA Special Agents have the authority to carry firearms while performing their duties. They can also execute and serve search warrants. They may arrest individuals who are committing an environmental crime or any other federal crime within their presence. If EPA Special Agents have reasonable grounds to believe that someone is committing a felony, they may arrest that person.

EPA Special Agents work on cases alone or with fellow investigators. They sometimes work on joint investigations with local, tribal, state, or other federal law enforcement agencies.

The nature of their work requires EPA Special Agents to travel frequently. They have a 40-hour week but often put in longer and irregular hours to perform their investigations. These federal law enforcement officers are required to retire upon reaching the age of 57.

## Salaries

Earnings for EPA Special Agents vary, depending on such factors as their education, experience, pay level, and geographical location. Most entry-level agents earn a salary beginning at the GS-5 or GS-7 level. (GS stands for General Schedule, the pay schedule for most federal employees). EPA Special Agents can advance to the GS-13 level in field nonsupervisory assignments. In 2005, the annual basic pay for GS-5 to GS-13 levels ranged from $24,677 to $83,819.

EPA Special Agents who live in metropolitan areas (such as Seattle and Boston) typically earn higher salaries.

## Employment Prospects

Special Agents work in the EPA's criminal investigation division offices, which are located throughout the United States. As of 2004, about 200 Special Agents were employed in the EPA criminal investigation division.

Job opportunities generally become available as Special Agents retire, transfer to other occupations, or advance to higher positions. Depending on the EPA's needs, Congress may increase or decrease the number of criminal investigators. The creation of additional EPA Special Agent positions is based on the availability of funds.

## Advancement Prospects

Many EPA Special Agents achieve advancement by earning higher pay and receiving greater levels of responsibilities. Agents with supervisory and managerial ambitions can pursue such positions within the criminal investigation division and the EPA as well as in other governmental agencies.

Upon retirement from the EPA, some Special Agents pursue second careers in environmental, security, educational, and other fields.

## Education and Training

Minimally, Special Agents must possess a bachelor's degree, in any field.

Recruits undergo an eight-week training program that covers basic federal law enforcement and criminal investigation, as well as physical conditioning and the use of firearms. Upon successful completion of their basic training, recruits receive another eight weeks of training that focuses on how to conduct environmental criminal investigations.

Throughout their careers, many EPA Special Agents enroll in educational programs, training seminars, conference workshops, and so on to increase their knowledge and update their skills.

## Experience, Skills, and Personality Traits

Applicants who qualify at the GS-5 level must have a minimum of three years of progressively responsible work experience in administrative, professional, technical, investigative, or other areas. All applicants must be U.S. citizens between the ages of 21 and 37 years upon the time of their appointment. They must also be in excellent physical condition.

EPA Special Agents need excellent writing, communication, analytical, organizational, and problem-solving skills for their job. They must also have effective interpersonal and teamwork skills, as they must deal with many people from diverse backgrounds.

Being dedicated, persistent, unbiased, ethical, resourceful, versatile, and tactful are some personality traits that successful EPA Special Agents share.

## Unions and Associations

EPA Special Agents are eligible to join the Federal Criminal Investigators Association and the Federal Law Enforcement

Officers Association. These professional associations provide opportunities for networking with peers, as well as professional services and resources. For contact information, see Appendix IV.

## Tips for Entry

1. As a high school student, begin learning about the various environmental problems and issues. For example, you might read books and magazines pertaining to the environment, talk with professionals in the environmental field, or volunteer for environmental projects.
2. As a college student, gain valuable experience with the EPA through its internship or work experience programs.
3. The EPA criminal investigation division sometimes hires college graduates who do not meet the work experience requirement. These graduates qualify as outstanding scholars. They graduated with a 3.45 or higher grade point average or graduated in the upper 10 percent of their class or major university subdivision.
4. Before submitting your job application, check it to be sure you have answered all questions completely. Also make sure that you have attached all forms and documents that have been requested.
5. You can learn more about the EPA and its criminal investigation division on the Internet at http://www. epa.gov. You can also find information about the EPA's career opportunities and job recruitment process. Additionally, you can read about the activities of the different EPA regional offices.

# POSTAL INSPECTOR

## CAREER PROFILE

**Duties:** Enforce federal postal laws; conduct criminal, civil, and administrative investigations

**Alternate Title(s):** None

**Salary Range:** $46,000 to $70,000

**Employment Prospects:** Fair

**Advancement Prospects:** Limited

**Prerequisites:**

**Education or Training**—Bachelor's degree; basic training program for Postal Inspectors

**Experience**—Meet one of the six experience requirements

**Special Skills and Personality Traits**—Teamwork, interpersonal, communication, researching, and writing skills; be tactful, persistent, ethical, resourceful, and dedicated

**Special Requirements**—Driver's license

## CAREER LADDER

```
┌─────────────────────────┐
│       Team Leader       │
└─────────────────────────┘

┌─────────────────────────┐
│     Postal Inspector    │
└─────────────────────────┘

┌─────────────────────────┐
│  Postal Inspector Trainee │
└─────────────────────────┘
```

## Position Description

Postal Inspectors are law enforcement officers who work for the U.S. Postal Inspection Service, which is part of the U.S. Postal Service. The U.S. Postal Inspection Service is responsible for the security and safety of the U.S. mail as well as for the U.S. Postal Service and its employees. This agency is also responsible for enforcing more than 200 federal postal laws.

Postal Inspectors assist with the responsibility of protecting the U.S. Postal Service's revenue and assets. Their primary role is to investigate criminal, civil, and administrative violations of the postal laws and regulations. Examples of their postal investigations include:

- theft of U.S. mail, postal money orders, and equipment
- assault or murder of postal employees
- burglary of a postal facility
- mailings of bombs, obscene material, child pornography, or drugs
- counterfeiting of postmarks, postage stamps, or postal money orders
- extortion
- mail fraud (the use of the mail to scam the public)

Their investigations involve collecting accurate information to link suspects to their crimes. Postal Inspectors gather physical evidence, interrogate suspects, interview victims and witnesses, and, if needed, do surveillance and undercover work. When Postal Inspectors have sufficient evidence for a case, they present it to U.S. Attorneys or other Department of Justice officials who decide what action should be taken. Postal Inspectors may help prepare evidence and provide testimony if a case is prosecuted in court.

Postal Inspectors carry firearms, and have the authority to serve warrants and subpoenas. They have, however, limited powers to arrest criminals. Postal Inspectors may only arrest persons who are committing a felony within their presence or if they have reasonable grounds to believe that persons are committing or have committed postal crimes.

On occasion, Postal Inspectors work with local, state, and other federal law enforcement officers on joint investigations in which the U.S. mail, the U.S. Postal Service, or postal employees are involved. For example, Postal Inspectors might work on a special task force to investigate a group of people who are sending fraudulent insurance claims through the mail.

Postal Inspectors work long and irregular hours. Their duties often involve frequent travel to other cities and states. Postal Inspectors may be reassigned to any Postal Inspection Service office at any time in their careers.

## Salaries

Earnings for Postal Inspectors vary, depending on such factors as their experience, education, and geographical location. Postal Inspectors who have reached the full performance level earn a salary comparable to the GS-11 and GS-12 levels on the General Schedule (GS), the pay schedule for most federal employees. In 2005, the annual basic pay for these GS levels ranged from $45,239 to $70,484. Postal Inspectors who live in metropolitan areas, such as New York and Chicago, typically earn higher salaries.

## Employment Prospects

Nearly 2,000 Postal Inspectors work in U.S. Postal Inspection Service field offices throughout the United States. Most job opportunities will be created to replace Postal Inspectors who are retiring, resigning for other occupations, or being promoted. Competition for the positions is high.

## Advancement Prospects

Supervisory and management opportunities are available, but limited. Many Postal Inspectors pursue career growth by way of wage increases and complexity of new assignments.

## Education and Training

Applicants must have a bachelor's degree (no specific major is required) as well as fulfill one of the experience requirements.

Postal Inspector recruits must complete a basic training program at the Inspection Service Academy in Potomac, Maryland. Trainees study subjects such as federal postal laws, court procedures, postal operations, audit functions, search and seizure procedures, arrest techniques, defensive tactics, and use of firearms.

## Special Requirements

The U.S. Postal Inspection Service requires that applicants hold a valid driver's license. Applicants must have been licensed for at least two years.

## Experience, Skills, and Personality Traits

Applicants must be U.S. citizens who are at least 21 years old and no older than 37 years upon receiving an appointment.

Applicants may qualify for a position under one of the following tracks.

- Language skills track. Applicants must be a fluent speaker in a foreign language that the Postal Inspection Service is currently seeking. Additionally, they must have one year of full-time work experience with the same company within two years of applying for a job.

- Postal experience track. Applicants are currently employed with the U.S. Postal Service. They have at least one year of full-time work experience as a supervisor, a U.S. Postal Inspection Service employee, or a postal employee in an area (such as computer analysis) that is critical to the U.S. Postal Inspection Service's needs.

Applicants may also qualify by having at least one year of full-time work experience within two years of applying for a job. In addition, they must meet one of the following requirements:

- possess a law degree
- have one or more appropriate professional certifications in auditing—such as the Certified Public Accountant (CPA) designation—or in protection, security, or fraud investigations—such as the Certified Fraud Examiner (CFE) designation
- hold a bachelor's degree in computer science, computer engineering, management information systems, telecommunications, electronic commerce, decision and information science, or computer information systems
- have a certification in computer systems, such as the Information Systems Security Professional (CISSP) designation
- possess specialized computer expertise in computer forensics, Internet investigations, Internet security, network security, or information systems security
- have law enforcement experience as a detective, criminalist, polygraph examiner, patrol officer, probation officer, parole officer, correction officer, or other related occupation

Postal Inspectors need excellent teamwork and interpersonal skills as well as strong communication, researching, and writing skills.

Some personality traits that successful Postal Inspectors share include being tactful, persistent, ethical, resourceful, and dedicated.

## Unions and Associations

Postal Inspectors may join the Federal Law Enforcement Officers Association or the Federal Criminal Investigators Association. These two professional societies serve the particular interests of law enforcement officers who work in federal agencies. They provide networking opportunities as well as various professional services and resources. For contact information for these organizations, see Appendix IV.

## Tips for Entry

1. For current recruitment information, contact a U.S. Postal Inspection Service office or a local U.S. Office of Personnel Management (OPM). You might find a listing for either agency in the U.S. Government pages of your local telephone book.

2. Gain work experience with the U.S. Postal Service as well as with the U.S. Postal Inspection Service, as many Postal Inspectors are recruited from within the U.S. Postal Services.

3. Applicants without work experience can apply as long as they possess an advanced degree or a bachelor's degree with a minimum grade point average of 3.0.

4. For more information about a career as a Postal Inspector, visit the U.S. Postal Inspection Service Web site at http://www.usps.com/postalinspectors. You can also call the agency's recruitment office at (866) 648-7472 or write to: Recruitment Office, U.S. Postal Inspection Service, Security Investigations Service Center, 225 N Humphreys Boulevard, 4th Floor, Memphis, TN 38161-0001.

5. You can learn more about the United States Postal Service on the Internet. Its Web address is http://www.usps.com.

# SPECIAL POLICE UNITS

# BIKE PATROL OFFICER

## CAREER PROFILE

**Duties:** Perform patrol duties by bicycle

**Alternate Title(s):** Police Cyclist, Bicycle Officer

**Salary Range:** $27,000 to $68,000

**Employment Prospects:** Fair

**Advancement Prospects:** Limited

**Prerequisites:**

    **Education or Training**—Certified police bicycle training
    **Experience**—Two to three years of patrol duty experience
    **Special Skills and Personality Traits**—Interpersonal, communication, teamwork, and self-management skills; be trustworthy, respectful, friendly, cheerful, and courteous

## CAREER LADDER

```
Police Cyclist Instructor or
Bike Patrol Unit Commander
```

```
Bike Patrol Officer
```

```
Police Officer
```

## Position Description

Bike Patrol Officers perform patrol duties on mountain bicycles, which are used for their effectiveness as crime-fighting tools. Their bicycles are equipped with all their necessary gear, such as two-way radios, first aid supplies, report forms, and bicycle maintenance kits. These officers are part of a special detail, usually known as the bicycle patrol unit, within their law enforcement agency. Bike patrol is a voluntary assignment to which officers are expected to commit themselves for a minimum number of years. Bike Patrol Officers perform bike patrol duties in addition to their regular assignments.

Unlike their peers in police vehicles, Bike Patrol Officers have the advantage of being unseen and unheard by criminals. In addition, they can be assigned to areas that are congested or inaccessible to patrol vehicles, including shopping centers, residential areas, downtown sections, campuses, parks, jogging trails, and bike trails. Their duties are similar to traditional patrol officers. Bike Patrol Officers:

- preserve the peace
- respond to calls for service
- enforce traffic laws
- keep an eye out for public hazards
- watch for suspicious criminal activities
- investigate crime
- apprehend lawbreakers
- keep detailed field logs and write police reports

Due to their mobility, Bike Patrol Officers are often assigned to perform crowd control and management at parades, marathons, festivals, and other special events.

Besides their patrol duties, Bike Patrol Officers may be assigned to work on various other operations, such as drug enforcement and community policing. Many of them also conduct bicycle safety workshops for their communities.

Bike Patrol Officers ride alone or in pairs. Many officers ride their bicycles for their entire work shift. Some officers attach their bicycles to their patrol car and put them in use for part of their shift or for specific areas of their beat. Bike Patrol Officers generally average between 15 to 25 miles daily on a work shift, according to the International Police Bike Association. Many of them ride in virtually all weather, except for extreme conditions.

In large bike patrol units, Bike Patrol Officers work rotating shifts. In smaller units, Bike Patrol Officers are assigned to work shifts when criminal activity is known to be most prevalent. Like other police officers, Bike Patrol Officers are on call 24 hours a day, seven days a week.

## Salaries

Earnings for Bike Patrol Officers vary, depending on such factors as their rank, education, experience, and geographical location. Most police patrol officers earned an estimated annual salary that ranged between $26,510 and $68,160, according to the November 2003 *Occupational Employment Statistics* survey by the U.S. Bureau of Labor Statistics.

Officers receive additional compensation for working overtime, weekends, holidays, and late night shifts. Many officers receive additional pay for performing special detail duty such as bike patrol.

## Employment Prospects

The International Police Mountain Bike Association reports that about 43 percent of all local police departments have a bike patrol unit, and 90 percent of that total number (5,600 departments) serve municipalities with a population of 100,000 or more. In addition to municipal police departments and county sheriff's offices, bike patrol units are used by airport, transit, campus, tribal, and state police departments as well as by local, state, and federal park law enforcement agencies.

The creation or expansion of bike patrol units for any police department is dependent on its budget. Many police departments have been able to start units with the support and financial assistance of their communities.

## Advancement Prospects

Police officers have the opportunity to develop a career according to their personal interests and ambitions. Volunteering for special police units such as bike patrol broadens their experience and may serve as a stepping stone in their careers. In addition to tackling special assignments, many officers pursue promotions to detective, sergeant, lieutenant, and so on. Depending on the police department, officers with administrative and managerial duties may be limited in their capacity to volunteer for special police units.

Many departments require that Bike Patrol Officers commit to a two-year assignment. Supervisory and administrative positions within the bike patrol detail are limited to unit commanders. Becoming certified police cyclist instructors is another career path for Bike Patrol Officers.

## Education and Training

Once selected to work the bike patrol detail, officers complete a certified police bike training course. They learn bicycle patrol procedures, pursuit tactics, traffic enforcement, bicycle maintenance, bicycle safety, and other basic tactical bicycle riding skills.

Bike Patrol Officers enroll in training and education programs throughout their careers to improve their skills and job performance.

## Experience, Skills, and Personality Traits

Police officers must complete two to three years of patrol duty before they are eligible to apply for a Bike Patrol Officer position.

Candidates must have some bicycle skills and be in excellent physical condition. They must have the strength and stamina to pedal a bicycle with 20 pounds of gear for several hours over different types of terrain, and sometimes at top speed.

Because they are in continued close contact with the community, Bike Patrol Officers must have effective interpersonal and communication skills. Additionally, they need excellent teamwork skills as well as self-management skills, which include the ability to work independently, follow instructions, handle stressful situations, and organize and prioritize tasks.

Some personality traits that successful Bike Patrol Officer have in common are being trustworthy, respectful, friendly, cheerful, and courteous.

## Unions and Associations

The International Police Mountain Bike Association (a division of the League of American Bicyclists) and the Law Enforcement Bicycle Association are two organizations specifically for Bike Patrol Officers. Both groups offer professional resources, services, networking opportunities, training, and certification. (For contact information, see Appendix IV.)

## Tips for Entry

1. As a police officer, let the bike patrol unit commander know of your interest, especially before you are eligible or before an opening is available.
2. Ride a bicycle regularly to build up and maintain physical stamina and endurance.
3. Get the community involved in starting or expanding a bike patrol unit. Many bike patrol units were started with community involvement, such as raising funds for buying bicycles and equipment.
4. Learn more about different law enforcement bike patrol units on the Internet. Enter the keywords *bike patrol unit* into a search engine to get a list of Web sites.
5. For more information about Bike Patrol Officers, visit these Web sites: International Police Mountain Bike Association, http://www.ipmba.org, and Law Enforcement Bicycle Association, http://www.leba.org.

# K9 HANDLER

## CAREER PROFILE

**Duties:** Search for suspects and evidence at a crime scene with a trained police dog

**Alternate Title(s):** K9 (Canine) Officer

**Salary Range:** $27,000 to $68,000

**Employment Prospects:** Fair

**Advancement Prospects:** Limited

**Prerequisites:**

    **Education or Training**—Certified police canine training

    **Experience**—Two to three years of patrol duty

    **Special Skills and Personality Traits**—Dog-handling skills; be mature, even-tempered, patient, and self-disciplined

## CAREER LADDER

```
┌─────────────────────────────────────┐
│  K9 Trainer or K9 Unit Commander     │
└─────────────────────────────────────┘

┌─────────────────────────────────────┐
│            K9 Handler                │
└─────────────────────────────────────┘

┌─────────────────────────────────────┐
│           Police Officer             │
└─────────────────────────────────────┘
```

## Position Description

K9 Handlers (or Canine Handlers) search for suspects and physical evidence with trained police dogs as their partners. Together, K9 Handlers and their dogs are known as K9 teams. They are part of a police department's K9 unit, a special detail for which police officers may volunteer. Officers perform canine duty in addition to their regular patrol, detective, or administrative duty.

Many departments require that officers commit to a minimum number of years to canine duty due to the cost and time required for training.

Canine teams are either trained for general patrol purposes or for specific purposes such as locating narcotics. They are called out to crime scenes when their specially trained support is needed. The teams are used for tracking criminals in rural, suburban, or urban settings. In addition, they are used to search buildings for suspects, evidence, drugs, or explosives.

Patrol officers are usually assigned to heavy crime areas, using their dogs as backups in dangerous situations. Their dogs also chase and apprehend criminals. In addition, many police departments use their K9 teams for search and rescue missions. The K9 teams help locate missing or lost persons. They also search for survivors and victims in human-made or natural disasters.

K9 Handlers are responsible for the well-being and safety of their dogs. They feed, water, groom, and exercise their dogs daily. They make sure their dogs get any necessary shots. And they train their dogs weekly, if not daily, on their tracking, obedience, aggression, and control skills. Most K9 Handlers keep their dogs at home with them.

K9 Handlers must have complete control over their dogs at all times. They decide in what situations to use their dogs, making sure there is no risk present for either themselves or their partners. For example, before having their dogs search a crime scene, K9 Handlers first inspect the area for hazards such as broken glass, harmful substances, and other dogs.

In departments with a large canine unit, K9 teams are assigned to any work shift. With small canine units, K9 teams are assigned an afternoon or midnight shift when there is more criminal activity. K9 Handlers and their partners are on call 24 hours a day, every day of the year.

## Salaries

Earnings for K9 Handlers vary, depending on such factors as their rank, experience, education, and geographical location. The estimated annual salary for most patrol officers ranged between $26,510 and $68,160, according to the November 2003 *Occupational Employment Statistics* survey by the U.S. Bureau of Labor Statistics.

Officers receive additional compensation for working overtime, weekends, holidays, and late-night shifts. Many officers receive additional pay for performing special detail duty, such as canine duty. Most officers receive compensation for taking care of police dogs in their homes.

## Employment Prospects

K9 units have become one of the fastest-growing crime prevention tools. Besides police departments, other law enforcement agencies also have K9 units—such as sheriff's departments, state police departments, fish and wildlife divisions, the U.S. Border Patrol, and Drug Enforcement Administration.

Opportunities for K9 Handlers are available, but the competition is keen as the jobs are popular and the turnover rate is low. The creation or expansion of K9 units depends on a police department's budget.

## Advancement Prospects

Police officers have the opportunity to carve out a career in accordance with their personal interests and ambitions. Volunteering for special police units such as canine duty broadens their experience and may serve as a stepping stone in their careers. Along with working special assignments, many officers pursue promotion to detective, sergeant, lieutenant, and so on. Depending on the police department, officers with administrative and managerial duties may be limited in their capacity to volunteer for special police units.

Supervisory and administrative positions within the canine detail are limited to unit commanders. Becoming certified police canine trainers is another career path for K9 Handlers.

## Education and Training

Police officers selected to be K9 Handlers are provided several weeks of training at an accredited police canine training school. The curriculum includes basics on dog temperaments and abilities, principles of dog training, training drills, dog maintenance and nutrition, and tracking skills. Those officers who will handle single-purpose dogs, such as for detecting narcotics, train for additional weeks.

Some departments require that K9 teams be recertified once or twice a year.

## Experience, Skills, and Personality Traits

After serving on their force for two or three years and meeting specific departmental requirements, police officers can apply for K9 duty. Police departments look for officers who show job stability.

K9 Handler candidates should enjoy being around dogs for long periods of time and must be perceptive to how dogs react with their environment. Most important, they should have the ability to train dogs. They should be physically fit in order to keep up with their dogs. And they should be willing to speak to and praise their dogs in soft tones in public.

Some personality traits that successful K9 Handlers share include being mature, even-tempered, patient, and self-disciplined.

## Unions and Associations

The North American Police Work Dog Association and the United States Police Canine Association are two national organizations to which many K9 Handlers belong. Both groups provide professional support services and networking as well as offer continuing education classes and certified training programs. (For contact information, see Appendix IV.) In addition, K9 Handlers might belong to state and local law enforcement canine associations.

## Tips for Entry

1. Get lots of experience being around, caring for, and training dogs.
2. As a police officer, let the K9 unit commander know of your interest, especially before you are eligible or before an opening is available.
3. Learn more about different law enforcement K9 units on the Internet. Enter the keywords *K9 unit* into a search engine to get a list of Web sites.
4. For more information about K9 Handlers, visit these Web sites: North American Police Work Dog Association, http://www.napwda.com, and United States Police Canine Association, http://www.uspcak9.com.

# OBSERVER

**Duties:** Perform patrol and tactical assistance from police aircraft

**Alternate Title(s):** Flight Officer or Tactical Flight Officer

**Salary Range:** $27,000 to $68,000

**Employment Prospects:** Fair

**Advancement Prospects:** Limited

**Prerequisites:**

**Education or Training**—In-house training

**Experience**—Three to five years of police work; knowledge of aircraft and Federal Airway regulations; knowledge of geography

**Special Skills and Personality Traits**—Observational, communication, and organization, skills; be mature, responsible, quick-witted, and sensible

**Licensure/Certification**—Pilot certificate and medical certificate may be required

```
┌─────────────────────────────────────────┐
│   Pilot or Air Support Unit Commander    │
└─────────────────────────────────────────┘

┌─────────────────────────────────────────┐
│                 Observer                  │
└─────────────────────────────────────────┘

┌─────────────────────────────────────────┐
│              Police Officer               │
└─────────────────────────────────────────┘
```

## Position Description

Observers are law enforcement officers who prevent, deter, and suppress crime from the air. These officers are part of their agency's air support unit, a special detail for which they may volunteer.

Air support units generally use helicopters or fixed-wing planes for their missions. Some units fly both types of aircraft. An Observer and a pilot (who is usually another law enforcement officer) comprise the flight crew for each mission. The pilot is responsible for the safe operation of the aircraft during a mission.

Flight crews are assigned to perform various types of missions, such as:

• patrolling assigned beats
• doing surveillance
• recovering stolen vehicles
• transporting prisoners
• protecting dignitaries

Flight crews also provide assistance to tactical ground operations. For example, a flight crew might help search for fleeing criminals, pursue high-speed drivers, or contain a crime scene. On occasion, flight crews assist other law enforcement agencies with their operations. They also help fire departments and other protective service agencies. They might perform search-and-rescue missions or aerial firefighting missions, or they might assess the damage and danger in man-made or natural disasters.

In the air, Observers are watchful of the activity on the ground and relay their observations to police ground units. For example, Observers might inform ground units about where fleeing suspects are hiding in bushes along a river. Observers operate specialized equipment from the police aircraft. They look through high-powered binoculars. They use high-powered searchlights and operate thermal imaging devices that detect the "heat signatures" of persons and objects. They also work with public address systems, video surveillance equipment, and tracking systems. In addition, Observers manage all police radio communications.

Observers assist the pilots by keeping watch on flight instruments and gauges. They look for wires, towers, and other air traffic. At the end of each flight, most Observers complete the flight log.

In some air support units, Observers fulfill the role of pilot or aircraft mechanic.

Air support duty may be part-time or full-time duty, depending on the police department. Part-time officers are assigned to work a few hours each week in the air support unit. The rest of their time is spent performing their regular duty as patrol officers, detectives, or administrators. Most departments rotate their aviation crew on an on-call schedule for nights and weekends.

## Salaries

Earnings for Observers vary, depending on such factors as their rank, experience, education, and geographical location. The estimated annual salary for most patrol officers ranged between $26,510 to $68,160, according to the November 2003 *Occupational Employment Statistics* survey by the U.S. Bureau of Labor Statistics.

Officers receive additional compensation for working overtime, weekends, holidays, and late-night shifts. Many officers receive additional pay for performing special detail duty such as air support duty.

## Employment Prospects

Besides police departments, air support units can be found in county, state, and federal law enforcement agencies. Job opportunities for Observers generally are more available in large police departments. Many departments require that officers commit to a minimum number of years for air support duty.

## Advancement Prospects

Police officers have the ability to develop a career commensurate with their personal interests and ambitions. Volunteering for special police units such as air support duty broadens their experience and serves as a stepping stone in their careers. In addition to working special assignments, many officers pursue promotions to detective, sergeant, lieutenant, and so on. Depending on the police department, officers with administrative and managerial duties may be limited in their opportunities to volunteer for special police units.

Supervisory and administrative positions within the air support detail are limited to unit commanders. Becoming pilots in the air support unit is another career path for Observers.

## Education and Training

At most departments, Observers receive in-house training. They learn the geographical layout of their jurisdiction, cockpit resource management, use of specialized equipment, search techniques, basic aircraft operation, and federal aviation regulations. Some agencies teach Observers basic aircraft maneuvers in case of emergencies.

Depending on the department, Observers participate in monthly in-service training.

## Special Requirements

If Observers also perform the role of pilot, they must possess a valid commercial pilot certificate with the appropriate ratings as well as a proper medical certificate. These certificates are granted by the Federal Aviation Administration, an agency within the U.S. Department of Transportation.

In some agencies, Observers are required to hold the necessary pilot and medical certifications even though they will not be flying a plane.

## Experience, Skills, and Personality Traits

Generally police officers need three to five years of police duty before they are eligible to apply for an Observer position. Knowledge about aircraft, federal aviation regulations, and geography is desirable.

To perform their job effectively, Observers need strong observational, communication, and organizational skills. Being mature, responsible, quick-witted, and sensible are some personality traits that successful Observers share.

## Unions and Associations

Many Observers belong to the Airborne Law Enforcement Association, a national organization that offers professional support, networking, and educational programs to all law enforcement officers who are involved in air-support duty. Many Observers also belong to the Law Enforcement Thermographers' Association, an international law enforcement society involved in promoting the use of thermal imaging in law enforcement operations. This group offers professional networking, training, and certification.

For contact information for the above associations, see Appendix IV.

## Tips for Entry

1. Young people might join the Civil Air Patrol to gain experience in aviation.
2. Talk with Observers to learn about high school classes or college courses that may be helpful for a career in their field.
3. As a police officer, let the air support unit commander know of your interest, especially before you are eligible or before an opening is available.
4. Learn more about different law enforcement air support units on the Internet. Enter the keywords *police air support unit* or *police aviation unit* into a search engine to get a list of Web sites.

# BOMB TECHNICIAN

## CAREER PROFILE

**Duties:** Neutralize and dispose of bombs and other explosive devices

**Alternate Title(s):** None

**Salary Range:** $27,000 to $68,000

**Employment Prospects:** Fair

**Advancement Prospects:** Limited

**Prerequisites:**

　**Education or Training**—FBI training for Bomb Technicians

　**Experience**—Five years of police work

　**Special Skills and Personality Traits**—Concentration, decision-making, and teamwork skills; be calm, composed, levelheaded, patient, and responsible

　**Licensure/Certification**—FBI certification required

## CAREER LADDER

```
┌─────────────────────────────────────┐
│  Specialist or Bomb Squad Commander  │
└─────────────────────────────────────┘

┌─────────────────────────────────────┐
│           Bomb Technician            │
└─────────────────────────────────────┘

┌─────────────────────────────────────┐
│            Patrol Officer            │
└─────────────────────────────────────┘
```

## Position Description

Bomb Technicians are law enforcement officers whose responsibility is to safely examine, neutralize, and dispose of explosives and hazardous devices within the communities that they serve. They handle bombs, ammunition, military ordnance, dynamite, pipe bombs, explosive chemicals, and other types of incendiary and improvised devices. In addition, Bomb Technicians deal with suspicious packages and hoax devices that may contain explosives.

Bomb Technicians are part of their agency's bomb squad, a special detail for which officers volunteer. (Many agencies call this special detail by such other names as the explosives unit, the explosive ordnance disposal (EOD) unit, or the hazardous device disposal squad.) Officers perform bomb squad duty in addition to their regular patrol, detective, or administrative duty. Many departments require that officers commit to a certain number of years for bomb squad duty because of the intensity and the cost of training involved.

Working in teams of two or more, Bomb Technicians investigate situations where explosive devices are or may be present. They are called out to homes, business offices and buildings, factories, colleges, schools, airports, sports arenas, parking lots, grassy fields, and other locations. They also examine vehicles, buses, and airplanes.

Bomb Technicians wear protective suits while working. They use hand tools, X-ray machines, remote-controlled robots, and other equipment. To defuse bombs, they might use counter-explosives or water cannons called disrupters.

Besides disarming explosive devices, Bomb Technicians perform other duties. For example, they:

- investigate "post blast" crime scenes where explosive devices may have been used
- assist in special operations such as providing support to tactical teams
- perform bomb sweeps to secure locations or areas where dignitaries will visit
- present bomb threat awareness and safety programs to public and private groups
- develop evacuation and search plans for government agencies and private companies
- collect and preserve evidence at crime scenes
- prepare and provide testimony as an expert witness

Bomb Technicians may be called upon to assist other law enforcement agencies—local, state, or federal agencies—within their jurisdiction as well as in nearby communities.

Bomb Technicians are available for duty 24 hours a day, seven days a week. In large bomb squad units, Bomb Technicians are rotated on an on-call schedule.

## Salaries

Earnings for Bomb Technicians vary, depending on such factors as their rank, experience, education, and geographical location. Most patrol officers earned an estimated annual salary that ranged between $26,510 and $68,160 according to the November 2003 *Occupational Employment Statistics* survey by the U.S. Bureau of Labor Statistics.

Officers receive additional compensation for working overtime, weekends, holidays, and late-night shifts. Many officers receive additional pay for performing special detail duty, such as bomb squad duty.

## Employment Prospects

Along with police departments, bomb squad units can be found in county, state, and federal law enforcement agencies. Some bomb squad units are formed using officers from different law enforcement agencies in an area or region.

Generally, opportunities on bomb squads become available as officers retire, advance to administrative positions, or resign from bomb squad duty. Law enforcement agencies will create additional positions to meet growing needs as long as funding is available.

## Advancement Prospects

Police officers have the ability to develop a career commensurate with their personal interests and ambitions. Volunteering for service in special police units, such as bomb squad duty broadens their experience and may serve as a stepping stone in their careers. In addition to taking on special assignments, many officers pursue promotions to detective, sergeant, lieutenant, and so on. Depending on the police department, officers with administrative and managerial duties may be limited in their capacity to volunteer for special police units.

Supervisory and administrative positions within the bomb squad detail are limited to unit commanders. Becoming a specialist in robotics, render safe procedures, or other technical area is another career path for Bomb Technicians.

## Education and Training

All public safety Bomb Technicians must successfully complete a monthlong training program provided by the FBI at the Hazardous Devices School located at Redstone Arsenal in Huntsville, Alabama. Through classroom and practical exercises, trainees learn basic procedures for handling hazardous and improvised explosive devices.

Bomb Technicians are required to complete a minimum number of hours of training each year to hone and develop their skills. Many Bomb Technicians also participate in training programs offered by the U.S. Bureau of Alcohol, Tobacco, Firearms and Explosives, the Drug Enforcement Agency, and other agencies to learn about handling and disposing of new types of explosive devices.

## Special Requirements

To be Bomb Technicians, local and state law enforcement officers must receive FBI certification, which is granted upon completion of an FBI-sponsored training program. Bomb Technicians must obtain recertification every three years.

## Experience, Skills, and Personality Traits

To be considered for a Bomb Technician position, police officers need at least five years of full-time experience. They may be patrol officers, detectives, or administrators. Applicants must be in excellent physical condition with exceptional eyesight and hearing. Having mechanical, electrical, or electronic experience is desirable.

To perform their work effectively, Bomb Technicians need superior concentration, decision-making, and teamwork skills. Being calm, composed, levelheaded, patient, and responsible are some personality traits that successful Bomb Technicians share.

## Unions and Associations

Bomb Technicians might join the International Association of Bomb Technicians and Investigators, an organization that provides professional support, networking, and education. For contact information, see Appendix IV.

## Tips for Entry

1. As a police officer, let the bomb squad commander know of your interest, especially before you are eligible or before an opening is available.
2. Get a background in mechanical, electronic, or electrical engineering.
3. Learn more about different law enforcement bomb squads on the Internet. Enter the keywords *police bomb squad* or *bomb squad unit* into a search engine to get a list of Web sites.

# SWAT SNIPER

## CAREER PROFILE

**Duties:** Provide disciplined, accurate marksmanship in high-risk operations

**Alternate Title(s):** Marksman

**Salary Range:** $27,000 to $68,000

**Employment Prospects:** Fair

**Advancement Prospects:** Limited

**Prerequisites:**

**Education or Training**—Certified sniper training

**Experience**—Be a SWAT team member

**Special Skills and Personality Traits**—Teamwork, interpersonal, and self-management skills; be calm, precise, focused, dedicated, and intelligent

## CAREER LADDER

```
┌─────────────────────────────┐
│      SWAT Instructor or      │
│    SWAT Unit Commander       │
└─────────────────────────────┘

┌─────────────────────────────┐
│        SWAT Sniper           │
└─────────────────────────────┘

┌─────────────────────────────┐
│      SWAT Team Member        │
└─────────────────────────────┘
```

## Position Description

SWAT Snipers are law enforcement officers who have been specially trained to provide weapons support in high-risk operations. They are part of their agency's Special Weapons and Tactics (SWAT) unit, a special detail for which officers volunteer.

SWAT teams are composed of Snipers, negotiators, gas specialists, and other specialists. Every SWAT team's primary mission is to protect and save lives. The teams respond to highly critical situations in which conventional police tactics are inadequate. For example, SWAT teams are called upon to assist in situations where:

- heavily armed suspects have barricaded themselves to resist arrest
- armed suspects have taken hostages
- suspects are shooting at others from hidden or faraway locations
- warrants are being executed to suspects who may be heavily armed

In addition, SWAT units are called out to help other law enforcement agencies. They might assist in drug arrests, protection of visiting dignitaries, riot suppression, and other special circumstances.

In a SWAT call-out, SWAT Snipers work together with SWAT observers, forming two-member sniper teams. Sniper teams locate the best positions for SWAT Snipers to take accurate aim on the suspects. Using camouflage and concealment techniques, sniper teams might scale high walls and fences, climb trees, run across wide open spaces, crawl on the ground, or creep through brush and grassy fields. Sniper teams keep in contact with the command post by two-way radios at all times. The observers are in charge of communication and relay information back and forth between the sniper teams and the command post.

Upon reaching an advantageous location, SWAT Snipers calculate distance, elevation, wind, and other factors to find the best firing position to aim at a suspect. When SWAT Snipers have settled comfortably into favorable firing positions, the observers notify the command post. SWAT Snipers stay in their positions, ready to fire when they receive the order from the command post.

According to the National Tactical Officers Association, most SWAT call-outs end in peaceful resolutions without any shots ever being fired.

SWAT team members are on call 24 hours a day, seven days a week. In large SWAT units, members may be rotated on an on-call schedule.

SWAT Snipers perform SWAT duty in addition to their regular patrol, detective, or administrative duties. Many departments require that officers commit to a minimum number of years of SWAT duty.

## Salaries

Earnings for SWAT Snipers vary, depending on their rank, experience, education, and geographical location. The estimated annual salary for most patrol officers ranged between $26,510 and $68,160, according to the November 2003 *Occupational Employment Statistics* survey by the U.S. Bureau of Labor Statistics.

Officers receive additional compensation for working overtime, weekends, holidays, and late-night shifts. Many officers receive additional pay for performing special detail duty, such as SWAT duty.

## Employment Prospects

Besides police departments, many county, state, and federal law enforcement agencies also have SWAT units or tactical details. The expansion or creation of SWAT units depends on the region or an agency's need for tactical details.

## Advancement Prospects

Police officers have the ability to develop a career commensurate with their personal interests and ambitions. Volunteering for special police units such as SWAT broadens their experience and may serve as a stepping stone in their careers. In addition to taking on special assignments, many officers pursue promotions to detective, sergeant, lieutenant, and so on. Depending on the police department, officers with administrative and managerial duties may be limited in their capacity to volunteer for special police units.

Supervisory and administrative positions within the SWAT detail are limited to unit commanders. Becoming certified SWAT instructors is another career path for SWAT Snipers.

## Education and Training

To become a SWAT Sniper, candidates must pass intensive, certified training, usually provided by their law enforcement agency.

SWAT Snipers are required to train monthly to maintain and hone their marksmanship skills. They also train with the whole SWAT unit on a monthly basis.

Most, if not all, departments require that Snipers be tested once or twice a year to ensure that they are retaining their high marksmanship skills. Many departments also require SWAT members to pass a physical training test once or twice a year.

## Experience, Skills, and Personality Traits

To qualify for a SWAT Sniper position, law enforcement officers must already be members of their agency's SWAT unit. Candidates must be in outstanding physical condition and should have excellent marksmanship and camouflaging skills.

To perform their job effectively, SWAT Snipers need superior teamwork and interpersonal skills. In addition, they have strong self-management skills, such as the ability to handle stressful situations, prioritize tasks, follow directions, and organize tasks. Being calm, precise, focused, dedicated, and intelligent are a few personality traits that successful SWAT Snipers share.

## Unions and Associations

Some SWAT Snipers join the American Sniper Association or the National Tactical Officers Association to take advantage of networking opportunities, training programs, and other professional services and resources. (For contact information, see Appendix IV.) State and regional SWAT associations are also available.

## Tips for Entry

1. As a SWAT candidate, let the unit commander know of your interest in becoming a SWAT Sniper.
2. Learn a form of martial arts, such as tae kwon do or karate. Many SWAT commanders have found the discipline of martial arts to be a valuable asset for performing SWAT duties.
3. Many law enforcement agencies have information about their SWAT units on the Internet. Enter the keywords *SWAT unit* into a search engine to get a list of Web sites.
4. To learn more about SWAT Snipers, visit the American Sniper Association Web site at http://www. americansniper.org.

# CRIME PREVENTION SPECIALIST

## CAREER PROFILE

**Duties:** Provide crime prevention and awareness programs to the community

**Alternate Title(s):** Crime Prevention Officer

**Salary Range:** $27,000 to $68,000

**Employment Prospects:** Fair

**Advancement Prospects:** Limited

**Prerequisites:**

    **Education or Training**—A college degree; certified training

    **Experience**—Two to five years of law enforcement experience; knowledge of and experience with crime prevention or community relations programs

    **Special Skills and Personality Traits**—Project management, writing, public speaking, teaching, communication, and interpersonal skills; be trustworthy, respectful, cooperative, and organized

## CAREER LADDER

> **Crime Prevention Unit Commander**

> **Crime Prevention Specialist**

> **Police Officer**

## Position Description

Crime Prevention Specialists provide crime prevention and awareness programs to the community. They are part of a police department's crime prevention unit, a special detail for which police officers may volunteer. The position may be full time or part time. Part-time officers perform crime prevention duty in addition to their regular patrol, detective, or administrative duty.

Many departments require that officers commit a minimum number of years to crime prevention duty.

Crime Prevention Specialists develop and organize many different crime prevention programs, such as neighborhood watch groups, tenant patrols, business watch groups, property identification programs, child safety programs, senior citizen safety programs, and driving safety programs. To create effective programs, they work directly with the community—individuals, businesses, churches, schools, non-profit groups, and other government agencies and law enforcement agencies.

Most Crime Prevention Specialists provide crime prevention and safety instruction, covering topics such as robbery, drugs in the workplace, rape prevention, child safety, bicycle safety, and security techniques. They conduct work-

shops for resident groups, businesses, schools, civic groups, and social organizations about crime prevention and personal safety. Some Crime Prevention Specialists teach other officers about crime prevention techniques. Some Crime Prevention Specialists also train volunteers and reserves to present workshops and seminars.

Other duties for Crime Prevention Specialists vary from department to department. Crime Prevention Specialists might:

- provide security inspections for businesses and residences
- provide escort services to banks
- check residences while owners are away
- provide victim assistance to local support agencies
- develop crime prevention materials such as brochures, public service announcements, and training worksheets
- compile crime statistics and perform other research tasks
- design crime prevention programs and procedures for other government agencies

Crime Prevention Specialists normally work a regular work shift. They also put in additional overtime hours—including nights, weekends, and holidays—to provide the many different crime prevention programs to the community.

## Salaries

Earnings for Crime Prevention Specialists vary, depending on their rank, experience, education, and geographical location. The estimated annual salary for most patrol officers ranged between $26,510 and $68,160, according to the November 2003 *Occupational Employment Statistics* survey by the U.S. Bureau of Labor Statistics.

Officers receive additional compensation for working overtime, weekends, holidays, and late-night shifts. Many officers receive additional pay for performing special detail duty, such as crime prevention duty.

## Employment Prospects

Along with police departments, many sheriff's departments and state police agencies have crime prevention units. Some agencies hire qualified civilians as Crime Prevention Specialists.

Community participation in crime prevention has increased in recent years. More and more departments are starting crime prevention units. Established units may create additional positions to meet growing needs, as long as funding is available.

## Advancement Prospects

Police officers have the opportunity to develop a career according to their personal interests and ambitions. Volunteering for special police units, such as for crime prevention, broadens their experience and may further their careers. In addition to taking on assignments, many officers pursue promotions to detective, sergeant, lieutenant, and so on. Depending on the police department, officers with administrative and managerial duties may be limited in their capacity to volunteer for special police units.

Supervisory and administrative positions within the crime prevention detail are limited to unit commanders.

Another career path for Crime Prevention Specialists is to work in the private sector for crime prevention businesses or nonprofit crime prevention agencies. Some former Crime Prevention Specialists become consultants or start their own business providing crime prevention services.

## Education and Training

Education requirements differ with every police department. Many police departments prefer candidates who have associate's or bachelor's degrees. They especially prefer applicants who have completed courses in communication, journalism, and education.

Training requirements also vary in each police department. Generally, police officers complete certified training programs before performing their duties as Crime Prevention Specialists.

## Experience, Skills, and Personality Traits

Experience requirements depend on the complexity of the Crime Prevention Specialist's duties in an agency. Depending on the department, applicants need two to five years of law enforcement experience. They should also have experience with crime prevention or community relations programs.

To perform their work effectively, Crime Prevention Specialists need strong project management, writing, public speaking, and teaching skills. Excellent communication and interpersonal skills are important, as Crime Prevention Specialists must be able to interact with children, adults, the elderly, businesspeople, professionals, and others from various backgrounds.

Being trustworthy, respectful, cooperative, and organized are some personality traits that successful Crime Prevention Specialists share.

## Unions and Associations

Crime Prevention Specialists might belong to local and state crime prevention councils and associations that offer professional support, networking, training, educational programs, and other services. Many also belong to professional organizations such as the International Society of Crime Prevention Practitioners and ASIS International. For contact information, see Appendix IV.

## Tips for Entry

1. Volunteer in Neighborhood Watch and other crime prevention programs to gain valuable experience.
2. As a police officer, let the crime prevention unit commander know of your interest, especially before you are eligible or before an opening is available.
3. Get experience developing, planning, and organizing programs by helping out with school, church, social, and other group functions.
4. Learn more about crime prevention on the Internet. You might start by visiting the National Crime Prevention Council Web site at http://www.ncpc.org. To get a list of other Web sites, enter the keywords *crime prevention* into a search engine.

# PARKING ENFORCEMENT OFFICER

## CAREER PROFILE

**Duties:** Enforce public parking laws, regulations, codes, and ordinances; perform patrol duties; issue parking citations or warnings

**Alternate Title(s):** Traffic Enforcement Agent, Parking Meter Attendant

**Salary Range:** $18,000 to $44,000

**Employment Prospects:** Good

**Advancement Prospects:** Fair

**Prerequisites:**

    **Education or Training**—High school diploma

    **Experience**—Have experience working with the public

    **Special Skills and Personality Traits**—Writing, math, analytical, problem-solving, customer service, interpersonal, communicational, and self-management skills; be courteous, calm, tactful, fair, and accurate

    **Licensure/Certification**—Driver's license; police officer certification may be required

## CAREER LADDER

```
┌─────────────────────────────────────┐
│  Lead Parking Enforcement Officer    │
└─────────────────────────────────────┘

┌─────────────────────────────────────┐
│    Parking Enforcement Officer       │
└─────────────────────────────────────┘

┌─────────────────────────────────────┐
│             Trainee                  │
└─────────────────────────────────────┘
```

## Position Description

Parking Enforcement Officers enforce public parking laws, regulations, codes, and ordinances that cover their jurisdictions. In some communities, these officers are also responsible for enforcing animal control laws, regulations, codes, and ordinances.

Parking Enforcement Officers are usually uniformed personnel. They work in the traffic units of municipal police departments as well as of special jurisdiction police agencies such as university police departments and airport police departments. Parking Enforcement Officers may be civilian employees or police officers, depending on the requirements of their agencies.

Parking Enforcement Officers are assigned a particular route to patrol, which may include downtown areas, business districts, residential streets, shopping centers, hospital areas, and public parking lots or garages. They patrol their route several times by foot or in a marked vehicle to make sure motorists have not exceeded the time limit of the public parking spaces. They check for vehicles in spaces with expired parking meters as well as vehicles that have exceeded the time limit of public parking spaces. To keep tabs on vehicles in limited-time parking spaces, Parking Enforcement Officers make chalk marks on the tires of the vehicles. When they make their rounds, they look for vehicles with chalk marks, which indicate the vehicles have occupied spaces beyond the time limit.

Parking Enforcement Officers also watch for other parking infractions as they make their rounds. For example, they keep an eye out for vehicles that are parked in loading zones; vehicles parked too close to fire hydrants; vehicles that are double-parked; and vehicles that are illegally parked in handicapped parking spaces.

When they find parking violations, Parking Enforcement Officers have the authority to issue parking citations or warnings to the vehicles' owners. The officers write tickets or complete them on handheld computers, providing such information as the description of the vehicle, the location of the parking space, and the parking violation. Tickets are left on the vehicles or given to the owners. Occasionally, Parking Enforcement Officers appear in court to testify about parking citations they have issued.

Parking Enforcement Officers can also issue notices to impound vehicles that owners have parked in restricted zones or that are in violation of parking ordinances. In those instances, tow trucks are dispatched to take the vehicles away to the appropriate parking lots or garages. The owners may retrieve their vehicles after paying all parking fines. In some communities, Parking Enforcement Officers have the authority to immobilize the vehicles of owners who have several unpaid parking tickets. The officers place wheel boots on these vehicles so that the owners cannot drive them. Once the owners have paid their fines, the wheel boot is removed from the vehicles.

In addition to their parking enforcement duties, officers keep their eyes open for traffic hazards, accidents, missing traffic signs, abandoned vehicles, and other problems. They report any trouble to the proper authorities.

When needed, Parking Enforcement Officers assist law enforcement officers or public safety officers with traffic control at accident scenes, at intersections with broken traffic lights, and in other emergency situations. Parking Enforcement Officers also assist at special events—such as parades, athletic events, or festivals—that require help maintaining an orderly flow of traffic.

Parking Enforcement Officers are responsible for performing general maintenance on their vehicle and equipment as well as on parking meters, machines, and signs. They also are responsible for completing daily logs, reports, and other forms. Additionally, they keep current with their agency's policies and procedures as well as with parking laws and regulations.

The job of Parking Enforcement Officers requires them to interact with the public on a daily basis. They answer questions about parking matters and provide motorists and pedestrians with directions to places. They assist motorists with flat tires, keys locked in their vehicles, and other problems. Parking Enforcement Officers also handle parking complaints as well as reports of suspected illegal activities. If any concerns are outside their areas of responsibility, Parking Enforcement Officers refer them to their supervisor or another proper authority. From time to time, Parking Enforcement Officers must deal with individuals who are argumentative, angry, upset, or discourteous.

Parking Enforcement Officers work outdoors in all types of weather conditions. Their job requires them to maneuver in moving and heavy traffic, in which they are regularly exposed to gas fumes and loud noise levels.

They are employed part-time or full-time. Many are assigned to rotating shifts. Some officers are assigned to work evenings, nights, or weekends.

## Salaries

Earnings for Parking Enforcement Officers vary, depending on such factors as their rank, education, experience, employer, and geographical location. Most Parking Enforcement Officers earned an estimated annual salary that ranged between $18,210 and $44,040, according to the November 2003 *Occupational Employment Statistics* survey by the U.S. Bureau of Labor Statistics (BLS).

## Employment Prospects

As of November 2003, about 9,690 Parking Enforcement Officers were employed nationwide, according to the BLS.

The number of positions available for Parking Enforcement Officers varies with the different agencies. In general, opportunities become available as Parking Enforcement Officers retire or transfer to other positions. Agencies generally create additional positions as their needs grow, as long as funding is available.

## Advancement Prospects

Lead officers and unit commanders are generally the only supervisory and administrative positions within the traffic detail. Hence, promotional opportunities are limited.

Parking Enforcement Officers who are police officers have the opportunity to develop a career according to their personal interests and ambitions. Police officers can pursue promotions to become detectives, sergeants, lieutenants, and so on. They can also apply for other special police details, such as the canine patrol unit, bomb squad, or aviation unit.

## Education and Training

Minimally, Parking Enforcement Officers must possess a high school diploma or a general equivalency diploma.

Recruits typically complete a training program that usually includes on-the-job training under the supervision of experienced officers. Some police agencies require that recruits complete police academy training prior to their parking enforcement training.

## Special Requirements

Applicants must possess a current driver's license.

Some agencies require that Parking Enforcement Officers possess a POST (Peace Officer Standards and Training) certificate, which is earned upon completion of basic training at a police academy.

## Experience, Skills, and Personality Traits

In general, employers require that entry-level candidates have previous experience working with the public.

To perform their work effectively, Parking Enforcement Officers must have strong writing, math, analytical, and problem-solving skills. In addition, they need excellent customer service, interpersonal, and communication skills. Parking Enforcement Officers should also have superior self-management skills, such as being able to work independently, organize tasks, handle stressful situations, and follow and understand instructions.

Being courteous, calm, tactful, fair, and accurate are just a few personality traits that successful Parking Enforcement Officers share.

## Unions and Associations

Parking Enforcement Officers may be able to join local or regional professional associations that serve their particular interests. By joining such societies, they can take advantage of networking opportunities, educational programs, and other professional resources and services.

Some Parking Enforcement Officers are members of a union, which represents them in negotiations and grievance processes.

## Tips for Entry

1. In some police departments, civilian volunteers assist officers with parking enforcement tasks. Contact your local police department for volunteer opportunities to gain valuable experience.
2. Contact the traffic unit at the agency where you would like to work. Find out what qualifications are needed to become a Parking Enforcement Officer.
3. A neat and well-groomed appearance can make a good impression at your job interview.
4. You can learn more about parking enforcement duty on the Internet. To get a list of relevant Web sites, enter the keywords *parking enforcement unit* or *parking enforcement officer* into a search engine.

# FORENSIC INVESTIGATIONS

# CRIME SCENE TECHNICIAN

## CAREER PROFILE

**Duties:** Collect and process physical evidence from crime scenes

**Alternate Title(s):** Crime Scene Examiner, Crime Scene Investigator

**Salary Range:** $20,000 to $68,000

**Employment Prospects:** Fair

**Advancement Prospects:** Limited

**Prerequisites:**

**Education or Training**—Requirements vary with the different departments

**Experience**—One to three years of police work with fingerprinting and crime scene experience; photography and photo processing experience

**Special Skills and Personality Traits**—Communication, interpersonal, teamwork, writing, and self-management skills; be objective, observant, detail-oriented, meticulous, ethical, honest, dependable, and courteous

**Licensure/Certification**—Professional certification may be required; driver's license

## CAREER LADDER

```
┌─────────────────────────────────┐
│   Senior Crime Scene Technician  │
└─────────────────────────────────┘

┌─────────────────────────────────┐
│      Crime Scene Technician      │
└─────────────────────────────────┘

┌─────────────────────────────────┐
│             Trainee              │
└─────────────────────────────────┘
```

## Position Description

Crime Scene Technicians collect and process physical evidence from crime scenes. They are part of a police department's crime scene unit, a special detail for which police officers may volunteer. Officers perform crime scene duty in addition to their regular patrol, detective, or administrative duty. In some agencies, Crime Scene Technicians may be civilian employees.

Their first task at any crime scene is to learn about the crime. Crime Scene Technicians talk with police officers and detectives to get the facts: what kind of crime took place, what happened, who was involved, and so on. With this information, Crime Scene Technicians plan their search for physical evidence that may link suspects to their crimes.

Crime Scene Technicians carefully document the crime scene. They write well-detailed notes as well as draw clear sketches of the scene. In addition, they take rolls and rolls of photographs. Some Crime Scene Technicians also videotape the crime scene.

Using special equipment and techniques, Crime Scene Technicians search thoroughly for all items that may relate to a crime. They look for physical clues, such as bullets, weapons, tools, drugs, papers, clothing, shoe prints, fingerprints, palm prints, and tire impressions. They also examine the area for trace evidence such as body fluids, hair, blood, tool marks, paint chips, glass fragments, and fibers.

Crime Scene Technicians follow certain procedures for collecting different types of evidence. They make sure that all evidence is noted, sketched, and photographed before being placed in proper containers. The containers are labeled accurately with their origins, the date and time when they were collected, and other necessary information. Crime Scene Technicians keep a precise inventory of everything that is collected. The whole process of collecting physical evidence may take several hours, and sometimes may take several days, to complete. The Crime Scene Technicians submit the collected physical evidence to crime labs for further processing.

Crime Scene Technicians also are responsible for preparing accurate and well-detailed reports and documentation for court cases. They may be called upon to testify as an expert witness on cases that they were assigned.

Besides crime scenes, Crime Scene Technicians might collect physical evidence at autopsies. They might also gather evidence at non-crime scenes such as suicides and serious car accidents.

Their other duties vary, depending on their department. Many Crime Scene Technicians process and develop film as well as maintain photographic equipment. Some may take fingerprints of living and deceased persons. Some may maintain files of fingerprints, photographic evidence, and other crime scene data. Others may maintain crime scene equipment.

Crime Scene Technicians work in any type of environment, indoors and outdoors. They often stand, bend, kneel, or crouch in awkward positions. They are on call 24 hours a day, seven days a week. In large crime scene units, they may be rotated on an on-call schedule.

## Salaries

Earnings for Crime Scene Technicians vary, depending on such factors as their rank, education, experience, job duties, employer, and geographical location.

Civilian employees typically earn lower salaries than police officers. According to the International Crime Scene Investigators Association Web site (http://www.icsia.com), the salary for Crime Scene Technicians ranges from $20,000 to more than $50,000. Most police and sheriff patrol officers earned an estimated annual salary that ranges between $26,510 and $68,160 according to the November 2003 *Occupational Employment Statistics* survey by the U.S. Bureau of Labor Statistics. Officers receive additional compensation for working overtime, weekends, holidays, and late-night shifts. Many officers receive additional pay for performing special detail duties such as crime scene duty.

## Employment Prospects

Most police departments have crime scene units as do sheriff's departments, state police departments, and federal law enforcement agencies. Job opportunities generally become available when Crime Scene Technicians retire, resign, or are promoted to higher positions.

Many departments require that officers commit to a minimum number of years for crime scene duty.

## Advancement Prospects

Police officers have the opportunity to develop a career in accordance with their personal interests and ambitions. Volunteering for special police units work such as crime scene duty broadens their experience and furthers their careers. In addition to volunteering for special assignments, many officers pursue promotions to detective, sergeant, lieutenant, and so on. Depending on the police department, officers with adminstrative and managerial duties may be limited in their capacity to volunteer for special police units.

Supervisory and administrative positions within the crime scene detail are limited to unit commanders. Another path for Crime Scene Technicians is to obtain additional education and become trace evidence examiners, firearms and toolmark examiners, or other forensic scientists who work in crime labs. Some Crime Scene Technicians become private consultants in crime scene reconstruction and investigation.

## Education and Training

Many departments require that applicants possess an associate's degree in police science or other related field. Some departments accept applicants with a high school diploma or general equivalency diploma if they have completed a minimum number of units in science, law enforcement, and other related fields.

Many agencies require that new Crime Scene Technicians complete certified training in crime scene investigations.

Crime Scene Technicians undergo intensive training programs in such areas as crime scene processing, latent fingerprint processing, photography, and advanced death investigation.

## Special Requirements

Many agencies require that Crime Scene Technicians possess professional certification from a recognized organization such as the International Association for Identification. In addition, they must have a valid state driver's license.

## Experience, Skills, and Personality Traits

Police officers need one to three years of police duty before they are eligible to apply for crime scene duty. Both police and civilian applicants must have experience in fingerprinting and the handling of physical evidence. They also need one to three years' experience in photography and photo processing and development. Some agencies allow applicants to substitute graduation from a certified professional school of photography for experience.

To perform their work effectively, Crime Scene Technicians need excellent communication, interpersonal, and teamwork skills, as they must be able to maintain positive working relationships. Crime Scene Technicians also need strong writing skills to compose accurate reports and correspondence. In addition, they need good self-management skills.

Some personality traits that successful Crime Scene Technicians share include being objective, observant, detail-oriented, meticulous, ethical, honest, dependable, and courteous.

**Unions and Associations**

Crime Scene Technicians might belong to state or regional organizations that serve professionals involved in crime scene investigations. At the national and international levels, Crime Scene Technicians might join the International Association for Identification, or the Association for Crime Scene Reconstruction, or the International Crime Scene Investigators Association. (For contact information, see Appendix IV.) Joining professional organizations gives officers the opportunity to network with peers and obtain professional support and services, such as training programs research resources, and job referrals.

**Tips for Entry**

1. College students might sign up for internships or do volunteer work with crime scene divisions.

2. Learn basic photography skills as well as how to process and develop both black-and-white and color films.

3. As a police officer, let the crime scene unit commander know of your interest, especially before you are eligible or before an opening is available.

4. Contact the law enforcement agencies where you are interested in working, and ask each of them what its requirements are for Crime Scene Technicians.

5. Learn more about crime scene investigations on the Internet. You might start by visiting these Web sites: Crime Scene Investigation, http://www.crime-scene-investigator.net, and Forensic Enterprises, Inc. (hosted by Hayden S. Baldwin), http://www.feinc.net.

# LATENT PRINT EXAMINER

## CAREER PROFILE

**Duties:** Identify latent print evidence that is found at crime scenes

**Alternate Title(s):** Latent Print Analyst, Criminalist

**Salary Range:** $26,000 to $71,000

**Employment Prospects:** Excellent

**Advancement Prospects:** Limited

**Prerequisites:**

**Special Requirements**—Pass a selection process

**Education or Training**—Bachelor's degree in physical science, forensic science, police science, or related field

**Experience**—One to five years' experience in crime scene investigation, fingerprinting, and latent print analysis; expert witness experience preferred

**Special Skills and Personality Traits**—Memory, writing, communication, and self-management skills; be self-disciplined, honest, patient, objective, and diligent

**Licensure/Certification**—Professional certification may be required

## CAREER LADDER

Senior Latent Print Examiner

Latent Print Examiner

Latent Print Examiner Trainee

## Position Description

Latent Print Examiners are criminalists who work in forensic labs, or crime labs, where they provide assistance in criminal investigations. Their expertise is in analyzing latent prints—fingerprints, palm prints, and footprints—and establishing their positive identity. Because everyone has a unique set of fingerprints, palm prints, and footprints, it is possible to link suspects to crime scenes by any prints that they leave behind.

Physical evidence is submitted to Latent Print Examiners to process for latent prints and to preserve or record for future comparisons. They do this in several ways. By using special chemicals, they can lift the latent prints from the surface of objects. They can take photographs of the latent prints. Or they can convert the latent prints into digital images and store them on a computer or other electronic media.

Latent Print Examiners compare the latent prints evidence with known prints of suspects, victims, and other persons. A positive identification is made when the small ridge details are clearly the same in both the prints evidence and the known prints.

Often Latent Print Examiners use a computer to find matching prints. They first categorize a set of latent prints by its type of pattern. With that information, they can then perform a computer database search through millions of latent print files. Within minutes, the Latent Print Examiners have a list of possible matches on their computer monitor. They then compare each file to make a positive identification of the unknown prints taken from the evidence.

As part of their investigations, Latent Print Examiners write reports of their findings and conclusions. They also testify in court as an expert witness on their conclusions and about latent print methods and procedures.

Depending on the crime lab, Latent Print Examiners perform other duties. They might organize and maintain latent print files, logs, and records. They might train identification technicians and other personnel. They might also take finger, palm, and foot prints from crime suspects, victims, and dead bodies. On occasion, they are called out to crime scenes to help locate, collect, and process latent print evidence. They might also assist in collecting other physical evidence such as impressions of shoe prints, tire tracks, and tool marks.

They work a regular 40-hour week but are on call 24 hours a day, seven days a week. In large crime labs, Latent Print Examiners may be rotated on an on-call schedule.

## Salaries

Earnings for Latent Print Examiners vary, depending on such factors as their education, experience, employer, and geographical location. The U.S. Bureau of Labor Statistics reports in its November 2003 *Occupational Employment Statistics* survey that the estimated annual salary for most forensic science technicians—including Latent Print Examiners—ranged between $26,520 and $70,830.

## Employment Prospects

Most Latent Print Examiners work in government crime labs at the local, state, and federal levels. Some of these specialists are employed by private forensic laboratories.

Latent Print Examiners are usually civilian employees. In some law enforcement agencies, they are sworn law enforcement officers who have volunteered for these positions. Officers perform latent print examination duties in addition to their regular patrol, investigative, or administrative duty.

Opportunities generally become available as Latent Print Examiners retire or transfer to other positions. An employer will create additional positions to meet growing demands, as long as funding is available.

## Advancement Prospects

Supervisory and management opportunities in crime labs are limited to a few positions—unit supervisor, assistant lab director, and lab director. Many Latent Print Examiners pursue career growth by way of salary increases and complexity of new assignments. Some examiners become private latent print consultants.

## Education and Training

Educational requirements vary with the different agencies. Many agencies require that Latent Print Examiners possess a bachelor's degree in chemistry, forensic science, police science, or a related field. Some agencies may hire candidates with a high school diploma (or a general equivalency diploma), an associate degree, or with some college training, if they have qualifying experience.

Throughout their careers, many Latent Print Examiners enroll in educational programs, training seminars, and conference workshops to increase their knowledge and update their skills.

## Special Requirements

Many agencies require that Latent Print Examiners possess professional certification from a recognized organization such as the FBI or the International Association for Identification. Those without certification are hired on the condition that they obtain proper certification within a specific time frame.

## Experience, Skills, and Personality Traits

Depending on their education, Latent Print Examiner candidates need one to five years of experience in crime scene investigation, fingerprinting, and latent print analysis. Many agencies prefer that candidates have some experience testifying in court as an expert witness.

Latent Print Examiners need excellent memory skills as well as strong writing and communication skills. They also must have strong self-management skills, such as the ability to work independently, handle stressful situations, follow instructions, and organize and prioritize tasks. Being self-disciplined, honest, patient, objective, and diligent are some personality traits that successful Latent Print Examiners share.

## Unions and Associations

Many Latent Print Examiners belong to one or more professional associations for their occupation as well as for criminalists in general. These associations are available at the local, state, regional, national, and international levels. For example, many Latent Print Examiners are members of the International Association for Identification or the American Academy of Forensic Sciences. (For contact information, see Appendix IV.)

By joining a professional association, Latent Print Examiners can take advantage of networking opportunities, educational programs, research findings, and other professional resources and services.

## Tips for Entry

1. Take chemistry, biology, and computer imaging courses in high school or college to gain useful knowledge and skills for work in latent print examination.
2. Contact crime labs directly to learn about current job opportunities as well as jobs that may become available soon.
3. Gain useful work experience as fingerprint technicians for police departments or other law enforcement agencies.
4. Learn more about Latent Print Examiners and their work on the Internet. You might start by visiting the following Web sites: Latent Print Examination: Fingerprints, Palmprints, and Footprints (hosted by Ed German), http://www.onin.com/fp, and Complete Latent Print Examination (hosted by Kasey Wertheim), http://www.clpex.com.

# FORENSIC CHEMIST

## CAREER PROFILE

**Duties:** Perform chemical analysis on physical evidence

**Alternate Title(s):** Criminalist, Forensic Scientist

**Salary Range:** $27,000 to $71,000

**Employment Prospects:** Good

**Advancement Prospects:** Limited

**Prerequisites:**

**Education or Training**—Bachelor's degree in chemistry

**Experience**—Knowledge of chemical principles, theories, and laboratory work

**Special Skills and Personality Traits**—Computer, technical writing, problem-solving, organizational, communication, public speaking, and self-management skills; be articulate, composed, impartial, credible, versatile, patient, ethical, and trustworthy

**Licensure/Certification**—Professional certification may be required

## CAREER LADDER

```
┌─────────────────────────────┐
│   Senior Forensic Chemist   │
└─────────────────────────────┘

┌─────────────────────────────┐
│      Forensic Chemist       │
└─────────────────────────────┘

┌─────────────────────────────┐
│           Trainee           │
└─────────────────────────────┘
```

## Position Description

Forensic Chemists are forensic scientists who assist in criminal investigations. They work in law enforcement forensic labs, or crime labs. Their expertise is to use chemical analysis and scientific principles to examine physical evidence. For example, a Forensic Chemist might analyze the content of fire debris for an arson investigation.

Before testing any evidence, Forensic Chemists need to know the type of criminal offense from which the evidence was obtained, what needs to be known about the evidence, and the chemical and physical properties of the substances involved. Forensic Chemists use this information to determine what specific data they need to obtain and the best approach, methods, and procedures to use.

Forensic Chemists perform several different tests to positively detect and identify a substance. Afterward, they evaluate and interpret the results. They make sure that all necessary data has been obtained, and they draw conclusions about their findings. They prepare reports, describing the results of the analyses and their conclusions. If necessary, they testify in court as expert witnesses on their findings.

Some Forensic Chemists work in chemistry labs that do specific investigative work. For example, in drug chemistry labs, Forensic Chemists analyze controlled substances in drug cases.

In all chemistry labs, Forensic Chemists do research. They are constantly developing new and better analytical and testing methods for forensic investigations.

Forensic Chemists work a regular 40-hour week. They are on call 24 hours a day. In large crime labs, Forensic Chemists are rotated on an on-call schedule. They work mostly in the chemistry lab, but from time to time, they are called out to a crime scene to help locate and collect physical evidence.

## Salaries

The salary for Forensic Chemists varies, depending on their experience, education, and job responsibilities, as well as the size and location of the crime lab for which they work. Generally, Forensic Chemists who have advanced degrees can expect higher wages. Also, they can usually earn more working for larger crime labs or for labs in metropolitan areas such as New York City and Los Angeles.

The U.S. Bureau of Labor Statistics reports in its November 2003 *Occupational Employment Statistics* survey that the estimated annual salary for most forensic science technicians—including Forensic Chemists—ranged between $26,520 and $70,830.

## Employment Prospects

Most Forensic Chemists work for crime labs in association with local, state, or federal law enforcement agencies. Some are employed by medical examiners' offices and private laboratories, as well as by academic laboratories that offer forensic services to law enforcement agencies on a contractual basis.

Most openings become available as Forensic Chemists are promoted, transfer to other jobs, or retire. The competition for jobs is high, but qualified Forensic Chemists should be able to find positions readily. Some experts report that opportunities should be particularly good in the area of DNA analysis.

## Advancement Prospects

Supervisory and management opportunities in crime labs are limited to a few positions—unit supervisor, assistant lab director, and lab director. Many Forensic Chemists pursue career growth by way of salary increases and complexity of new assignments.

Another career path for Forensic Chemists is to become an expert in an area such as trace evidence analysis or drug analysis. Some Forensic Chemists become private consultants.

## Education and Training

Entry-level applicants need a bachelor's degree in chemistry. Some agencies accept applicants who have a bachelor's degree in a life science or other physical science if they have a required number of hours in chemistry.

Throughout their careers, many Forensic Chemists enroll in conference workshops, training seminars, and educational programs to increase their knowledge and update their skills.

## Special Requirements

Employers may require Forensic Chemists to possess professional certification that is granted by the state where they work or from a recognized organization such as the American Board of Criminalistics. Employers will hire qualified candidates without certification on the condition that they obtain it within a specific time frame.

## Experience, Skills, and Personality Traits

Previous crime lab work is not needed for entry-level positions. However, crime labs hire candidates who have knowledge of chemical principles, theories, practices, and laboratory work.

Forensic Chemists must have strong computer and technical writing skills as well as excellent problem-solving and organizational skills. They should have good communication and public speaking skills in order to be effective as expert witnesses. Furthermore, they need strong self-management skills.

Being articulate, composed, impartial, credible, versatile, patient, ethical, and trustworthy are some personality traits that successful Forensic Chemists share.

## Unions and Associations

Forensic Chemists belong to regional and state professional associations for forensic scientists or criminalists, which offer networking opportunities, training and educational programs, and other professional services. Many also belong to the American Academy of Forensic Sciences, an international organization that promotes education and high professional standards in forensic science. In addition, some Forensic Chemists are members of the American Chemical Society.

For contact information for these organizations, see Appendix IV.

## Tips for Entry

1. Take as many science and math courses as possible in high school.
2. If possible, gain experience at crime labs as an intern or volunteer.
3. Contact professional associations such as the American Academy of Forensic Sciences to learn about job openings.
4. Learn more about Forensic Chemists on the Internet. Enter the keywords *forensic chemist* into a search engine to get a list of Web sites. For information on crime labs, or forensic labs, enter the keywords *forensic lab.*

# TRACE EVIDENCE EXAMINER

## CAREER PROFILE

**Duties:** Analyze and identify small particles of physical evidence

**Alternate Title(s):** Trace Evidence Analyst, Trace Evidence Specialist, Criminalist

**Salary Range:** $27,000 to $71,000

**Employment Prospects:** Good

**Advancement Prospects:** Limited

**Prerequisites:**

**Education or Training**—Bachelor's degree in chemistry

**Experience**—One to three years of crime lab or related experience; expert witness experience

**Special Skills and Personality Traits**—Concentration, technical writing, computer, communication, public speaking, and self-management skills; be detail-oriented, patient, persistent, impartial, ethical, and trustworthy

**Licensure/Certification**—Professional certification may be required

## CAREER LADDER

```
┌─────────────────────────────────┐
│  Senior Trace Evidence Examiner  │
└─────────────────────────────────┘

┌─────────────────────────────────┐
│     Trace Evidence Examiner      │
└─────────────────────────────────┘

┌─────────────────────────────────┐
│             Trainee              │
└─────────────────────────────────┘
```

## Position Description

Trace Evidence Examiners are criminalists who assist in criminal investigations. They work in law enforcement forensic labs, or crime labs. Their expertise is analyzing small particles of physical evidence, or trace evidence, from a crime scene or a victim's body. For example, they might examine hair, tissue, saliva, blood, body fluids, fibers, soil, glass, plastic, metal, fire debris, explosives, or paint chips. Their findings help establish facts in criminal investigations.

Using various techniques and methods, Trace Evidence Examiners may be able to identify the contents or composition of trace evidence and their origins. They work on the principle that when two objects have come together, each object will leave particles on the other. With computers, microscopes, and instruments, Trace Evidence Examiners compare the composition, color, shade, and makeup of unknown particles with known ones. For example, cat hair is collected as evidence at a crime scene. Detectives want to know if that cat hair matches a certain cat. A Trace Evidence Examiner would examine a known sample of the cat hair alongside the cat hair evidence.

After performing complex chemical and physical analyses, Trace Evidence Examiners interpret test results and draw conclusions. They prepare written reports of their findings and conclusions. And, when requested, they testify in court as expert witnesses about their findings and conclusions.

Trace Evidence Examiners also conduct research in developing new and better analytical and testing methods for forensic investigations. In some crime labs, Trace Evidence Examiners analyze other evidence such as fingerprints, footwear, tire impressions, and track impressions. They might also examine vehicle speedometers, headlamps, and tail-lights.

From time to time, Trace Evidence Examiners leave the crime lab to assist at crime scenes, locating and collecting physical evidence. They work a regular 40-hour week but are on call 24 hours a day. Those working in large crime labs may be rotated on an on-call schedule.

## Salaries

Salaries depend on the size and location of a crime lab, as well as the experience, education, and job responsibilities of

Trace Evidence Examiners. Generally, examiners earn more working for larger crime labs or for labs in metropolitan areas such as New York City and Los Angeles. In addition, earnings are higher for those who perform supervisory duties.

According to the November 2003 *Occupational Employment Statistics* survey by the U.S. Bureau of Labor Statistics (BLS), the estimated annual salary for most forensic science technicians—including Trace Evidence Examiners—ranged between $26,520 and $70,830.

## Employment Prospects

Most Trace Evidence Examiners are employed by government crime labs at the local, state, and federal levels. Some are employed by private labs that offer forensic services on a contractual basis.

According to the BLS, employment for forensic science technicians in general is expected to grow by 10 to 20 percent through 2012. In addition to new opportunities, jobs will become available to replace Trace Evidence Examiners who have retired, been promoted, or transferred to other occupations.

## Advancement Prospects

Supervisory and management opportunities in crime labs are limited to a few positions—unit supervisor, assistant lab director, and lab director. Many Trace Evidence Examiners pursue career growth by way of salary increases and complexity of new assignments. Some examiners become private consultants.

## Education and Training

Entry-level applicants need a bachelor's degree in chemistry. Some agencies accept applicants who have a bachelor's degree in a life science or other physical science if they have a required number of hours in chemistry.

Throughout their careers, many Trace Evidence Examiners enroll in educational programs, training seminars, and conference workshops to increase their knowledge and update their skills.

## Special Requirements

Many agencies require that Trace Evidence Examiners possess professional certification granted by the American Board of Criminalistics or another recognized organization.

Those without certification are hired on the condition that they obtain it within a specific time frame.

## Experience, Skills, and Personality Traits

Depending on the crime lab, an applicant needs one to three years of crime lab or related work experience in addition to experience testifying in court as an expert witness. Some crime labs accept an equivalent combination of experience, training, and education that provides the required knowledge, skills, and abilities for the job.

To perform the various aspects of their job effectively, Trace Evidence Examiners need strong concentration, technical writing, computer, communication, and public speaking skills. In addition, they must have excellent self-management skills, such as the ability to work independently, meet deadlines, organize and prioritize tasks, and follow directions.

Being detail-oriented, patient, persistent, impartial, ethical, and trustworthy are some personality traits that successful Trace Evidence Examiners share.

## Unions and Associations

Trace Evidence Examiners might belong to the American Academy of Forensic Sciences and the International Association for Identification. For contact information, see Appendix IV.

Some Trace Evidence Examiners belong to regional and state forensic science associations. Joining professional organizations gives officers the opportunity to network with peers and obtain professional support and services, such as certified training programs, research findings, and job listings.

## Tips for Entry

1. Take police science, criminal justice, law, or other courses related to law enforcement to gain valuable skills and knowledge for a career in the crime lab.
2. Learn about job openings on the Internet. Many law enforcement agencies, professional associations, and forensic science organizations post job opportunities on their Web sites.
3. Learn more about Trace Evidence Examiners and trace evidence examination on the Internet. Enter the keywords *trace evidence analyst* or *trace evidence examiner* into a search engine to get a list of Web sites. For information on crime labs, or forensic labs, enter the keywords *forensic lab*.

# FIREARMS AND TOOLMARK EXAMINER

## CAREER PROFILE

**Duties:** Determine whether firearms and tools left at crime scenes were used in crimes

**Alternate Title(s):** Firearms and Toolmark Specialist; Criminalist

**Salary Range:** $27,000 to $71,000

**Employment Prospects:** Good

**Advancement Prospects:** Limited

**Prerequisites:**

**Education or Training**—Minimum high school diploma, but varies with each agency

**Experience**—Three to five years in firearms and toolmarks examinations; expert witness experience

**Special Skills and Personality Traits**—Concentration, public speaking, technical writing, computer, communication, and self-management skills; be ethical, trustworthy, impartial, patient, detail-oriented, and persistent

**Licensure/Certification**—Professional certification may be required

## CAREER LADDER

```
┌─────────────────────────────────────────┐
│  Senior Firearms and Toolmark Examiner   │
└─────────────────────────────────────────┘

┌─────────────────────────────────────────┐
│     Firearms and Toolmark Examiner        │
└─────────────────────────────────────────┘

┌─────────────────────────────────────────┐
│                 Trainee                   │
└─────────────────────────────────────────┘
```

## Position Description

Firearms and Toolmark Examiners are criminalists who assist in criminal investigations. They work in law enforcement forensic labs, or crime labs. Their expertise covers two areas of physical evidence—firearms and toolmarks. They determine if firearms and tools found at a crime scene were used in the crime, based on the fact that all firearms and tools produce their own unique markings. For example, two screwdrivers may be identical in size, shape, and makeup, but each makes individual markings.

As firearms experts, Firearms and Toolmark Examiners can make a positive match between a specific gun and recovered bullets. Every firearm has microscopic markings that are unique to itself. When it is fired, its markings are transferred to the fired bullets or other ammunition. Thus, the Firearms and Toolmark Examiners test fire a gun in question, and then compare the test bullets with those in evidence under a special microscope that allows them to see the bullets side by side. If the markings are the same on both bullets, the Firearms and Toolmark Examiners have proof that the bullets in evidence came from the gun in question.

On occasion, Firearms and Toolmark Examiners may be asked to determine the path bullets may have taken and re-create possible crime scene scenarios. They may also be asked to estimate the distance from which a gun was shot by examining the gunpowder residue on clothing or around wounds.

As toolmarks experts, they can determine if tools and tool marks recovered from a crime scene match. The Firearms and Toolmark Examiners compare test toolmarks made by the tools in question with the tool markings in evidence. For example, if a crowbar found at a crime scene is suspected of being used to pry open a door, the crowbar and a piece of the door frame with markings on it are brought to the crime lab. A Firearms and Toolmark Examiner makes test marks with the crowbar and then compares them with the markings on the door frame. If the markings match, the Firearms and Toolmark Examiner has proof that the markings on the door frame were made by the crowbar.

After making their analyses and evaluations, Firearms and Toolmark Examiners draw conclusions and prepare necessary reports. They may be called upon to testify as expert witnesses in court about their findings and conclusions.

Other duties may include establishing new or better policies and procedures for their crime lab. Some examiners also perform other forensic examinations such as those involving footwear, tire impressions, metal, and plastics.

Firearms and Toolmark Examiners work mostly in the crime lab. Sometimes they are called out to examine crime scenes to help locate and collect physical evidence. They work a 40-hour week but are on call 24 hours a day, seven days a week. In large crime labs, they may be rotated on an on-call schedule.

## Salaries

Salaries depend on the size and location of a crime lab, as well as the experience, education, and job duties of Firearms and Toolmark Examiners. Generally, examiners earn more working for larger crime labs or for labs in metropolitan areas such as New York City and Los Angeles. In addition, earnings are higher for those who perform supervisory duties.

According to the November 2003 *Occupational Employment Statistics* survey by the U.S. Bureau of Labor Statistics (BLS), the estimated annual salary for most forensic science technicians—including Firearms and Toolmark Examiners—ranged between $26,520 and $70,830.

## Employment Prospects

Most Firearms and Toolmark Examiners are employed by government crime labs at the county, state, and federal levels. Some are employed by private labs that offer forensic services on a contractual basis.

According to the BLS, employment for forensic science technicians in general is expected to grow by 10 to 20 percent through 2012. In addition to newly created openings, opportunities will become available as Firearms and Toolmark Examiners retire, are promoted, or transfer to other occupations.

## Advancement Prospects

Supervisory and management opportunities in crime labs are limited to a few positions—unit supervisor, assistant lab director, and lab director. Many Firearms and Toolmark Examiners pursue career growth by way of salary increases and complexity of new assignments. Some examiners become private consultants.

## Education and Training

Education requirements vary with each agency. Applicants need at least a high school diploma or general equivalency diploma. Some agencies do not require a bachelor's degree but prefer that candidates have one. Other agencies require a bachelor's degree in physical, natural, or forensic science.

Throughout their careers, many Firearms and Toolmark Examiners enroll in training seminars, educational pro-grams, and conference workshops to increase their knowledge and update their skills.

## Special Requirements

Many agencies require that Firearms and Toolmark Examiners possess professional certification granted by the Association of Firearm and Tool Mark Examiners or another recognized organization. Those without certification are hired on the condition that they obtain it within a specific time frame.

## Experience, Skills, and Personality Traits

Depending on the crime lab, applicants need three to five years of experience in firearms and toolmark examination and evidence identification techniques. They also must have experience testifying in court as expert witnesses.

Firearms and Toolmark Examiners must have excellent concentration, public speaking, technical writing, computer, and communication skills. Their job also requires that they have effective self-management skills, such as the ability to meet deadlines, organize and prioritize tasks, follow directions, and work independently.

Some personality traits that successful Firearms and Toolmark Examiners share include being ethical, trustworthy, impartial, patient, detail-oriented, and persistent.

## Unions and Associations

The Association of Firearm and Tool Mark Examiners is a professional organization specifically for Firearms and Toolmark Examiners. They also belong to the International Association for Identification. (For contact information, see Appendix IV.)

Many examiners are members of regional and state professional forensic scientist associations. Joining professional organizations affords examiners the opportunity to network with peers and obtain professional support and services, such as education programs, research findings, and job listings.

## Tips for Entry

1. Join one or more professional associations as many crime labs prefer to hire applicants with professional affiliations.
2. Go to professional conventions and network with other forensic scientists. You may be able to learn about upcoming job openings at various crime labs.
3. Learn more about Firearms and Toolmark Examiners on the Internet. You might start by visiting the Association of Firearm and Tool Mark Examiners Web site at http://www.afte.org. To get a list of other relevant Web sites, enter the keywords *firearm examination* or *toolmark examination* into a search engine.

# QUESTIONED DOCUMENT EXAMINER

## CAREER PROFILE

**Duties:** Determine if documents are authentic or forgeries; identify types of inks, papers, writing instruments, and business machines

**Alternate Title(s):** Questioned Documents Specialist, Forensic Document Examiner

**Salary Range:** $27,000 to $71,000

**Employment Prospects:** Good

**Advancement Prospects:** Limited

**Prerequisites:**

**Education or Training**—Bachelor's degree preferred

**Experience**—Knowledge of computer, photography, microscopy, and job-related examination techniques

**Special Skills and Personality Traits**—Writing, observation, communication, interpersonal, and self-management skills; be ethical, trustworthy, patient, persistent, and organized

**Licensure/Certification**—Professional certification may be required

## CAREER LADDER

```
┌─────────────────────────────────────────┐
│  Senior Questioned Document Examiner      │
└─────────────────────────────────────────┘

┌─────────────────────────────────────────┐
│     Questioned Document Examiner          │
└─────────────────────────────────────────┘

┌─────────────────────────────────────────┐
│              Trainee                      │
└─────────────────────────────────────────┘
```

## Position Description

Questioned Document Examiners are forensic scientists who assist in criminal investigations. They work in law enforcement forensic labs, or crime labs. Their expertise is analyzing documents such as checks, currency, vouchers, invoices, contracts, certificates, business correspondence, passports, wills, notes, and personal letters. They determine facts about documents that may help establish a link between suspects and crime scenes. For example, they can analyze documents and determine:

- if documents are real or counterfeit
- if handwriting or signatures are authentic or forgeries
- if any changes have been made to documents
- what words and sentences have been erased or crossed out

Questioned Document Examiners are also trained to identify the types of inks and papers that are used for a document. They can determine the type of writing instrument or typewriter, printer, copy machine, or other business machine that produced a document.

As part of their job, Questioned Document Examiners obtain authentic handwriting samples and other documents to make comparisons with the physical evidence. They use various microscopes, magnifiers, measuring devices, and special instruments. They write and submit reports of their findings and conclusions. They also testify in court as expert witnesses on their findings and conclusions.

Questioned Document Examiners are usually civilian employees. In some law enforcement agencies, they are sworn law enforcement officers who have volunteered for these positions. Many agencies require that officers commit to a minimum number of years for the assignment. Officers perform document examination duties in addition to their regular patrol, investigative, or administrative duty.

Questioned Document Examiners work mostly in the crime lab. Occasionally, they are called out to crime scenes to help locate and collect physical evidence. They work a regular 40-hour week but are on call 24 hours a day, every day of the year. In large crime labs, they may be rotated on an on-call schedule.

## Salaries

Salaries depend on the size and location of a crime lab as well as the experience, education, and job responsibilities of Questioned Document Examiners. Generally, examiners earn more working for larger crime labs or for labs in metropolitan areas such as New York City and Los Angeles. In addition, earnings are higher for those who perform supervisory duties.

According to the November 2003 *Occupational Employment Statistics* survey by the U.S. Bureau of Labor Statistics (BLS), the estimated annual salary for most forensic science technicians—including Questioned Document Examiners—ranged between $26,520 and $70,830.

## Employment Prospects

Most Questioned Document Examiners are employed by government crime labs at the local, state, and federal levels. Job opportunities generally become available as examiners retire or transfer to other positions. However, the number of job openings at a crime lab will depend upon its budget.

## Advancement Prospects

Supervisory and management opportunities in crime labs are limited to a few positions—unit supervisor, assistant lab director, and lab director. Many Questioned Document Examiners pursue career growth by way of salary increases and complexity of new assignments. Some examiners become private consultants.

## Education and Training

Many agencies require Questioned Document Examiners to have a bachelor's degree, preferably in forensic science, criminal justice, chemistry, or other related field. In addition, they must complete an apprenticeship with either a crime lab or a certified private Questioned Document Examiner. The apprenticeship is usually two years long.

Throughout their careers, many Questioned Document Examiners enroll in training seminars, conference workshops, and educational programs to increase their knowledge and update their skills.

## Special Requirements

Many agencies require that Questioned Document Examiners possess professional certification that is granted by the American Board of Forensic Document Examiners or another recognized organization. Those without certification are hired on the condition that they obtain it within a specific time frame.

## Experience, Skills, and Personality Traits

Requirements for Questioned Document Trainee positions vary from agency to agency. Many agencies prefer trainees who have at least one year's work experience in a crime scene unit, forensic science lab, or other related field. Trainees should have a working knowledge of computers, photography, and microscopy as well as examination techniques that are related to the job.

To perform well at their job, Questioned Document Examiners must have strong writing, observation, communication, and interpersonal skills. Effective self-management skills are also essential. Being ethical, trustworthy, patient, persistent, and organized are some personality traits that successful Questioned Document Examiners share.

## Unions and Associations

Questioned Document Examiners might belong to one or two national associations: the American Society of Questioned Document Examiners or the National Association of Document Examiners. Both organizations offer networking opportunities, research and education programs, referral services, and other professional services and support. For contact information, see Appendix IV.

## Tips for Entry

1. Earn a bachelor's degree, as more and more agencies are making that a requirement for Questioned Document Examiners.
2. Contact certified private Questioned Document Examiners about apprenticeship opportunities.
3. Learn more about Questioned Document Examiners on the Internet. Enter the keywords *questioned documents* into a search engine to get a list of Web sites. For information on crime labs, or forensic labs, enter the keywords *forensic lab.*

# FORENSIC PATHOLOGIST

## CAREER PROFILE

**Duties:** Perform autopsies to determine the cause and manner of a person's death

**Alternate Title(s):** Medical Examiner

**Salary Range:** $40,000 to $200,000

**Employment Prospects:** Good

**Advancement Prospects:** Good

**Prerequisites:**

**Education or Training**—Bachelor's degree; medical school degree; residency training

**Experience**—Residency in forensic pathology

**Special Skills and Personality Traits**—Interpretive, analytical, communication, and interpersonal skills; be energetic, outgoing, honest, detail-oriented, and ethical

**Licensure/Certification**—Physician licensure; board certification

## CAREER LADDER

```
┌─────────────────────────────────────┐
│   Deputy Chief Medical Examiner      │
└─────────────────────────────────────┘

┌─────────────────────────────────────┐
│ Forensic Pathologist (Medical Examiner) │
└─────────────────────────────────────┘

┌─────────────────────────────────────┐
│   Resident in Forensic Pathology     │
└─────────────────────────────────────┘
```

## Position Description

Forensic Pathologists are medical doctors who specialize in death investigations. They have been specially trained to perform autopsies in medicolegal investigations of persons who have died suddenly, unexpectedly, or violently. Forensic Pathologists work for state and local medical examiner systems and are also known as medical examiners. (Note: Not all medical examiners are Forensic Pathologists.)

Through their autopsies, Forensic Pathologists attempt to answer questions such as time of death; whether the manner of death was natural, accidental, suicidal, or homicidal; the cause of death; what type of instrument may have been used if the death was the result of injury; and whether the death occurred where the body was found as well as if the body was moved after death.

Forensic Pathologists are often called out to crime scenes or other locations to do brief, preliminary examinations of dead bodies before they are moved. They gather information about a death, such as what the person was doing at the time he or she died. They also obtain information about the person's medical history.

At the laboratory, Forensic Pathologists do a thorough external and internal examination of the body. They perform various laboratory tests. They take X-rays. They remove tissue, fluids, and organs for microscopic, chemical, and toxicological studies. They also look for medical evidence on and inside the body, properly documenting, collecting, and processing any evidence such as bullets, hair, fibers, fingernail clippings, blood, and body fluids. All evidence is forwarded to forensic specialists, such as trace evidence examiners, for identification and analysis. If the identity of a body is unknown, Forensic Pathologists obtain help from other forensic specialists. For example, a forensic odontologist may be able to determine an identity by investigating dental records.

Forensic Pathologists evaluate the autopsy and lab results with the case history and draw a conclusion as to the cause and manner of death. They prepare comprehensive reports of their findings and conclusions, and may testify in court as expert witnesses. When natural deaths have been determined, Forensic Pathologists might meet with the family of the deceased to discuss the circumstances and cause of death.

Besides medicolegal investigations, Forensic Pathologists do research for publication in scientific journals. They also design protocol and standards for specialized death investigations such as infant deaths.

Sometimes Forensic Pathologists are involved in the practice of clinical forensic pathology for law enforcement agencies. They examine patients who may be victims or who may be suspected of being victimized to determine whether their injuries are accidental or intentional. For example, a Forensic Pathologist might examine a child's injuries to determine if he or she has been abused.

Forensic Pathologists work 40 hours a week but are on call 24 hours a day, every day of the year. In large medical examiner offices, Forensic Pathologists may be rotated on an on-call schedule.

## Salaries

Earnings for Forensic Pathologists vary, depending on various factors, such as their position, experience, employer, and geographical location. Annual salaries for forensic pathology residents generally range from $40,000 to $50,000 or more. Chief medical examiners, holders of the highest-ranking positions in medical examiner's offices, may earn up to $200,000 per year.

## Employment Prospects

Job opportunities are good at the present time and are expected to grow into the next decade. Forensic Pathologists are mostly hired by county and state government medical examiner offices. Some may find jobs with medical schools, military services, and the federal government. A few may find jobs with private groups or hospitals that perform forensic autopsies on a contractual basis.

Most job openings become available as Forensic Pathologists retire, advance to higher positions, or transfer to other jobs. Opportunities for this occupation may increase due to the small number of Forensic Pathologists being trained in comparison to the number of those retiring each year, according to the Wake Forest University Baptist Medical Center (Winston-Salem, North Carolina) Forensic Pathology Fellowship Program Web page (http://www.wfubmc.edu/pathology/training/forensic.htm).

## Advancement Prospects

After completing a residency in forensic pathology, these specialist doctors are usually hired as either assistant or associate medical examiners. Those seeking supervisory responsibilities become deputy chief medical examiners. The top positions in medical examiner systems are chief medical examiners.

Because there are so few Forensic Pathologists, advancement opportunities are good. However, many Forensic Pathologists change locations in order to move up to higher positions. Some may leave small offices at high ranks to work at lower ranks at larger offices in order to perform more interesting or challenging cases. Some Forensic Pathologists become private consultants.

## Education and Training

Forensic Pathologists must complete at least 13 years of study before they are qualified to enter the field. Students first complete a bachelor's degree, in any field, which may take four to five years. They next complete four years of medical training to earn either a doctor of medicine (M.D.) or doctor of osteopathy degree (D.O.). This is followed by four to five years of graduate medical education (more commonly known as a residency) to gain experience in the practice of pathology. Future Forensic Pathologists may choose to complete either four years of training in anatomic pathology or five years of training in both anatomic and clinical pathology. This is followed by another year of advanced training in forensic pathology, which includes practical experience performing autopsies and participating in death investigations.

## Special Requirements

Forensic Pathologists must be licensed to practice medicine in the state or territory where they plan to work.

Employers usually require that Forensic Pathologists be board-certified by the American Board of Pathology.

## Experience, Skills, and Personality Traits

In addition to their technical training, Forensic Pathologists must have strong interpretive and analytical skills for medicolegal investigations. They also need excellent communication and interpersonal skills.

Being energetic, outgoing, honest, detail-oriented, and ethical are some personality traits that successful Forensic Pathologists share.

## Unions and Associations

Different professional organizations that Forensic Pathologists might belong to are the National Association of Medical Examiners, the American Society for Clinical Pathologists, the American Medical Association, and the American Academy of Forensic Sciences. (For contact information, see Appendix IV.) Joining professional organizations gives Forensic Pathologists the opportunity to network with peers and obtain professional support and services, such as certified training, continuing education programs, current research findings, and job listings.

## Tips for Entry

1. Obtain the best training possible in anatomic and/or clinical pathology.
2. While you are waiting to get into a medical school, become a medical technologist and work in a medical examiner office's crime lab to gain exposure to the field.

3. Contact the Accreditation Council for Graduate Medical Education to get information about forensic pathology residency programs. The address is 515 North State Street, Suite 2000, Chicago, IL 60610-4322. The telephone number is (312) 775-5000.

4. To learn about job openings as well as fellowships, contact professional societies or visit their Web sites on the Internet.

5. Learn more about forensic pathology investigations on the Internet. You might start by visiting the National Association of Medical Examiners Web site at http://www.thename.org. To get a list of other relevant Web sites, enter the keywords *forensic pathology* or *medical examiner* into a search engine.

# POLYGRAPH EXAMINER

## CAREER PROFILE

**Duties:** Determine if people are being truthful or deceptive about issues in criminal investigations

**Alternate Title(s):** Polygraphist, Forensic Psychophysiologist

**Salary Range:** $27,000 to $68,000

**Employment Prospects:** Good

**Advancement Prospects:** Limited

**Prerequisites:**

**Education or Training**—College degree is preferred

**Experience**—Five years of investigative experience in law enforcement

**Special Skills and Personality Traits**—Interviewing, organizational, communication and interpersonal skills; be impartial, calm, levelheaded, ethical, and unbiased

**Licensure/Certification**—Professional licensure or certification may be required

## CAREER LADDER

```
┌─────────────────────────────────┐
│    Polygraph Unit Commander     │
└─────────────────────────────────┘

┌─────────────────────────────────┐
│       Polygraph Examiner        │
└─────────────────────────────────┘

┌─────────────────────────────────┐
│    Polygraph Examiner Intern    │
└─────────────────────────────────┘
```

## Position Description

Police Polygraph Examiners assist in criminal investigations by providing another investigative tool. They perform authorized polygraph examinations on suspects, victims, witnesses, and informants to determine if they are being truthful about specific issues under investigation.

Polygraph Examiners operate a polygraph instrument, which is more commonly known as a lie detector machine. It measures a person's pulse, blood pressure, breathing, and sweat gland activity as that person is asked a set of questions pertaining to a criminal case. Police investigators use the results from polygraph examinations to help them determine investigative leads, confirm allegations that cannot be disproved by other evidence, or establish probable cause to seek a search warrant. All authorized polygraph examinations are voluntary and they follow state laws and department policies.

A polygraph examination may be about one or more issues that are under investigation. Polygraph Examiners develop a series of questions for each issue. So if a polygraph exam is about two issues—such as two robberies—a Polygraph Examiner develops one series of questions for each issue.

Before administering a polygraph test, Polygraph Examiners get background information about the case and the person, or subject, they will be testing. They talk with investigators and other sources. They review the case file along with all other pertinent documents and records. Upon reviewing all available information, Polygraph Examiners develop the questions to ask the subject.

The structured polygraph examination is conducted in a room free of distractions. The test has two stages and takes about two to three hours. The first stage is the pretest interview. Polygraph Examiners explain the testing process, how the polygraph works, and the subject's legal rights. They discuss the issue under investigation. They also review the series of questions that the subject will be asked about that issue. The Polygraph Examiners then confirm that the subject understands the proceedings.

The second stage is the in-test. Attachments are placed on the subject to monitor physiological responses during the exam. The subject is asked the series of questions. It is repeated a second, and sometimes, a third time. The questions do not change. If an additional issue needs to be addressed, a second series of questions is then developed.

Polygraph Examiners interpret the polygraph charts and determine one of three conclusions: the subject answered the questions truthfully; the subject did not answer the questions truthfully; or the test results were inconclusive. For inconclusive results, Polygraph Examiners decide whether to conduct another examination. They write and submit reports on their findings and conclusions, and may testify in court as expert witnesses. (Currently, polygraph results are admissible as evidence at trials in only some federal circuits and some states.)

Many Polygraph Examiners also perform polygraph examinations on job applicants for law enforcement positions.

Most Polygraph Examiners are law enforcement officers who have volunteered to be part of their agency's polygraph detail. They usually perform polygraph examination duty in addition to their patrol, administrative, or other primary duties. Many agencies require that officers commit to a minimum number of years for the assignment. In some law enforcement agencies, Polygraph Examiners are civilian employees. Police Polygraph Examiners are on call 24 hours a day, seven days a week.

## Salaries

Earnings for police Polygraph Examiners vary, depending on such factors as their rank, education, experience, and geographical location. Most patrol officers earn an estimated annual salary that ranged between $26,510 and $68,160, according to the November 2003 *Occupational Employment Statistics* survey by the U.S. Bureau of Labor Statistics. Officers receive additional compensation for working overtime, weekend, holidays, and late-night shifts. Many officers receive additional pay for performing special detail duty, such as polygraph duty.

## Employment Prospects

In addition to police departments, Polygraph Examiners work in county, state, and federal law enforcement agencies. They also work for lawyers, courts, private detective agencies, and security agencies. Some Polygraph Examiners are self-employed or run their own polygraph services. In recent years, the polygraph examination has become part of the selection process for many jobs in government and the private sector. Hence, highly qualified Polygraph Examiners should be able to readily find employment.

Job opportunities generally become available as Polygraph Examiners retire or transfer to another occupation. An agency will create additional positions to meet demands, as long as funding is available.

## Advancement Prospects

Police officers have the chance to develop a career in keeping with their personal interests and ambitions. Volunteering for special police units such as polygraph units broadens their experience and may provide a stepping stone in their career advancement. In addition to taking on special assignments, many officers pursue promotions to detective, sergeant, lieutenant, and so on. Depending on the police

department, officers with administrative and managerial duties may be limited in their opportunity to volunteer for special police units.

Supervisory and administrative positions within the polygraph detail are limited to unit commanders. Many retired police Polygraph Examiners start their own business and contract with law enforcement agencies to do polygraph examinations.

## Education and Training

Most law enforcement agencies prefer candidates with associate's or bachelor's degrees in criminal justice, law, police science, or other related fields. Candidates must complete a certified training program and field training with a senior Polygraph Examiner.

Many states require that Polygraph Examiners have a license. Qualifications for a license differ in each state. Generally, Polygraph Examiners need a bachelor's degree and certification from an accredited polygraph school. In addition, they must complete an internship and pass their state's licensing exam.

Throughout their careers, many Polygraph Examiners enroll in educational programs, training seminars, and conference workshops to increase their knowledge and update their skills.

## Special Requirements

In 2004, the American Polygraph Association reported that 29 states and three counties in the United States required Polygraph Examiners to possess professional licensure or certification. Requirements for licensure differs from state to state, as well as from county to county. For more information, contact the governmental agency that regulates Polygraph Examiner licensure in the state or county where you plan to work.

You can find a listing of polygraph licensing agencies at the American Polygraph Association Web site: http://www.polygraph.org/statelicensing.htm.

## Experience, Skills, and Personality Traits

Polygraph Examiners need excellent interviewing, organizational, and communication skills to perform effectively at their job. They must also have superior interpersonal skills, as they will need to relate with people of diverse backgrounds. Being impartial, calm, levelheaded, ethical, and unbiased are some personality traits that successful Polygraph Examiners share.

## Unions and Associations

The American Polygraph Association and the American Association of Police Polygraphists are two professional organizations specifically for Polygraph Examiners. Both associations have a certification program recognized by law enforcement agencies. For contact information, see Appendix IV.

Polygraph Examiners might also be members of professional state polygraph associations. Joining professional organizations gives officers the opportunity to network with peers and obtain professional support and services, such as certified training, continuing education programs, current research findings, and job listings.

## Tips for Entry

1. If you are planning to enroll in a polygraph school, make sure it is recognized by professional associations and law enforcement agencies.

2. Keep up with the current polygraph training and technology as well as relevant legislation.

3. As a police officer, let the polygraph unit commander know of your interest, especially before you are eligible or before an opening is available.

4. Learn more about polygraph examinations on the Internet. You might start by visiting the American Polygraph Association Web site at http://www.polygraph.org. To get a list of other relevant Web sites, enter the keywords *polygraph examination* into a search engine.

# PRIVATE INVESTIGATIONS

# PRIVATE INVESTIGATOR

## CAREER PROFILE

**Duties:** Conduct investigations and provide protection for clients

**Alternate Title(s):** Private Detective

**Salary Range:** $19,000 to $58,000

**Employment Prospects:** Good

**Advancement Prospects:** Limited

**Prerequisites:**

**Education or Training—**High school diploma

**Experience—**Requirements differ with each agency

**Special Skills and Personality Traits—**Problem-solving, organizational, writing, research, computer, self-management, interpersonal, and communication skills; be objective, curious, adaptable, innovative, honest, ethical, loyal, and reliable

**Licensure/Certification—**Private investigator's license and firearms license may be required; business license needed for agency owners

## CAREER LADDER

```
┌─────────────────────────────┐
│    Manager or Owner,        │
│  Private Investigations Firm │
└─────────────────────────────┘

┌─────────────────────────────┐
│    Private Investigator     │
└─────────────────────────────┘

┌─────────────────────────────┐
│  Private Investigator Trainee │
└─────────────────────────────┘
```

## Position Description

Private Investigators perform investigative or protection services for their clients. They are hired by individuals, attorneys, businesses, corporations, and organizations for services that may involve:

- locating missing persons, assets (such as cash and property), documents, or information
- performing background checks—that is, verifying that information about individuals, businesses, or groups is true (Example: A Private Investigator might verify information on job applications for employers.)
- verifying information on insurance claims
- determining if a theft, fraud, or other criminal activity has occurred
- collecting evidence for criminal or civil trials
- gathering information about the activities of a person, group, or business
- protecting clients or their property from theft, robbery, personal harm, or other danger
- serving subpoenas or other processes

Many Private Investigators provide almost any kind of investigative or protective service that clients want. Other Private Investigators specialize in a few areas such as background investigations, arson investigations, surveillance work, or personal protection services.

When conducting investigations, Private Investigators perform any number of tasks. They search for information on computer databases and in public records such as courthouse records. They review documents, computer files, and other materials that clients give them. They examine scenes where a crime, accident, suicide, or other incident took place. They interview people, sometimes traveling to other cities and states.

Some cases require Private Investigators to do surveillance work. For example, a client might hire a Private Investigator to observe a stepparent to determine if he or she is abusing the client's mother or father. Private Investigators may take photographs or shoot videotapes to document the actions of individuals under surveillance.

For some cases, Private Investigators might perform undercover work. For example, a Private Investigator might pose as a worker in a warehouse to discover who may be stealing merchandise.

Private Investigators generally do not use firearms on the job. They may carry a gun if an assignment warrants the need for one.

With every case, Private Investigators maintain accurate, well-detailed notes. They provide verbal or written progress reports to their clients as well as submit a comprehensive summary of their investigation. On occasion, Private Investigators testify in court as expert witnesses about their findings.

Private Investigators who have their own agency oversee daily business operations. For example, they may do accounts, invoice clients, and pay bills and salaries. They may supervise both investigative and support staffs. They may maintain file systems and do routine office work.

Their jobs involve constant travel and meeting new people. They work long and irregular hours, including nights, week-ends, and holidays.

## Salaries

Earnings for Private Investigators vary, depending on such factors as their experience, abilities, specialties, and geographical location. According to the November 2003 *Occupational Employment Statistics* (OES) survey by the U.S. Bureau of Labor Statistics (BLS), most Private Investigators earned an estimated annual salary that ranged between $18,800 and $57,860.

## Employment Prospects

Private Investigators are employed full-time or part-time by private detective agencies, law firms, banks, insurance companies, employment services, and other establishments. Some Private Investigators are self-employed. The BLS reports in its November 2003 OES that an estimated 33,420 Private Investigators were employed in the United States.

Many job openings are created to replace Private Investigators who retire or leave the occupation for various reasons. According to the BLS, employment for this occupation is expected to grow by 21 to 35 percent through 2012. Much of this is due to such factors as an increase in litigation, the fear of crime, and other reasons.

## Advancement Prospects

Supervisory and management positions are limited to case managers. Thus, many Private Investigators pursue career growth by way of wage or fee increases and complexity of new assignments. The goal for some Private Investigators is to start their own agencies.

## Education and Training

Education requirements for entry-level Private Investigators vary from agency to agency. However, more and more agen-cies are hiring applicants who have associate's or bachelor's degrees in any field. Entry-level Private Investigators receive on-the-job training, performing basic tasks such as searching for information on computer databases.

## Special Requirements

Depending on where they are located, Private Investigators must hold either a state or local private investigator's license to practice. License requirements, which include age, education, and experience qualifications, vary from state to state or city to city. (For a listing of state private investigative licensing agencies, see Appendix III.)

Private Investigators who carry firearms as part of performing their job must possess the proper state licensure for owning firearms. In addition, agency owners must hold a valid business license issued by their local government.

Private Investigator trainees are covered by the licenses of the Private Investigators for whom they work.

## Experience, Skills, and Personality Traits

Requirements for entry-level positions vary with the different employers. Some employers are willing to hire individuals with little or no investigative work experience. Others prefer hiring entry-level Private Investigators who have law enforcement or military backgrounds and experience conducting investigations.

Private Investigators need strong problem-solving, organizational, writing, research, and computer skills for their job. They also must have excellent self-management skills—the ability to prioritize tasks, meet deadlines, follow instructions, work independently, and handle stressful situations. In addition, they should have superior interpersonal and communication skills, as they must be able to handle people with diverse backgrounds.

Some personality traits that successful Private Investigators have in common include being objective, curious, adaptable, innovative, honest, ethical, loyal, and reliable.

## Unions and Associations

Many Private Investigators join one or more professional associations to take advantage of educational programs, training programs, job referrals, networking opportunities, and other professional resources and services. These organizations are available at the local, state, regional, and national levels. Some national groups that serve the interests of Private Investigators are National Association of Investigative Specialists, ASIS International, and Global Investigators Network. For contact information, see Appendix IV.

## Tips for Entry

1. Contact local Private Investigators about part-time or full-time trainee positions.

2. Take speech, psychology, English, history, sociology, business law, and physical education courses in high school or college to obtain valuable knowledge and skills for this field.

3. You can learn more about the private investigation field on the Internet. You might start by visiting the Private Investigations Portal at http://www.infoguys.com.

# BACKGROUND INVESTIGATOR

## CAREER PROFILE

**Duties:** Verify that the information individuals and businesses state about themselves is true

**Alternate Title(s):** None

**Salary Range:** $19,000 to $58,000

**Employment Prospects:** Good

**Advancement Prospects:** Limited

**Prerequisites:**

**Education or Training—**High school diploma

**Experience—**Requirements vary with the different agencies

**Special Skills and Personality Traits—**Computer, research, interviewing, communication, interpersonal, organizational, and self-management skills; be detail-oriented, persistent, innovative, flexible, creative, honest, and ethical

**Licensure/Certification—**Private investigator's license may be required; business license needed for agency owners

## CAREER LADDER

```
┌─────────────────────────────────┐
│        Manager or Owner,         │
│  Background Investigations Firm  │
└─────────────────────────────────┘

┌─────────────────────────────────┐
│     Background Investigator      │
└─────────────────────────────────┘

┌─────────────────────────────────┐
│  Background Investigator Trainee │
└─────────────────────────────────┘
```

## Position Description

Background Investigators specialize in verifying information for clients who include individuals, nonprofit groups, businesses, corporations, and government agencies. Their investigations help clients decide whether to:

- hire people for jobs
- marry people or become personally involved with people
- contribute money to organizations
- give loans to individuals or companies
- do business with companies or individuals
- buy or sell companies
- invest money in companies

A background check on an individual may involve verifying personal information such as name, social security number, date of birth, past and current addresses, and family history. Clients may also request Background Investigators to collect or verify facts about people's education or employment history and professional licenses, military service, financial history, criminal or driving record, medical history, group memberships, and so forth.

A background check on a business or company might consist of verifying information about its operations—for example, how long it has been in existence, what products it makes or sells, how many employees it has, and who its executive and management officers are. Background Investigators might check licenses, certificates, and public filing information such as Occupational Safety and Health Administration records. In addition, they might verify facts about the business's or company's financial history, including credit reports.

Background Investigators perform their information searches in several ways. They search many different computer databases that are available on the Internet and from information services, industry sources, and government offices. Sometimes they visit libraries, schools, courthouses, and other institutions to research public records, directories, yearbooks, and other sources. Background Investigators also interview people who can verify information. They talk with personnel departments, bank managers, landlords, teachers, professors, school counselors, job counselors, medical personnel, neighbors, friends, relatives, and others. These interviews may be conducted by phone or in person.

Background Investigators who have their own agencies are responsible for the daily administration of their operations. They perform various tasks such as record keeping, invoicing clients, paying bills and taxes, and maintaining the office. If they have staff, they are responsible for supervising, directing, and evaluating their work.

Background Investigators work a 40-hour week but may work extra hours to complete rush requests.

## Salaries

Earnings for Background Investigators vary, depending on their experience, employer, fees, geographical location, and other factors. According to the November 2003 *Occupational Employment Statistics* survey by the U.S. Bureau of Labor Statistics (BLS), the estimated annual salary for most private investigators—including Background Investigators—ranged between $18,800 and $57,860.

## Employment Prospects

Background Investigators work for private detective agencies or have their own firms. Some investigators are self-employed. The job opportunities for the private investigation field are expected to grow faster than the average of all other occupations through 2012, according to the BLS.

## Advancement Prospects

Supervisory and management positions are limited to case managers. So, many Background Investigators pursue career growth by way of wage or fee increases and complexity of new assignments. The goal for some Background Investigators is to start their own agencies.

## Education and Training

Most agencies require trainees to have a high school or general equivalency diploma. Many agencies, however, are hiring trainees who have associate's or bachelor's degrees in any field.

## Special Requirements

Most Background Investigators need either a state or local private investigator's license to practice. License require-ments, which include age, education, and experience qualifications, vary from state to state or city to city. (For a listing of state private investigative licensing agencies, see Appendix III.)

Background Investigator trainees are covered by their employers' licenses.

Agency owners must possess a business license issued by their local government.

## Experience, Skills, and Personality Traits

Small agencies are willing to hire applicants with little or no investigative work experience.

Background Investigators need excellent computer, research, and interviewing skills for their job. In addition, they need strong communication and interpersonal skills as well as organizational and self-management skills. Being detail-oriented, persistent, innovative, flexible, creative, honest, and ethical are some personality traits that successful Background Investigators share.

## Unions and Associations

Background Investigators may join local, state, or national professional associations to take advantage of networking opportunities and other professional resources and services. At the national level, they are eligible to join such organizations as National Association of Investigative Specialists, ASIS International, and Global Investigators Network. For contact information, see Appendix IV.

## Tips for Entry

1. Take investigative courses through community colleges and continuing education programs.
2. Some detective agencies hire trainees for part-time work. Call up agencies in your area to find out if they are currently hiring or planning to hire soon.
3. Get an idea of the different services that Background Investigators offer clients. Read about some detective agencies on the Internet. Enter the keywords *background investigations* into a search engine to get a list of Web sites.

# ARSON INVESTIGATOR

## CAREER PROFILE

**Duties:** Investigate fires that may have been started on purpose for money or other reasons; provide expert witness testimony

**Alternate Title(s):** Fire Investigator

**Salary Range:** $19,000 to $58,000

**Employment Prospects:** Good

**Advancement Prospects:** Limited

**Prerequisites:**

**Education or Training**—College work and certified training desirable

**Experience**—Three years of firefighting experience

**Special Skills and Personality Traits**—Communication, presentation, report writing, and computer skills; be objective, detail-oriented, organized, honest, ethical, and reliable

**Licensure/Certification**—Private investigator's license may be required

## CAREER LADDER

```
┌─────────────────────────────┐
│   Manager or Owner,         │
│   Arson Investigations Firm │
└─────────────────────────────┘

┌─────────────────────────────┐
│   Arson Investigator        │
└─────────────────────────────┘

┌─────────────────────────────┐
│   Firefighter               │
└─────────────────────────────┘
```

## Position Description

Private Arson Investigators are hired by attorneys and insurance companies to investigate fires in which properties may have been burned down on purpose so that owners can get money from their insurance companies for the loss of property. Their cases include suspicious burning of homes, apartment buildings, office buildings, churches, schools, hotels, stores, factories, automobiles, boats, and aircraft.

With every investigation, Arson Investigators gather evidence in the form of documents, witnesses, and physical proof to substantiate that a fire was arson. They carefully examine fire scenes to determine where a fire began and how it was started. They look for signs such as burn patterns and physical evidence that show the fire was set intentionally. They also keep an open mind to the possibility that a fire may have started naturally or by accident.

Arson Investigators document all fire scenes. They write well-detailed notes about their observations. They make clear diagrams of the burnt structure and physical evidence of arson. They take photographs of the scene and may make videotapes of it. In addition, they review police and fire marshal reports. Throughout their investigation, they may exchange information with police officers and fire marshals who are also investigating the case.

Interviewing people for pertinent information is an essential part of an arson investigation. Arson Investigators interview police and firefighters who were at the fire scene as well as people who witnessed the fire. In addition, the investigators interview the owners and occupants of the property to learn more about them. They also interview neighbors, friends, relatives, bank managers, and any other persons who may have knowledge about the fire, the property, the owners, and the occupants.

Furthermore, Arson Investigators do background checks on the scorched property and its owners. They examine insurance policies, and learn pertinent facts about the structure such as its age, its purpose, what kind of fire alarm systems it had, and who had access to the building. They do intensive background checks on suspects, including owners and occupants.

Arson Investigators complete and submit well-detailed reports, which include witness statements, documents, photographs, and physical evidence. In addition, Arson Investigators may testify in court as expert witnesses about their findings and their expertise in arson investigations.

Arson Investigators who have their own agencies are responsible for overseeing the day-to-day operations. They perform various tasks such as record keeping, invoicing clients, paying bills and taxes, and maintaining the office. If they have staff, the investigators are responsible for supervising, directing, and evaluating their staff's work.

Arson Investigators often work evenings and weekends in order to interview people when they are most available.

## Salaries

Earnings for Arson Investigators vary, depending on such factors as their experience, job status (staff or self-employed), and geographical location. According to the November 2003 *Occupational Employment Statistics* survey by the U.S. Bureau of Labor Statistics (BLS), the estimated annual salary for most private investigators—which includes Arson Investigators—ranged between $18,800 and $57,860.

## Employment Prospects

Most private Arson Investigators work for detective agencies. Some Arson Investigators have their own agencies, while some are self-employed. Job opportunities for private investigators, including Arson Investigators, are expected to grow faster than the average of all other occupations through 2012, according to the BLS.

## Advancement Prospects

Supervisory and management positions are limited to case managers. So, many Arson Investigators pursue career growth by way of wage or fee increases and complexity of new assignments. The goal for some Arson Investigators is to start their own agencies.

## Education and Training

Many agencies desire applicants who have a college degree in fire science, criminal justice, or other related field. They also prefer applicants who have taken courses in fire protection engineering and fire investigation.

Arson Investigator trainees must complete certified training programs from recognized organizations such as the International Association of Arson Investigators.

## Special Requirements

Most Arson Investigators need either a state or local private investigator's license to practice. Trainees are cov-

ered by their employers' licenses. License requirements, which include age, education, and experience qualifications, vary from state to state or city to city. (For a listing of state private investigative licensing agencies, see Appendix III.)

Agency owners must possess a valid business license issued by their local government.

## Experience, Skills, and Personality Traits

Arson Investigator trainees should have three years of firefighting experience plus a strong background in the chemistry of fire. In recent years, more and more agencies are hiring applicants who have backgrounds in fire protection engineering.

Skills especially needed by Arson Investigators are related to communication, presentation, and report-writing. Computer skills are also necessary for this occupation.

Being objective, detail-oriented, organized, honest, ethical, and reliable are some personality traits that successful Arson Investigators share.

## Unions and Associations

Many Arson Investigators belong to the International Association of Arson Investigators, a professional organization that offers seminars and certification programs as well as resources and networking. For contact information, see Appendix IV.

Arson Investigators might also belong to regional, state, and national professional associations for private investigators and firefighters. Joining professional organizations gives investigators the opportunity to network with peers and obtain certified training, job listings, and other professional services and support.

## Tips for Entry

1. Take business courses. Having an understanding of business is valuable in arson investigations.
2. Learn about job openings from professional associations and at professional conventions.
3. Keep a competitive edge in your field by taking relevant classes and training programs from colleges and professional organizations.
4. Get an idea of the different services that private Arson Investigators provide. Read about some detective agencies on the Internet. Enter the keywords *fire investigations* or *arson investigations* into a search engine to get a list of Web sites.

# INSURANCE INVESTIGATOR

## CAREER PROFILE

**Duties:** Verify that the information on insurance claims are true for insurance companies

**Alternate Title(s):** Insurance Claims Investigator

**Salary Range:** $27,000 to $72,000

**Employment Prospects:** Good

**Advancement Prospects:** Limited

**Prerequisites:**

**Education or Training**—High school diploma, but college degree is preferred

**Experience**—Requirements vary with the different agencies

**Special Skills and Personality Traits**—Organizational, self-management, analytical, observational, communication, writing, research, and interviewing skills; be ingenious, persistent, assertive, tactful, and calm

**Licensure/Certification**—Private investigator's license may be required

## CAREER LADDER

```
┌─────────────────────────────────┐
│        Manager or Owner,         │
│  Insurance Investigations Firm   │
└─────────────────────────────────┘

┌─────────────────────────────────┐
│      Insurance Investigator      │
└─────────────────────────────────┘

┌─────────────────────────────────┐
│  Insurance Investigator Trainee  │
└─────────────────────────────────┘
```

## Position Description

Insurance Investigators examine insurance claims that insurance companies suspect may be fraudulent or in which criminal activity may be involved. They investigate claims filed by individuals, businesses, hospitals, and various organizations covered by automobile, home, health, worker's compensation, life, and other types of insurance policies. Insurance claims can range from a few hundred dollars to millions of dollars. Investigators' assignments may involve claims for:

- damaged, wrecked, or stolen vehicles
- damaged, lost, or stolen computers, jewelry, or other valuables
- damaged or destroyed homes
- medical and hospital costs
- loss of income due to injuries or illnesses
- injuries, illnesses, or deaths resulting from using a company's products or a business's services
- deaths or disappearances of insured persons

Insurance Investigators are responsible for verifying that the information claimants provide is accurate and true. In other words, they make sure that the claims are in fact valid. For example, they seek to verify that a burnt building was not the work of arson; a car accident was not staged; costs for medical treatments were not overstated; or an employee did not fake an injury on the job.

Insurance Investigators generally start each case by reviewing the claim and insurance policy of a claimant. They plan and organize their investigations. They determine what types of evidence they should seek to back up the information on claims as well as proof of fraud or criminal activity.

Their investigations typically require collecting and reviewing various facts about the claimant as well as the claim. They search for information on computer and Internet databases. They also visit police departments, fire departments, courthouses, public health offices, medical offices, and other places to find documents related to a claim. For example, for an injury claim resulting from a car accident, an Insurance Investigator might seek and review medical records, traffic reports, police investigation reports, and so on.

Most investigations involve a lot of travel to meet with people. Insurance Investigators interview the claimant, witnesses, doctors, police, and other people who have information about an incident. Those interviewed sign a formal statement written by themselves or by the Insurance Investigators. Many Insurance Investigators also tape-record interview sessions with the permission of those interviewed.

Insurance Investigators examine the insured property as well as the scene where the loss, injury, or death took place. They look for evidence that backs up the information on an insurance claim in addition to possible evidence of fraud. They write well-detailed notes about their observations. They take photographs and draw clear sketches. Some Insurance Investigators may make videotapes.

Depending on the case, Insurance Investigators may perform surveillance or undercover work to learn relevant information. For example, an Insurance Investigator may conduct surveillance on a claimant to determine if he or she is truly unable to use his or her back because of a job injury.

Throughout an investigation, Insurance Investigators maintain a proper and accurate case file that includes notes, documents, photographs, sketches, and formal statements. Upon completion of the investigation, they write a summary report and submit it and the case file to the insurance company.

Insurance Investigators usually set their own work schedule, working nights and weekends in order to interview people when they are available.

## Salaries

Earnings for Insurance Investigators vary, depending on such factors as their experience, education, employer, and geographical location. According to the November 2003 *Occupational Employment Statistics* survey by the U.S. Bureau of Labor Statistics, most Insurance Investigators earned an estimated annual salary that ranged between $26,970 and $72,080.

## Employment Prospects

Many Insurance Investigators are employed by insurance companies and insurance agencies. Some work for private investigation agencies, and some are self-employed.

Openings generally become available as Insurance Investigators retire or transfer to other occupations. Competition for jobs is usually high.

## Advancement Prospects

Supervisory and management positions are limited to case managers. Many Insurance Investigators pursue career growth by way of wage or fee increases and complexity of new assignments. The goal for some Insurance Investigators is to start their own agencies.

## Education and Training

The minimum education requirement is a high school or general equivalency diploma. Many employers prefer hiring trainees with bachelor's degrees in business administration or liberal arts.

## Special Requirements

Depending on their location, Insurance Investigators must hold either a state or local private investigator's license to practice. License requirements, which include age, education, and experience qualifications, vary from state to state or city to city. (For a listing of state private investigative licensing agencies, see Appendix III.)

Insurance Claims Investigator trainees are covered by the licenses of the investigators for whom they work.

## Experience, Skills, and Training

Employers typically choose candidates who have a general knowledge of the insurance industry, particularly in the areas in which the employers specialize. Most employers prefer to hire applicants who have previous experience conducting insurance investigations. Many Insurance Investigators are former law enforcement officers and private investigators, as well as experienced claims adjusters and examiners.

To perform well on their job, Insurance Investigators must have excellent organizational and self-management skills, as well as strong analytical and observational skills. They also need strong communication, writing, research, and interviewing skills. Being ingenious, persistent, assertive, tactful, and calm are some personality traits that successful Insurance Investigators share.

## Unions and Associations

Two professional societies that serve the interests of Insurance Investigators are the International Association of Special Investigation Units and the National Society of Professional Insurance Investigators. Both organizations offer networking opportunities and professional support and services such as training and education programs. For contact information, see Appendix IV.

## Tips for Entry

1. As a college student, gain experience by obtaining an internship or job with an insurance company.
2. Gain valuable experience in the insurance business by first working as an insurance customer service representative, claims adjuster, claims examiner, or in a similar position.
3. Many insurance companies recruit on college campuses. Find out if any insurance companies may be attending job fairs at the colleges in your area.

4. Learn how to use computers and word processing pro-grams. In addition, learn basic photography and videotaping skills—valuable skills to have in the private investigation field.
5. On the Internet, you can learn about the types of services some private investigators offer in insurance claims investigations. Enter the keywords *insurance claims investigations* into a search engine to get a list of Web sites.

# LEGAL INVESTIGATOR

## CAREER PROFILE

**Duties:** Gather evidence for attorneys who are preparing for criminal or civil trials

**Alternate Title(s):** None

**Salary Range:** $19,000 to $58,000

**Employment Prospects:** Good

**Advancement Prospects:** Limited

**Prerequisites:**

**Education or Training**—Some college education is preferred

**Experience**—Requirements vary with the different agencies

**Special Skills and Personality Traits**—Problem-solving, organizational, writing, communication, interpersonal, and self-management skills; be independent, objective, curious, honest, responsible, flexible, and enthusiastic

**Licensure/Certification**—Private investigator's license may be required

## CAREER LADDER

```
┌─────────────────────────────┐
│     Manager or Owner,       │
│ Legal Investigation Service │
└─────────────────────────────┘

┌─────────────────────────────┐
│     Legal Investigator      │
└─────────────────────────────┘

┌─────────────────────────────┐
│    Assistant Investigator   │
└─────────────────────────────┘
```

## Position Description

Legal Investigators are hired by attorneys to help them prepare cases for court trials. They gather documentary, testimonial, and physical evidence that allows attorneys to put together a sound and logical case.

Legal Investigators conduct investigations for criminal or civil trials. In criminal trials, Legal Investigators usually work for lawyers of the defendant—the person who is accused of committing a crime. They work for lawyers of either party in civil trials—the defendant (the one who is being sued), or the plaintiff (the one who is suing).

Legal Investigators perform similar tasks when investigating for either criminal or civil cases. One task is gathering and reviewing documents that are pertinent to a case. For example, in a lawsuit that involves injuries from a car accident, a Legal Investigator might obtain insurance policies, claims applications, insurance investigators' reports; police accident reports and traffic citations; medical and hospital records; and driving records of both drivers in the accident.

Another important task is locating persons who may be potential witnesses for the attorneys. For example, a Legal Investigator working on a case in which the attorney's client is accused of embezzling thousands of dollars from his employer would look for coworkers, neighbors, and other persons willing to testify on behalf of the client. In addition, Legal Investigators look for expert witnesses, such as physicians, forensic scientists, forensic accountants, and other private investigators, who may be able to develop evidence for the lawyers.

Legal Investigators may examine the locations where injuries or crimes occurred. They carefully document the scenes. They write well-detailed notes about their observations. They make clear sketches. They take photographs of the scene and may make videotapes of it. In addition they look for physical evidence that may help the lawyers' cases.

Other duties that Legal Investigators might perform are:

- serving subpoenas
- preparing exhibits for the trial
- testifying in court

Legal Investigators might work nights, weekends, and holidays in order to complete their investigations.

## Salaries

Earnings for Legal Investigators vary, depending on such factors as their experience and geographical location. The estimated annual salary for most private investigators—which includes Legal Investigators—ranged between $18,800 and $57,860, according to the November 2003 *Occupational Employment Statistics* survey by the U.S. Bureau of Labor Statistics (BLS).

## Employment Prospects

Some Legal Investigators are employees of law firms. Other Legal Investigators work on a contractual basis, as independent contractors or as members of detective agencies.

Staff positions usually become available as individuals retire or transfer to other positions. Opportunities, in general, for the private investigation field are expected to increase by 21 to 35 percent through 2012, according to the BLS.

## Advancement Prospects

Supervisory and management positions are limited to case managers. Many Legal Investigators pursue career growth by way of wage or fee increases and complexity of new assignments. The goal for some Legal Investigators is to start their own agencies.

Some Legal Investigators take positions, such as a Federal Public Defender Office Investigator, in government agencies.

## Education and Training

Requirements vary with each law firm and detective agency. Many law firms require Legal Investigators on their staffs to have at least an associate's degree in any field. Some employers prefer applicants who have taken courses in criminal justice, law enforcement, business administration, or journalism.

Every agency and law firm has its own way of conducting investigations. So all newly hired Legal Investigators, experienced or inexperienced, receive extensive training on the job.

## Special Requirements

Most Legal Investigators need either a state or local private investigator's license to practice. License requirements, which include age, education, and experience qualifications, vary from state to state or city to city. (For a listing of state private investigative licensing agencies, see Appendix III.)

Legal Investigator trainees are covered by their employers' licenses.

## Experience, Skills, and Personality Traits

Many employers prefer hiring trainees who have law enforcement, journalism, or business management backgrounds. Some employers are willing to hire inexperienced applicants who have a desire to learn, are not easily convinced, and genuinely like to work with people.

Legal Investigators need strong problem-solving, organizational, writing, communication, and interpersonal skills. In addition, they must have excellent self-management skills, such as the ability to handle stressful situations, prioritize tasks, make sound judgments, and meet deadlines.

Being independent, objective, curious, honest, responsible, flexible, and enthusiastic are some personality traits that successful Legal Investigators share.

## Unions and Associations

Legal Investigators might belong to the National Association of Legal Investigators and the National Association of Investigative Specialists. (For contact information, see Appendix IV.) Joining professional organizations gives investigators the opportunity to network with peers and obtain certified training, continuing education, professional resources, job listings, and other professional services and support.

## Tips for Entry

1. Talk with Legal Investigators about their job to find out if their career is one that interests you.
2. Take courses in criminal justice, law, and paralegal studies to enhance your qualifications for trainee positions.
3. Network with attorneys and Legal Investigators in your area to learn about career resources and job opportunities. Some businesses offer summer internships to college students, giving them the chance to work with experienced Legal Investigators.
4. Get an idea of the different services that Legal Investigators offer clients. Read about some detective agencies on the Internet. Enter the keywords *legal investigations* or *legal investigator* into a search engine to get a list of Web sites.
5. To learn more about Legal Investigators on the Internet, visit the National Association of Legal Investigators Web site at http://www.nalionline.org.

# FINANCIAL INVESTIGATOR

## CAREER PROFILE

**Duties:** Investigate or protect financial matters for businesses, companies, organizations, and individuals; provide expert witness testimony

**Alternate Title(s):** Finance Detective, Fraud Investigator

**Salary Range:** $19,000 to $58,000

**Employment Prospects:** Good

**Advancement Prospects:** Limited

**Prerequisites:**

**Education or Training**—Bachelor's degree in accounting

**Experience**—Requirements vary with each agency

**Special Skills and Personality Traits**—Computer, research, problem-solving, interpersonal, and communication skills; be creative, clever, persistent, assertive, and calm

**Licensure/Certification**—Private investigator's license may be required; business license needed for agency owners

## CAREER LADDER

```
┌─────────────────────────────────┐
│       Manager or Owner,         │
│   Financial Investigations Firm  │
└─────────────────────────────────┘

┌─────────────────────────────────┐
│       Financial Investigator     │
└─────────────────────────────────┘

┌─────────────────────────────────┐
│   Financial Investigator Trainee │
└─────────────────────────────────┘
```

## Position Description

Financial Investigators are private detectives who specialize in the field of finance. They are hired by businesses, companies, and organizations to investigate or protect various financial matters. With a strong background in forensic accounting (investigative accounting), much of a Financial Investigator's work involves examining financial statements, inventory records, and other business records and correspondence.

Financial Investigators offer several different services. They develop financial profiles on companies and individuals with whom clients are thinking about doing business. They perform background checks on potential executive officers and business partners for clients. They investigate companies or businesses that clients may want to buy or sell. They gather financial information about competitors.

Financial Investigators also do asset investigations. They locate missing or stolen assets that a company or individual owns. For example, a Financial Investigator might recover thousands of dollars worth of missing shipments for a company. Another Financial Investigator might uncover hundreds of thousands of dollars of missing money hidden in various bank accounts of his client's former employees. And

still another Financial Investigator might track how a client's stolen stocks had been converted by the client's broker to buy a home in another state.

Financial Investigators also conduct investigations that involve fraud, theft, embezzlement, scams, or other criminal activity. For example, a client might ask a Financial Investigator to determine if employees are stealing office equipment or if vendors are defrauding a company by delivering fewer products to the company.

Financial Investigators perform various tasks when they work on their different cases. For example, they might:

- audit financial records
- develop financial models
- reconstruct financial statements
- forecast a company's financial status
- search for information on computer databases
- interview employees, executives, and other people pertinent to a case
- conduct surveillance
- do undercover work
- provide expert witness testimony in court and depositions

Financial Investigators who have their own agencies are responsible for the daily administration of their operations. They perform various tasks such as record keeping, invoicing clients, paying bills, and generating new clients. Investigators also are responsible for supervising, directing, and evaluating their staff.

Financial Investigators generally work a 40-hour week, but work longer hours as needed.

## Salaries

Earnings for Financial Investigators vary, depending on such factors as their experience, employer, and geographical location. According to the November 2003 *Occupational Employment Statistics* survey by the U.S. Bureau of Labor Statistics (BLS), the estimated annual salary for most private investigators—including Financial Investigators—ranged between $18,800 and $57,860.

## Employment Prospects

Financial Investigators work for detective agencies or have their own agencies. The BLS reports that opportunities in the private detective field are expected to increase by 21 to 35 percent through 2012. It predicts that due to the growth of global financial activity, there should be an increase in demand for investigators to control internal and external financial losses.

## Advancement Prospects

Supervisory and management positions are limited to case managers. Many Financial Investigators pursue career growth by way of wage or fee increases and complexity of new assignments. The goal for some Financial Investigators is to start their own agencies.

## Education and Training

There are no specific educational requirements in this field, but most Financial Investigators have a bachelor's degree in accounting. Financial Investigators are trained on the job.

## Special Requirements

Depending on location, Financial Investigators must hold a state or local private investigator's license in order to practice. Trainees are covered by employers' licences. License requirements, which include age, education, and experience qualifications, vary from state to state or city to city. For a listing of state private investigative licensing agencies, see Appendix III.

Agency owners must possess a business license, which is issued by their local government.

## Experience, Skills, and Personality Traits

Some agencies are willing to hire recent accounting graduates as trainees. Other agencies prefer to hire trainees who have experience as forensic accountants and as expert witnesses in court.

Financial Investigators must have competent computer, research, and problem-solving skills to perform well at their job. They also need strong interpersonal and communication skills, as they must be able to deal with people from different backgrounds. Being creative, clever, persistent, assertive, and calm are some personality traits that successful Financial Investigators share.

## Unions and Associations

Financial Investigators might belong to different professional groups that represent their different areas of expertise such as the National Association of Investigative Specialists, Association of Certified Fraud Examiners, International Association of Financial Crime Investigators, and American Institute of Certified Public Accountants. (For contact information, see Appendix IV.) Joining professional organizations gives investigators an opportunity to network with peers and obtain certified training, continuing education, professional resources, job listings, and other professional services and support.

## Tips for Entry

1. To keep a competitive edge in this field, obtain professional certification such as becoming a Certified Public Accountant or a Certified Fraud Examiner.
2. As an accountant, specialize in forensic accounting, a field that combines accounting skills and investigative methods. You can find forensic accountant jobs with accounting firms as well as with detective agencies.
3. Learn about job openings from professional organizations.
4. Build a network of contacts by attending conferences sponsored by professional associations.
5. On the Internet, you can learn about the types of services some Financial Investigators offer clients. Enter the keywords *financial investigator* or *financial investigations* into a search engine to get a list of Web sites.

# STORE DETECTIVE

## CAREER PROFILE

**Duties:** Protect retail business's cash, stock, and other assets; detect and apprehend shoplifters; other duties vary from store to store

**Alternate Title(s):** Loss Prevention Specialist

**Salary Range:** $19,000 to $58,000

**Employment Prospects:** Excellent

**Advancement Prospects:** Good

**Prerequisites:**

**Education or Training**—High school diploma

**Experience**—Requirements vary from store to store

**Special Skills and Personality Traits**—Organizational, self-management, writing, communication, interpersonal, and teamwork skills; be honest, dependable, assertive, and observant

## CAREER LADDER

```
┌─────────────────────────────┐
│   Senior Store Detective    │
└─────────────────────────────┘


┌─────────────────────────────┐
│      Store Detective        │
└─────────────────────────────┘


┌─────────────────────────────┐
│  Store Detective Trainee    │
└─────────────────────────────┘
```

## Position Description

Store Detectives are responsible for protecting a store's assets—cash, merchandise, and property. As part of a store's loss prevention department, they watch out for suspicious activity among shoppers, store employees, vendors, and delivery people. Their primary job is to detect and apprehend shoplifters. Store Detectives do not have the authority to arrest; but they can question suspects and hold them in custody until law enforcement officers arrive at the store.

Depending on the store, Store Detectives either help or conduct investigations. They might work on external investigations that involve trouble with customers such as shoplifting, credit card fraud, and refund scams. In addition, they might work on internal investigations that involve losses or theft committed by employees, vendors, and delivery people.

Some Store Detectives perform audits to make sure that employees are following the store's policies and procedures. Some Store Detectives are also responsible for periodic safety inspections to make sure that a store's safety program is effective and follows government laws.

In many stores, Store Detectives conduct various training programs for store employees. Some workshops cover loss prevention topics such as how to handle theft, fraud, and potentially dangerous situations. Other workshops cover employee safety concerns such as avoiding injuries and reporting safety hazards.

Other duties that Store Detectives may perform are:

- maintain and test physical security equipment such as locks, security alarms, and fire alarms
- help open and close the store
- prepare loss prevention and security reports
- file complaints with the police
- testify in court about apprehensions or investigations in which they took part

Store Detectives work either full time or part time. They work on rotating schedules that include nights, weekends, and holidays. Store Detectives who work for corporate chain stores might work a rotation of several stores.

## Salaries

Earnings for Store Detectives vary, depending on such factors as their experience, position, employer, and geographical location. According to the November 2003 *Occupational Employment Statistics* by the U.S. Bureau of Labor Statistics (BLS), most private detectives—including Store Detectives—earned an estimated annual salary that ranged between $18,800 and $57,860.

## Employment Prospects

Store Detectives work for department stores, general merchandise stores, corporate chain stores, and shopping malls. They are also employed by security agencies that provide contractual services to retail businesses. Retail employers are in constant need for full-time and part-time Store Detectives, especially for entry-level positions. The number of jobs may increase as retail loss prevention is a fast-growing field.

The BLS reports that the best opportunities can be found with large discount chains and discount stores.

## Advancement Prospects

Advancement depends upon an employee's ambition, skills, commitment to a company's ideals, and a willingness to relocate, particularly for district and regional loss prevention positions.

Store Detectives can advance to senior, or lead, Store Detectives and loss prevention managers who may manage one store, several stores, or several districts. The highest position in the retail loss prevention field is director or vice president, depending on the retail company. Other career options for Store Detectives are becoming loss prevention trainers or loss prevention investigators.

## Education and Training

Store Detectives need a high school or general equivalency diploma. However, more and more retail stores are hiring applicants with associate's and bachelor's degrees.

Store Detectives usually complete an in-store training program that covers safety, auditing, investigative methods, and interviewing and interrogation techniques.

In some parts of the country, Store Detectives are required to be trained in state certified security courses or through police officer training centers.

## Experience, Skills, and Personality Traits

Experience requirements for Store Detective differ with every retail business. Many stores are willing to hire applicants with little or no experience who show a willingness to learn. In addition, stores hire candidates who can think fast on their feet and are not afraid of being confrontational.

Store Detectives need strong organizational and self-management skills, such as the ability to work independently, follow directions, and handle stressful situations. Their job also requires that they have effective writing, communication, interpersonal, and teamwork skills. Being honest, dependable, assertive, and observant are some personality traits that successful Store Detectives share.

## Unions and Associations

Some Store Detectives belong to local, state, or national professional associations to take advantage of networking opportunities, educational programs, job banks, and professional services and resources. The Loss Prevention and Security Association and the National Association of Investigative Specialists are two national organizations that Store Detectives are eligible to join. For contact information, see Appendix IV.

## Tips for Entry

1. Stores hire Store Detectives for temporary part-time and full-time positions for the Christmas holiday shopping season. Begin applying for these positions in September and October.

2. Research potential retail employers and find a company that is committed to career development and training of its employees.

3. Get a job as a sales worker, stock clerk, office worker, or other position in a retail store. This experience is valuable for understanding the role of Store Detectives and retail loss prevention professionals.

4. Use the Internet to learn more about the retail prevention field. To get a list of Web sites to visit, enter the keywords *retail loss prevention* in a search engine.

# PERSONAL PROTECTION SPECIALIST

## CAREER PROFILE

**Duties:** Protect clients from danger and invasion of privacy

**Alternate Title(s):** Bodyguard, Executive Protection Agent

**Salary Range:** $19,000 to $58,000+

**Employment Prospects:** Good

**Advancement Prospects:** Limited

**Prerequisites:**

**Education or Training**—High school diploma

**Experience**—Security or law enforcement experience preferred

**Special Skills and Personality Traits**—Observational, planning, critical thinking, decision-making, interpersonal, and communication skills; be personable, calm, trusting, discreet, and detail-oriented

**Licensure/Certification**—Private investigator's license and firearms license may be required; business license needed for agency owners

## CAREER LADDER

```
┌─────────────────────────────┐
│      Manager or Owner,       │
│  Personal Protection Firm    │
└─────────────────────────────┘

┌─────────────────────────────┐
│   Personal Protection Agent  │
└─────────────────────────────┘

┌─────────────────────────────┐
│  Personal Protection Trainee │
└─────────────────────────────┘
```

## Position Description

Personal Protection Specialists, or bodyguards, protect their clients from physical harm, kidnapping threats, and invasion of privacy. Their clients are individuals who need to safeguard their security, such as entertainers, sport figures, diplomats, politicians, business executives, military officials, threatened family members, victims of stalkers, and high-risk witnesses.

Personal Protection Specialists provide a safe place in which their clients can live, work, play, and travel. They guard clients in their homes and workplaces. They escort clients to work, appointments, speaking engagements, stores, restaurants, and other locations. They accompany clients on trips to other cities and countries.

At all times, Personal Protection Specialists are on the alert for potential trouble. They are watchful for suspicious individuals, constantly observing people and keeping track of activity around their clients. They also check out suspicious packages that may hold bombs. Some Personal Protection Specialists perform searches of their clients' homes, offices, and vehicles before their clients enter them.

In order to prevent dangerous situations, Personal Protection Specialists plan and organize security in advance. They choose suitable cars and plan the safest driving routes. They inspect clients' homes and set up necessary security systems, including closed circuit television systems. They make sure they have adequate access to their clients' offices.

In confrontational situations, Personal Protection Specialists act quickly to divert attackers and act as shields for their clients. They may use deadly force on attackers if that is the only way to preserve the life of their clients.

Before starting an assignment, Personal Protection Specialists and clients agree on their non-security duties. These duties might include chauffeuring and planning travel arrangements for clients. Personal Protection Specialists make sure the clients understand that they are not personal servants or valets.

Personal Protection Specialists who have their own agencies are responsible for the daily administration of their operations. They perform various tasks such as record keeping, invoicing clients, paying bills and taxes, and maintaining the office. If they have staff, they are responsible for supervising, directing, and evaluating their staff's work.

Personal Protection Specialists might be hired to protect a client for several days, months, or years. Most Personal Protection Specialists do not perform 24-hour duty. They are normally assigned to a work shift that may include nights, weekends, and holidays.

## Salaries

Earnings for Protective Protection Specialists vary, depending on their experience, job status (staff or self-employed), clientele, types of assignments, and other factors. Formal salary information for this occupation is not available, but a general idea can be gained by looking at what private detectives earn. The U.S. Bureau of Labor Statistics reports in its November 2003 *Occupational Employment Statistics* survey that the estimated annual salary for most private detectives ranged between $18,800 and $57,860.

Experienced specialists who work for celebrities and corporate figures can earn higher incomes.

## Employment Prospects

Most Personal Protection Specialists are employed by private detective and security agencies that provide personal protective services. Some specialists are self-employed or run their own agencies.

Experts in the field expect the demand for personal protective services to grow as more executives, celebrities, and other high-profile individuals become increasingly concerned with issues of privacy and personal security.

## Advancement Prospects

Supervisory and management positions are limited to case managers. Many Personal Protection Specialists pursue career growth by way of wage or fee increases and complexity of new assignments. The goal for some Personal Protection Specialists is to become independent contractors or head their own agencies.

## Education and Training

Employers generally require applicants to have only a high school or general equivalency diploma. Many Personal Protection Specialists, however, have college degrees. Some agencies also require Personal Protection Specialists to complete certified training programs in which they learn specialized skills such as protective driving and use of fire arms.

## Special Requirements

Depending on where they are located, Personal Protection Specialists must hold a state or local private investigator's license in order to practice. Trainees are covered by their employers' licenses. License requirements, which include age, education, and experience qualifications, vary from state to state or city to city. For a listing of state private investigative licensing agencies, see Appendix III.

Personal Protection Specialists who carry firearms in connection with their job must possess the proper state licensure for having firearms. In addition, agency owners must possess a business license that is issued by their local government.

## Experience, Skills, and Personality Traits

Many Personal Protection Specialists are former military personnel, law enforcement officers, and security guards who are experienced in performing protection and security.

Requirements vary with the different employers. In general, applicants must be in excellent physical condition. Being skilled in self-defense techniques and martial arts as well as protective driving and the proper use of firearms is usually preferred. Applicants should also have a general knowledge of security technology and prevention methods.

To perform their job effectively, Personal Protection Specialists need excellent observational, planning, critical-thinking, and decision-making skills. They must also have excellent interpersonal and communication skills, as they must be able to work well with their clients. Being personable, calm, trusting, discreet, and detail-oriented are some personality traits that successful Personal Protection Specialists share. They should also have excellent manners and maintain a neat appearance.

## Unions and Associations

Personal Protection Specialists can join professional associations to take advantage of networking opportunities, training programs, and other professional resources and services. The International Association of Personal Protection Specialists and ASIS International are two national associations that they may join. They are also eligible to join various associations that serve the interests of private detectives and security professionals.

## Tips for Entry

1. Enroll in a personal protection school that is recognized by detective agencies and professional associations.
2. Maintain a regular physical fitness program to stay in top physical and mental shape.
3. To enhance your employability, consider obtaining voluntary certification as a personal protection professional. One source of certification is ASIS International. For more information, visit its Web site at http://www.asisonline.org.
4. You can learn more about Personal Protection Specialists on the Internet. Enter any of these keywords— *personal protection specialist, executive protection agent,* or *bodyguard*—into a search engine to get a list of Web sites.

# PUBLIC SAFETY

# PUBLIC SAFETY DISPATCHER

## CAREER PROFILE

**Duties:** Handle telephone requests for police, fire, rescue, and emergency medical help; dispatch appropriate units and equipment to emergency and non-emergency sites

**Alternate Title(s):** Emergency Communications Officer, Emergency Operator, 911 Operator, Police Dispatcher, Fire Dispatcher

**Salary Range:** $18,000 to $44,000

**Employment Prospects:** Fair

**Advancement Prospects:** Fair

**Prerequisites:**

**Education or Training**—High school diploma

**Experience**—Varies from agency to agency; some experience preferred

**Special Skills and Personality Traits**—Organizational, communication, reading, writing, telephone, computer, teamwork, interpersonal, and self-management skills; be calm, patient, levelheaded, and decisive

## CAREER LADDER

```
+-------------------------------+
|          Supervisor           |
+-------------------------------+

+-------------------------------+
|    Public Safety Dispatcher   |
+-------------------------------+

+-------------------------------+
| Public Safety Dispatcher Recruit |
+-------------------------------+
```

## Position Description

Public Safety Dispatchers work in emergency communications centers or public safety dispatch centers. Their job is to process telephone calls from the general public who are seeking emergency and nonemergency help. Some dispatchers work in emergency communications centers that are part of law enforcement agencies, fire departments, or emergency medical services. Other dispatchers work in centers that are part of public safety departments. (A public safety department oversees the police, fire, and emergency services organizations within a municipality or region.)

Public Safety Dispatchers receive various requests for police, fire, rescue, or emergency medical assistance. For example, they receive calls about thefts, burglaries, shootings, vandalism, heart attacks, injuries, fires, chemical spills, car accidents, missing persons, suicide attempts, bomb threats, illegal parking, traffic hazards, prowling wild animals, and obnoxious drunks. Some Public Safety Dispatchers also handle requests from public safety agencies such as police departments and fire departments.

Upon receiving requests, Public Safety Dispatchers ask standard questions to determine what type of units and equipment should be dispatched. For example, for a call requesting police help for a theft, a Public Safety Dispatcher would gather facts about the crime, location, suspects, victims, and injuries.

Public Safety Dispatchers transmit orders by radio or computer to the appropriate police, fire, rescue, or ambulance units. They monitor dispatched units, answering requests for additional backup or for other services such as rescue units.

In medical emergencies, Public Safety Dispatchers stay on the line with callers and relay updated information about the patients' conditions to hospital or emergency medical staff. Public Safety Dispatchers who are certified emergency medical service personnel may give certain medical assistance when necessary.

In large emergency communications centers, Public Safety Dispatchers work in teams. Some dispatchers perform as call-takers (or 911 Operators). They answer calls, gather information, then transfer the information to other Public Safety Dispatchers who send out the appropriate response units.

Public Safety Dispatchers maintain well-detailed daily reports and logs. In addition, they perform other duties such as filing and other routine office tasks; monitoring city-wide radio channels; checking weather monitors; and operating mobile communications vans. In law enforcement agencies, dispatchers might process police records, process prisoners, and conduct computer searches for warrants and other data.

Sitting for long periods of time, Public Safety Dispatchers work with computers, telephones, two-way radios, and other electronic equipment. Their job is very stressful as they perform multitask duties and handle many highly emotional callers.

Emergency communication centers are open 24 hours a day. Thus, Public Safety Dispatchers work rotating shifts that include weekends and holidays. Dispatchers may work full time or part time.

## Salaries

Earnings for Public Safety Dispatchers vary, depending on such factors as their experience, job status, employer, and geographical location. The U.S. Bureau of Labor Statistics (BLS) reports in its November 2003 *Occupational Employment Statistics* survey that the estimated annual salary for most police, fire, and ambulance dispatchers ranged between $18,470 and $43,880.

## Employment Prospects

Public Safety Dispatchers are hired by public safety departments, law enforcement agencies, fire departments, emergency medical services, and 911 centers. The BLS estimates that about 90,490 police, fire, and ambulance dispatchers were employed in the United States as of November 2003. The job growth for dispatchers is expected to increase by 10 to 20 percent through 2012. Most opportunities will become available as dispatchers transfer to other occupations, retire, or leave the workforce for other reasons.

## Advancement Prospects

Supervisory and management positions are available, but limited. Many Public Safety Dispatchers pursue career growth by way of wage increases and complexity of new assignments. For some, this position is a stepping stone for pursuing a career as a police officer, deputy sheriff, firefighter, emergency medical technician, or other protective service career.

## Education and Training

Education requirements vary with the different agencies. Most agencies require that applicants have a high school or general equivalency diploma. Some agencies require some college work in police science or other related field.

Recruits must complete training programs, which vary with the different agencies. Some agencies supplement field training with formal study at law enforcement academies or community colleges where trainees study topics such as basic radio broadcasting, public safety telecommunications systems, and interpersonal communications.

## Experience, Skills, and Personality Traits

Requirements vary from agency to agency. Some agencies prefer applicants with previous experience in dispatching or working with the public. With some agencies, applicants must be sworn law enforcement officers, firefighters, or emergency medical service personnel.

To perform their work effectively, Public Safety Dispatchers must have strong organizational, communication, reading, writing, telephone, and computer skills. Strong teamwork and interpersonal skills are also essential. In addition, they need adequate self-management skills, such as the ability to work independently, prioritize tasks, handle stressful situations, and follow and understand directions. Being calm, patient, levelheaded, and decisive are some personality traits that successful Public Safety Dispatchers have in common.

## Unions and Associations

Public Safety Dispatchers may join professional associations to take advantage of networking opportunities, educational programs, and other professional services and resources. These societies are available at the local, state, and national levels. Some professional associations at the national level are the Association of Public-Safety Communication Officials International, Inc., the International Municipal Signal Association, and the National Emergency Number Association. For contact information for these organizations, see Appendix IV.

## Tips for Entry

1. Qualifications vary with every agency. In general, applicants must be U.S. citizens who are at least 18 years old and do not have felony convictions.
2. Contact agencies directly to learn about job openings.
3. Obtain work experience in which you deal directly with the public. Sales clerks, receptionists, hotel clerks, and customer service representatives are some workers who use work skills similar to those that dispatchers need.
4. Many emergency communications centers have Web sites on the Internet. To get a list of Web sites, enter the keywords *emergency communications center* or *police communications center* into a search engine.

# FIREFIGHTER

## CAREER PROFILE

**Duties:** Control and put out fires; save lives and property; inspect buildings for fire hazards; provide fire safety and fire prevention information; respond to other emergency calls

**Alternate Title(s):** Volunteer Firefighter; a title that reflects a specialty such as Firefighter/Paramedic, Airport Firefighter, or Wildland Firefighter

**Salary Range:** $19,000 to $60,000

**Employment Prospects:** Fair

**Advancement Prospects:** Good

**Prerequisites:**

  **Education or Training—**High school diploma

  **Experience—**Some fire service experience preferred

  **Special Skills and Personality Traits—**Communication, interpersonal, teamwork, reading, writing, and self-management skills; be courageous, calm, dependable, honest, open-minded, flexible, self-disciplined, caring, and dedicated

  **Licensure/Certification—**Firefighter certification

## CAREER LADDER

```
┌─────────────────────────────────┐
│   Fire Lieutenant; or a specialty │
│   such as Firefighter/EMT,        │
│   Firefighter/Driver Operator     │
└─────────────────────────────────┘

┌─────────────────────────────────┐
│           Firefighter             │
└─────────────────────────────────┘

┌─────────────────────────────────┐
│       Firefighter Recruit         │
└─────────────────────────────────┘
```

## Position Description

Firefighters are responsible for responding immediately to fire alarms within their jurisdictions. Their job is to put out fire as well as to protect lives and property from its danger.

Firefighters work in cities, the suburbs, and rural areas. They are involved in structural and wildland firefighting. (Firefighters who specifically fight fires in forests and grassland areas are known as wildland Firefighters.) Firefighters may be employees or volunteers. In many areas, particularly rural areas, fire departments are staffed by all-volunteer Firefighters.

Firefighters are highly trained to determine the best methods to suppress and control fires. Because firefighting is dangerous and complex work, Firefighters work in a very organized and coordinated manner. Firefighters perform preassigned tasks such as connecting hose lines to hydrants; operating pumps; and holding hoses to direct water or chemicals on the fires. Firefighters enter burning buildings to rescue people or to reach the source of a fire. They raise and place ladders to climb to windows. They use axes or saws to

hack their way into or through buildings. They also use cutting torches, saws, and other rescue equipment to retrieve people trapped within. Furthermore, Firefighters provide first aid and emergency medical treatment to victims.

After fires are put out, Firefighters help salvage property, such as ventilating smoke-filled rooms, removing broken glass, or covering objects to prevent water damage. They inspect utilities and appliances to make sure they can be safely turned on. They may help search for clues that show how a fire started; and if arson is suspected, they may help search for evidence.

In most communities, Firefighters also respond to various emergency requests. They answer emergency medical calls as well as assist at cleanups of hazardous materials, such as oil spills. They also participate in search-and-rescue missions, and provide assistance when human-made and natural disasters (such as floods, mudslides, hurricanes, and earthquakes) occur.

Between calls, Firefighters clean and service fire trucks and firefighting equipment as well as maintain fire stations and grounds. They practice fire drills and do physical training. They also do office work, prepare reports, and study new firefighting technology.

Some Firefighters perform inspection services in their communities, checking homes, schools, hospitals, and other buildings for fire hazards. Some Firefighters teach fire safety and fire prevention classes and make presentations to schools and civic organizations.

While on duty, Firefighters work and live at their fire stations, which have kitchens, dining rooms, sleeping quarters, and training rooms. Firefighters work in shifts. Some Firefighters work a 24-hour duty tour in which they work a 24-hour day, followed by 48 hours off. Other Firefighters work a split-shift tour; for example, they might be assigned to work three 10-hour days, followed by three days off.

Firefighters sometimes work overtime during fires and emergency situations. They are constantly at risk of being injured as well as being exposed to smoke, gases, chemicals, and hazardous materials that may affect their health.

## Salaries

Annual earnings for Firefighters vary, depending on such factors as their rank, experience, employer, and geographical location. The estimated annual salary for most Firefighters ranged between $19,420 and $59,610 according to the November 2003 *Occupational Employment Statistics* (OES) survey by the U.S. Bureau of Labor Statistics (BLS).

Wages are generally higher in large cities and less in small cities and rural areas. In some smaller cities and rural areas, Firefighters are volunteers and receive no compensation.

## Employment Prospects

Most of the professional urban Firefighters are employed by municipal and county fire departments. Some Firefighters are employed by fire departments owned by airport authorities and military bases, while others work for private firefighting companies. Wildland Firefighters can find employment with state and federal forest and wildland protection agencies. The BLS reports in its November 2003 OES study that an estimated 274,590 Firefighters were employed in the United States.

The competition for paid positions is high, and the turnover rate for these positions is low. Job openings are expected to grow by 10 to 20 percent through 2012. Most job openings will become available as personnel retire or transfer to other positions.

## Advancement Prospects

Firefighters can develop satisfying and diverse fire protection careers. With further training, they can apply for specialized positions such as paramedics, fire equipment operators, hazardous waste specialists, technical rescue specialists, and underwater recovery specialists. They can also pursue careers such as fire inspectors, fire investigators, or fire protection engineers.

Advancement through the ranks—engineer, lieutenant, captain, battalion chief, assistant chief, deputy chief, and chief—is based on competitive exams, job performance, interviews, and seniority. In many fire departments, candidates for battalion chief or beyond, must have a bachelor's degree, preferably in fire science, public administration, or a related field.

## Education and Training

Minimally, applicants must possess a high school or general equivalency diploma. Some departments may also require that applicants have completed some college work. Other departments may require that applicants possess either an associate's or bachelor's degree in fire science or a related field.

Recruits usually complete several weeks of formal training at a fire academy, vocational school, or community college. Their studies include firefighting techniques, fire prevention, emergency medical procedures, local building codes, and hazardous materials. They also learn to use firefighting and rescue equipment such as ladders, axes, saws, fire hoses, and fire extinguishers.

Throughout their careers, Firefighters enroll in educational programs, training seminars, conference workshops, and so on to increase their knowledge and update their skills.

## Special Requirements

Recruits are usually required to become certified Firefighters within one year of their appointment.

Applicants may be required to possess certification as emergency medical technicians. Agencies may hire applicants without this certification on the condition that they obtain it within a certain time frame.

Every fire department has specific age, residency, medical, and other qualifications that applicants must fulfill. Applicants must also pass a physical exam that tests physical strength, stamina, coordination, and agility.

## Experience, Skills, and Personality Traits

In general, fire departments choose physically fit candidates who have strong leadership qualities and a sense of community service. Applicants for entry-level positions should have fire service experience, which they may have gained as volunteer or paid Firefighters.

To perform well at their job, Firefighters need excellent communication, interpersonal, and teamwork skills. They must also have adequate reading and writing skills. In addition, they need superior self-management skills, which include the ability to handle stressful situations, work independently, take initiative, prioritize tasks, and follow and understand directions. Being courageous, calm, dependable, honest, open-minded, flexible, self-disciplined, caring, and dedicated are some personality traits that successful Firefighters share.

## Unions and Associations

Firefighters are usually members of a union, such as the International Association of Fire Fighters, which represents them in contract negotiations with their employers. In addition, many Firefighters belong to local, state, or national professional associations to take advantage of networking opportunities, educational programs, and other professional services and resources. Two national societies that some Firefighters join include the National Fire Protection Association and the Women in the Fire Service, Inc. Volunteer Firefighters might join the National Volunteer Fire Council.

For contact information for the above organizations, see Appendix IV.

## Tips for Entry

1. Gain valuable firefighting experience by becoming a volunteer Firefighter.

2. Some fire departments offer cadet or apprenticeship programs for young people. Find out if these programs are available in your community.

3. Contact the fire departments where you would like to work to learn about their volunteer and professional opportunities as well as their hiring needs and selection processes.

4. Apply for positions in fire departments that fit your interests and goals. For example: Do you want to work in a small or large fire department? What kind of advancement opportunities does a department offer? Does a department offer the type of specialized units in which you'd eventually like to work? Many fire departments maintain a Web site on the Internet. To find a specific one, enter the name of the city and the keywords *fire department,* such as *Seattle Fire Department.*

5. Use the Internet to learn more about the firefighting profession. You might start by visiting the following Web sites: United States Fire Administration, http://www.usfa.fema.gov; Firehouse.com, http://www.firehouse.com; and Women in the Fire Service, Inc., http://www.wfsi.org. To find other relevant Web sites, enter the keyword *firefighting* or *firefighter* into a search engine.

# EMERGENCY MEDICAL TECHNICIAN

## CAREER PROFILE

**Duties:** Provide emergency treatment for ill or injured persons and transport them to hospital emergency rooms

**Alternate Title(s):** None

**Salary Range:** $16,000 to $42,000

**Employment Prospects:** Excellent

**Advancement Prospects:** Fair

**Prerequisites:**

**Education or Training**—High school diploma

**Experience**—Varies with the different employers

**Special Skills and Personality Traits**—Teamwork, interpersonal, communication, reading, writing, and driving skills; be calm, levelheaded, caring, dedicated, and stable

**Licensure/Certification**—State licensure or professional certification

## CAREER LADDER

```
┌─────────────────────────────┐
│      Emergency Medical      │
│    Technician—Paramedic     │
└─────────────────────────────┘

┌─────────────────────────────┐
│      Emergency Medical      │
│   Technician—Intermediate   │
└─────────────────────────────┘

┌─────────────────────────────┐
│ Emergency Medical Technician—Basic │
└─────────────────────────────┘
```

## Position Description

Emergency Medical Technicians (EMTs) provide ill and injured persons with emergency medical care and transport them to hospital emergency rooms. Receiving orders from public safety dispatchers, EMTs drive to emergency scenes in ambulances equipped with special communication equipment, medical equipment, and medical supplies. They attend to emergency medical situations such as heart attacks, gun wounds, car accident injuries, drug overdoses, unconsciousness, drowning, broken hips, and unexpected child births.

EMTs respond to emergencies according to their certified skill level. All EMTs are certified to perform these medical procedures: provide first aid, restore breathing (by giving oxygen or doing pulmonary or cardiopulmonary resuscitation), control bleeding, treat for shock, bandage wounds, and immobilize fractures. They can treat and help heart attack victims, using automated external defibrillators; treat poison and burn victims; manage emotionally disturbed patients; or assist in childbirth.

Emergency Medical Technicians with more advanced training can use more intensive care procedures. For example, they can administer intravenous fluids; use manual defibrillators to give lifesaving shocks to a stopped heart; and use advanced techniques and equipment to help patients with respiratory emergencies. The most advanced EMTs—or EMT-Paramedics—provide advanced emergency care such as administering drugs and interpreting electrocardiograms (EKGs).

EMTs usually work in teams of two. Upon reaching emergency scenes, they examine the patients to determine the nature and degree of their illness or injury. In addition, EMTs learn whether patients have any pre-existing medical conditions such as diabetes, epilepsy, or heart disease. Following standard operating procedures, EMTs provide appropriate medical treatment that they are certified to perform. They monitor patients' vital signs and give additional care, if necessary, as they transport them to hospital emergency rooms. With complicated problems, EMTs provide care according to instructions given by medical personnel over two-way radios.

After each response call, EMTs prepare and maintain written logs and reports. They clean and sterilize ambulances and equipment as well as restock supplies. They also make sure that ambulances are in top maintenance form.

EMTs work both indoors and outdoors in all types of weather. They risk back injuries from lifting patients and may be exposed to diseases such as Hepatitis B and AIDS.

From time to time, they may handle violent or distressed patients and bystanders.

EMTs typically work between 45 to 60 hours a week—working nights, weekends, and holidays. In some fire and police departments, EMTs are on call.

## Salaries

Earnings for EMTs vary, depending on such factors as their rank, experience, education, and geographical location. According to the U.S. Bureau of Labor Statistics (BLS) in its November 2003 *Occupational Employment Statistics* survey, the estimated annual salary for most EMTs ranged between $15,680 and $42,320.

## Employment Prospects

EMTs work for hospitals, ambulance services, emergency medical service centers, rescue squads, fire departments, and police departments. In many communities, especially rural areas, Emergency Medical Technicians are volunteers.

The turnover rate is generally high, and jobs are expected to be continuously available. Competition is higher for EMT positions with fire, police, and rescue squad departments due to job security, higher pay, and generous benefits packages.

The BLS predicts that employment of EMTs and paramedics is expected to grow by 21 to 35 percent through 2012. This will mostly be due to population growth, expanding urban areas, and the aging of baby boomers.

## Advancement Prospects

With additional training and certification, EMTs can advance from entry-level to intermediate-level to paramedic positions. As they progress, EMTs earn higher salaries and perform greater responsibilities.

EMTs with supervisory and management ambitions can rise through the ranks as supervisor, operations manager, administrative director, and executive director. Usually at the higher positions, EMTs are no longer doing fieldwork. For many EMTs, their training and experience are stepping-stones to careers as firefighters, public safety dispatchers, nurses, and doctors.

## Education and Training

To become EMTs, applicants need a high school or general equivalency diploma. They must complete formal EMT training programs offered at colleges and universities, in hospitals, or by police, fire, and health departments. (To qualify for EMT training programs, applicants must be at least 18 years old, have valid driver's licenses, and no felony records.)

EMT training has three progressive levels: EMT-Basic, the entry-level position, EMT-Intermediate, and EMT-Paramedic. Upon completing each level of training, students are eligible to take the state or NREMT certification examination.

## Special Requirements

All 50 states and the District of Columbia require that EMTs hold proper certification. Some states grant EMT licenses to qualified individuals. Other states require that EMTs be certified by and registered with the National Registry of Emergency Medical Technicians (NREMT).

## Experience, Skills, and Personality Traits

Requirements vary with the different employers. To be EMTs with police and fire departments, applicants must be qualified police officers or firefighters. To apply for EMT-basic positions in hospitals and ambulance services, work experience is not necessary, but preferred.

Employers generally choose mature applicants who are willing to perform community service. They also must be physically fit, agile, strong, and have the stamina and coordination to lift, carry, and balance heavy loads.

EMTs need effective teamwork, interpersonal, and communication skills for their line of work. In addition, they must have adequate reading and writing skills as well as excellent driving skills.

Some personality traits that successful EMTs share include being calm, levelheaded, caring, dedicated, and stable.

## Unions and Associations

EMTs may join professional associations at the local, state, and national level to take advantage of networking opportunities, educational programs, job banks, and other professional services and resources. For example, some EMTs belong to the National Association of Emergency Medical Technicians or the National Volunteer Fire Council. (For contact information for these organizations, see Appendix IV.)

Many EMTs are also members of a union that represents them in contract negotiations for pay, benefits, and working conditions. Their union can also handle any grievances that EMTs may have against their employers.

## Tips for Entry

1. To learn about EMT training and job openings with emergency medical services, contact employers for whom you want to work.
2. Take health, science, and driver's education classes in high school to prepare for an EMT career.

3. If you are interested in a career in emergency medical services, talk with EMTs in your area.

4. Consult a school, college, or job counselor to find out about EMT training programs that are available in your area.

5. Use the Internet to learn more about the field of emergency medical services. To get a list of relevant Web sites, enter the keywords *emergency medical services* or *emergency medical technicians* into a search engine.

# RESCUE TECHNICIAN

## CAREER PROFILE

**Duties:** Perform search and rescue missions for missing and lost persons; perform technical rescues

**Alternate Title(s):** Rescue Specialist

**Salary Range:** Voluntary; no salary or additional pay

**Employment Prospects:** Good

**Advancement Prospects:** Limited

**Prerequisites:**

Education or Training—High school diploma; completion of certified training programs

Experience—No experience necessary

**Special Skills and Personality Traits**—Interpersonal, teamwork, communication and self-management skills; be calm, levelheaded, dedicated, caring, and stable

**Licensure/Certification**—Certification for each type of technical work to be performed

## CAREER LADDER

> Rescue Team Leader

> Rescue Technician

> Rescue Trainee

## Position Description

Rescue Technicians are emergency responders. They perform search and rescue missions for lost or missing persons in urban and wilderness settings. They also search for victims in fires, collapsed buildings, airplane crashes, hurricanes, earthquakes, and other human-made or natural disasters.

Many rescues are performed in dangerous situations that call for Rescue Technicians who are trained in particular technical disciplines. For example:

- those trained in high-angle rescue might recover people who are stranded on high cliff ledges
- those trained in confined-space rescue might recover people who are lodged in manholes
- those trained in water rescue might save people who are caught in rushing flood waters
- those trained in vehicle-extrication rescue might remove people trapped in crushed cars

Rescue Technicians work for rescue squads or search-and-rescue units that are administered by police departments, sheriff's offices, fire departments, public safety departments, or emergency service offices. Typically, rescue squads are volunteer units composed of law enforcement

officers, firefighters, emergency medical personnel, and private citizens.

Rescue work is performed quickly, but deliberately, in organized teams. Standard procedures are followed in every aspect of rescue work, from planning to finding and removing victims.

Each rescue situation begins with careful planning and assigning appropriate rescue teams. Rescue Technicians learn about a victim's identity and current mental and physical state to decide which rescue and first aid/lifesaving equipment is needed. They assess both real and potential hazards present within the area to be searched. In a technical rescue such as a confined space rescue, Rescue Technicians must decide the best way to enter a site, perform the rescue, and exit without causing any injury to the victims or themselves.

Rescue Technicians search hills, forests, ditches, culverts, ponds, rivers, swamps, and other areas that are not easily accessible. Searches may be performed by foot, horse, mountain bikes, all-terrain vehicles, boats, skis, helicopters, or other specialized means of transportation. Some Rescue Technicians are trained as canine handlers to track missing or lost persons.

Upon locating or reaching victims, Rescue Technicians check vital signs and examine victims for trauma and injuries. They provide first aid and emergency medical help (such as immobilizing fractures) for which they are trained. They then secure victims to stretchers or backboards for carrying or hoisting out of the site.

As part of their duties, Rescue Technicians attend regular meetings, drills, and training sessions. They maintain rescue and lifesaving equipment, making sure all equipment is clean, in working order, and always ready to be used. Rescue Technicians also prepare and maintain incident reports, activity logs, staff files, and training records.

Rescue squads often work with other local, regional, and state rescue squads. They are on call 24 hours a day, 365 days a year.

## Salaries

Rescue work is a voluntary assignment. Law enforcement officers, firefighters, emergency medical personnel, and park rangers rarely receive additional compensation for rescue duties.

## Employment Prospects

Police departments, sheriff's departments, fire departments, public safety departments, emergency service offices, and federal and state park services have rescue squads. New rescue squads form every year. Existing rescue squads continually welcome new volunteers, including private citizens.

## Advancement Prospects

Volunteers stay with this work as long as they are interested and qualified. Supervisory positions are limited to team and squad leaders.

Becoming certified rescue trainers or rescue equipment sales representatives or manufacturing consultants are other career paths for Rescue Technicians.

## Education and Training

Generally, applicants need a high school or general equivalency diploma in order to obtain the necessary rescue work certifications.

Rescue Technicians must complete certified training in basic land search and rescue techniques, first aid, and lifesaving skills.

## Special Requirements

Most agencies require Rescue Technicians to be certified in each type of technical rescue work that they will perform, such as vehicle extrication, confined space rescue, high-angle rescue, tracking, canine handling, cadaver recovery, and underwater recovery.

Some squads require Rescue Technicians to become certified as first emergency responders or emergency medical technicians.

Private citizen volunteers must meet certain qualifications which vary from squad to squad. Some rescue squads require volunteers to pass police background checks and/or driving record checks.

## Experience, Skills, and Personality Traits

Applicants do not need any previous experience, but they should have the basic skills for the type of rescue work they will perform. For example, volunteers for wilderness rescue units should have outdoor survival skills, and volunteers for water rescue units should have strong swimming skills.

Rescue squads typically look for mature, confident volunteers who have positive attitudes and strong commitments to serve the public. They show that they have the ability to react quickly to situations and stay calm under stressful conditions. In addition, applicants must be in excellent health with excellent physical strength and stamina.

Rescue Technicians need excellent interpersonal, teamwork, communication, and self-management skills. Being calm, levelheaded, dedicated, caring, and stable are some personality traits that successful Rescue Technicians have in common.

## Unions and Associations

Rescue Technicians can join local, state, and national professional associations to take advantage of networking opportunities, educational programs, certification programs, technical information, and other professional services and resources. At the national level, they might join the National Association for Search and Rescue, the Mountain Rescue Association, or the International Rescue and Emergency Care Association. For contact information for these organizations, see Appendix IV.

## Tips for Entry

1. Teenagers might be able to join rescue squads as part of a participating Explorer group.
2. As a police officer, firefighter, park ranger, or emergency service staff member, let your supervisor or rescue squad commander know of your interest in joining the rescue squad.
3. Learn first aid, CPR, wilderness survival skills, knot tying skills, and other skills that are useful for professional rescue work. Also maintain a regular exercise program to stay physically fit.
4. Contact your local fire department, law enforcement agency, or public safety department to learn about volunteer opportunities in its rescue division.
5. You can learn more about the rescue field on the Internet. To get a list of relevant Web sites, enter any of these keywords into a search engine: *rescue squad, rescue unit, technical rescue,* or *rescue technicians.*

# PARK RANGER

## CAREER PROFILE

**Duties:** Enforce park laws and regulations; may enforce criminal laws; protect park resources and park visitors; patrol assigned park areas; provide park visitors with natural, historical, and other information

**Alternate Title(s):** Park Police, Protection Ranger, Park Interpreter

**Salary Range:** $20,000 to $90,000

**Employment Prospects:** Fair

**Advancement Prospects:** Limited

**Prerequisites:**

**Education or Training**—Completion of employer's training programs; law enforcement training may be required

**Experience**—Several years of park or park-related experience needed

**Special Skills and Personality Traits**—Interpersonal, customer service, communication, problem-solving, writing, teamwork, self-management, and outdoor skills; be courteous, tactful, outgoing, calm, patient, impartial, and flexible

**Licensure/Certification**—Law enforcement officer certification may be required

## CAREER LADDER

```
┌─────────────────────────────┐
│     Senior Park Ranger      │
└─────────────────────────────┘

┌─────────────────────────────┐
│        Park Ranger          │
└─────────────────────────────┘

┌─────────────────────────────┐
│  Seasonal Park Ranger or    │
│    Park Ranger Trainee      │
└─────────────────────────────┘
```

## Position Description

Park Rangers are responsible for enforcing conservation laws and regulations in local, state, and national park systems. They work in urban, rural, and wilderness settings that include parks, natural reserves, recreational areas, and historical sites. Their job requires them to perform several roles, such as being a compliance inspector, conservationist, naturalist, teacher, public relations representative, police officer, firefighter, and rescue technician. Along with the primary duty of protecting park resources, Park Rangers provide for public safety. In other words, Park Rangers ensure the safety and security of park visitors within their park's boundaries.

Many Park Rangers are sworn law enforcement officers. They have the authority to enforce criminal laws within their jurisdiction. They can carry firearms, issue citations, make arrests, collect and process evidence, and conduct criminal investigations.

In some park systems, Park Rangers may be hired as protection rangers, who primarily perform law enforcement duties, or as interpretive specialists, who specifically are involved in developing and providing park education programs. In other park systems, all Park Rangers are commissioned officers.

Regardless of their primary job responsibility, Park Rangers are involved in many of the same general duties. Most of them patrol assigned areas within their park, which they perform on foot or by truck, boat, bicycle, or other specialized vehicle. They keep an eye out for violations, safety hazards, litter, and fire. Other general duties that they might perform include:

- answering visitors' questions
- collecting park fees
- registering park visitors

- issuing permits for camping, backpacking, or other park uses
- monitoring and controlling traffic
- handling visitors' complaints
- doing custodial work; for example, picking up garbage
- repairing trails, campgrounds, and picnic areas
- performing safety inspections
- studying plants and animals in the park
- writing reports and maintaining files

Park Rangers are always ready to respond to emergency situations, ranging from fighting fires to searching for lost campers to rescuing hikers from high cliffs to transporting injured campers to emergency rooms. Some Park Rangers are certified as emergency medical technicians and rescue technicians.

All Park Rangers help visitors learn about the natural, cultural, and historical aspects of their parks. They answer questions about such topics as natural resources, recreational activities, and topography. In addition, they prepare exhibits and create written materials. They also conduct group hikes, history presentations, crafts classes, and other recreational programs.

Park Rangers also assist in the management of natural resources. For example, they may supervise or participate in special programs such as habitat restoration, monitoring wildlife behavior, or monitoring air quality.

Park Rangers perform strenuous work in all types of weather and terrain. They work rotating shifts, including weekends and holidays. During tourist seasons, they frequently work overtime. Many Park Rangers are on call 24 hours a day.

## Salaries

Annual earnings for Park Rangers vary, depending on their job status, experience, education, employer, and geographical location. According to the Career Prospects in Virginia Web site, Park Rangers generally earn between $20,000 and $40,000, while supervisory rangers earn between $60,000 and $90,000.

In the National Park Service, entry-level, seasonal Park Rangers earn a salary that ranges from GS-4 to GS-7 on the GS schedule, while entry-level, permanent rangers earn a salary that ranges from GS-5 to GS-9. (The GS schedule is the pay schedule for many federal employees.) In 2005, the annual basic pay for GS-4 to GS-9 levels ranged from $22,056 to $48,604.

## Employment Prospects

Park Rangers are uniformed, government employees. They work for federal, state, regional, county, and municipal park systems throughout the United States. At the federal level, most Park Rangers work for the National Park Service (an agency within the U.S. Department of the Interior). Some federal Park Rangers are also employed by the U.S. Army Corps of Engineers.

The turnover rate for Park Rangers is low, and the competition for available positions (seasonal or permanent, part-time or full-time) is high. Opportunities usually become available when Park Rangers retire, advance to higher positions, or transfer to other locations.

## Advancement Prospects

Supervisory and management opportunities are available, and based on an agency's needs and individual merit. Possessing a master's degree is helpful for advancement to high supervisory positions such as federal district ranger or state park manager.

## Education and Training

The minimum educational requirement varies among the different state and local agencies. Some agencies require that applicants have at least a high school diploma, while others prefer to hire applicants who have completed some college work or possess an associate's or a bachelor's degree. Federal agencies prefer to hire applicants who possess a bachelor's degree in park and recreation management, natural resource management, earth science, history, law enforcement, or another related field.

Most employers allow relevant work experience or a combination of experience and education to be substituted for a college degree.

All seasonal and permanent recruits complete training programs provided by their employers. Candidates for law enforcement positions must successfully complete a law enforcement training program. For example, recruits for local park systems fulfill this requirement by attending a police officer academy.

Throughout their careers, Park Rangers enroll in educational programs, training seminars, conference workshops, and so on to increase their knowledge and update their skills.

## Special Requirements

In general, local and state Park Rangers who perform law enforcement duties must possess a POST (Peace Officer Standard and Training) certificate. This certificate is earned upon completion of basic training at a police academy.

Agencies usually require that applicants hold a valid driver's license. In addition, applicants may need current CPR, Emergency Medical Technician or other certifications, upon being appointed or within a certain time after being hired.

## Experience, Skills, and Personality Traits

Requirements vary among the different agencies, as well as for the different ranger positions. In general, applicants for permanent entry-level positions should have several years of park or park-related experience, which may have been gained through part-time, seasonal, or volunteer work.

Because they deal with the public on a daily basis, Park Rangers must have effective interpersonal, customer service, and communication skills. Their job also requires them to have strong problem-solving, writing, teamwork, and self-management skills. In addition, Park Rangers are expected to have strong outdoor skills such as swimming, hiking, and rock climbing.

Some personality traits that successful Park Rangers have in common include being courteous, tactful, outgoing, calm, patient, impartial, and flexible.

## Unions and Associations

Many Park Rangers belong to professional associations to take advantage of networking opportunities, educational programs, and other professional services and resources. Some national societies that serve the interests of Park Rangers include the National Recreation and Park Association and the Park Law Enforcement Association. Park Rangers who work in the national park system might join the Association of National Park Rangers.

Some Park Rangers are members of a union, which represents them in contract negotiations with their employers. At the federal level, Park Rangers are eligible to join the U.S. Park Ranger Lodge, which is part of the Fraternal Order of Police.

For contact information for the above organizations, see Appendix IV.

## Tips for Entry

1. Every agency has special requirements that applicants must meet. For example: to apply for a position with law enforcement duties in the National Park Service, applicants must be U.S. citizens between 21 and 37 years old without criminal records.

2. Contact the human resources department at each park where you would like to work to learn about volunteer, seasonal, or permanent opportunities.

3. The National Park Service usually hires permanent employees from their ranks of experienced seasonal employees or volunteers. To learn about the National Park Service's Seasonal Employment Program, call (877) 554-4550 or visit its Web page at http://www.sep.nps.gov.

4. Many national and state parks have Web sites on the Internet. To learn about national parks, start at the NPS Web site, http://www.nps.gov. For state parks, enter the name of the state plus the keywords *State Parks* into a search engine to get a list of Web sites (Example: *Idaho State Parks*).

# LIFEGUARD

## CAREER PROFILE

**Duties:** Prevent drownings, injuries, and other accidents at swimming pools, water parks, oceans, lakes, and rivers

**Alternate Title(s):** Water Safety Officer, Ocean Water Lifeguard

**Salary Range:** $6 to $27 per hour

**Employment Prospects:** Fair

**Advancement Prospects:** Limited

**Prerequisites:**

**Education or Training**—High school diploma; lifeguard training programs

**Experience**—Previous lifeguarding experience usually required

**Special Skills and Personality Traits**—Leadership, management, decision-making, teamwork, communication, public relations, interpersonal, and self-management skills; be calm, friendly, courteous, fair, firm, observant, reliable, and stable

**Licensure/Certification**—Lifeguard certification

## CAREER LADDER

```
┌─────────────────────────────────┐
│   Head (Pool) Lifeguard or      │
│      (Beach) Team Leader        │
└─────────────────────────────────┘

┌─────────────────────────────────┐
│           Lifeguard             │
└─────────────────────────────────┘

┌─────────────────────────────────┐
│        Lifeguard Trainee        │
└─────────────────────────────────┘
```

## Position Description

Lifeguards supervise all water activity and prevent drownings, injuries, and other accidents within their assigned areas. Pool Lifeguards protect swimmers at public and private swimming pools and water parks, while beach Lifeguards protect swimmers in open beach areas at oceans, rivers, and lakes.

Lifeguards usually work in pairs. They observe swimmers, with the help of binoculars, from towers and stations. Using megaphones and bullhorns, they warn swimmers about unsafe areas as well as unruly behavior. They also keep an eye out for poor swimmers and summon them back from deep waters.

Upon seeing swimmers in danger, Lifeguards respond immediately to rescue them. They provide first aid, CPR, or other appropriate emergency medical attention that they are qualified to provide. Lifeguards also complete necessary reports such as emergency incident reports, medical treatment reports, and daily activity logs.

In addition, pool Lifeguards enforce facility safety rules such as "no running around the pool." They also inspect dressing rooms for cleanliness and safety hazards. Plus, they clean and refill the pool. This includes determining the chlorine content and pH value of the water. Pool Lifeguards may give swimming lessons, help at swim meets, and do cashier duties at snack bars.

Beach Lifeguards patrol public beach areas by foot or by vehicle, enforcing ordinances, rules, and regulations that govern beach activities and shore water usage. In addition, beach Lifeguards are responsible for identifying ocean and beach hazards such as high surf and strong currents. Some beach Lifeguards act as harbor police officers with limited law enforcement authority; however, they do not carry firearms.

Rescue work for beach Lifeguards involves both ocean rescues and cliff rescues. They operate rescue boats and all-terrain vehicles as well as emergency medical equipment such as resuscitators. They also operate switchboards or two-way radios to coordinate activities with emergency rescue units.

Professional Lifeguards work part time or full time. They may work year-round or temporarily during the summer months. Many beach Lifeguards in California, Florida, and Hawaii work full time on a year-round basis.

## Salaries

Annual earnings for professional Lifeguards vary, depending on such factors as experience, job status, employer, and geographical location. Formal salary information for professional Lifeguards is unavailable. An informal search on the Internet found hourly wages for professional Lifeguards ranging as low as $6 to as high as $27.

## Employment Prospects

Professional Lifeguards can find employment with city park and recreation departments, county and state park systems, national parks, private campgrounds, water parks, hotels and resorts, health and fitness centers, and colleges and universities. Additionally, professional Lifeguards work for pool management firms that offer lifeguarding services to private swim clubs, hotels, apartment complexes, and other businesses or organizations.

Job opportunities for pool and beach Lifeguard positions are available year round; most openings are available for summer positions. Mostly high school and college students fill these seasonal positions, and the turnover rate is high.

Competition for professional Lifeguard positions is high. Returning seasonal Lifeguards generally receive better work schedules and assignments. Some employers hire permanent Lifeguards from seasonal ranks.

## Advancement Prospects

Professional Lifeguards pursue career paths according to their interests and ambitions. Administrative and management positions, such as supervisor and facility manager, are available but limited. Those interested in teaching might become swimming teachers, lifeguard trainers, water sports instructors, or water sports coaches.

Beach Lifeguards have better promotion opportunities, advancing up the ranks from team leader to sergeant, lieutenant, and then chief. In addition, Beach Lifeguards can pursue specialized duty such as rescue boat patrol, underwater recovery unit, marine firefighting, cliff rescue, and river rescue.

With additional training and experience, Lifeguards can pursue careers in such fields as education, fitness training, emergency services, health care, or law enforcement.

## Education and Training

Minimally, applicants for professional positions must possess a high school or general equivalency diploma. Some employers prefer applicants with college degrees.

Applicants for pool Lifeguard positions must have completed certified lifeguard training programs from the Red Cross or another recognized organization. Beach Lifeguard applicants must complete a certified training program that meets the curriculum requirements of the United States Lifesaving Association.

## Special Requirements

Applicants are usually required to possess appropriate lifeguard certification from a nationally recognized organization, such as the American Red Cross. Some employers also prefer that applicants be certified in performing first aid and CPR.

Applicants for county and state beaches may be required to obtain certification as first responders or emergency medical technicians. In addition, they may be required to possess a valid driver's license.

## Experience, Skills, and Personality Traits

Employers generally hire applicants who have previous lifeguarding experience, which may have been gained through seasonal, part-time, or permanent employment.

Lifeguards need excellent leadership, management, decision-making, and teamwork skills to be effective at their job. Because they deal with the public, Lifeguards must also have superior communication, public relations, and interpersonal skills. In addition, they need excellent self-management skills.

Some personality traits that successful Lifeguards share include being calm, friendly, courteous, fair, firm, observant, reliable, and stable.

Furthermore, professional Lifeguards are expected to maintain a high level of physical fitness throughout their career.

## Unions and Associations

Lifeguards might join local, state, or national professional associations to take advantage of networking opportunities, educational programs, certification programs, and other professional services and resources. For example, beach Lifeguards may belong to the United States Lifesaving Association. (Contact information for this organization can be found in Appendix IV.)

## Tips for Entry

1. The Junior Lifeguarding program teaches basic water safety and first aid techniques and provides valuable training for future Lifeguards. To find out about programs in your area, contact aquatic programs at YMCA, community parks, or community colleges.
2. Most employers hire for summer seasonal Lifeguards in the spring. Contact the employers for whom you want to work at the beginning of the year to find out when they are recruiting for summer Lifeguard jobs.

3. You do not have to wait until you get a Lifeguard job to obtain first aid, CPR, and Red Cross Lifeguard certifications. You can enroll in these certification programs at any time. Contact local Red Cross offices, community colleges, or community parks to find out about Lifeguard training programs.

4. The minimum age for most permanent Lifeguard positions is 18 years old.

5. Use the Internet to learn more about professional lifeguarding. To find relevant Web sites, enter the keywords *lifeguarding, lifeguard career,* or *professional lifeguards* into a search engine.

# PHYSICAL SECURITY

# LOCKSMITH

## CAREER PROFILE

## CAREER PROFILE

**Duties:** Install and repair mechanical locks; make keys; open locks and safes when keys are lost or missing; may install and repair electronic security systems

**Alternate Title(s):** None

**Salary Range:** $18,000 to $47,000

**Employment Prospects:** Good

**Advancement Prospects:** Limited

**Prerequisites:**

**Education or Training**—High school diploma; apprenticeship

**Experience**—Some knowledge of locksmithing as well as electricity and electronics

**Special Skills and Personality Traits**—Math, reading, writing, communication, interpersonal, and self-management skills; be composed, calm, and self-motivated

**Licensure/Certification**—Locksmith license; driver's license may be required

## CAREER LADDER

```
┌─────────────────────────────────────┐
│  Manager or Owner, Locksmith Business │
└─────────────────────────────────────┘

┌─────────────────────────────────────┐
│             Locksmith                 │
└─────────────────────────────────────┘

┌─────────────────────────────────────┐
│        Locksmith Apprentice           │
└─────────────────────────────────────┘
```

## Position Description

Locksmiths install and repair mechanical locks, deadbolts, and other locking devices for residents, businesses, industries, and institutions. They help safeguard the security of homes, safes, vehicles, apartment complexes, schools, stores, office buildings, corporate complexes, warehouses, laboratories, factories, refineries, and many other types of facilities.

Traditionally, Locksmiths own shops or work for other Locksmiths. Along with lock installations and repairs, Locksmiths offer other services. Some Locksmiths install and service electronic security systems for vehicles, homes, and businesses. These systems include burglar alarms, smoke detectors, electronic access control systems (such as electronic card-operated locks), and closed circuit television systems.

Most Locksmiths make duplicates of original keys for customers. They also make replacements for lost keys by inserting key blanks into locks to get impressions of the lock tumblers. In addition, they make master keys that open different locks. For example, a Locksmith might make a master key for a hotel that opens several hotel rooms.

Many Locksmiths offer a service to design and maintain security systems for commercial, industrial, and institu-

tional customers. Locksmiths might rekey all the door locks in a facility—that is, changing locks completely for a new set of original keys. They might make different sets of master keys. They might install access control systems or other security systems.

Another service is responding to emergency calls from people who have lost or forgotten their keys and have locked themselves out of their vehicles, homes, or businesses. Locksmiths use lockpicks or key impressions to open locks; when necessary, they use other methods to force locks to open or break. Most Locksmiths offer emergency services 24 hours a day.

Some Locksmiths specialize in safes. They might sell different types of safes to customers, such as money, jewelry, and gun safes. They might install and service safes. They might open safes when combinations are lost by safecracking, or listening for the contact points when turning the wheels. When that fails, drilling holes into the locks might be necessary.

Besides locksmith shops, Locksmiths work for corporations, universities, and other institutions as part of their security forces. They are usually known as in-house or institutional Locksmiths. Institutional Locksmiths are responsible for maintaining mechanical locks and electronic devices, such as padlocks, furniture locks, computer security locking devices, and access control systems. As part of their job, they learn and stay up-to-date with government safety codes, ordinances, and laws as well as their facilities' internal security procedures.

Locksmiths use different types of tools and equipment. These include files, screwdrivers, tweezers, electric drills, soldering equipment, key-cutting machines, and special tools such as lock picks.

Locksmiths work alone, but often work around other people. They may work indoors or outdoors, day or night, in any type of weather. Institutional Locksmiths work a 40-hour week, occasionally working overtime to complete jobs. Traditional Locksmiths work between 35 to 60 hours a week.

## Salaries

Earnings depend on a Locksmith's level of experience and work skills as well as the size and location of an employer. Typically, Locksmiths earn higher wages in metropolitan areas such as Chicago, San Francisco, and New York City. According to the November 2003 *Occupational Employment Statistics* survey by the U.S. Bureau of Labor Statistics (BLS), the estimated annual salary for most Locksmiths ranged between $17,640 and $46,920.

## Employment Prospects

Locksmiths have their own shops or work for other locksmiths. Institutional Locksmiths are hired by universities, colleges, corporations, government agencies, and other institutions. The BLS reports that an estimated 18,730 Locksmiths and safe repairers were employed in the United States as of November 2003.

Experienced Locksmiths are expected to be in constant demand due to the great concern for adequate security to deter crime. Competition is keen for trainee positions as many locksmith shops have small staffs and prefer to hire experienced Locksmiths.

## Advancement Prospects

Supervisory and management positions are limited in both retail and institutional fields. Many Locksmiths pursue career growth by earning higher incomes or specializing in particular skills such as safecracking and installing electronic security systems. The goal for some Locksmiths is to start their own shop.

## Education and Training

Locksmithing is an apprenticeship trade in which trainees work with experienced Locksmiths while mastering basic skills on the job. Some apprentices participate in on-the-job programs that offer both classroom and practical training. Apprenticeships last from three months to four years, depending on the area of specialty and level of expertise that is required.

Many employers prefer trainees to have a high school or general equivalency diploma.

## Special Requirements

Many states and cities require Locksmiths to have locksmithing licenses. Requirements differ with each state and city. The process generally involves being fingerprinted and having their fingerprints on file with local authorities; passing a police background check; and passing a state examination. Many states and cities also require that Locksmiths be bonded or have a specific amount of insurance coverage. Locksmiths may need to get additional licensing if they install electronic security devices.

Some employers require candidates to have a valid driver's license.

## Experience, Skills, and Personality Traits

Employers prefer to hire trainees who have some knowledge of the locksmithing trade along with knowledge of electricity and electronics.

Locksmiths must have adequate math, reading, and writing skills as well as strong communication and interpersonal skills. In addition they need strong self-management skills—the ability to meet deadlines, follow directions, work independently, handle pressure, and organize and prioritize tasks. Being composed, calm, and self-motivated are a few personality traits that successful Locksmiths share.

## Unions and Associations

Many Locksmiths are members of state and regional locksmith associations. Many also belong to the Associated Locksmiths of America, a national group that offers a professional certification program. Institutional Locksmiths might join the Institutional Locksmiths' Association. Joining professional organizations gives Locksmiths the opportunity to network with peers and obtain professional support and services such as certified training and job listings. (Contact information for the above organizations can be found in Appendix IV.)

## Tips for Entry

1. Talk directly with Locksmiths about opportunities for apprenticeships.
2. To prepare for a Locksmith career while in high school, take courses in mathematics, mechanical drawing, metalworking, basic electronics, physics, English, and business education.

3. Enroll in a locksmithing school or program that is recognized by professional Locksmiths and locksmith associations. Contact Locksmiths in your area for recommendations.

4. On the Internet, you can learn about the types of services some Locksmiths offer. Enter the keywords *Locksmiths* into a search engine to get a list of Web sites.

# ALARM INSTALLER

## CAREER PROFILE

**Duties:** Install electronic security and fire alarm systems in residences and businesses; may inspect, repair, and service systems

**Alternate Title(s):** Burglar Alarm Installer, Fire Alarm Installer, Alarm Service Technician, Security Technician, Security Alarm Installer

**Salary Range:** $21,000 to $56,000

**Employment Prospects:** Good

**Advancement Prospects:** Limited

**Prerequisites:**

**Education or Training**—High school diploma; on-the-job training

**Experience**—Knowledge of electricity and electronics; use of hand tools and power tools

**Special Skills and Personality Traits**—Communication, interpersonal, and self-management skills; be calm, friendly, and self-motivated

**Licensure/Certification**—Alarm installer license; driver's license may be required

## CAREER LADDER

```
┌─────────────────────────────────┐
│   Alarm Installer Supervisor    │
└─────────────────────────────────┘

┌─────────────────────────────────┐
│        Alarm Installer          │
└─────────────────────────────────┘

┌─────────────────────────────────┐
│     Alarm Installer Trainee     │
└─────────────────────────────────┘
```

## Position Description

Alarm Installers put in and repair electronic security and fire alarm systems in vehicles, homes and businesses. The different types of systems they might install are:

- burglar alarms
- fire alarms
- special alarms, such as smoke detectors
- alarm systems to protect metal containers such as safes and files
- alarm monitoring systems, which transmit signals to a police station, security firm's central station, or other location upon sensing intrusion, break-ins, or fire on the premises
- intercom systems
- surveillance systems such as closed-circuit televisions
- access control systems (such as electronic card-operated locks)

Before installing any security system in a building, Alarm Installers look at building blueprints and electrical layouts to determine where wires, sensors, switches, and various parts of a system will be placed. Alarm Installers also read the operations manuals and manufacturer's specifications for the systems they are installing.

An installation involves putting in the necessary electronic equipment such as wire, conduits, motion sensors, horns, lights, and control panels throughout the building. The Alarm Installer also programs the systems according to the manufacturer's specifications and then tests the systems to make sure they are working properly.

Many Alarm Installers perform regular inspection checks on security systems to make sure the systems are working properly. They tighten loose connections as well as repair or replace defective parts and wiring. They test electrical circuits and sensors, making any necessary adjustments. Detailed records are kept on every alarm system.

Alarm Installers use different hand tools, power tools, and other equipment for their work; for example, they use wire cutters, wire strippers, screwdrivers, electric drills, soldering irons, voltmeters, and ohmmeters. As part of their duties, Alarm Installers keep detailed records of each installation or service job they perform.

Their work is performed both indoors and outdoors. They often need to climb ladders, crawl into small spaces, stoop, kneel, or crouch to do their work. They usually carry equipment that weighs 25 to 50 pounds.

Alarm Installers work 40 hours a week, which may include Saturdays and evenings. They may be rotated on an on-call schedule for emergency repair work. Large companies have three work shifts, in which case Alarm Installers might be assigned a permanent shift or be rotated.

## Salaries

Earnings for Alarm Installers vary, depending on such factors as their experience, job duties, employer, and geographical location. According to the November 2003 *Occupational Employment Statistics* survey by the U.S. Bureau of Labor Statistics (BLS), the estimated annual salary for most security and fire alarm systems installers ranged between $21,470 and $55,970.

## Employment Prospects

According to the BLS, an estimated 47,690 security and fire alarm systems installers were employed in the United States as of November 2003.

Job opportunities for Alarm Installers generally become available as individuals retire, transfer to another occupation, or leave the workforce. Employers may create additional staff positions to meet growing demands.

## Advancement Prospects

Supervisory and management positions are limited. In large companies, most managers have bachelor's degrees. Many Alarm Installers pursue career growth by way of wage increases. The goal for some Alarm Installers is to start their own companies.

## Education and Training

Many employers prefer to hire applicants who have a high school or general equivalency diploma. In addition, they seek applicants who have completed basic electricity and electronic courses in high school, community colleges, or vocational schools.

Trainees receive on-the-job training, learning their employers' specific installation procedures.

## Special Requirements

Many states and cities require Alarm Installers to have licenses for installing security systems. Requirements differ with each state and city. The process generally involves being fingerprinted and passing a police background check. Trainees are usually required to have their fingerprints and other identification registered with local authorities. In some states, applicants must pass an alarm installer examination. Some states also require Alarm Installers to complete a certified training program that includes basic alarm system electronics.

Many employers require Alarm Installers to have a valid driver's license.

## Experience, Skills, and Personality Traits

Trainee applicants do not need prior work experience, but they should have knowledge of electricity and electronics. They should be able to read schematic diagrams and follow operation manuals. In addition, they should know how to safely operate many of the hand tools and power tools that are used on the job.

Alarm Installers need good communication and interpersonal skills along with self-management skills. In addition, they should be in good health and physically fit.

Being calm, friendly, and self-motivated are some personality traits that successful Alarm Installers share.

## Unions and Associations

Many Alarm Installers belong to the National Burglar and Fire Alarm Association, which offers professional training and certification. (For contact information, see Appendix IV.)

## Tips for Entry

1. Apply directly to companies for trainee positions. To find out what companies are in your area, look in the yellow pages of your telephone book under *Burglar Alarm Systems, Fire Alarm Systems,* and *Automobile Alarm and Security Systems.*
2. Take mathematics, electricity, electronics, mechanical drawing, science, and shop courses in high school to obtain valuable knowledge and skills for this field.
3. On the Internet, you can learn about the types of services some security alarm companies offer customers. Enter the keywords *security alarms* into a search engine to get a list of Web sites.

# FIRE PROTECTION ENGINEER

## CAREER PROFILE

**Duties:** Design building features to reduce the risk of fire damage; design, install, and maintain fire detection and fire suppression systems; analyze fire hazards to determine the degree of fire risk in a facility; conduct research projects

**Alternate Title(s):** None

**Salary Range:** $31,000 to $94,000

**Employment Prospects:** Excellent

**Advancement Prospects:** Good

**Prerequisites:**

**Education or Training**—Bachelor's degree in engineering

**Experience**—Requirements vary from employer to employer

**Special Skills and Personality Traits**—Teamwork, interpersonal, communication, computer, and writing skills; be curious, creative, innovative, persistent, determined, and confident

**Licensure/Certification**—Professional Engineer (P.E.) license

## CAREER LADDER

```
┌─────────────────────────────────────────┐
│  Senior or Lead Fire Protection Engineer │
└─────────────────────────────────────────┘

┌─────────────────────────────────────────┐
│        Fire Protection Engineer          │
└─────────────────────────────────────────┘

┌─────────────────────────────────────────┐
│     Fire Protection Engineer Trainee     │
└─────────────────────────────────────────┘
```

## Project Description

Fire Protection Engineers are engineers who specialize in limiting the destruction of fire on lives and property. They create comprehensive fire safety plans for high-rise residence and office buildings, shopping center complexes, hospitals, schools, libraries, museums, parking garages, warehouses, factories, oil refineries, airports, and other various kinds of facilities. Their employers include government agencies, insurance companies, private corporations, architect firms, and engineering firms.

Fire Protection Engineers work in several different areas. Some Fire Protection Engineers help plan the design of buildings to reduce the risk of fire damage, working with building owners, architects, other engineers (such as civil and electrical engineers), and fire marshals. For example, Fire Protection Engineers recommend materials and structures that are more fire resistant. They design features that can act as fire barriers, such as windows constructed to block the spread of fire between buildings. They plan emer-

gency lighting systems as well as plan where fire escapes, fire stairs, and fire exits should go.

Some Fire Protection Engineers design various fire safety systems for employers or clients. They configure alarm and detector systems that upon detecting heat, smoke, or flames trigger off warning signals. They also design fire suppression systems, such as automatic sprinkler systems, that extinguish fires using water, foam, dry chemical, or other agents. In addition, they plan out adequate water supply systems for a facility.

Along with installing fire safety systems, Fire Protection Engineers maintain them. They perform routine inspections and tests on the different fire safety systems to make sure they are in working order as well as provide preventive maintenance on those systems.

Some Fire Protection Engineers analyze fire hazards to determine the risk of fire losses in a facility. They test and evaluate existing fire safety systems and survey all potential fire hazards in the facility. In addition, they recommend how to prevent the fire losses.

Some Fire Protection Engineers work on research projects for government agencies, universities, professional organizations, standards testing facilities, or corporations. Examples of research projects are:

- developing new fire suppression methods
- analyzing the behavior of fire in various materials, such as construction materials, children's clothing, or fire fighting gear
- estimating the time it takes occupants to safely clear burning rooms
- determining fire risk in consumer products, such as appliances, clothing, furniture, and computers

As part of their professional duty, Fire Protection Engineers stay up-to-date with the constantly changing developments in fire research and technologies. In addition, Fire Protection Engineers are responsible for knowing current governmental fire codes and standards.

Fire Protection Engineers work a 40-hour week. Occasionally, they work overtime to meet deadlines.

## Salaries

Earnings for Fire Protection Engineers vary, depending on such factors as their education, experience, employer, and geographical location. Experts in the field report that Fire Protection Engineers generally earn higher salaries than engineers in other disciplines. The U.S. Bureau of Labor Statistics reports in its November 2003 *Occupational Employment Statistics* survey that the estimated annual salary for most engineers (from all engineering disciplines) ranged between $31,480 to $93,680.

## Employment Prospects

Fire Protection Engineers can find opportunities both nationwide and worldwide. They are hired by insurance companies, large corporations, government agencies, architectural and engineering firms, testing laboratories, academic institutions, and others.

Experts in the field report that employment is readily available for qualified Fire Protection Engineers. Currently, job opportunities exceed the number of fire protection engineering graduates.

## Advancement Prospects

Fire Protection Engineers can pursue several paths in their field. Supervisory and management positions are readily available. Fire Protection Engineers can seek promotions to senior and team leader positions, assistant project managers, and managers. Some Fire Protection Engineers start their own consulting businesses. Other career paths in fire protection engineering lead to such positions as university professors, fire investigators, and sales representatives for the various fire safety systems.

## Education and Training

Entry-level Fire Protection Engineers need a bachelor's degree in fire protection engineering, mechanical engineering, civil engineering, electrical engineering, or another related-field. Newly hired Fire Protection Engineers receive on-the-job training.

## Special Requirements

Fire Protection Engineers must be licensed as professional engineers (P.E.) if they offer engineering services directly to the public or if they perform work that affects the life, health, or property of the public. Requirements for professional engineer licensure vary among the states, territories, and Washington, D.C. For specific information, contact the state board of engineering examiners where you wish to practice.

## Experience, Skills, and Personality Traits

Many employers hire newly graduated engineering students for entry-level positions. Applicants must have fundamental knowledge of the nature and characteristics of fire and fire combustion.

To perform their job effectively, Fire Protection Engineers must have excellent teamwork, interpersonal, and communication skills. Additionally, they must have strong computer and writing skills. Being curious, creative, innovative, persistent, determined, and confident are some personality traits that successful Fire Protection Engineers share.

## Unions and Associations

Among the professional associations that Fire Protection Engineers might belong to are Society of Fire Protection Engineers, National Fire Protection Association, and National Society of Professional Engineers. (For contact information, see Appendix IV.) Joining professional organizations gives Fire Protection Engineers the opportunity for networking with peers and obtaining professional support and services such as educational programs, research findings, and job listings.

## Tips for Entry

1. To begin preparing for a career in fire protection engineering, take these courses in high school: math, chemistry, physics, English, and computer science.
2. As an engineering student, do internships with fire protection employers. Not only will you get valuable work experience but also a chance to decide if fire protection engineering is a field you want to pursue.

**3.** Join professional organizations such as the Society of Fire Protection Engineers to keep up to date with valuable information and resources in the constantly changing field as well as learn about available job openings.

**4.** Learn more about fire protection engineering on the Internet. You might start by visiting the Society of Fire Protection Engineers Web site at http://www.sfpe.org.

# SECURITY GUARD

**Duties:** Protect property, assets, information, employees, tenants, and visitors from criminal activity, fire, and other danger; enforce employer's policies, security procedures, and safety plans.

**Alternate Title(s):** Security Officer

**Salary Range:** $14,000 to $33,000

**Employment Prospects:** Excellent

**Advancement Prospects:** Good

**Prerequisites:**

**Education or Training**—High school diploma preferred

**Experience**—No experience is necessary

**Special Skills and Personality Traits**—Reading, writing, observational, self-management, interpersonal, and communication skills; be alert, calm, self-motivated, ethical, dependable, and levelheaded

**Licensure/Certification**—Security guard license, firearms license, and driver's license may be required

```
┌─────────────────────────────────┐
│   Security Guard Supervisor      │
└─────────────────────────────────┘

┌─────────────────────────────────┐
│        Security Guard            │
└─────────────────────────────────┘

┌─────────────────────────────────┐
│    Security Guard Trainee        │
└─────────────────────────────────┘
```

## Position Description

Security Guards are hired to protect their employer's building, grounds, assets, employees, tenants, and visitors against criminal activity, accidents, fires, and natural disasters. Additionally, Security Guards enforce their employers' policies, rules, and regulations for maintaining order and safety on the premises. Banks, office complexes, government buildings, data processing centers, restaurants, malls, airports, museums, libraries, universities, hospitals, laboratories, factories, and refineries are some facilities where Security Guards work. Security guards also work temporary assignments, such as at concerts, sports games, conferences, weddings, and construction sites.

Security Guards are assigned to guard posts that may be gatehouses, building lobbies, or reception areas along with sensitive and dangerous locations in the facilities. Most Security Guards are unarmed. They carry two-way radios to communicate with other guards and command posts. Some Security Guards monitor surroundings on closed-circuit televisions.

From their guard posts, Security Guards are watchful for suspicious persons, packages, and activities. They make sure unauthorized persons do not enter restricted areas. Security Guards might check for employee and vendor identification. They might inspect vehicles and packages as well as monitor deliveries. In addition, they might screen visitors for weapons, explosives, and other contraband. They may call employees to verify visitors' appointments and have visitors sign in and sign out on visitor registers. Security Guards may also escort visitors to their destinations within the facilities.

Some Security Guards answer questions for visitors and employees as part of their duty. Some Security Guards direct traffic on the premises and issue parking permits. Security Guards also respond to emergency situations such as providing first aid and sounding appropriate security and fire alarms.

Security Guards also perform patrol duty, making regular rounds in their assigned areas. They check for safety problems such as blocked fire exits. They may inspect fire protection equipment to make sure it is working properly. They are on alert for unusual sounds or odors (such as gas) and any hazardous conditions. At night, Security Guards check gates, entrances, doors, windows, and vents to ensure that they are locked and secure against break-ins.

In some states, Security Guards can obtain certification as special police officers that gives them the authority to make some arrests while on duty. Security Guards may make citizen's arrests if persons are committing crimes in front of them or they have reasonable grounds to believe that persons have committed crimes. Security Guards can interview suspects to determine facts and, if warranted, detain them while investigating the situation or until police arrive. Security Guards may only use force to control attackers who are using force to create bodily harm or are using deadly force.

Keeping a record of their daily activities is part of Security Guards' job. They include reports of employee violations, accidents, unauthorized persons, criminal incidents, safety problems, and hazardous or dangerous conditions. In some facilities, Security Guards enter their information into computers.

Security guards may work part time or full time. Many work a rotating shift that includes nights, weekends, and holidays.

## Salaries

Salaries for Security Guards depend on several factors, including level of experience and education; job duties (such as being armed or unarmed); and type, size, location, and budget of an employer.

The estimated annual salary for most Security Guards ranged between $14,180 and $32,940, according to the November 2003 *Occupational Employment Statistics* (OES) survey by the U.S. Bureau of Labor Statistics (BLS).

Typically, Security Guards with higher education and/or certified training can earn higher wages. In addition, armed Security Guards usually earn more than unarmed Security Guards. Furthermore, wages are typically higher in the largest cities and lower in smaller cities and rural areas.

## Employment Prospects

Security Guards are employed by businesses, corporations, retailers, manufacturers, educational institutions, hospitals, apartment complexes, government agencies, nonprofit organizations, and various other organizations. They also work for investigation and security companies that provide security services on a contractual basis. The BLS reports in its November 2003 OES survey that about 961,660 Security Guards were employed in the United States.

Employment for Security Guards in the United States is expected to grow by 21 to 35 percent through 2012, according to the BLS. Much of this will be due to the growing concern for the need for increased security by businesses, corporations, and other organizations. In addition, opportunities will become available as Security Guards retire or transfer to other occupations. The best opportunities can be found with contract security guard agencies.

Applicants can expect keen competition for the higher paying and more responsible Security Guard positions as many retired law enforcement officers and military personnel begin second careers in security.

## Advancement Prospects

Security Guards in small companies pursue advancement through salary increases because of limited opportunities. Those working for large companies can pursue supervisory and managerial positions along with higher wages; however, employers usually prefer Security Guards who have bachelor's degrees (in any field) for managerial positions and advanced degrees for administrative positions.

Other career paths for Security Guards are becoming law enforcement officers, corrections officers, private investigators, and personal protection agents.

## Education and Training

Most employers prefer applicants who have at least a high school or general equivalency diploma.

All employers have an on-the-job training program that covers their rules and regulations, security procedures, first aid, fire rescue, and other basic skills. Many security guard firms include both classroom instruction and field training. Armed Security Guards complete a more intense training program that covers areas such as the use of firearms and the laws pertaining to their use.

## Special Requirements

Most states and many cities require Security Guards to have licenses. Licensing requirements vary with the different states and cities. For example, some states require trainees to complete certified training in order to get licenses.

Security Guards who carry firearms in the performance of their duties must possess the proper state licensure for using firearms.

Many employers require that Security Guards possess a valid driver's license.

## Experience, Skills, and Personality Traits

Many employers hire applicants without any experience for entry-level Security Guard positions, but applicants should have some experience handling emergencies and other stressful situations. Applicants should be in good health, physically fit, and emotionally stable.

Important skills that Security Guards need for their job are reading, writing, observational, and self-management skills. They should also have adequate interpersonal and communication skills, as they must be able to handle people from various backgrounds.

Some personality traits that successful Security Guards share include being alert, calm, self-motivated, ethical, dependable, and levelheaded. Furthermore, Security Guards maintain a professional appearance and attitude at all times.

## Unions and Associations

Many Security Guards join professional associations to take advantage of networking opportunities and other professional services and resources. Two societies that serve the security profession are the International Foundation of Protective Officers and the National Police and Security Officers Association of America. (For contact information, see Appendix IV.)

Some Security Guards are members of a local union, which represents them in contract negotiations for pay, ben-

efits, and working conditions. It also handles any grievances that Security Guards may have against their employers.

## Tips for Entry

1. Apply directly to companies, government agencies, institutions, and security guard agencies for jobs.
2. Read the job want ads in local newspapers, particularly the Sunday edition, for notices about Security Guard openings.
3. On the Internet, you can learn about the different protective services that some security firms offer clients. Enter the keywords *security guard services* or *security guard company* into a search engine to get a list of Web sites.

# GAMING SURVEILLANCE OFFICER

## CAREER PROFILE

**Duties:** Monitor movements and activities of casino patrons and employees to ensure they are not violating any governmental laws or regulations nor casino policies and rules

**Alternate Title(s):** Surveillance Operator, Surveillance Agent, Surveillance Investigator

**Salary Range:** $17,000 to $42,000

**Employment Prospects:** Good

**Advancement Prospects:** Fair

**Prerequisites:**

**Education or Training**—High school diploma

**Experience**—One to two years of experience in security operations may be required

**Special Skills and Personality Traits**—Observational, communication, writing, teamwork, interpersonal, and self-management skills; be enthusiastic, respectful, calm, focused, and trustworthy

**Licensure/Certification**—Occupational license usually required

## CAREER LADDER

> **Lead Gaming Surveillance Officer**

> **Gaming Surveillance Officer**

> **Trainee**

## Position Description

Gaming Surveillance Officers play an essential role in the security of casino operations. They monitor the movements and activities of patrons and employees to ensure that governmental laws and regulations as well as casino policies and rules are not being violated. For example, Gaming Surveillance Officers keep an eye open for patrons or employees who may be in the act of stealing money or cheating at card games on the casino floor.

Surveillance officers are employed throughout the gaming industry, which includes commercial operations that may be land-based, riverboat, dock side, or racetrack casinos. The industry also consists of casinos owned by Native American tribes that are run on tribal grounds. Besides gaming, many casinos offer various hospitality and entertainment services, such as hotels, restaurants, boutiques, spas, concerts, comedy shows, family arcades, golf, bowling centers, and amusement parks.

Surveillance officers are usually part of the security departments of casino operations. Like security guards, sur-

veillance officers are assigned areas to patrol that may include casino floors, hotel lobbies, shops, parking lots, employee areas, restricted areas, and so on. Instead of patrolling by foot or vehicle, Gaming Surveillance Officers use closed-circuit surveillance cameras that are installed inside and outside of buildings and grounds. The officers are stationed in a central monitoring room above the casino floor where they view multiple monitor screens. Each screen shows a different area of the casino, its facilities, and its grounds. Gaming Surveillance Officers can control cameras to focus on particular individuals, activities, or locations that may concern them. These officers might also observe people through one-way mirrors that may be installed above the casino floor, cashier's cages, hotel front desks, and other locations.

The primary concern of Gaming Surveillance Officers is to monitor monetary transactions for possible theft by patrons and employees—card dealers, keno runners, cashiers, security guards, managers, and others. The Officers watch closely as money is transferred to and from slot machines, video machines, and other money dispensers. They also monitor rooms where money is brought, counted, and bagged by employees. Additionally, the officers observe how money is handled by employees and patrons at card games, keno, roulette, slot machines, and other casino games. Furthermore, these officers watch over monetary transactions that take place in casino hotels, restaurants, lounges, shops, arcades, and so forth.

Gaming, Surveillance Officers observe patrons for incidents of cheating the casino. For example, a poker player may exchange his playing cards. The Officers also keep track of patrons who are acting suspicious, being obnoxious, or are intoxicated.

Some surveillance officers are assigned to conduct undercover work on the casino floor. While maintaining their anonymity, they walk and sit among the patrons and employees, as they watch for cheating, theft, and other violations. While working undercover, surveillance officers maintain communication with the other officers in the central monitoring room.

When Gaming Surveillance Officers suspect any wrongdoing by employees or patrons, they immediately inform their supervisors. The officers also document their observations. They write accurate and well-detailed reports that describe the incidents and the violations.

Gaming Surveillance Officers perform various tasks each day, such as putting in blank videotapes as needed, completing daily shift reports, and maintaining surveillance equipment. They are also expected to keep up-to-date with all laws, regulations, and ordinances related to gaming operations.

Gaming Surveillance Officers work 40 hours a week. They usually work varied shifts, which may include nights, weekends, and holidays.

## Salaries

Earnings for Gaming Surveillance Officers vary, depending on such factors as their experience, job responsibilities, employer, and geographical location. According to the November 2003 *Occupational Employment Statistics* survey by the U.S. Bureau of Labor Statistics (BLS), most Gaming Surveillance Officers earned an estimated salary that ranged between $16,550 and $42,220.

## Employment Prospects

The BLS estimates that about 8,170 Gaming Surveillance Officers were employed in the United States as of November 2003. Gaming Surveillance Officers are employed in states and American Indian reservations where gambling is legal. The American Gaming Industry reports that there were 443 commercial casinos in 11 states in 2003. According to the National Indian Gaming Association Web site, http://www.indiangaming.org, there are 354 tribal government gaming operations in 28 states.

The job market for Gaming Surveillance Officers is predicted to grow by 36 percent or more through 2012. Opportunities are increasing due to the expansion of small and large casinos throughout the country. Casinos will create additional positions to keep pace with their security needs. In addition, many opportunities will become available as surveillance officers transfer to other occupations, retire, or leave the field for various reasons.

Indian casinos hire tribal members as well as local, non-Indian people from the surrounding areas. They usually give first preference for jobs to their tribal members.

Surveillance officers can also find employment with non-gaming employers, such as hotels, department stores, shopping malls, airports, and construction sites.

## Advancement Prospects

Many Gaming Surveillance Officers realize advancement by earning higher wages and receiving greater responsibilities. Those with supervisory and managerial ambitions can advance through the ranks as lead surveillance officers, supervisors, and managers.

Some Surveillance Officers use their experience as a stepping-stone to follow career paths in law enforcement, security, or other fields of interest.

## Education and Training

Minimally, Gaming Surveillance Officers must possess a high school diploma or a general equivalency diploma. Some employers require that applicants have some postsecondary training.

Employers provide new surveillance officers with training programs.

## Special Requirements

Gaming Surveillance Officers are usually required to possess an occupational license granted by the state casino control commission that monitors the casino where they work. Requirements vary with different state agencies. Some employers make arrangements for new employees to obtain the proper licensure, while others direct new employees to apply for licensing on their own.

## Experience, Skills, and Personality Traits

Requirements vary with the different employers. In some casinos, this position is considered entry-level and requires no previous experience. Other casinos require one to two years of work experience in security operations. Experience with or knowledge of casino games is desirable.

Gaming Surveillance Officers must have excellent observational, communication, writing, and teamwork skills to execute their job effectively. Their job also requires that they have strong interpersonal skills, as they must work with many people of diverse backgrounds. In addition, officers need good self-management skills, which include the ability to work independently, handle stressful situations, follow directions, and prioritize tasks.

Being enthusiastic, respectful, calm, focused, and trustworthy are some personality traits that successful Gaming Surveillance Officers have in common.

## Unions and Associations

Gaming Surveillance Officers are eligible to join the International Association of Certified Surveillance Professionals. This is a professional association that offers its members networking opportunities, educational programs, and other professional resources and services. For contact information, see Appendix IV.

## Tips for Entry

1. Casinos generally hire candidates who live locally or in nearby communities.
2. Some experts advise that individuals without experience apply for jobs at smaller casinos. As they gain experience, they can seek higher-paying jobs at larger casinos.
3. When you apply for a job in person, be ready to interview. Sometimes employers conduct job interviews as soon as individuals turn in their applications.
4. Learn more about casino surveillance and Gaming Surveillance Officers on the Internet. Two Web sites you might visit are International Association of Certified Surveillance Professionals, http://iacsp.org, and Casino Surveillance News, http://www.casinosurveillancenews.com.

# SECURITY SUPERVISOR

## CAREER PROFILE

**Duties:** Oversee the daily activities of the guard operations; complete all necessary reports and record-keeping; may perform guard post or patrol duties

**Alternate Title(s):** None

**Salary Range:** $14,000 to $33,000

**Employment Prospects:** Excellent

**Advancement Prospects:** Good

**Prerequisites:**

**Education or Training**—High school diploma preferred

**Experience**—Six months to two years experience in guard work

**Special Skills and Personality Traits**—Leadership, teamwork, interpersonal, communication, and writing skills; be energetic, self-motivated, dedicated, trustworthy, and enthusiastic

**Licensure/Certification**—Security guard license, firearms license, and driver's license may be required

## CAREER LADDER

```
┌─────────────────────────────┐
│      Security Manager       │
└─────────────────────────────┘


┌─────────────────────────────┐
│     Security Supervisor     │
└─────────────────────────────┘


┌─────────────────────────────┐
│       Security Guard        │
└─────────────────────────────┘
```

## Position Description

Security Supervisors directly oversee the activities of the security guard staff on a day-to-day basis. Staffs vary, depending on the size of the facilities, but Security Supervisors may supervise as few as two or as many as 25 or more guards. Their job is to make sure that security guards understand and enforce the policies, security procedures, and emergency plans of their employers against criminal activity, accidents, fires, and natural disaster.

All work shifts have Security Supervisors. Their responsibilities vary from employer to employer. Most Security Supervisors draw up work schedules and make guard post or patrol assignments. They also perform regular inspections of security and fire safety equipment to make sure they are in working order. Many perform investigations of security and safety problems such as theft or employee accident. Some continue to perform regular guard duties.

Security Supervisors also train and retrain their staff regarding employers' rules, protective procedures, first aid, fire safety, and other pertinent security matters. In addition, Security Supervisors regularly evaluate the job performance of each staff member, usually completing and signing performance appraisals. When staff members are performing poorly, Security Supervisors recommend disciplinary actions to their superiors. If staff members must be disciplined (such as being docked pay for tardiness), Security Supervisors are responsible for handling the appropriate discipline.

They meet regularly with security management, giving updates on daily operations, reporting any problems or potential trouble spots, and requesting any necessary equipment or personnel changes. From time to time, Security Supervisors might suggest ways to improve procedures or modify existing policies to provide better protection. Furthermore, Security Supervisors may take part in the selection process for new staff members and make recommendations.

Security Supervisors prepare various administrative reports, such as payroll, overtime, and part-time reports. They also write business correspondence and reports such as monthly theft reports.

Security guard firms have either on-site or field supervisors, or both. Field Security Supervisors are usually responsible for security crews at one or more locations. They visit locations on a rotating basis, often performing unscheduled and unannounced spot inspections to make sure the security guards are performing their jobs satisfactorily.

In-house Security Supervisors work 40 hours a week. Security Supervisors work part time or full time for security guards firms.

## Salaries

Salaries for Security Supervisors vary with different employers, and generally are higher in urban areas. Typically, supervisors with more experience and education can earn higher wages.

Specific salary information for Security Supervisors is unavailable. They typically earn higher wages than security guards. According to the November 2003 *Occupational Employment Statistics* survey by the U.S. Bureau of Labor Statistics (BLS), the estimated annual salary for most security guards ranged between $14,180 and $32,940.

## Employment Prospects

Security Supervisors work for businesses, corporations, manufacturers, retailers, apartment complexes, educational institutions, hospitals, government agencies, nonprofit organizations, and various other organizations. They are also employed by investigation and security companies that provide security services on a contractual basis.

Opportunities generally become available as Security Supervisors retire, advance to higher positions, or transfer to other occupations. The BLS reports that employment for Security Guards in the United States is expected to grow by 21 to 35 percent through 2012. The growing concern about crime and terrorism will result in demands for increased security by businesses, corporations, and other organizations.

## Advancement Prospects

Security Supervisors can pursue management and administrative positions, such as security directors, security managers, security chiefs, and vice presidents or presidents of security. Many employers prefer that managerial and administrative officers have a college degree in any field. Security Supervisors choose to go into law enforcement, become security specialists, or head their own security guard agencies.

## Education and Training

Employers usually hire applicants who have a high school or general equivalency diploma; many prefer applicants with some college background.

Security Supervisors receive on-the-job training. Type and length of training varies with the different employers.

## Special Requirements

In most states and many cities, Security Supervisors must be licensed. Licensing requirements vary with the different states and cities.

Security Supervisors who carry firearms in the performance of their duties must possess the proper state licensure for using firearms.

Many employers require that Security Supervisors possess a valid driver's license.

## Experience, Skills, and Personality Traits

Requirements vary with the different employers. For example, an employer might require that applicants have at least six months of security guard experience, while another employer might require that applicants have two or more years of experience. Along with guard experience, applicants should be able to demonstrate the ability to maintain schedules, payroll reports, and other routine records.

Security Supervisors must have effective leadership, teamwork, and interpersonal skills. In addition, they should have excellent communication and writing skills. Being energetic, self-motivated, dedicated, trustworthy, and enthusiastic are some personality traits that successful Security Supervisors share.

## Unions and Associations

Security Supervisors may join professional associations to take advantage of professional services and resources, such as networking opportunities, certification programs, and educational programs. The International Foundation for Protection Officers, the National Police and Security Officers Association of America, and ASIS International are three professional associations that are available to Security Supervisors. For contact information, see Appendix IV.

## Tips for Entry

1. Apply directly to security guard firms for jobs. To find out what companies are in your area, look in the yellow pages of your telephone book under *Security Guard* and *Patrol Services*.

2. To improve your chances for supervisory and management positions in security, take courses in law, police science, security, business management, and personnel. Courses in computer science, communications, electronics, and information technology are also valuable for a career in security.

3. Enhance your employability by obtaining professional certification from an organization that is recognized by employers, such as ASIS International or International Foundation for Protection Officers.

4. Use the Internet to learn more about security service. You might start by visiting the International Foundation for Protection Officers Web site. Its URL is http://www.ifpo.com.

# SECURITY MANAGER

## CAREER PROFILE

**Duties:** Be responsible for the day-to-day physical security operations that safeguard their employers' buildings, grounds, assets, employees, tenants, and visitors

**Alternate Title(s):** None

**Salary Range:** $30,000 to $109,000

**Employment Prospects:** Excellent

**Advancement Prospects:** Good

**Prerequisites:**

　**Education or Training**—Bachelor's degree

　**Experience**—Requirement varies with the different employers

　**Special Skills and Personality Traits**—Leadership, negotiation, interpersonal, communication, planning, organizational, and self-management skills; be intelligent, articulate, analytical, detail-oriented, flexible, decisive, and inspirational

　**Licensure/Certification**—Protection professional certification may be required

## CAREER LADDER

```
+---------------------------+
|     Security Director     |
+---------------------------+

+---------------------------+
|     Security Manager      |
+---------------------------+

+---------------------------+
|    Security Supervisor    |
+---------------------------+
```

## Position Description

Security Managers are in charge of the day-to-day physical security operations that safeguard their employers' buildings, grounds, assets, employees, tenants, and visitors. They make sure that the security force, security systems, fire safety systems, security procedures, and safety plans are in effect against criminal activity, accidents, fires, and natural disasters.

Security Managers oversee the whole security guard force. They organize the security force so that there are adequate guard posts and patrols to cover the grounds and buildings, particularly sensitive and dangerous areas. They also make sure there is sufficient staff for 24-hour coverage. Additionally, they delegate responsibilities to supervisors and maintain close communication with them.

They make sure security controls are in place to keep unauthorized persons—visitors as well as employees—out of restricted areas and to prevent criminal activity in shipping, warehousing, cash handling, and other sensitive areas. When security problems arise, such as theft or hazardous conditions, Security Managers oversee the investigations. If law enforcement and fire agencies are involved, Security Managers are the liaisons for their employers.

Security Managers make regular reviews of the security procedures and safety plans to ensure their effectiveness. That involves inspecting the condition of security barriers, protective equipment, communication systems, and so on. They also audit security controls as well as review the performance, appearance, and competence of the security guards.

Security Managers are also responsible for allocating funds for staff salaries, security equipment, and other operational costs within the established department budget. They hire and fire security personnel as well as make recommendations for promotions. Security Managers also handle any grievance matters that any security personnel have. In addition, Security Managers develop security training programs as well as establish staff evaluation procedures and oversee disciplinary actions. They may develop security and safety education programs for all the employees.

Depending on the structure and size of their employer's physical security operations, Security Managers may be involved in mid-level or top-level security management. Mid-level Security Managers are usually found in organizations in which the security operations are responsible for several facilities or are divided into several departments (such as physical security, personnel security, and information technology security divisions). In midsize and large organizations, Security Mangers may oversee the physical security of one or more facilities, and it is not uncommon for some Security Managers to be responsible for facilities located in different cities or states.

Depending on their position (mid-level or top-level management), Security Managers may be responsible for, or assist with:

- developing and evaluating physical security plans and programs that meet the security needs of their employer
- developing and revising physical security goals, standards, guidelines, policies, and procedures
- preparing the annual budget for the physical security department
- developing security or risk assessments

Security Managers perform other duties as required of their position. Top-level Security Managers usually report to an organization's owner or an executive administrative officer.

Security Managers sometimes work beyond their 40-hour week. They are on call 24 hours a day to attend to emergencies.

## Salaries

Earnings for Security Managers vary, depending on such factors as their education, experience, position, employer, and the size and the complexity of their security department. Top-level Security Managers who oversee a large security staff and several facilities for a large private corporation typically earn the highest wages. These managers usually hold a bachelor's or master's degree as well as professional certification from ASIS International or another recognized security association.

The November 2003 *Occupational Employment Statistics* survey by the U.S. Bureau of Labor Statistics (BLS), reports that the estimated annual salary for most administrative services managers, which includes Security Managers, ranged between $29,920 and $108,780.

## Employment Prospects

Security Managers are employed by private companies, manufacturers, department stores, shopping malls, educational institutions, hospitals, utility companies, government agencies, nonprofit organizations, and various other organizations. They are also employed by investigation and security companies that provide physical security services on a contractual basis. Organizations with large and complex security operations usually have several layers of management.

Job openings generally become available as Security Managers retire, advance to higher positions, or transfer to other jobs.

## Advancement Prospects

Security Managers can advance in number of ways. Those working for small organizations can pursue positions with higher incomes and more complex responsibilities in other establishments. In midsize and large organizations with complex security operations, Security Managers can rise through the ranks from mid-level to top-level management positions. They are generally required to hold a college degree as well as professional certification to qualify for a higher position. In addition, they must be knowledgeable about and experienced in other security areas (such as personnel and information technology) besides physical security.

## Education and Training

Many employers require Security Managers to possess at least a bachelor's degree, preferably in business administration, law enforcement, or a related field. Some employers prefer to hire Security Managers who hold a master's degree.

Throughout their careers, Security Managers enroll in educational programs, training seminars, conference workshops, and so on to increase their knowledge and update their skills.

## Special Requirements

Many employers require that Security Managers possess professional certification from a recognized professional association. For example, many Security Managers obtain the Certified Protection Professional (CPP) designation, which is granted by ASIS International. Those without certification may be hired on condition that they obtain proper certification within a specific time frame.

## Experience, Skills, and Personality Traits

Requirements vary among employers, as well as for the different levels of management positions. In general, applicants should have several years of professional experience in security or law enforcement, which includes performing supervisory and management duties. Applicants also need to be familiar with the type of setting and industry in which they would be working.

Because they must be able to establish strong working relationships with various people, Security Managers must have effective leadership, negotiation, interpersonal, and communication skills. In addition, they need excellent planning and organizational skills. Furthermore, they must have superior self-management skills, which include the ability to meet deadlines, organize and prioritize several tasks, resolve problems quickly, and handle stressful situations.

Being intelligent, articulate, analytical, detail-oriented, flexible, decisive, and inspirational are some personality traits that successful Security Managers share.

## Unions and Associations

Security Managers join professional associations to take advantage of professional services and resources, such as networking opportunities, certification programs, and educational programs. One such organization is ASIS International (formerly known as the American Society for Industrial Society). For contact information, see Appendix IV.

## Tips for Entry

1. Network with other professionals to learn about job openings that are currently available or will be available soon.
2. Stay current with the latest security trends, issues, and concerns.
3. Courses in security, computer science, business management, law, police science, personnel, and information management can provide you with valuable knowledge and skills for a career in security.
4. To learn more about the security field, visit the ASIS International Web site at http://www.asisonline.org.

# AVIATION SAFETY
# AND SECURITY

# AIR TRAFFIC CONTROLLER

## CAREER PROFILE

**Duties:** Manage air traffic so it flows safely, orderly, and smoothly; give pilots permission and instruction for aircraft taxiing, takeoffs, and landings; monitor aircraft in flight

**Alternate Title(s):** Air Traffic Specialist; Flight Service Specialist

**Salary Range:** $55,000 to $136,000

**Employment Prospects:** Good

**Advancement Prospects:** Limited

**Prerequisites:**

    **Education or Training**—Bachelor's degree: complete FAA training program

    **Experience**—Three years' experience without college degree; pilot, navigator, or military air traffic controller experience preferred

    **Special Skills and Personality Traits**—Concentration, teamwork, interpersonal, communication, self-management, problem-solving, and decision-making skills; be alert, precise, calm, decisive, and flexible

    **Licensure/Certification**—FAA certification and facility rating

## CAREER LADDER

```
┌─────────────────────────────────────┐
│     Air Traffic Control Specialist   │
└─────────────────────────────────────┘

┌─────────────────────────────────────┐
│       Air Traffic Controller         │
└─────────────────────────────────────┘

┌─────────────────────────────────────┐
│     Air Traffic Control Trainee      │
└─────────────────────────────────────┘
```

## Position Description

Air Traffic Controllers (ATCs) are responsible for coordinating air traffic in the air and on airport grounds. Every day, ATCs manage and separate thousands of aircraft as they pass through their assigned airspace, runways, and taxiways. Using radar equipment, computer systems, and other procedures and techniques, ATCs monitor several aircraft at the same time to make sure traffic is flowing smoothly and safely. ATCs also communicate constantly with pilots to give them important instructions and advice about air traffic as well as potential hazards, weather, navigational sites, and other matters.

In the United States, most ATCs are employees of the Federal Aviation Administration (FAA), an agency within the U.S. Department of Transportation. (The FAA is responsible for overseeing the U.S. air traffic control system along with enforcing federal aviation laws and regulations.) FAA Air Traffic Controllers are stationed in different types of facilities—terminal facilities, air route traffic control centers, and flight service stations.

ATCs at FAA terminal facilities are responsible for the separation of aircraft as they arrive or depart from an airport and as they taxi on the ground. Some ATCs work in control towers, while others work in terminal radar approach control (TRACON) facilities, which may be housed within control towers or in nearby buildings. Different tower controllers review flight plans, give pilots permission to depart or land, and guide aircraft between terminal gates or hangars and runways. The various TRACON controllers are responsible for monitoring aircraft during their departure and landing phases. Along with serving the airport where they are stationed, TRACON controllers provide air traffic service to smaller airports that fall within the airspace they monitor.

The FAA has 21 air route traffic control centers (ARTCC) across the United States. Each facility manages air traffic that passes through its assigned airspace, which covers hundreds of thousands of miles. ARTCC Air Traffic Controllers, who are often known as en route controllers, work in teams of two or three to monitor aircraft. When necessary, these controllers communicate with pilots to advise them about flight conditions, such as bad weather, the status of military operating areas, and potential hazards in their particular jurisdictions.

FAA flight service stations are located at airports throughout the United States. ATCs who work at these facilities are not involved with the separation of air traffic. Their job is to help pilots avoid potential flight hazards within their service areas. Also known as flight service station specialists, these ATCs provide pilots with essential information about weather conditions and hazards, routes, terrain, airport conditions, and other flight matters.

Monitoring air traffic is complex and stressful work that requires a high level of teamwork. Various Air Traffic Controllers work together to guide and monitor aircraft from takeoff to landing. For example, if a commercial jet is waiting to depart from an airport, a flight plan has already been filed with the control tower. The pilots developed the flight plan after receiving vital information from flight service station ATCs. After approving their flight plan, a tower controller contacts the pilots and gives them permission to depart from the airport. Another controller guides the pilots from their spot at a terminal gate to a runway, where the pilots wait for final clearance from a third controller.

Upon takeoff, the pilots receive instruction from a TRACON controller. This ATC guides the pilots out of the airport's airspace, instructing the pilots on which direction, speed, and rate of ascent to take along the departure route. When the aircraft has left the TRACON controller's airspace, a pilot notifies the appropriate ARTCC facility. ARTCC controllers then track the jet as it travels through its assigned airspace.

Each time the jet enters a different airspace, new controllers monitor the jet and give pertinent information to the pilots. For instance, if the jet is scheduled to arrive at the same time, location, and altitude as another aircraft in the next airspace, a controller instructs the pilots on how to change course. Pilots also maintain contact with flight service station traffic controllers to stay up to date with conditions, such as wind turbulence, that may affect their flight.

When the jet enters the TRACON airspace for its destination airport, a TRACON controller guides the pilots. As they near the airport, another TRACON controller prepares the pilots for landing by telling them what speed, altitude, and direction to fly and on which runway to land. At the airport, pilots receive landing clearance and instructions from a tower controller. Upon landing, the pilots are then guided to a terminal gate by another tower controller.

ATCs work rotating shifts. They usually work a 40-hour week and, whenever required, work overtime.

## Salaries

Earnings for Air Traffic Controllers vary, depending on such factors as their education, experience, facility, job responsibilities, and geographical location. According to the November 2003 *Occupational Employment Statistics* survey by the U.S. Bureau of Labor Statistics, the estimated annual salary for most Air Traffic Controllers ranged between $55,340 and $136,170.

FAA controllers usually start at the GS-7 level on the general schedule, the pay schedule for most federal employees. In 2005, the basic pay rate for GS-7 employees ranged between $30,567 and $39,738.

## Employment Prospects

The majority of civilian Air Traffic Controllers work for the FAA. Some civilian controllers work for the U.S. Department of Defense. Others are employed by private firms that provide air traffic control services on a contractual basis to the FAA.

Job vacancies typically become available as ATCs retire, advance to higher positions, or transfer to other occupations. Opportunities are expected to increase in the coming years due to the large number of ATCs who will become eligible for retirement. According to the National Air Traffic Controllers Association, about half of the ATC workforce in the United States is expected to retire by 2010.

## Advancement Prospects

Supervisory and management positions are available, but limited. Many Air Traffic Controllers pursue career growth by way of wage increases and increased responsibilities. ATCs can also seek specialist positions, such as a quality assurance specialist, in which they perform support roles for their facilities. Research and training positions are also available for those interested in pursuing those career options.

FAA Air Traffic Controllers are required to retire upon reaching the age of 56. They are eligible for retirement at age 50 if they have completed 20 years of service or at any age if they have completed 25 years of service.

## Education and Training

Applicants may qualify for entry-level ATC positions if they have earned a bachelor's degree with an emphasis in air traffic control from an academic institution that offers FAA-certified air traffic control programs. Applicants may also qualify if they have completed air traffic control training in the military.

Recruits must successfully complete basic training at the FAA Academy in Oklahoma City, in which they study such areas as the air traffic control system, federal aviation regulations, job procedures, and aircraft performance. The length of their training varies, depending on the type of facility in which they would be working. For example, recruits for control tower positions complete a 15-week program.

After completing their basic training, recruits are assigned to a facility where they receive on-the-job training from senior controllers. They also continue to participate in classroom training and independent study. It generally takes several years before trainees become certified as full performance-level ATCs.

## Special Requirements

ATCs must obtain and maintain professional certification and facility ratings from the FAA.

To qualify for an entry-level position, applicants must meet the following requirements:

- be a U.S. citizen
- be under 31 years old when initially hired (for positions at airport and ARTCC facilities)
- be able to speak, read, write, and understand English fluently
- meet vision, color vision, hearing, and other medical standards
- achieve a qualifying score on the FAA prequalification exam, which is an aptitude test designed to identify the cognitive skills required by Air Traffic Controllers

Air Traffic Controllers are required to pass an annual physical exam and a job performance exam that is given twice a year. They must also be able to pass random drug screenings.

## Experience, Skills, and Personality Traits

Without a bachelor's degree, entry-level applicants must have three years of general work experience that demonstrate they are capable of becoming Air Traffic Controllers. Applicants may also be eligible if they have previous experience as pilots, navigators, military controllers, or aircraft dispatchers.

ATCs need superior memories and concentration skills for their line of work. In addition, they need excellent team-work, interpersonal, and communication skills. Having strong self-management, problem-solving, and decision-making skills is also essential.

Some personality traits that successful ATCs share include being alert, precise, calm, decisive, and flexible.

## Unions and Associations

Many ATCs belong to a labor union that represents them in contract negotiations for better wages, benefits, and working conditions. Flight service station ATCs usually join the National Association of Air Traffic Specialists, while ATCs from the other air traffic facilities join the National Air Traffic Controllers Association.

ATCs also join professional associations to take advantage of networking opportunities, educational programs, and other professional services and resources. The Air Traffic Control Association and the Professional Women Controllers, Inc. are two such societies.

For contact information for the above organizations, see Appendix IV.

## Tips for Entry

1. Visit the different air traffic control facilities and see which environment might suit you best.
2. To learn about job openings, contact a U.S. Office of Personnel Management (OPM) office, which may be listed under the U.S. government pages in your telephone book. Or visit the OPM Web site (http://www.usajobs.opm.gov) on the Internet.
3. The FAA has special hiring policies for applicants who are veterans, former military, civilian controllers, or graduates of FAA-certified ATC programs.
4. To learn more about ATCs, check out the following Web sites: Air Traffic Control Association, http://www.atca.org; National Air Traffic Controllers Association, http://www.natca.org; National Association of Air Traffic Specialists, http://www.naats.org; and FAA Academy, http://www.academy.jccbi.gov.

# AIRCRAFT DISPATCHER

## CAREER PROFILE

**Duties:** Manage daily airline flight operations; prepare flight plans; monitor flights

**Alternate Title(s):** Airline Dispatcher

**Salary Range:** $24,000 to $90,000 or more

**Employment Prospects:** Fair

**Advancement Prospects:** Fair

**Prerequisites:**

**Education or Training**—High school diploma

**Experience**—Varies with the different airlines

**Special Skills and Personality Traits**—Decision-making, communication, teamwork, interpersonal, and self-management skills; be calm, quick-witted, detail-oriented, enthusiastic, and flexible

**Licensure/Certification**—FAA Aircraft Dispatcher certificate

## CAREER LADDER

```
┌─────────────────────────────────┐
│   Senior Aircraft Dispatcher     │
└─────────────────────────────────┘

┌─────────────────────────────────┐
│      Aircraft Dispatcher         │
└─────────────────────────────────┘

┌─────────────────────────────────┐
│     Aircraft Trainee or          │
│  Assistant Aircraft Dispatcher   │
└─────────────────────────────────┘
```

## Position Description

Aircraft Dispatchers are licensed by the Federal Aviation Administration (FAA) to manage daily flight operations. Aircraft Dispatchers are responsible for managing several flights, which may be domestic or international flights, at the same time. In commercial airlines, Aircraft Dispatchers and aircraft captains are jointly responsible for the safety of flights. In fact, Aircraft Dispatchers are often described as "captains on the ground."

One of the main duties that Aircraft Dispatchers perform is preparing flight plans for their assigned flights. They gather and analyze such data as weather conditions and air traffic flow along flight routes. They also compute the amount of fuel that aircraft need to complete flights as well as determine which airports that aircraft can be diverted to in case of emergencies. In addition, dispatchers make sure that flights are in compliance with company policies and protocols as well as with aviation laws and regulations.

Aircraft Dispatchers also prepare the dispatch release form, a legal document that gives authorization for a flight to depart. This document must be cosigned by captains and Aircraft Dispatchers. If Aircraft Dispatchers think conditions may threaten the safety of a flight, they will delay or cancel it.

Monitoring assigned flights is another duty that Aircraft Dispatchers perform. Dispatchers keep track of aircraft from their departure airports until they have landed or have gone beyond the dispatchers' jurisdiction. They also maintain communication with pilots throughout flights via two-way radios, satellite communications, or computer text-messaging systems. They provide pilots with updates of conditions that may affect the successful completion of their flights. For example, they warn pilots of sudden changes in weather, air traffic, or airport field conditions. When necessary, Aircraft Dispatchers recommend changes in the flight plans—such as changing altitudes or landing at different airports—for safety and economic reasons. Furthermore, Aircraft Dispatchers assist in any flight emergencies.

As liaisons between flight crews and ground service operations, Aircraft Dispatchers prepare and distribute flight information to other employees, including those working at reservation desks and gate stations. Their data is usually the source for all information that is provided to the traveling public.

In order to perform their tasks, Aircraft Dispatchers must be knowledgeable in many different areas. For example, they must be familiar with all airports and airline routes; the different types of aircraft operated by their airlines, including takeoff, cruising, and landing characteristics; meteorology; air traffic control procedures; and instrument flight procedures.

Aircraft Dispatchers keep up with changing technologies, company policies, and federal air regulations by participating in regular training sessions, continuing education programs, and self-study. In addition, the FAA requires Aircraft Dispatchers to ride in the cockpit with flight crews at least five hours each year to observe flight routes and working conditions.

Dispatch centers operate on a 24-hour basis; thus, Aircraft Dispatchers work rotating shifts that include weekends and holidays. They may also work overtime.

## Salaries

Earnings for Aircraft Dispatchers vary, depending on such factors as their experience, education, seniority, employer, and geographical location. According to the Sheffield School of Aeronautics (http://www.sheffield.com), entry-level Aircraft Dispatchers generally earn an annual salary between $24,000 and $28,000. Experienced Aircraft Dispatchers with major airlines can earn an annual salary of $80,000 to $90,000.

## Employment Prospects

In addition to commercial airlines, Aircraft Dispatchers are employed by air charter companies that offer scheduled and on-demand flights. Some Aircraft Dispatchers work for corporations that own and use aircraft specifically for business transportation.

Opportunities generally become available when Aircraft Dispatchers retire, transfer to other occupations, or leave the workforce altogether. Employers may create additional positions as their companies grow, as long as funding is available.

## Advancement Prospects

Supervisory and management positions, which vary from airline to airline, are available. Many Aircraft Dispatchers pursue career growth by way of wage increases and additional responsibilities that often involve changing jobs or locations.

## Education and Training

Minimally, applicants must have a high school or general equivalency diploma. Some employers prefer to hire applicants who have a college degree, which may be in any major.

Trainees must complete airline training programs that include company orientation and formal flight dispatcher training. Trainees then receive on-the-job training under the supervision of senior Aircraft Dispatchers. Field training may last several weeks or months or even over a year, depending on the employer.

## Special Requirements

Aircraft Dispatchers who work for commercial airlines must possess an aircraft dispatcher certificate, which is granted by the FAA. Other employers may require or strongly prefer that dispatchers possess this certificate.

To be eligible for the aircraft dispatcher certificate, individuals must be at least 23 years old. They must also meet other qualifying requirements, which may be fulfilled through experience as a pilot, flight navigator, meteorologist, flight dispatcher, or air traffic controller. Applicants may also qualify by completing an Aircraft Dispatcher training program from an FAA-approved school.

## Experience, Skills, and Personality Traits

Requirements vary with different employers. Many airlines hire applicants who have no prior dispatch work experience if they have completed FAA-approved training programs and hold FAA certification.

Aircraft Dispatchers must have excellent decision-making and communication skills as well as strong teamwork and interpersonal skills. They also need adequate self-management skills, such as the ability to follow directions, meet deadlines, work independently, and handle stressful situations. Being calm, quick-witted, detail-oriented, enthusiastic, and flexible are some personality traits that successful Aircraft Dispatchers share.

## Unions and Associations

Many Aircraft Dispatchers join the Airline Dispatchers Federation, a professional society, to take advantage of networking opportunities, educational programs, and other professional services and resources. (For contact information, see Appendix IV.) Many dispatchers also belong to a labor union that represents them in contract negotiations with their employers.

## Tips for Entry

1. After submitting job applications, contact personnel offices on a regular basis by phone or mail to let them know you are still available. Many Flight Dispatchers have been hired because they contacted an airline at a time when an opening just became available.

2. Individuals who are at least 21 years old and are eligible for the FAA Aircraft Dispatcher certificate can take the test. If they pass, they will be issued a Letter of Aeronautical Competency and receive the Aircraft Dispatcher certificate upon reaching their 23rd birthday.

3. To learn more about Aircraft Dispatchers, visit the Airline Dispatchers Federation Web site at http://www.dispatcher.org.

# AIRPORT FIREFIGHTER

## CAREER PROFILE

**Duties:** Provide firefighting, rescue, fire protection, and emergency medical services; respond to all aircraft emergencies

**Alternate Title(s):** None

**Salary Range:** $19,000 to $60,000

**Employment Prospects:** Limited

**Advancement Prospects:** Good

**Prerequisites:**

**Education or Training**—High school diploma; FAA-approved training program

**Experience**—Previous firefighting experience

**Special Skills and Personality Traits**—Teamwork, communication, interpersonal, reading, writing, and self-management skills; be calm, dependable, cooperative, courteous, honest, alert, and courageous

**Licensure/Certification**—Firefighting and emergency medical technician certification may be required; driver's license may be needed

## CAREER LADDER

```
┌─────────────────────────────┐
│        Lieutenant           │
└─────────────────────────────┘

┌─────────────────────────────┐
│      Airport Firefighter    │
└─────────────────────────────┘

┌─────────────────────────────┐
│  Airport Firefighter Trainee │
└─────────────────────────────┘
```

## Position Description

Airport Firefighters are stationed at municipal airports, international airports, and military air bases where they are responsible for providing firefighting, rescue, fire protection, and emergency medical services on a 24-hour basis. They respond to various types of calls, including aircraft fires, structural fires, aircraft crashes, car accidents, terrorism alerts, bomb threats, medical emergencies, and hazardous waste emergencies.

Airport Firefighters are specially trained to provide aircraft rescue and firefighting services. They execute a different strategy than that of structural or building firefighting. Their first priority is to rescue the passengers and crew, who will be suffering from traumatic injuries and burns, and may need to be extricated from the aircraft. Airport Firefighters must work quickly, as aviation fuels burn at temperatures between 3,000 and 4,000 degrees Fahrenheit, and the aircraft cabin can reach unbearable temperatures within minutes.

They fight only that part of the fire that interferes with the rescue to allow more time for the rescue. For example, they might spray the outside of the fuselage with overflowing streams of foam or water to draw off heat from the inside of the aircraft. Once a rescue is completed, Airport Firefighters then redirect their energies to suppressing the fire.

Firefighters perform other duties that may include:

- conducting routine fire and safety inspections of fuel farms, hangars, and other airport property
- teaching fire safety training classes to airport and airline employees
- participating in routine drills and training sessions
- performing routine inspections and maintenance of all rescue and firefighting vehicles and equipment
- maintaining fire stations and grounds
- performing desk watch duty

Some Airport Firefighters are also certified peace officers who perform police duties.

Aircraft rescue and firefighting work is hard and dangerous. Airport Firefighters are exposed to high noise levels, extreme heat, toxic chemicals (such as nitrogen dioxide and carbon monoxide), and hazardous materials. They often lift and carry persons or objects weighing over 100 pounds.

Fire stations are located at airports, near runways, and are equipped with special heavy-duty and complex aircraft rescue and firefighting vehicles and equipment. Firefighters are required to reach aircraft emergencies within a few minutes. As they cross runways to reach an emergency, they are alert to incoming and outgoing flights. In addition, they are in communication with the airport control tower, the local fire dispatcher and, at some airports, with the National Guard.

Airport Firefighters live and work at their fire stations during their duty tours, which vary from department to department. Airport Firefighters often work 50 or more hours a week.

## Salaries

Earnings for Airport Fire Fighters vary, depending on such factors as their rank, experience, employer, and geographical location. According to the November 2003 *Occupational Employment Statistics* survey by the U.S. Bureau of Labor Statistics, the estimated annual salary for most firefighters ranged between $19,420 and $59,610.

## Employment Prospects

Most Airport Firefighters work for local or state fire departments. Some work for private firms that offer aircraft rescue and firefighting services.

Most job openings will become available as personnel retire or transfer to other positions. The turnover rate for Airport Firefighter positions is low, and the competition for available positions is high. Employers may increase or reduce their staff, depending on the needs of their units.

## Advancement Prospects

Advancement through the ranks—engineer, lieutenant, captain, battalion chief, assistant chief, deputy chief, and chief—is based on competitive exams, job performance, interviews, and seniority. Many fire departments prefer candidates who possess a bachelor's degree in fire science, public administration, or another related field for the positions of battalion chief and higher.

With further training, Airport Firefighters can apply for specialized positions such as fire equipment drivers/operators or firefighter/paramedics. They might pursue other firefighting careers such as fire inspectors, fire investigators, or fire protection engineers.

## Education and Training

Fire departments require a high school or general equivalency diploma. Some departments require additional college work or college degrees, preferably in fire science or other related field.

Recruits must complete Federal Aviation Administration (FAA) approved training programs. Among the subjects that trainees study are airport operations; aircraft construction

and equipment; personnel safety; airport emergency plans; use of aircraft rescue and firefighting equipment and appliances; and emergency aircraft evacuation.

Airport Firefighters fulfill mandatory training requirements on a regular basis to maintain and update firefighting skills and knowledge. For example, they are required to complete a live-fire drill at least once a year. This drill includes a pit fire with an aircraft mock-up to simulate the type of aircraft fire they may encounter.

## Special Requirements

Every fire department has specific age, residency, medical, and other qualifications that applicants must fulfill. Applicants may be required to hold firefighting and emergency medical technician certifications as well as a valid driver's license. Employers may hire candidates without the proper licensure or certifications on the condition that they obtain them within a specific time frame.

## Experience, Skills, and Personality Traits

Requirements vary from department to department. For example, some departments hire only applicants who have aircraft rescue and firefighting experience. In general, applicants should have previous firefighting and rescue technician experience.

To perform their work effectively, Airport Firefighters must have excellent teamwork, communication, and interpersonal skills. They must also have adequate reading and writing skills and strong self-management skills. Being calm, dependable, cooperative, courteous, honest, alert, and courageous are some personality traits that successful Airport Firefighters share.

## Unions and Associations

Airport Firefighters are eligible to join a union, such as the International Association of Fire Fighters, that represents them in contractual negotiations.

Many firefighters join local, state, or national professional associations to take advantage of networking opportunities, educational programs, certification programs, job banks, and other professional services and resources. Two national associations that serve the interests of Airport Firefighters are the National Fire Protection Association and the Aircraft Rescue and Fire Fighting Working Group. For contact information, see Appendix IV.

## Tips for Entry

1. Improve your chances of getting a job at the fire departments where you would like to work by being able to fill all required—as well as desired—job qualifications. For example, if having paramedic certifica-

tion or particular technical rescue (confined space rescue, high-level rescue) certification is a high priority, then obtain the necessary certification.

2. As a firefighter, let the commander of the aircraft rescue and firefighting unit know of your interest even if positions are not currently available.

3. You can learn more about Airport Firefighters on the Internet. Enter the keywords *airport firefighters, airport fire department,* or *aircraft rescue and firefighting* into a search engine for a list of relevant Web sites to browse. Or, visit the Aircraft Rescue and FireFighting Working Group at http://www.arffwg.org.

# AIRPORT POLICE OFFICER

## CAREER PROFILE

**Duties:** Provide law enforcement services and airport security; enforce local, state, and federal laws and regulations; preserve the peace, protect life and property, and provide public service

**Alternate Title(s):** Airport Public Safety Officer

**Salary Range:** $27,000 to $68,000

**Employment Prospects:** Good

**Advancement Prospects:** Excellent

**Prerequisites:**

**Education or Training**—High school diploma; police academy training, airport security training

**Experience**—Previous law enforcement experience preferred

**Special Skills and Personality Traits**—Writing, computer, problem-solving, observational, teamwork, communication, interpersonal, public relations, and self-management skills; be honest, dependable, courteous, trustworthy, levelheaded, quick-witted, and cooperative

**Licensure/Certification**—Police officer certificate; driver's license

## CAREER LADDER

```
┌─────────────────────────────────────┐
│  Special Assignments, Detective,     │
│           or Sergeant                │
└─────────────────────────────────────┘

┌─────────────────────────────────────┐
│       Airport Police Officer         │
└─────────────────────────────────────┘

┌─────────────────────────────────────┐
│    Airport Police Officer Trainee    │
└─────────────────────────────────────┘
```

## Position Description

Airport Police Officers are stationed on airport grounds to ensure a safe and secure environment. Like all other local law enforcement officers, Airport Police Officers are responsible for preserving the peace, protecting life and property, and providing public service. Their job involves enforcing local and state laws, regulations, and ordinances as well as federal laws and regulations relating to aviation security.

As uniformed officers, Airport Police Officers carry firearms and have the authority to issue warnings and citations and make arrests. Their work involves patrolling assigned areas (terminal buildings, parking lots, runways, and grounds), and keeping an eye out for theft, trespassing, vandalism, and all other criminal activity. They make their rounds by foot, in patrol vehicles, or on bicycles. Some officers are trained as canine handlers and conduct their duties with police dogs.

Airport Police Officers also receive dispatches to help airport employees, tenants, travelers, and the general pub-

lic. Airport Police Officers investigate trouble such as shoplifting, theft, assault, rape, or other criminal activity, and look into problems such as lost items or missing persons. They also respond to emergency situations such as vehicle accidents, heart attacks, or childbirth, and provide first aid, CPR (cardiovascular pulmonary resuscitation), or other emergency medical care that they are certified to perform.

Airport Police Officers perform a variety of other duties, such as:

- monitor security checkpoints in the airport terminals
- investigate security breaches, and if necessary, secure areas and evacuate people from the airport
- screen passengers for guns, bombs, and other contraband
- coordinate police efforts for special events (such as the arrival of visiting dignitaries) that require heightened security
- enforce traffic laws in the airport

- provide traffic control in and out of airports and on nearby highways during emergencies or special events
- provide general information about airport facilities to travelers and the general public

At some airports, Airport Police Officers are part of departments that oversee all law enforcement, aircraft rescue and firefighting, and emergency medical care activities. These officers are cross-trained to provide all these services on their work shifts.

Furthermore, Airport Police Officers cooperate with other local and state law enforcement agencies as well as federal agencies (such as the FBI, the Drug Enforcement Administration, the U.S. Secret Service and the U.S. Department of Homeland Security) on various activities such as narcotics surveillance or antiterrorism programs.

As part of their duties, Airport Police Officers keep a daily field notebook on their activities as well as complete accidents and incidents reports. All logs and reports must be accurate and detailed, as they become permanent public records that can be placed as evidence in trials.

Airport Police Officers work rotating shifts that include nights, weekends, and holidays. Officers who also perform aircraft rescue and firefighting duty work a shift that schedules those duties.

## Salaries

Earnings for Airport Police Officers vary, depending on such factors as their rank, experience, education, and geographical location. The estimated annual salary for most police patrol officers ranged between $26,510 and $68,160, according to the November 2003 *Occupational Employment Statistics* survey by the U.S. Bureau of Labor Statistics.

## Employment Prospects

Since terrorist acts took place in the United States on September 11, 2001, the demand for stronger airport security has increased. Airport police departments will create additional positions to meet security needs as long as funding is available. In general, most opportunities for Airport Police Officers will become available as officers retire, resign, or are promoted to higher positions.

## Advancement Prospects

Officers interested in supervisory or administrative duties can seek promotions as sergeants, lieutenants or captains. They must have additional experience and education as well as pass competitive exams and reviews.

In larger airport police departments, officers can volunteer for special duty, such as canine patrol or hostage negotiations, when they become eligible. Airport Police Officers can also pursue a career in police investigations. After completing two or three years of patrol duty, they become eligible to take the detective exam.

## Education and Training

Applicants must have a high school or general equivalency diploma. Many departments also require applicants to have a minimum of college credits with courses in police science or other related study. Some police departments require applicants to have either an associate's or bachelor's degree.

Recruits must complete police academy training in addition to separate airport security training, which covers use of firearms; procedures for detentions, search, arrest, and other aviation security activities; and law enforcement responsibilities in airport security. Those recruits who will perform aircraft rescue and firefighting duties must also complete fire academy training. Along with formal training, recruits complete field training under the supervision of senior officers.

## Special Requirements

Airport Police Officers must possess a current POST (Peace Officer Standard and Training) certificate, which is earned upon completion of basic training at a police academy. In addition, they must hold a current driver's license.

Every law enforcement agency has specific age, vision, hearing, weight, and height requirements that applicants must meet in order to become Airport Police Officers. Usually, applicants must be U.S. citizens. Furthermore, applicants must not have any criminal record nor misdemeanor conviction of domestic violence, which disqualifies individuals from obtaining a permit to carry weapons.

## Experience, Skills, and Personality Traits

Requirements vary from department to department. Most departments prefer one or more years of experience in law enforcement. For positions with aircraft rescue and firefighting duty, departments prefer applicants with structural firefighting or aircraft rescue and firefighting experience.

Airport Police Officers need strong writing, computer, problem-solving, observational, and teamwork skills. Their job also requires that they have effective communication, interpersonal, and public relations skills, as they must work with the general public on a daily basis. They also need exceptional self-management skills, such as the ability to handle stressful situations, work independently, prioritize tasks, and understand and follow directions. Being honest, dependable, courteous, trustworthy, levelheaded, quick-witted, and cooperative are some personality traits that successful Airport Police Officers share.

## Unions and Associations

Many Airport Police Officers belong to professional associations to take advantage of networking opportunities, educational programs, and other professional services and resources. Some professional societies that Airport Police Officers might join include the American Federation of Police and Concerned Citizens, the International Association of Airport and Seaport Police, the Fraternal Order of Police, and the International Association of Women Police. (For contact information, see Appendix IV.)

In addition, many Airport Police Officers join a union that represents them in contract negotiations with their employers. The union seeks to get the best contract terms in regard to pay, benefits, and working conditions. It also handles any grievances that officers may have against their employers.

## Tips for Entry

1. To learn about job openings or career information, contact airport police departments. In the city, county, or state government pages of your telephone book, look under *Airports* or *Airport Commissions.*

2. As a police officer, let the commander of the airport patrol unit or division know of your interest even if positions are not currently available.

3. Check out local unions and professional associations for job listings.

4. Use the Internet to learn more about Airport Police Officers. To get a list of relevant Web sites, enter the keywords *airport police officers, airport police unit,* or *airport police department* into a search engine.

# TRANSPORTATION SECURITY SCREENER

## CAREER PROFILE

**Duties:** Screen passengers and baggage for dangerous and lethal items; operate various screening equipment and machines

**Alternate Title(s):** Airport Security Screener

**Salary Range:** $24,000 to $35,000

**Employment Prospects:** Good

**Advancement Prospects:** Fair

**Prerequisites:**

**Education or Training**—High school diploma; complete a security screener training program

**Experience**—Must have one year of qualifying work experience without a high school diploma

**Special Skills and Personality Traits**—English proficiency; interpersonal, customer service, communication, and self-management skills; be honest, trustworthy, dependable, alert, and courteous

## CAREER LADDER

```
┌─────────────────────────────────────────┐
│  Lead Transportation Security Screener    │
└─────────────────────────────────────────┘

┌─────────────────────────────────────────┐
│    Transportation Security Screener       │
└─────────────────────────────────────────┘

┌─────────────────────────────────────────┐
│                 Trainee                   │
└─────────────────────────────────────────┘
```

## Position Description

Throughout the United States, Transportation Security Screeners work in more than 440 commercial airports. They play an essential role in providing security and protection to airports, aircraft, travelers, and the general public every day. Their job is to identify dangerous or lethal items on passengers' bodies and in their carry-on and checked baggage as well as to prevent those objects from being brought aboard aircraft.

In November 2002, the Transportation Security Screeners at U.S. commercial airports became federal employees, as a provision of the Aviation and Transportation Security Act. The screener workforce is under the supervision and management of the Transportation Security Administration (TSA), an agency within the U.S. Department of Homeland Security.

Transportation Security Screeners are stationed at various security checkpoints within commercial airports. They use standard security procedures as well as electronic and imaging technologies to look for firearms, knives, swords, explosives, and other objects that can be used as weapons for criminal or terrorist purposes aboard aircraft. They also keep their eyes open for flammable liquids and other hazardous materials that may cause fatal accidents during flights.

Screeners at baggage checkpoints monitor passengers' luggage before they are loaded into the cargo section of an aircraft. These screeners operate various types of X-ray machines to view the contents of all checked items. Senior screeners may be assigned to operate equipment that detects explosives.

Screeners at passenger checkpoints have the duty of screening passengers and their carry-on items. Some screeners are assigned passenger screening. They are responsible for screening every individual, from baby to elderly person, before they proceed to their gates. Passengers walk through a metal-detector machine after emptying their pockets of any coins, keys, and metal objects as well as after removing any pieces of clothing that may set off the machine's alarm. When passengers set off the alarm, Transportation Security Screeners perform a secondary screening, which includes passing a metal-detector wand closely over passengers' bodies. In addition, screeners may perform pat down searches of passengers.

Other screeners are assigned to inspect carry-on items by using X-ray machines. Passengers place purses, backpacks, briefcases, luggage, and other items on conveyor belts. As each item passes through the machine, screeners look for specific clues that indicate suspicious organic, metal, and other inorganic items. If they believe a closer inspection is needed, Transportation Security Screeners have the authority to perform hand searches on the bags. In other words, they may open bags and examine their contents.

Transportation Security Screeners work within a stressful environment, which involves the pressure of dealing with long lines and meeting deadlines. At all times, screeners are expected to be continually alert for potentially threatening situations. They often lift objects weighing up to 70 pounds. They stand for long periods of time and deal with the constant noise of people and machinery as they perform their duties.

Their job requires them to make effective decisions in routine and crisis situations. Additionally, they are expected to act in a calm and professional manner as they deal with the public. On occasion, Transportation Security Screeners must handle individuals who are upset, angry, or disruptive.

Besides screening duties, Transportation Security Screeners perform other tasks. For example, they maintain security logs, write incident reports and statements, and attend meetings. They may assist with inquiries or investigations into security issues.

Transportation Security Screeners are hired to work full-time or part-time. Some screeners are employed on a temporary basis, particularly during peak travel seasons in the summer and during holidays. All screeners are assigned to work shifts, which may include working nights, weekends, and holidays. On occasion, they are required to work overtime.

## Salaries

Earnings for Transportation Security Screeners vary, depending on such factors as experience, job rank, and geographical location. In 2005, the base annual salary for Transportation Security Screeners ranged from $23,600 to $35,400. Screeners working in areas with high costs of living, such as New York and Los Angeles, typically receive higher wages.

Private screening companies are required by law to provide their employees with compensation and employee benefits that are at least equivalent to those received by federal screeners.

## Employment Prospects

The TSA is continually recruiting for full-time and part-time positions at airports nationwide. As of September 30, 2004, the TSA could employ up to 45,000 permanent, full-time Transportation Security Screeners. The U.S. Congress may increase or decrease the total number of screener positions to meet the changing demands of airport security. The number of full-time and part-time screeners who are employed at a commercial airport varies, depending on the needs of the airport.

In November 2004, the TSA began accepting applications from commercial airports that wanted to use private screening contractors. The first groups of private Transportation Security Screeners were expected to begin working in late 2005. Although they would be nonfederal employees, the private screeners would be trained and certified to use security procedures and technologies that are established by the TSA.

## Advancement Prospects

Transportation Security Screeners can advance through the ranks to become lead screeners and supervisory screeners. Most screeners measure success by earning higher wages and receiving greater responsibilities.

Some screeners gain experience on the job and move on to pursue a career in law enforcement, security, airport administration, or other fields that interest them.

## Education and Training

Minimally, applicants must possess a high school diploma or general equivalency diploma.

Newly hired Transportation Security Screeners receive a minimum of 40 hours of classroom training and 60 hours of on-the-job training. They are trained in security procedures and technologies for performing both passenger and baggage screening.

All screeners are required to complete recurrent training on a regular basis. In addition, they receive training on new security procedures and equipment.

## Experience, Skills, and Personality Traits

Applicants who do not possess the minimum educational requirements must have at least one year of full-time work experience in aviation security screening, security, or X-ray technician work. All applicants must be U.S. citizens or U.S. nationals (individuals who are born in U.S. territories such as American Samoa). Additionally, they need to be physically fit and in good health.

To perform well on the job, Transportation Security Screeners must be proficient in speaking, reading, and writing the English language. They must also have excellent interpersonal, customer service, and communication skills. Furthermore, they need strong self-management skills, which includes the ability to follow directions, handle stressful situations, and organize multiple tasks.

Some personality traits that successful Transportation Security Screeners share include being honest, trustworthy, dependable, alert, and courteous.

## Unions and Associations

Transportation Security screeners may join a union that can represent them at grievance and discrimination hearings as well as advance their interests and rights in Congress and in the courts. (For example, federal screeners may join the American Federation of Government Employees.) Unions may not represent federal screeners for the purpose of collective bargaining. Transportation Security Screeners—federal or private contractor employees—do not have the right to strike.

## Tips for Entry

1. Candidates must pass a selection process that includes an aptitude test, English-language proficiency test, medical examination, physical abilities test, oral interview, drug screening, background investigation, and security check. The selection process takes several weeks to complete.

2. An intensive background check is performed on all applicants, which includes a credit check. An applicant who owes delinquent federal or state taxes or child support payments or has defaulted on a debt of $5,000 or more is ineligible for the Transportation Security Screener position.

3. You may apply online at the TSA website. Go to http://www.tsa.gov, then click on the *Employment* link for information. You may also apply by phoning the TSA Recruitment Center at (800) 887-1895. Applicants with hearing impairments can call (800) 887-5506.

4. You can learn more about the TSA on the Internet at http://www.tsa.gov.

# COMPUTER SECURITY

# DATA SECURITY SPECIALIST

## CAREER PROFILE

**Duties:** Safeguard information assets from theft, damage, and destruction; administer policies that control access to computer data files

**Alternate Title(s):** Data Security Administrator

**Salary Range:** $40,000 to $96,000

**Employment Prospects:** Good

**Advancement Prospects:** Good

**Prerequisites:**

**Education or Training**—Varies from employer to employer

**Experience**—Previous work experience in data security or information systems

**Special Skills and Personality Traits**—Writing, communication, interpersonal, and teamwork skills; be logical, focus, detail-oriented, patient, and trustworthy

## CAREER LADDER

Senior Data Security Specialist

Data Security Specialist

Data Security Specialist Trainee

## Position Description

Data Security Specialists are responsible for protecting the valuable information that is stored and managed on computer-based information systems in banks, schools, hospitals, companies, and other institutions. For example, some information assets that a department store might hold in computer systems are store accounts, inventory records, bills, invoices, and employee information.

While working alone and in teams, Data Security Specialists safeguard electronic information from theft, tampering, and unauthorized access by employees, as well as by hackers who attempt to access computer files through trial and error methods. These specialists are particularly concerned with crackers—criminal hackers—whose objective is to destroy data, undermine computer security, or perform other criminal activities. Furthermore, Data Security Specialists protect data from virus corruption, systems failures, and natural disasters.

One of their main responsibilities is maintaining the confidentiality of the various databases in an institution's computer systems. They make sure that employees have access only to computer files and applications for which they have authorization. For example, a personnel worker might have access to employee files but not to executive files.

Data Security Specialists maintain the authorization and authentication systems. They assign passwords, log-on iden-

tifications, smart cards, and other forms of identification to employees for the particular databases, applications, and computers that they are allowed to access for their jobs. They help users when they have access problems. They reassign passwords and other identification when users forget or lose them. When necessary, Data Security Specialists remove names of employees from the authorization and authentication systems as well as add names of new employees. In addition, they report any problems or potential trouble to their supervisors.

Another major responsibility is maintaining the integrity of the databases. Data Security Specialists monitor access and transaction logs to check for possible security violations and break-ins. They regularly check the different software for viruses, trojan horses, and worms. From time to time, they use the hacker's techniques to get into the security systems to find their flaws and weaknesses. As critical problems and potential trouble spots are found, the Data Security Specialists report them to their supervisors.

Other duties that Data Security Specialists might perform include:

- gather information for risk assessment surveys
- help develop security policies

- work with programmers and other security personnel to improve methods or procedures that strengthen security measures
- advise employees on ways to practice preventative security measures
- keep up to date with security software revisions
- make recommendations for new security software

Data Security Specialists work 40 hours a week; they work overtime during emergencies. Many Data Security Specialists are on call for emergencies 24 hours a day.

## Salaries

Earnings for Data Security Specialists vary, depending on such factors as their education, experience, job duties, employer, and geographical location. Specific salary information for Data Security Specialists is unavailable. The estimated annual salary for most computer systems analysts—which includes Data Security Specialists—ranged between $40,650 and $95,860 according to the November 2003 *Occupational Employment Statistics* survey by the U.S. Bureau of Labor Statistics (BLS).

## Employment Prospects

Data Security Specialists are employed by financial institutions, government agencies, educational institutions, hospitals, data processing centers, private companies, nonprofit groups, and other organizations. In addition, they work for consulting firms that provide data security services on a contractual basis.

According to the BLS, employment of computer systems analysts is expected to increase by 36 percent or more though 2012. Opportunities specifically created for information security professionals should be plentiful due to the increasing need by organizations to safeguard their electronic information. Besides the job growth factor, job openings will be created to replace Data Security Specialists who are promoted, transfer to other jobs, or leave the workforce.

## Advancement Prospects

There are different paths that Data Security Specialists can take. They can pursue supervisory and managerial positions in Data Security by becoming team leaders, project managers, data security managers, and, eventually, information security officers.

Another path is to get into other areas of information systems security such as network security analysis, security software development, or computer forensic work. In addition, Data Security Specialists might become self-employed consultants or start their own data security consulting firms.

## Education and Training

Most employers prefer applicants with a bachelor's degree, particularly in computer science, management information systems, or other related majors. Many employers hire applicants with a high school diploma, general equivalency diploma, or some college background if they have the required number of years of experience in data security.

## Experience, Skills, and Personality Traits

Requirements vary with the different employers, and depend on the complexity of job responsibilities that entry-level Data Security Specialists perform. In general, applicants should have a background in programming, systems analysis, and telecommunications along with one to four years of work experience in data security or information systems. Applicants need a broad knowledge of computers and computer networks, and should have knowledge in the operating systems that prospective employers use. Having knowledge in networking systems is desirable.

Data Security Specialists must have strong writing and communication skills as they must be able to explain technical terms and procedures in language that is understood by everyone. They also need strong interpersonal and teamwork skills. Being logical, focused, detail-oriented, patient, and trustworthy are some personality traits that successful Data Security Specialists share.

## Unions and Associations

Many Data Security Specialists join professional associations to take advantage of networking opportunities, certification programs, educational programs, and other professional resources and services. Two national organizations that specifically serve the interests of computer security professionals are the Information Systems Security Association and the Computer Security Institute. For contact information, see Appendix IV.

## Tips for Entry

1. Talk with data security professionals about the current security needs and hiring requirements of their employers. Some places where you can make contacts are professional computer security associations, university or college computer departments, and data security consulting firms.
2. If there is a particular industry such as manufacturing, banking, or healthcare in which you are interested in working, become familiar with that industry. Take college courses that may be useful for working in the industry as well as obtain paid or voluntary experience.
3. Research the companies for which you are interested in working before you apply or interview for a job. Learn about what they do, their assets, and their commitment to employee career development.
4. Get an idea of the type of work involved in data security by looking at Web sites of data security consulting firms on the Internet. In a search engine, enter the keywords *data security consulting* to get a list of relevant Web sites to visit.

# INFORMATION SYSTEMS SECURITY (INFOSEC) SPECIALIST

## CAREER PROFILE

**Duties:** Implement information systems security policies and procedures; evaluate computer security systems for their effectiveness; help develop ways to reduce the risks of unauthorized entry, theft, or damage

**Alternate Title(s):** Computer Security Specialist

**Salary Range:** $36,000 to $89,000

**Employment Prospects:** Good

**Advancement Prospects:** Good

**Prerequisites:**

**Education or Training**—Bachelor's degree preferred

**Experience**—Three to five years of work in computer security

**Special Skills and Personality Traits**—Writing, communication, analytical, presentation, interpersonal, and teamwork skills; be patient, detail-oriented, adaptable, creative, persistent, energetic, self-motivated, and trustworthy

## CAREER LADDER

```
┌─────────────────────────────────┐
│     Senior Infosec Specialist    │
└─────────────────────────────────┘

┌─────────────────────────────────┐
│         Infosec Specialist       │
└─────────────────────────────────┘

┌─────────────────────────────────┐
│     Infosec Specialist Trainee   │
└─────────────────────────────────┘
```

## Position Description

Information Systems Security (Infosec) Specialists work for companies, government agencies, and other institutions. Their job is to safeguard information assets and the computer-based information system from theft, tampering, accidental erasures, system failures, virus corruption, natural disasters, and so on. Information systems are made up of computer hardware, software, and databases. Networks in which computers are connected through telecommunications are also part of information systems: local area networks (LANs) connect computers to each other within an institution; wide area networks (WANs) connect an institution's computers to computers outside the institution; and internetworks, such as the Internet, connect an institution's computers to many different networks at the same time. In addition, computer-based information systems include the procedures for running the various systems and the people who input, process, and output information.

Infosec Specialists are constantly evaluating all aspects of their employers' information systems, particularly with regard to network security, to identify flaws within the systems that are security threats. They often use the trial and error techniques of a hacker to find ways to illegally access computer systems and networks to shore up security. Infosec Specialists also examine computer logs and log files to check for possible break-ins by hackers and crackers (criminal hackers) who have gained unauthorized access.

Infosec Specialists work with other security personnel to find solutions to security problems or issues. For example, in a corporate retail store, Infosec Specialists might work on the problem of finding the best encryption methods to send and receive sensitive data over the Internet. In addition, Infosec Specialists help develop plans and security measures to reduce security risks. In many infosec divisions, the Infosec Specialists are responsible for implementing new security procedures once they are approved.

Other duties Infosec Specialists may perform include:

- be responsible for data security
- write security manuals for the various networks and stand-alone computer systems as well as update manuals when needed

- install new security software and updates, making sure they are compatible with security measures
- talk with users who have violated security policies

Infosec Specialists work 40 hours a week. On occasion, they may work evenings and weekends to finish projects or to resolve emergency situations. In large computer installations, Infosec Specialists work on different shifts.

## Salaries

Earnings for Infosec Specialists vary, depending on such factors as their education, experience, employer, industry, and geographical location. The estimated annual salary for most network and computer systems administrators—including computer security specialists—ranged between $36,390 and $89,460, according to the November 2003 *Occupational Employment Statistics* survey by the U.S. Bureau of Labor Statistics (BLS).

## Employment Prospects

Infosec Specialists are employed throughout the private sector, from small businesses to startup companies and established corporations. They also find employment with government agencies, educational institutions, nonprofit organizations, and other institutions. In addition, they work for consulting firms that offer information technology security services on a contractual basis.

According to the BLS, opportunities specifically created for information security professionals should be plentiful due to the growth in electronic commerce as well as to the increasing concern by organizations to safeguard their information systems. Besides the job growth factor, job openings will be created to replace Infosec Specialists who are promoted, transfer to other jobs, or leave the workforce. Keep in mind that during economic downturns, fewer jobs and more layoffs can be expected.

## Advancement Prospects

Infosec Specialists can advance to senior and lead positions as well as to managerial positions. In addition, Infosec Specialists might become self-employed consultants or start their own consulting firms.

## Education and Training

Educational requirements vary with the different employers. Many employers prefer to hire candidates who possess a bachelor's degree in computer science or a related field. Some employers will hire candidates without a college degree, if they have relevant infosec experience as well as the technical skills that employers seek.

Throughout their careers, Infosec Specialists enroll in educational programs, training seminars, and conference workshops to increase their knowledge and learn new skills. In addition, employers typically provide their employees with in-service training programs.

## Experience, Skills, and Personality Traits

Depending on the job duties, applicants need between three and five years work of infosec experience. In addition, they must have experience in the specific technologies, such as operating systems, networking systems, firewalls, and Internet architecture, that are used by prospective employers. Infosec Specialists must have excellent writing, communication, analytical, and presentation skills. They also need interpersonal and teamwork skills, as they work with many different people, including infosec staff, users, and vendors.

Some personality traits that successful Infosec Specialists have in common include being patient, detail-oriented, adaptable, creative, persistent, energetic, self-motivated, and trustworthy.

## Unions and Associations

Many Infosec Specialists join professional associations to take advantage of educational programs, certification programs, networking opportunities, and other professional resources and services. Some societies that serve the interests of these professionals include the Information Systems Security Association and the Computer Security Institute. Many professionals also belong to the Association for Computing Machinery's SIGMOD (Special Interest Group on Management of Data). For contact information on these organizations, see Appendix IV.

## Tips for Entry

1. To learn about job openings in computer security, contact college and university placement centers, and professional associations. Also apply directly to companies and institutions for which you would like to work.
2. While in college, participate in internship or co-op programs, working in the information security divisions of companies or other institutions.
3. Enhance your employability by obtaining the Certified Information Systems Security Professional (CISSP) designation when you become eligible. This professional certification is granted by the International Information Systems Security Certification Consortium, which is recognized by many employers. For further information, visit http://www.cissp.com.
4. You can learn more about the infosec field on the Internet. In a search engine, enter the keywords *infosec, computer security,* or *information systems security.* You will get a list of Web sites that include consulting firms, infosec products, and professional organizations.

# INFORMATION SYSTEMS SECURITY (INFOSEC) MANAGER

## CAREER PROFILE

**Duties:** Plan, execute, and oversee the security of the computer-based information systems in companies, government agencies, and other institutions

**Alternate Title(s):** Director of Information Security, Chief Security Officer

**Salary Range:** $52,000 to $200,000+

**Employment Prospects:** Good

**Advancement Prospects:** Fair

**Prerequisites:**

    **Education or Training**—Bachelor's degree preferred

    **Experience**—Five to 10 years of Infosec experience; experience in security management, project management, and application development

    **Special Skills and Personality Traits**—Writing, decision-making, project management, leadership, team-building, communication, and interpersonal skills; be cooperative, decisive, tactful, energetic, enthusiastic, organized, flexible, and creative

## CAREER LADDER

```
┌─────────────────────────────┐
│         Consultant          │
└─────────────────────────────┘

┌─────────────────────────────┐
│       Infosec Manager       │
└─────────────────────────────┘

┌─────────────────────────────┐
│    Infosec Specialist or    │
│   other Infosec Profession  │
└─────────────────────────────┘
```

## Position Description

Information Systems Security (Infosec) Managers are responsible for the overall computer security operations for companies, government agencies, and other institutions. Their job is to develop, implement, and administer security policies and programs that safeguard their employers' computer-based information systems 24 hours a day.

An institution's information systems include its information assets—various databases about organizational accounts, inventory, customer accounts, and employee records. These systems also include all computer hardware and software as well as communication networks that connect computers to each other within the company (local access networks or LANs), to computers outside the company (wide access networks or WANs), and to networks such as the Internet. So, Infosec Managers make sure that their staff protects every part of these information systems from loss or damage.

Infosec Managers manage all aspects of computer security, such as:

- physical security and fire safety measures for the computer systems
- emergency plans for recovering data in case of power failures, fires, or natural disasters
- authorization and authentication systems to make sure that access to computer files or software programs are given only to authorized personnel who have the proper identification
- selection, testing, and installation of new security software and hardware
- the detection, reporting, and investigation of security violations by employees as well as security breaches by crackers (criminals who use trial and error, or hacking, techniques to gain access into databases)
- training programs that teach employees the safe and proper use of computer systems

To keep tabs on the different security areas, Infosec Managers meet regularly with staff managers and team leaders. Infosec Managers also review audits, risk management surveys, and other reports to check on the continuing effectiveness of the various security measures. Upon finding weaknesses or potential trouble, Infosec Managers direct staff members to find solutions and develop new security procedures.

Infosec Managers are the liaisons for the infosec departments. They meet with user departments, such as data processing, to discuss the security needs or issues that those departments may have. Infosec Managers also make presentations about infosecurity programs to organizational executive officers. When necessary, Infosec Managers represent their employers in meetings with law enforcement agencies.

Infosec Managers also handle routine administrative tasks. For example: they manage departmental budgets; negotiate contracts with vendors and consulting firms; hire and fire infosec staff members as well as suggest that staff members earn promotions or salary raises; handle personnel grievances or complaints; and develop staff training programs.

Infosec Managers work a regular 40-hour week but often put in many overtime hours to complete responsibilities or handle emergencies.

## Salaries

Earnings for Infosec Managers vary, depending on such factors as their experience, education, employer, and geographical location. Experienced Infosec Managers generally command high salaries. For example, it is not uncommon for executive-level infosecurity managers to earn annual salaries of $150,000 to $200,000 or more.

The U.S. Bureau of Labor Statistics reports in its November 2003 *Occupational Employment Statistics* survey that the estimated annual salary for most computer and information systems managers ranged between $52,040 and $145,600.

## Employment Prospects

Infosec Managers are employed throughout both the public and private sectors. Some experts in the information security field report that opportunities for Infosec Managers should increase in the coming years as computer security is increasingly becoming a major concern with various organizations in many industries. In addition, job openings will result from the need to replace managers who retire, transfer to other positions, or move into other occupations. Keep in mind that during economic downturns, fewer jobs and more layoffs can be expected.

## Advancement Prospects

Infosec Managers are generally the highest-level position in the information systems security department. In some institutions, they report to the chief information systems officers; in others, Infosec Managers report to the chief executive officers or presidents of the institutions.

Infosec Managers can pursue further advancement by way of salary increases and changes in title, such as to chief security officer or vice president of information security. Some Infosec Managers also pursue career growth by finding employment with companies that have new or developing infosec departments. In addition, some Infosec Managers become consultants or start their own firms in information systems security.

## Education and Training

Requirements vary from employer to employer. Many employers prefer to hire candidates with at least a bachelor's degree, while others prefer to hire candidates with advanced degrees. Some employers are willing to hire candidates without any college degree if they have the experience in information systems security.

## Experience, Skills, and Personality Traits

Applicants generally need between five and 10 years of information systems security experience, depending on the responsibilities of the jobs that they are applying for. Along with infosec experience, employers look for experience in security management, project management, and application development. Furthermore, employers seek candidates who have strong business skills as well as a general background in the industry in which they would be working.

Essential skills that Infosec Managers need are writing, decision-making, project management, leadership, and team-building abilities. In addition, they must have excellent communication and interpersonal skills, as their job requires them to work effectively with various people, including infosec staff, vendors, and consultants, as well as organizational managers and executives. Being cooperative, decisive, tactful, energetic, enthusiastic, organized, flexible, and creative are some personality traits that successful Infosec Managers share.

## Unions and Associations

Many Infosec Managers join professional associations to take advantage of networking opportunities, certification programs, educational programs, research findings, job listings, and other professional services and resources. Some organizations that are available to them include the Information Systems Security Association, the Computer Security Institute, the Association for Computing Machinery, and ASIS International. For contact information, see Appendix IV.

## Tips for Entry

1. Join professional organizations and attend professional conventions to take advantage of networking with peers who may know of job openings.

2. Enhance your employability by obtaining professional certification from a recognized organization.

3. Early in your career as a computer security specialist, seek a mentorship with an information technology security manager whom you respect and trust, and from whom you would like to learn.

4. To get an idea of the extent of different responsibilities an Information Security Manager has at different companies, browse job openings on the Internet. In a job bank, such as "America's Job Bank," enter the keywords *information systems security manager* or *Infosec Manager.*

# COMPUTER FORENSICS SPECIALIST

## CAREER PROFILE

**Duties:** Conduct investigations of computer crime and computer-related crimes; examine computers to discover and recover electronic data that may be potential evidence of crimes

**Alternate Title(s):** Computer Investigative Specialist, Computer Forensics Examiner, Computer Forensics Investigator

**Salary Range:** $32,000 to $84,000

**Employment Prospects:** Fair

**Advancement Prospects:** Fair

**Prerequisites:**

**Education or Training**—Requirements vary with the different law enforcement agencies

**Experience**—Requirements vary with the different law enforcement agencies

**Special Skills and Personality Traits**—Critical-thinking, problem-solving, writing, communication, and interpersonal skills; be credible, trustworthy, persistent, patient, competent, and self-motivated

## CAREER LADDER

```
+------------------------------------------+
|             Unit Commander               |
+------------------------------------------+

+------------------------------------------+
|       Computer Forensics Specialist      |
+------------------------------------------+

+------------------------------------------+
|   Computer Forensics Specialist Trainee  |
+------------------------------------------+
```

## Position Description

Many law enforcement agencies have computer crime units, or high-technology crime units, that are responsible for investigating computer and computer-related crimes. The law enforcement officers working these special details are called Computer Forensics Specialists. Their job is to discover and recover data from computers to uncover potential evidence for arresting and convicting criminals.

Computer Forensics Specialists are involved in the investigation of such crimes as the theft of computer systems, trade secrets, and information assets (data), as well as the destruction or damage of computer files. These specialists also conduct or assist in investigations in which computers were used to commit a crime such as embezzlement, credit fraud, selling narcotics, kidnapping, or murder. For example, a bank employee might keep a file of all the customer account numbers from which she steals money on her personal computer at home.

Before examining the data in a computer, Computer Forensics Specialists gather information about the crime for which the data is potential evidence. With those facts, they plan what they should look for on the computer's hard disk and backup media. Throughout their examination, they follow standard procedures so that potential evidence is not destroyed or damaged thus establishing a chain of custody so that the evidence can be admitted at a court trial. Computer Forensics Specialists also make sure that all the data in a computer system is safe and intact throughout their examination.

Using special software and utilities, they perform a thorough search for relevant data, looking for and examining existing files as well as hidden files. They find and access relevant encrypted files and files that are protected by passwords. They probe every portion of unused space in the computer disk, searching for sites that may have evidence that had been created and then deleted, or erased. After completing their examination, they prepare a detailed report of their findings, including a list of files that may be potential evidence and how the files were discovered or recovered.

Computer Forensics Specialists perform other investigative duties, including interviewing witnesses and victims, interrogating suspects, performing surveillance or undercover work, participating in evidence searches and seizures, and arresting criminals.

Like all law enforcement officers, Computer Forensics Specialists work a 40-hour week with many overtime hours. They are on call 24 hours a day, seven days a week.

## Salaries

Earnings for Computer Forensics Specialists vary, depending on their rank, experience, education, and geographical location. According to the November 2003 *Occupational Employment Statistics* survey by the U.S. Bureau of Labor Statistics (BLS), the estimated annual salary for most detectives and criminal investigators ranged between $31,760 and $84,060.

Law enforcement officers receive additional compensation for working overtime, weekends, holidays, and late-night shifts. Many officers receive additional pay for performing special detail duty, such as the computer forensic detail.

## Employment Prospects

Computer Forensics Specialists are part of computer crime or high-technology crime units in local, state, and federal law enforcement agencies, as well as in the U.S. military forces. Some Computer Forensics Specialists are private consultants or work for computer forensics firms.

Most job opportunities become available when officers retire, resign, transfer to other positions, or become promoted to higher positions. The creation or expansion of a computer investigation unit is dependent on an agency's needs and budget.

## Advancement Prospects

Computer investigation is a voluntary assignment. In all law enforcement agencies, officers can pursue supervisory and administrative positions. In local agencies, officers may have to resign from computer investigation duty in order to perform supervisory or administrative duties. Supervisory and administrative positions within the computer investigation detail are limited to unit commanders.

Many retired law enforcement and military Computer Forensics Specialists start a second career by becoming computer forensics consultants, working for a private computer forensics firm, or starting their own firm.

## Education and Training

Educational requirements vary with the different agencies. A bachelor's degree in computer science is desirable but not necessarily required.

Throughout their careers, Computer Forensics Specialists enroll in educational programs, training seminars, and conference workshops to increase their knowledge and update their skills.

## Experience, Skills, and Personality Traits

Employers generally seek candidates who have the aptitude to learn the necessary skills to work in computer forensics. These candidates usually are knowledgeable about computer hardware as well as software programming.

To work effectively at their job, Computer Forensics Specialists must have excellent critical-thinking and problem-solving skills. They also need strong writing, communication, and interpersonal skills. Being credible, trustworthy, persistent, patient, competent, and self-motivated are some personality traits that successful Computer Forensics Specialists share.

## Unions and Associations

Computer Forensics Specialists from both law enforcement and the private sector might belong to the High Technology Crime Investigation Association. Law enforcement officers might also belong to the International Association of Computer Investigative Specialists (For contact information, see Appendix IV.) Joining such organizations allows Computer Forensics Specialists to network with peers and obtain professional support and services, such as training programs, and technical information.

## Tips for Entry

1. When you apply or interview for a law enforcement position, let the agency know of your interest in computer forensics investigations.
2. Learn as much as you can about computers—how they are built, how they function, how data is stored, and so on.
3. Take college courses in criminal justice, law, police science, computer science, and other related fields. A college degree in any of these subjects is a valuable asset in this field.
4. You can learn more about the forensics computing field on the Internet. To look at Web sites about law enforcement crime units, enter the keywords *high-technology crime* or *computer crime units* into a search engine. To look at Web sites of computer forensics consultants, enter the keywords *forensics computer* or *forensics computing*.

# QUALITY ASSURANCE SPECIALIST

## CAREER PROFILE

**Duties:** Evaluate the performance and integrity of new software before it is sold to the public; check that programs work according to specifications; find flaws in the programs

**Alternate Title(s):** Software Tester, Software Test Engineer

**Salary Range:** $45,000 to $90,000

**Employment Prospects:** Good

**Advancement Prospects:** Good

**Prerequisites:**

**Education or Training**—College degree usually preferred

**Experience**—Have a computer background

**Special Skills and Personality Traits**—Communication, interpersonal, teamwork, problem-solving, and organizational skills; be calm, patient, logical, persistent, self-motivated, and detail-oriented

## CAREER LADDER

Senior Quality Assurance Specialist

Quality Assurance Specialist

Quality Assurance Specialist Trainee

## Position Description

Quality Assurance Specialists evaluate the performance and integrity of software before it is sold to the public. They check that software programs work according to developers' instructions, making sure that the software is compatible with the various computer systems on which they will be used. Additionally, they look for bugs, or flaws, in the applications while testing them.

Upon completion of the final version of new software or updated versions of existing software, developers turn the software over to Quality Assurance Specialists. They also provide a set of specifications upon which Quality Assurance Specialists create a test plan. The specifications include information such as:

- who will use a software and the kind of environment (office, elementary school, medical lab) where the software will be used
- the purpose and objectives for the software
- the different platforms upon which the software can be used
- how the software is expected to work
- any specific features that need to be tested
- specific types of tests that are needed
- when the testing needs to be completed

In addition Quality Assurance Specialists review any accompanying documents such as charts, diagrams, programmers' notes and correspondence, and reviews by customers who tested beta, or developmental, versions of the software.

Once they understand the specifications, Quality Assurance Specialists begin planning the test processes. They develop test scenarios; they estimate the number of tests they must perform and how many times they will perform each test; and they create time schedules.

They keep well-detailed notes for each test they perform, writing down positive results as well as problems. They describe any bugs, and note the number of times they appear. Each time the program crashes, they reconstruct the moves or computer commands that brought on a crash and write down the sequence for programmers to examine and fix. Throughout the testing, they submit written and oral progress reports to their managers. As part of their final report, Quality Assurance Specialists might include suggestions for improving applications, such as how to make them easier to use.

On occasion, Quality Assurance Specialists are given software to evaluate without any specifications. They must then define test procedures for the software. Usually that involves talking with programmers as well as customers who have tested the software to gather enough information to create a specifications outline from which to work.

Quality Assurance Specialists generally work 40 hours a week, but may work more hours to meet deadlines.

## Salaries

Earnings for software Quality Assurance Specialists vary, depending on such factors as their education, experience, employer, and geographical location. According to Wetfeet. com, the annual salary for quality assurance professionals ranged between $45,000 and $90,000.

Generally, quality assurance professionals who work in large cities and metropolitan areas receive higher wages. Also, professionals who have college degrees earn higher wages.

## Employment Prospects

Software Quality Assurance Specialists work for software and hardware companies, as well as for consulting firms that offer software quality assurance services. Some specialists are employed by academic institutions and private companies.

Most openings become available as Quality Assurance Specialists are promoted, transfer to other jobs, or leave the workforce. An employer may create additional positions to meet growing demands as long as funds are available. During economic downturns, fewer jobs and more layoffs can be expected.

## Advancement Prospects

Quality Assurance Specialists have several options to pursue. Within the quality assurance field, they can become quality assurance analysts and engineers as well as pursue supervisory and managerial positions.

With additional training and experience, Quality Assurance Specialists can follow other career paths by becoming programmers, software engineers, research computer scientists, or computer security professionals.

## Education and Training

Education requirements for entry-level positions vary with different employers. Many employers prefer applicants who have college degrees with some classes in computer science or a related field. Some are willing to hire applicants who have a high school or general equivalency diploma.

Training varies with the employers as well. Some employers provide entry-level Quality Assurance Specialists with formal training programs while others give new employees informal on-the-job training.

## Experience, Skills, and Personality Traits

Requirements vary with the different employers. In general, employers prefer to hire applicants who have one or more years of work experience performing software quality control or quality assurance. Some employers hire applicants for entry-level positions who have no previous experience if they demonstrate that they have the aptitude to learn quality assurance duties.

Because they work with people from different backgrounds, Quality Assurance Specialists must have strong communication and interpersonal skills. In addition, their job requires that they have effective teamwork, problem-solving, and organizational skills. Being calm, patient, logical, persistent, self-motivated, and detail-oriented are some personality traits that successful Quality Assurance Specialists share.

## Unions and Associations

Quality Assurance Specialists might belong to the American Society for Quality. This organization offers networking opportunities, training and education programs, job listings, research resources, and other professional services. For contact information, see Appendix IV.

## Tips for Entry

1. Contact the quality assurance department at companies for which you are interested in working and ask about job openings that are available or may soon be available.
2. Gain experience by becoming volunteer testers for software companies. Contact software companies directly, and ask them if they need beta testers for the types of software of which you are familiar.
3. To enhance your employability, you might obtain professional certification from the American Society for Quality or another organization recognized by many employers.
4. You can learn more about the software quality assurance field on the Internet. In a search engine, enter the keywords *software quality assurance.* You will get a list of Web sites that include consulting firms, professional organizations, and general information.

# CORRECTIONS

# BAILIFF

## CAREER PROFILE

**Duties:** Call courts to order; maintain order in courtrooms; protect judges, juries, and all those in attendance at trials

**Alternate Title(s):** None

**Salary Range:** $18,000 to $55,000

**Employment Prospects:** Fair

**Advancement Prospects:** Fair

**Prerequisites:**

**Education or Training**—Varies with the different law enforcement agencies

**Experience**—Knowledge of office practices, court procedures, and legal terminology and forms

**Special Skills and Personality Traits**—Communication, interpersonal, reading, writing, and self-management skills; be perceptive, focused, dependable, trustworthy, respectful, friendly, patient, and calm

**Licensure/Certification**—Peace officer certification for local positions; firearms certification may be required

## CAREER LADDER

```
┌─────────────────────────┐
│     Unit Commander      │
└─────────────────────────┘

┌─────────────────────────┐
│         Bailiff         │
└─────────────────────────┘

┌─────────────────────────┐
│     Deputy Sheriff      │
└─────────────────────────┘
```

## Position Description

Bailiffs are law enforcement officers whose job is to maintain peace and order in the courts. They enforce courtroom rules of behavior as well as provide security during court trials. They work in federal, state, and municipal courts.

In the federal court system, the U.S. Marshals Service (part of the U.S. Department of Justice) is responsible for providing bailiff services. In the state court systems, county sheriffs' offices are responsible for providing bailiff services to the courts within their jurisdiction. Deputy sheriffs may be assigned to bailiff detail on a part-time or full-time basis. Responsibility for bailiff services in municipal courts varies from city to city. Municipal court Bailiffs can be law enforcement officers from the city marshal's office, the city police department, or the county sheriff's office.

As officers of the court, Bailiffs usually work in groups of two or more, performing a variety of tasks. They inspect courtrooms for security and cleanliness before court sessions begin. They also check that courtrooms have sufficient light, heat, and ventilation. In addition, they scan for concealed weapons, such as guns and bombs, as well as for other haz-ards. As people enter the courtroom, they keep their eyes open for weapons and confiscate them accordingly.

It is the duty of the Bailiffs to call the court to order and announce the entry of the judge. During court sessions, Bailiffs call defendants and witnesses to the stand as well as swear them in before they testify. When necessary, Bailiffs warn persons who are disturbing court procedures, and may physically remove unruly persons from courtrooms.

Bailiffs are responsible for the security of juries throughout court trials. They must prevent jurors from talking about a trial with the public lest a mistrial is called—that is, the trial is stopped and the suspects are set free. Bailiffs escort juries between courtrooms and jury rooms as well as stand guard outside the jury rooms. In addition, Bailiffs attend to the jurors' needs, such as relaying their requests or questions to the judges. Bailiffs also arrange for food to be delivered to the juries or escort them to restaurants. Bailiffs may run personal errands for jurors if they are sequestered (held overnight or longer). Furthermore, they make any necessary arrangements for jurors, such as overnight lodging or transportation.

Bailiffs work under the supervision of judges or court administrators, performing any errands or tasks that are required by the court. Upon the request of judges, Bailiffs might summon attorneys to the judge's chambers. They might maintain court documents and exhibits during trials. They might deliver court files, court minutes, and law books to judges or other court personnel. They might fetch necessary supplies or forms. When courts are not in session, Bailiffs might do routine clerical tasks such as photocopying court calendars and completing forms. Bailiffs who have legal training might serve as legal assistants to the judge.

Bailiffs perform other duties, which depend on the specific needs of the courts they serve. For example, in criminal courts, Bailiffs might guard and escort defendants (the persons who are accused of committing crimes) into courtrooms. Or, for example, some municipal court Bailiffs have the additional duty of serving civil orders, such as physical eviction orders, civil documents, and subpoenas.

Their job requires them to stand or sit for long periods of time, while being alert and watchful at all times. Bailiffs interact with many people from diverse backgrounds on a daily basis. They sometimes handle individuals who are in highly emotional states such as being angry, unhappy, or upset.

Bailiffs work regular court hours, Monday to Friday. They may work nights and weekends if they are escorting or guarding jurors.

## Salaries

Earnings for Bailiffs vary, depending on such factors as their experience, education, employer, and geographical location. The estimated annual salary for most Bailiffs who served in local and state courts ranged between $18,170 and $54,720, according to the November 2003 *Occupational Employment Statistics* survey by the U.S. Bureau of Labor Statistics (BLS).

## Employment Prospects

The BLS reports that about 16,690 Bailiffs were employed in local and state courts as of November 2003. Most of them were law enforcement officers who applied voluntarily for the Bailiff detail within their agency.

Opportunities for Bailiffs in a local, state, or federal court generally become available as officers retire or transfer to other assignments. Additional positions may be created by a court to meet needs, as long as funding is available.

## Advancement Prospects

Advancement in Bailiff details is limited. Bailiffs can become lead and supervisory Bailiffs.

As law enforcement officers, Bailiffs have the ability to develop a career according to their interests and ambitions. For example, deputy sheriffs can rise through the ranks to become sergeants, lieutenants, captains, and so on. They may stay with the Bailiff detail for as long as they are quali-

fied for the job. They can also seek assignments in other special details within their agency.

## Education and Training

Education requirements vary with the different agencies. Most sheriff's departments require Bailiffs to have a high school or general equivalency diploma. Some departments require an associate's degree or a minimum of 60 credits from an accredited college, preferably with course work in police science or other related fields. To become deputy U.S. marshals, applicants must have bachelor's degrees in law, criminal justice or other related field.

Law enforcement agencies or court systems train new Bailiffs for their positions. Through on-the-job training and formal instruction, they learn how to protect judges and juries, defend themselves in close quarters, handle prisoners and evidence, and so forth.

## Special Requirements

Most Bailiffs in municipal and state courts are required to be certified law enforcement officers. All Bailiffs must possess a valid driver's license. If Bailiffs are required to carry firearms while performing their duties, they must possess proper licensure.

## Experience, Skills, and Personality Traits

Requirements vary with the different agencies. For example, deputy sheriffs may volunteer for Bailiff duty after serving a specific number of years on their force.

Bailiffs must have effective communication and interpersonal skills as they must deal with coworkers, judges, attorneys, jurors, courtroom staff, and the general public. Having adequate reading and writing skills is also important. Additionally, Bailiffs need strong self-management skills, such as the ability to follow directions, work independently, handle stressful situations, meet deadlines, and organize and prioritize tasks.

Being perceptive, focused, dependable, trustworthy, respectful, friendly, patient, and calm are some personality traits that successful Bailiffs share.

## Unions and Associations

Bailiffs may join professional associations to take advantage of networking opportunities, educational programs, and other professional services and support. One association that specifically serves the interests of Bailiffs is the International Association of Court Officers and Services, Inc.

Bailiffs, who are deputy sheriffs, belong to regional or state sheriff unions and associations. They might also join the National Sheriffs' Association or its affiliate, the American Deputy Sheriffs' Association.

For contact information for the above organizations, see Appendix IV.

**Tips for Entry**

1. Knowledge of office practices, court procedures, legal terminology, and legal forms can enhance your chances of obtaining a Bailiff position.
2. Talk with Bailiffs to learn more about their jobs. Ask them to suggest paralegal, law, or criminal justice courses that may be helpful to prepare for a career as a Bailiff.
3. As a deputy sheriff, let the unit commander know of your interest, especially before you are eligible or before an opening is available.
4. To learn more about state and federal court systems on the Internet, enter the keywords *judicial systems* or *state court systems* into a search engine to get a list of Web sites.

# CORRECTIONAL OFFICER (SHERIFF'S DEPARTMENT)

## CAREER PROFILE

**Duties:** Maintain order, enforce rules and regulations, supervise prisoners and their activities in county jails and other county correctional facilities

**Alternate Title(s):** Jailer, Detention Officer

**Salary Range:** $22,000 to $54,000

**Employment Prospects:** Excellent

**Advancement Prospects:** Good

**Prerequisites:**

**Education or Training**—High school diploma

**Experience**—Requirements vary with the different sheriff's departments

**Special Skills and Personality Traits**—Critical-thinking, supervisory, interpersonal, communication, writing, and self-management skills; be organized, calm, trustworthy, self-motivated, and reliable

## CAREER LADDER

```
┌─────────────────────────────────┐
│           Sergeant              │
└─────────────────────────────────┘

┌─────────────────────────────────┐
│      Correctional Officer       │
└─────────────────────────────────┘

┌─────────────────────────────────┐
│   Correctional Officer Trainee  │
└─────────────────────────────────┘
```

## Position Description

Sheriff's Correctional Officers are responsible for the supervision of inmates in county jails and other correctional facilities to prevent escapes, fights, and other disturbances. These correctional facilities hold persons who have been arrested and are awaiting court hearings or trials, as well as those who have been convicted and sentenced to serve time in jails. State or federal prisoners are sometimes housed in county correctional facilities when there is insufficient space in state or federal prisons.

Correctional Officers are sworn law enforcement officers whose authority extends only to within correctional facilities. They are responsible for maintaining safe, secure, and orderly environments. Correctional Officers supervise inmates and their activities, such as eating, exercising, showering, working, seeing visitors, and making phone calls. When needed, Correctional Officers obtain or provide medical help for inmates. In addition, they settle arguments and break up fights between inmates. They enforce discipline when prisoners become disorderly or break rules or regulations. When it is warranted, Correctional Officers use physical means to control inmates who become violent. Correctional officers keep a daily record of every inmate's activities, such as what they did, who visited them and any violations they committed.

Correctional Officers make routine checks throughout the institution for unsanitary conditions and fire hazards as well as signs of tampering around windows, doors, locks, or gates. They also perform routine inspections of cells and of prisoners for weapons, drugs, and other contraband. Furthermore, Correctional Officers monitor mail and screen visitors for any prohibited items.

In direct supervision jails, Correctional Officers work in the same space where prisoners live. There are no bars or gates to separate the Correctional Officers from the prisoners. Correctional Officers do not carry firearms in those jails. To maintain order and enforce regulations among prisoners, Correctional Officers use interpersonal and communication skills. Surveillance equipment is also used to help Correctional Officers monitor prisoner activity.

Sheriff's Correctional Officers perform various duties, such as:

• book prisoners into the facilities, which includes preparing arrest reports, fingerprinting prisoners, and taking their photographs

- interrogate prisoners about the charges against them
- take prisoner's belongings into custody, maintain them, and return them when prisoners are released
- distribute commissary items such as candy, snacks, and toilet articles as well as record payments on vouchers
- escort inmates to locations inside the jail as well as outside, such as to courtrooms and medical facilities
- help investigate any disturbances or crimes that are committed within the facilities
- search for escaped prisoners
- admit visitors as well as release them
- maintain a daily log of their activities

Correctional Officers work rotating shifts that include night, weekends, and holidays. On occasion, they may be required to work overtime.

## Salaries

Earnings for Correctional Officers vary, depending on such factors as their education, experience, job duties, and geographical location. The estimated annual salary for most Correctional Officers ranged between $22,440 and $54,260, according to the November 2003 *Occupational Employment Statistics* survey by the U.S. Bureau of Labor Statistics (BLS).

## Employment Prospects

Correctional Officers for county correctional facilities are employed by sheriff's departments. In many sheriff's departments, rookie deputy sheriffs are assigned to jail duty for a certain length of time before performing patrol duty. Some sheriff's departments have two distinct career lines—Correctional Officers and deputy sheriffs.

The BLS reports that employment for Correctional Officers, in general, is expected to increase by 21 to 35 percent through 2012. In addition to newly created positions, job openings will become available as officers retire, advance to higher positions, or transfer to other occupations. Some correctional facilities have trouble attracting and retaining qualified Correctional Officers due to low salaries and the rural location of the facilities.

## Advancement Prospects

With experience and further education and training, Correctional Officers can advance through the ranks of sergeant, lieutenant, and captain. Some Correctional Officers pursue other careers in corrections such as specialists, instructors, and parole officers.

## Education and Training

Sheriff's departments require a high school or general equivalency diploma. Some departments require an associate's degree or a minimum of 60 credits from an accredited

college, preferably with course work in police science, psychology, criminal justice, or other related field.

Many departments have a formal training program that trainees must complete before starting on the job or within their probationary period. Trainees receive instruction on institutional policies, regulations, and operations: custody and security procedures; self-defense skills; use of firearms; and other pertinent subject matter. Upon graduation, trainees receive on-the-job training under the supervision of senior officers.

## Experience, Skills, and Personality Traits

Requirements vary with the different sheriff's departments. Many departments hire applicants without any previous work experience in corrections. In departments that have no career Correctional Officer positions, applicants must first qualify as deputy sheriffs. (To learn more about deputy sheriff requirements, see pages 13–14.)

To perform well at their job, Correctional Officers must have excellent critical-thinking, supervisory, interpersonal, and communication skills. They also need adequate writing skills and strong self-management skills—such as the ability to get to work on time, follow directions, work independently, and handle stressful situations.

Being organized, calm, trustworthy, self-motivated, and reliable are some personality traits that successful Correctional Officers share.

## Unions and Associations

Sheriff's Correctional Officers might belong to the American Jail Association, an organization that provides professional support, networking, and training programs for jail personnel. (For contact information, see Appendix IV.) In addition, Correctional Officers might join regional and state deputy sheriff's associations or correctional officer organizations.

Many Correctional Officers are members of a union that represents them in contract negotiations for pay, benefits, and working conditions. It also handles any grievances that officers may have against their employers.

## Tips for Entry

1. Contact sheriff's departments or police departments to learn about job requirements and opportunities.
2. Obtain a bachelor's degree in criminal justice, public administration, social services, or other related field, if you are interested in pursuing a career in jail management and administration.
3. To learn about different county jail systems on the Internet, enter the keywords *county jail* or *county corrections facility* into a search engine to get a list of Web sites.

# CORRECTIONAL OFFICER (STATE OR FEDERAL)

## CAREER PROFILE

**Duties:** Enforce regulations of state or federal prisons and other correctional facilities; supervise the conduct and activities of prisoners; maintain the general well-being of prisoners

**Alternate Title(s):** Corrections Officer

**Salary Range:** $22,000 to $54,000

**Employment Prospects:** Excellent

**Advancement Prospects:** Good

**Prerequisites:**

**Education or Training**—High school diploma for state facilities; bachelor's degree for federal facilities; formal training and field training

**Experience**—Varies with the different institutions

**Special Skills and Personality Traits**—Leadership, supervisory, interpersonal, communication, and self-management skills; be calm, self-motivated, reliable, and trustworthy

## CAREER LADDER

```
┌─────────────────────────────┐
│   Supervisor or Sergeant    │
└─────────────────────────────┘

┌─────────────────────────────┐
│    Correctional Officer     │
└─────────────────────────────┘

┌─────────────────────────────┐
│ Correctional Officer Trainee│
└─────────────────────────────┘
```

## Position Description

Many Correctional Officers are employed by state and federal prisons, penitentiaries, and other correctional facilities. They are responsible for maintaining a safe, secure, and orderly environment for adults or juvenile prisoners. Along with enforcing institutional policies and regulations, Correctional Officers supervise the conduct and activities of the prisoners.

Assigned to a variety of duty posts, Correctional Officers oversee prisoners 24 hours a day. They supervise inmates while they eat, bathe, exercise, work, attend educational programs, talk with visitors and pursue other activities. They conduct accurate counts of inmates. They keep constant watch for violations as well as for signs of unruly and unusual behavior that may turn into fights or disturbances. If inmates need medical attention, Correctional Officers provide basic first aid, CPR, or get medical help. In some facilities, Correctional Officers provide individual or group counseling.

Correctional Officers also make routine inspections of cells and of prisoners for weapons, drugs and other contraband. Furthermore, Correctional Officers monitor mail and screen visitors for any prohibited items. Correctional Offi-

cers escort high-security inmates to locations within the facilities. Correctional Officers may also transport prisoners to outside locations such as courts, medical centers, and other correctional facilities.

When fights or disturbances occur, Correctional Officers break them up immediately, using physical force, firearms, chemical agents, and other necessary equipment, if necessary. In addition, Correctional Officers make daily written and oral reports of prisoners' activities—what activities they did, who visited them, any violations they committed, and so on.

Security duties are also part of Correctional Officers' jobs. They perform routine security and safety checks throughout the institution. They also stand guard at gates and in courtyards as well as hold security positions in security towers above the premises.

Depending on the facilities, Correctional Officers may have specialized duties. In maximum security facilities where very dangerous offenders are housed, Correctional Officers monitor inmates' activities with surveillance equipment from a centralized control center. In direct supervision prisons, Correctional Officers do not carry firearms. They work in the same space where prisoners live without any bars or gates to separate them from the prisoners. In these facilities, Correctional Officers use interpersonal communication skills to maintain order and enforce regulations among prisoners.

Correctional Officers work eight-hour days, five days a week. They work rotating shifts, which include nights, weekends, and holidays. They are sometimes required to work overtime.

## Salaries

Earnings for Correctional Officers vary, depending on such factors as their education, experience, job duties, employer, and geographical location. According to the November 2003 *Occupational Employment Statistics* survey by the U.S. Bureau of Labor Statistics (BLS), the estimated annual salary for most Correctional Officers ranged between $22,440 and $54,260.

Entry-level federal Correctional Officers earn a salary that begins at either the GS-5 or GS-6 level. (GS stands for General Schedule, the pay schedule for most federal employees). In 2005, the annual basic pay for GS-5 to GS-6 levels ranged from $24,677 to $35,760.

## Employment Prospects

State and federal prisons, penitentiaries, community correctional work centers, and other correctional facilities hire Correctional Officers. Most job opportunities are for replacements for Correctional Officers who are retiring, resigning, or transferring to other positions. This field is considered one of the fastest-growing occupations through the year 2012. Additional positions are expected to be created due to the increasing rate of criminal convictions and longer sentencing as well as the expansion and construction of prisons and other correctional facilities.

## Advancement Prospects

With additional experience, education, and training, Correctional Officers can advance to supervisory and administrative positions, including warden—the highest position in corrections. They can also pursue other careers within corrections, such as probation and parole officers, specialists, and instructors.

Federal Correctional Officers are eligible for retirement after 25 years of service or upon reaching age 50 if they have 20 years of service.

## Education and Training

State institutions require applicants to have a high school or general equivalency diploma. Federal institutions require bachelor's degrees unless applicants fulfill the work experience requirement.

Entry-level Correctional Officers must complete formal instruction and field training, which cover areas such as institutional regulations and operations, constitutional law,

cultural awareness, self-defense, and use of firearms. Federal Correctional Officer trainees complete specialized instruction at the Federal Bureau of Prisons residential training center in Glynco, Georgia.

## Experience, Skills, and Personality Traits

Experience requirements vary with the different state institutions. Some institutions require previous work experience in corrections or other related area, including military service. For federal entry-level Correctional Officer positions, applicants without bachelor's degrees must have three years of general work experience that has involved supervision, teaching, social casework, rehabilitation counseling, management, or professional sales.

In general, applicants must be U.S. citizens who are between 18 and 21 years old and must have no felony convictions. The maximum age for federal applicants is 36 years old. Applicants must meet other requirements that vary with the state and federal institutions.

State and federal Correctional Officers must have excellent leadership, supervisory, interpersonal, and communication skills. They also need observational skills as well as self-management skills—such as the ability to follow directions, work independently, handle stressful situations, and organize and prioritize tasks. Some personality traits that successful Correctional Officers share include being calm, self-motivated, reliable, and trustworthy.

## Unions and Associations

Correctional Officers might belong to regional or state professional Correctional Officer associations, including labor unions. A national organization that Correctional Officers might join is the American Correctional Association. (For contact information, see Appendix IV.) Joining such organizations affords Correctional Officers the opportunity to network with peers and obtain certification, continuing education, job listings, and other professional services and support.

## Tips for Entry

1. Contact the state or federal correctional facility where you are interested in working, and obtain information about job requirements and openings.
2. To enhance your opportunities in this field, take college courses in psychology, criminal justice, police science, criminology, and other related areas.
3. Participate in volunteer programs that work with juvenile and adult offenders and prisoners to gain valuable experience as well as learn if corrections is the field you want to pursue.
4. Many state correctional facilities have Web sites on the Internet. To get a list of Web sites, enter the keywords *state department of corrections*. To learn about the federal prison systems, visit the Federal Bureau of Prisons Web site. Its address is http://www.bop.gov.

# PROBATION OFFICER

## CAREER PROFILE

**Duties:** Conduct pre-sentence investigations of convicted offenders to help courts determine the appropriate type of sentence; supervise convicted offenders while they complete the terms of their probations

**Alternate Title(s):** None

**Salary Range:** $26,000 to $66,000

**Employment Prospects:** Fair

**Advancement Prospects:** Limited

**Prerequisites:**

**Education or Training**—Bachelor's degree; certified training

**Experience**—One to two years of related work experience

**Special Skills and Personality Traits**—Communication, interpersonal, computer, writing, supervisory, investigative, teamwork, and self-management skills; be patient, persistent, ethical, detail-oriented, flexible, courteous, objective, and realistic

## CAREER LADDER

```
+-----------------------------+
|   Senior Probation Officer  |
+-----------------------------+

+-----------------------------+
|      Probation Officer      |
+-----------------------------+

+-----------------------------+
|   Probation Officer Trainee |
+-----------------------------+
```

## Position Description

Probation Officers work with convicted offenders who receive suspended sentences—that is, they are placed on probation rather than serve time in jail or prison. Often characterized as part police officer and part social worker, Probation Officers oversee juvenile or adult probationers, or offenders. They make sure that probationers are completing the specified court plans under which they were conditionally released back into their communities. In addition, Probation Officers ensure the safety and protection of the communities. Because of the danger involved in their jobs, some Probation Officers are authorized to carry firearms.

Probation Officers perform several duties. One major duty is conducting pre-sentence investigations on offenders to help the courts determine suitable sentences for them, which may include probation, jail or prison sentence, or both. Probation Officers gather background information about the offenders, including their criminal history, work history, and so on. They review various records such as police reports, police records, medical files, and personnel records. They interview victims, police officers, and other individuals who have relevant information about the crime

or offense. In addition, they interview offenders, family members, employers, counselors, and other individuals and professionals who may have pertinent facts about the offenders. Probation Officers evaluate all the facts and recommend rehabilitation or treatment plans for the offenders.

Another major duty is supervising convicted offenders who are on probation. All probationers have their own set of conditions for probation. For example, a convicted offender might get these conditions to complete during her 12 months on probation: do 500 hours of community service; meet regularly with a psychologist to deal with emotional problems; and stay away from certain individuals.

Probation Officers make sure each client (probationer who is on their caseload) understands the terms of his or her probation. They help every client obtain proper services and enroll in appropriate programs that may help him or her. In addition, Probation Officers make sure each client pays the fines, restitution, or reparations that courts have ordered him or her to pay. They keep in contact with every client, meeting regularly with each one. Furthermore, Probation Officers keep accurate case records on each client's progress and file written or oral reports with their supervisors. If progress for any client becomes negative, Probation Officers may submit a recommendation to court to suspend a client's probation.

In some agencies, Probation Officers are also assigned to work with parolees, or prisoners who are released before their sentence is completed. Probation Officers may have additional responsibilities, such as:

- represent the probation department in court to present probation reports or answer questions about probation recommendations
- operate work furloughs or other community correction programs
- perform intake services (the interviewing of offenders to determine if they should be placed under supervision rather than be brought to trial)
- enforce court orders such as arresting clients, performing searches for specific evidence, and seizing evidence
- train probation assistants and volunteers

Their work can be very stressful at times. In addition to carrying heavy caseloads, Probation Officers handle individuals who may be disturbed, upset, angry, hostile, or manipulative. They frequently travel to meet with clients. They work 40 hours a week, which may include nights and Saturdays to accommodate meetings with individuals who are unavailable during the day or weekdays. Probation Officers are on call 24 hours a day.

## Salaries

Earnings for Probation Officers vary, depending on such factors as their education, experience, employer, and geographical location. The estimated annual salary for most Probation Officers—who were employed by local and state governments—ranged between $26,070 and $65,850, according to the November 2003 *Occupational Employment Statistics* (OES) survey by the U.S. Bureau of Labor Statistics (BLS).

## Employment Prospects

More than 4,000 Probation Officers are employed by the U.S. Probation Offices in the 94 federal court districts. At the local and state level, the BLS reports (in its November 2003 OES survey) that an estimated 87,200 Probation Officers and correctional treatment specialists were employed in the United States.

According to the BLS, employment for Probation Officers is expected to increase by 10 to 20 percent through 2012. In addition to the creation of new positions, opportunities will become available as Probation Officers retire, advance to higher positions, or transfer to other occupations. A large number of Probation Officers are expected to retire through 2012. However, the creation of additional positions

or the maintenance of the current levels of staffing is dependent upon the availability of funding within an agency.

## Advancement Prospects

Supervisory and management opportunities in probation departments are limited to a few positions—supervisors, chief probation officers, and directors of probation departments. Many Probation Officers pursue career growth by way of salary increases and complexity of new assignments.

## Education and Training

In most agencies, the minimum education requirement is a bachelor's degree, preferably in criminal justice, social work, sociology, or other related field. Some agencies require an additional year of graduate level studies.

Probation Officer trainees must complete certified formal training as well as field training within their first year of employment.

## Experience, Skills, and Personality Traits

Requirements for entry-level positions vary from agency to agency. Many agencies hire recent college graduates without any previous related work experience. Some agencies hire non-college graduates if they have two years of full-time work experience in related areas, such as intake work, rehabilitation counseling, or community work that involves supervising ex-offenders.

Federal positions generally require one to three years of progressively responsible work in probation, pretrial services, parole, corrections, criminal investigations, or related fields.

In general, applicants must be U.S. citizens without any felony convictions. They must be in good physical shape and be emotionally stable. They usually need to be at least 21 years old. Applicants for federal positions must not have reached their 37th birthday upon their appointment.

Probation Officers must have excellent communication and interpersonal skills, as they must be able to work with people from diverse backgrounds. Their job also requires that they have strong computer and writing skills to complete the task of preparing accurate, concise, and comprehensive reports. Additionally, they must have supervisory, investigative, and teamwork skills as well as self-management skills, such as the ability to work independently, meet deadlines, handle stressful situations, and organize and prioritize tasks.

Being patient, persistent, ethical, detail-oriented, flexible, courteous, objective, and realistic are some personality traits that Probation Officers share.

## Unions and Associations

Probation Officers might belong to regional and state correctional associations as well as probation and parole officer associations. Two national organizations that Probation Officers might belong to are the American Probation and Parole Association and the American Correctional Association. (For contact information see Appendix IV.) Joining such organizations allows Probation Officers an opportunity to network with peers and obtain continuing education, training, and other professional services and support.

**Tips for Entry**

1. Contact probation departments directly, to learn about job openings, or job requirements.
2. While in college, do internships with probation departments, juvenile halls, or community-based programs that work with ex-offenders.
3. Many county probation departments use volunteers to assist probation officers with some of their routine office tasks. Find out if there are any programs in your area and join one to obtain valuable experience.
4. You can learn more about Probation Officers on the Internet. To find a list of relevant Web sites, enter the keywords *probation officers* or *probation departments* into a search engine. For a list of Web sites specifically about federal Probation Officers, enter the keywords *U.S. Probation Office.*

# PAROLE OFFICER

<table>
<tr><td>

## CAREER PROFILE

**Duties:** Help parolees adjust to living and working in their communities; supervise and counsel parolees until they have completed their sentences

**Alternate Title(s):** Parole Agent

**Salary Range:** $26,000 to $66,000

**Employment Prospects:** Fair

**Advancement Prospects:** Limited

**Prerequisites:**

    **Education or Training**—Bachelor's degree; certified training

    **Experience**—Some casework experience

    **Special Skills and Personality Traits**—Interpersonal, communication, computer, writing, supervisory, investigative, teamwork, and self-management skills; be calm, persistent, ethical, assertive, courteous, flexible, respectful, and confident

</td><td>

## CAREER LADDER

```
┌─────────────────────────────┐
│    Senior Parole Officer     │
└─────────────────────────────┘


┌─────────────────────────────┐
│       Parole Officer         │
└─────────────────────────────┘


┌─────────────────────────────┐
│    Parole Officer Trainee    │
└─────────────────────────────┘
```

</td></tr>
</table>

## Position Description

Parole Officers work with prisoners who have been granted a conditional release from prison before the end of their prison sentences. They help juvenile and adult prisoners adjust to living and working within society and staying away from further criminal activities. In addition, Parole Officers watch over parolees for the public safety, supervising them until they have completed the time left on their prison sentences.

As part of their responsibilities, Parole Officers help their clients (parolees who are on their caseloads) find jobs and residences. They refer clients to educational and training programs, counseling services, drug rehabilitation programs, and other services or programs that may help their clients make honest livings and lead productive lives. In addition, they enforce any fines or other payments that their clients are ordered to pay for their crimes.

Furthermore, Parole Officers monitor the progress of their clients by maintaining regular contact with them. For some clients, Parole Officers might contact them once every two weeks; with others, contact may be needed every few days. Parole Officers meet with their clients in parole offices and sometimes in clients' homes. Parole Officers may also talk with employers, family members, counselors, and others to learn how their clients are doing.

Parole Officers maintain accurate records on their clients, and submit regular oral and written reports to their supervisors and parole board on their clients' progress. If a client violates any terms of his or her parole, Parole Officers may recommend to the parole board that the client's parole be suspended. If the parole board agrees, the client is sent back to prison.

On occasion, Parole Officers may enforce court orders such as arresting their clients, conducting searches, and seizing evidence. Because of the danger involved in their jobs, some Parole Officers are authorized to carry firearms.

Many Parole Officers also perform pre-parole investigations to help parole boards decide whether prisoners should be granted parole and, if so, determine the terms of their parole. Parole Officers review prisoner records and any other pertinent reports. They interview correction officers and other correction staff. Through interviews with prisoners, family members, and others in the community, Parole Officers gather facts about prisoners' lives before their incarceration along with information about their families and job prospects.

Depending on the agency, Parole Officers might also work with probationers, or convicted offenders who receive suspended prison or jail sentences and instead serve probation under specified conditions.

Parole Officers' work can be very stressful at times. Their job requires them to carry heavy caseloads and continually meet deadlines. In addition, they handle individuals who may be disturbed, upset, angry, hostile, or manipulative.

Parole Officers often travel in their job to meet with clients and other individuals pertinent to their clients. They work 40 hours a week, usually with a flexible schedule in order to accommodate meetings with clients and others who are unavailable during the day and weekdays. Parole Officers are on call 24 hours a day.

## Salaries

Earnings for Parole Officers vary, depending on such factors as their education, experience, employer, and geographical location. The U.S. Bureau of Labor Statistics (BLS) reports in its November 2003 *Occupational Employment Statistics* survey that the estimated annual salary for most probation officers and correctional treatment specialists ranged between $26,070 and $65,850 (Note: The estimates are for Parole Agents who were employed by local and state governments.)

## Employment Prospects

Parole Officers are hired by parole divisions at the county and state levels. At the federal government levels, probation officers perform the duties of Parole Officers.

Most openings become available when Parole Officers retire, resign, or become promoted to higher positions. The creation of additional positions or maintenance of current level of staffing is dependent upon agencies' budgets.

## Advancement Prospects

Supervisory and management opportunities are limited to a few positions—supervisors, unit managers, and directors. Many Parole Officers pursue career growth by way of salary increases and complexity of new assignments.

## Education and Training

Most agencies require applicants to have bachelor's degrees, preferably in criminal justice, social work, sociology, or other related field. Some employers require an additional year of graduate level studies. Some employers are willing to hire applicants without college degrees if they have sufficient work experience.

Parole Officer trainees must complete certified training within their first year of employment.

## Experience, Skills, and Personality Traits

Many agencies require entry-level applicants to have one to three years of casework experience in a social service, correctional institution, or other agency.

In addition, applicants must be U.S. citizens without any felony convictions. They must also be in good physical shape and be emotionally stable.

Parole Officers need effective interpersonal and communication skills, as they must be able to work with people from diverse backgrounds. Their job also requires that they have strong computer, writing, supervisory, investigative, and teamwork skills. In addition, they must have excellent self-management skills, such as the ability to work independently, meet deadlines, handle stressful situations, and organize and prioritize tasks.

Some personality traits that successful Parole Agents share include being calm, persistent, ethical, assertive, courteous, flexible, respectful, and confident.

## Unions and Associations

Parole Officers might belong to regional and state correctional associations and probation and parole officer associations. Two national organizations that they might belong to are the American Probation and Parole Association and the American Correctional Association. (For contact information, see Appendix IV.) Joining such organizations gives Parole Officers the opportunity to network with peers and obtain continuing education, training, and other professional services and support.

## Tips for Entry

1. To learn about job openings or job requirements, contact parole divisions directly.
2. While in college, do internships with probation departments, juvenile halls, or community programs that work with ex-offenders.
3. Volunteer with police departments or sheriff's departments to gain useful experience for this field.
4. To learn about some parole divisions on the Internet, enter the keywords *parole division* or *parole services* into a search engine to get a list of Web sites.

# COMPLIANCE INSPECTIONS

# FOOD INSPECTOR

## CAREER PROFILE

**Duties:** Enforce federal laws and regulations relating to the production of fresh and processed meat, poultry, and eggs; perform inspections of slaughterhouses or processing plants

**Alternate Title(s):** None

**Salary Range:** $25,000 to $40,000 for entry-level positions

**Employment Prospects:** Good

**Advancement Prospects:** Limited

**Prerequisites:**

**Education or Training**—Bachelor's degree

**Experience**—Work experience in the food industry or a food processing environment

**Special Skills and Personality Traits**—Teamwork, communication, writing, and observational skills; be detail-oriented, responsible, decisive, accurate, calm, and impartial

## CAREER LADDER

```
+---------------------------+
|   Senior Food Inspector   |
+---------------------------+

+---------------------------+
|      Food Inspector       |
+---------------------------+

+---------------------------+
|  Food Inspector Trainee   |
+---------------------------+
```

## Position Description

Food inspectors in the U.S. Food Safety and Inspection Service (FSIS) play a vital role in ensuring the safety and freshness of the meat, poultry, and egg products that are eaten every day in the United States. The FSIS, part of the U.S. Department of Agriculture (USDA), is responsible for enforcing federal agricultural laws and regulations that relate to the production of raw meat, chicken, and eggs as well as their processed by-products. The FSIS Food Inspectors' job is to perform inspections at slaughterhouses and processing plants to ensure that these companies are in compliance with the appropriate laws and regulations.

Food Inspectors examine raw beef, pork, lamb, chicken, and turkey and eggs to make sure that products are wholesome and free of disease. In addition, they inspect about 250,000 different processed meat and poultry products. These include hams, sausage, soups, stews, pizzas, frozen dinners, and any product containing 2% or more of cooked poultry or at least 3% of raw meat. They also inspect liquid, frozen, and dried egg products.

Food Inspectors normally work in teams at the sites. At slaughterhouses, they perform antemortem (before animals are slaughtered) and postmortem (after animals are slaugh-

tered) inspections. Antemortem inspections involve visual examinations of livestock or poultry in confined areas where they are kept. Food Inspectors also make sure that sanitary equipment and handling practices are used. The postmortem inspection involves examining carcasses and animal body parts for visible defects that can affect safety and quality. Food Inspectors use sharp steel knives or hooks to perform their inspections, working rapidly and accurately.

At processing plants, Food Inspectors monitor all stages of the processing operations to ensure that approved procedures are followed. Food Inspectors not only inspect the processed meat and poultry but also all the other ingredients that make up the final products. Additionally, they test for the presence of salmonella and other bacteria that may cause food poisoning. Furthermore, they check that nutrition guidelines and safe food handling labels are accurate.

Food Inspectors work in hazardous working environments. They must be attentive to slippery floors, vats of extremely hot water, high voltage equipment, and large machines. In addition, they work in extreme climates (cold, damp, dry) throughout the plant. Furthermore, their duties often require moderate lifting, walking, and long hours of standing.

Food Inspectors generally work 40 hours per week. Some Food Inspectors are hired to intermittent positions; they are limited to working a certain number of hours in a service year. (In 2004, these inspectors were limited to working 1,280 hours.)

## Salaries

Earnings for Food Inspectors vary, depending on such factors as their education, experience, pay level, and geographical location. Most FSIS Food Inspectors enter at either the GS-5 or GS-7 level on the general schedule (GS), the pay schedule for most federal employees. In 2005, the annual basic pay for the GS-5 and GS-7 levels ranged from $24,677 to $39,738. Employees who live in metropolitan areas, such as Dallas and Chicago, typically earn higher salaries.

## Employment Prospects

The FSIS employs more than 7,500 Food Inspectors throughout the United States and Puerto Rico. In general, most job opportunities become available as Food Inspectors retire, resign, or advance to higher positions. Experts in the field expect opportunities to be favorable in the next few years due to the high number of Food Inspectors who are becoming eligible for retirement.

## Advancement Prospects

Supervisory and management opportunities are available, but limited. Many Food Inspectors pursue career growth by way of wage increases and complexity of new assignments.

FSIS Food Inspectors can pursue other career paths within the U.S. Department of Agriculture such as becoming consumer safety inspectors or import inspectors. With additional experience and education, individuals can also seek professional and scientific careers within the agency.

## Education and Training

To qualify at the GS-5 level, applicants must have bachelor's degrees with at least twelve semester hours in biology, physical science, mathematics, or agricultural science.

New employees receive on-the-job training in their duties and responsibilities, federal laws and regulations, and inspection procedures. When required, they receive classroom training at the FSIS Training Center in College Station, Texas.

Throughout their careers, Food Inspectors enroll in educational programs, training seminars, conference workshops, and so on to increase their knowledge and update their skills.

## Experience, Skills, and Personality Traits

Applicants must be U.S. citizens.

If applicants do not have a bachelor's degree, they may qualify for a position based on their work experience. To qualify at the GS-5 level, applicants must have one year of specialized work experience in the food industry or in a food-processing environment at which they followed standards of quality and approved production methods to make food products. For example, applicants may have gained experience through such positions as being a meat butcher, quality control technician in a food manufacturing plant, food processor, large restaurant chef, or chicken farm manager.

Applicants may qualify at the GS-7 level by having one year of full-time experience performing regulatory duties as a Food Inspector. They may have worked for a state or federal agency or for a military service.

To perform their work effectively, Food Inspectors need excellent teamwork and communication skills as well as strong writing and observational skills. Being detail-oriented, responsible, decisive, accurate, calm, and impartial are some personality traits that successful Food Inspectors share.

## Unions and Associations

FSIS Food Inspectors may join the American Federation of Government Employees, the largest federal employee union. In addition to union representation, members can obtain legal representation, technical expertise, informational services, and other professional support and services.

## Tips for Entry

1. Students who will be earning a bachelor's degree may apply for a Food Inspector position up to nine months before they graduate.
2. For information about FSIS jobs and its application process, visit the Food Safety Jobs Web site at http://www.foodsafetyjobs.gov. You can also call the FSIS human resources department at (800) 370-3747.
3. Applicants must be able to lift and carry heavy objects. They also need good eye-hand coordination and dexterity of the arms, hands, and fingers.
4. Many Food Safety and Inspection Service offices hire Food Inspectors for part-time work or for an on-call basis. These positions may eventually lead to full-time work.
5. You can learn more about the Food Safety and Inspection Service on the Internet. Its Web address is http://www.fsis.usda.gov.

# AGRICULTURAL COMMODITY GRADER

## CAREER PROFILE

**Duties:** Inspect, grade, and certify the quality of over 200 commodities based on federal regulations and standards

**Alternate Title(s):** None

**Salary Range:** $25,000 to $40,000 for entry-level positions

**Employment Prospects:** Limited

**Advancement Prospects:** Limited

**Prerequisites:**

**Education or Training**—Bachelor's degree

**Experience**—Three years work experience without a bachelor's degree

**Special Skills and Personality Traits**—Organizational, critical-thinking, decision-making, interpersonal, communication, report-writing, and self-management skills; be tactful, courteous, respectful, precise, unbiased, reliable, efficient, and self-motivated

## CAREER LADDER

> **Senior Agricultural Commodity Grader**

> **Agricultural Commodity Grader**

> **Agricultural Commodity Grader Trainee**

## Position Description

Agricultural Commodity Graders work for the Agricultural Marketing Service, a division of the United States Department of Agriculture (USDA). Their job is to inspect, grade, and certify the quality of over 200 commodities, including cotton and cotton products, dairy products, dried beans, eggs, fruits, live cattle, meat, peanuts, poultry and poultry products, rabbits, sheep, swine, tree nuts, tobacco, vegetables, and wool.

USDA standards are developed for each particular product. For example, Agricultural Commodity Graders would follow a set of standards for grading each type of milk product—whole milk, low-fat milk, buttermilk, cream, non-fat dry milk, and so on.

When performing an inspection, Agricultural Commodity Graders choose samples from the container, lot, or line of products that are to be certified. They examine the samples to determine their conformance to weight, quantity, packing, packaging, labeling, and other specifications. They also look for abnormal growths, spoilage, and other defects. They may collect samples of suspected material or pests and send them to laboratories for analysis.

Upon completing their evaluation of the samples, Agricultural Commodity Graders assign a grade to the commodity being certified. For example, a container of fresh apples may be given one of seven grades, of which the top three are U.S. Extra Fancy, U.S. Fancy, and U.S. No. 1. Agricultural Commodity Graders issue certification papers or apply official grade markings directly to products or containers.

Agricultural Commodity Graders also perform inspections of processing plants and other facilities to determine their compliance with regulations. They check that sanitation is maintained throughout the plant as well as proper processing, packaging, storage, and transportation procedures are in compliance. Furthermore, they make sure only approved chemicals and pesticides are used.

The Agricultural Commodity Graders meet with owners or their representatives to discuss their findings. They may suggest to owners methods of improving quality or correcting any problems. In addition, Agricultural Commodity Graders complete all necessary reports and records.

Agricultural Commodity Graders work in many different settings, such as meat plants, fruit canneries, fish processing plants, milk processing plants, cheese factories, and chicken ranches. Whatever the setting, their duties often require moderate lifting, walking, and long hours of standing throughout their shift.

## Salaries

Earnings for Agricultural Commodity Graders vary, depending on such factors as their education, experience, pay level, and geographical location. These compliance inspectors usually enter at either the GS-5 or GS-7 level on the general schedule (GS), the pay schedule for most federal employees. In 2005, the annual basic pay for the GS-5 and GS-7 levels ranged from $24,677 to $39,738. Employees who live in metropolitan areas, such as San Francisco and New York, typically earn higher salaries.

## Employment Prospects

Agricultural Commodity Graders are stationed at Agricultural Marketing Service field offices throughout the United States. Job growth for Agricultural Commodity Graders is expected to increase by 3 to 9 percent through 2012. Most job opportunities will become available as officers retire, resign, or become promoted. The creation of additional job openings depends on the agency's needs and budget.

## Advancement Prospects

Supervisory and management opportunities are available, but limited. Many Agricultural Commodity Graders pursue career growth by way of wage increases and complexity of new assignments.

## Education and Training

Applicants who have no work experience need a bachelor's degree to qualify at the GS-5 grade. A combination of college credits and work experience may also qualify applicants at GS-5. To qualify at the GS-7 grade (without work experience), applicants must have a bachelor's degree and meet specific academic achievements. Applicants may also qualify by having completed one year of graduate-level work in agriculture, mathematics, engineering, science, business, or economics.

Trainees must successfully complete a training program that combines classroom and field training.

## Experience, Skills, and Personality Traits

Applicants must be U.S. citizens. Without a college degree, applicants must have three years of progressively responsible work experience to qualify at the GS-5 level. Their experience should demonstrate their abilities, skills, and knowledge to perform the duties of the position for which they are applying. They may have gained experience from jobs in quality assurance, food processing, administrative, and other related work.

To qualify at the GS-7 level, applicants must have one year of specialized experience in production, processing, quality control, inspection, research, or receiving in which they were making quality determinations of agricultural commodities based on standards.

Agricultural Commodity Graders must have excellent organizational, critical-thinking, and decision-making skills. They also need strong interpersonal, communication, and report-writing skills. Additionally, they should have adequate self-management skills. Being tactful, courteous, respectful, precise, unbiased, reliable, efficient, and self-motivated are some personality traits that successful Agricultural Commodity Graders share.

## Unions and Associations

Agricultural Commodity Graders may join a labor union, such as the American Federation of Government Employees, to represent them in contract negotiations. The union seeks to get the best contract terms in regard to pay, benefits, and working conditions.

## Tips for Entry

1. Contact a local Agricultural Marketing Service office for further information about work experience programs, internships, career information, and job vacancies.
2. For many positions, a valid driver's license is required.
3. Carefully read the qualifications for each pay grade level and determine the grade level at which you best qualify. If you qualify for a position, the agency will hire you only at the grade level at which you apply.
4. After you have filled out your job application, carefully go over it and make sure you have followed the instructions and answered all the questions completely.
5. You can learn more about the Agricultural Marketing Service on the Internet. Its Web address is http://www.ams.usda.gov.

# CONSUMER SAFETY INSPECTOR

## CAREER PROFILE

**Duties:** Enforce laws and regulations related to the production, handling, storing, and marketing of products sold to the general public; conduct inspections of facilities or products; investigate complaints

**Alternate Title(s):** None

**Salary Range:** $25,000 to $40,000, for entry-level positions

**Employment Prospects:** Good

**Advancement Prospects:** Limited

**Prerequisites:**

    **Education or Training**—Bachelor's degree

    **Experience**—Varies from agency to agency

    **Special Skills and Personality Traits**—Communication, interpersonal, public relations, teamwork, report-writing, and problem-solving skills; be observant, ethical, impartial, fair, tactful, courteous, and responsible

## CAREER LADDER

```
┌─────────────────────────────────────┐
│   Senior Consumer Safety Inspector   │
└─────────────────────────────────────┘

┌─────────────────────────────────────┐
│      Consumer Safety Inspector       │
└─────────────────────────────────────┘

┌─────────────────────────────────────┐
│  Consumer Safety Inspector Trainee   │
└─────────────────────────────────────┘
```

## Position Description

Consumer Safety Inspectors make sure that companies comply with federal and state laws that govern the production, handling, storing, and marketing of products that are sold to the public. These products include foods, infant formulas, animal feeds, drugs, medical equipment, blood products, vaccines, cosmetics, fabrics, clothing, toys, household products, appliances, furniture, sports equipment, computer software, paints, pesticides, bicycles, vehicles, and many others.

Working individually or in teams, Consumer Safety Inspectors examine products as well as the facilities where they are manufactured or processed. They make routine inspections and conduct investigations of complaints made by customers, employees, vendors, or consumer activist groups.

When examining products, Consumer Safety Inspectors look for impurities and defects that may be harmful to health. They use various tools—such as portable scales, cameras, ultraviolet lights, thermometers, chemical testing kits, and radiation monitors—to identify substances and sources of contamination. They may send product samples, collected as part of their examinations, to laboratories for analysis. Furthermore, Consumer Safety Inspectors check for improper packaging and labeling that may be deceptive or inaccurate.

As part of their facility inspections, Consumer Safety Inspectors monitor manufacturing practices or production processes and review quality control systems. They watch for violations of standards. After completing their inspections, they discuss their findings with plant managers or officials, cite violations, and suggest corrective measures.

Consumer Safety Inspectors prepare comprehensive reports and correspondence regarding their inspections; and, when necessary, compile evidence that may be used in legal proceedings. In addition, Consumer Safety Inspectors may be called to testify as expert witnesses on their findings and inspection methods.

Consumer Safety Inspectors work irregular hours. Some compliance officers work part-time or on an on-call basis. For many positions, officers travel to other cities and states to perform their duties.

## Salaries

Earnings for Consumer Safety Inspectors vary, depending on such factors as their experience, education, employer, and geographical location. Formal salary information for this occupation is unavailable. Entry-level inspectors in the Food Service and Inspection Service, an agency in the U.S.

Department of Agriculture, and other federal agencies, usually start at the GS-5 or GS-7 level on the General Schedule (GS), the pay schedule for most federal employees. In 2005, the annual basic pay for the GS-5 and GS-7 levels ranged from $24,677 to $39,738.

## Employment Prospects

Consumer Safety Inspectors work for various federal and state agencies that regulate products and processes that affect the public good. The Food and Drug Administration, the Consumer Product Safety Commission, and the Environmental Protection Agency are just a few federal agencies that employ Consumer Safety Inspectors.

Most job opportunities will become available as officers retire, resign, or become promoted. The creation of additional job openings depends on an agency's needs and budget.

## Advancement Prospects

Supervisory and management opportunities are available, but limited. Promotion is generally based on agency needs and individual merit. Many Consumer Safety Inspectors pursue career growth by way of wage increases and complexity of new assignments.

## Education and Training

Education requirements vary with the different agencies. In general, entry-level applicants must have a bachelor's degree, preferably in subjects that are related to the areas in which applicants would work. For example, Consumer Safety Inspectors who perform fish processing inspections might have a bachelor's degree in biological sciences, chemistry, food technology, nutrition, veterinary medical science, or other related scientific field.

Consumer Safety Inspectors must successfully complete training in applicable laws and inspection procedures. Training programs vary with the different agencies, but generally combine classroom and on-the-job training.

## Experience, Skills, and Personality Traits

Experience requirements vary with the different agencies. In general, applicants should have knowledge of the properties and characteristics of the products they would be inspecting along with basic skills in the techniques of collecting samples and performing field tests and examinations.

To perform effectively, Consumer Safety Inspectors must have excellent communication, interpersonal, and public relations skills. Additionally, they need strong teamwork, report-writing, and problem-solving skills. Being observant, ethical, impartial, fair, tactful, courteous, and responsible are some personality traits that successful Consumer Safety Inspectors share.

## Unions and Associations

Consumer Safety Inspectors might join professional associations to take advantage of networking opportunities, educational programs, and other professional services and resources. Some are also members of a labor union, which represents them in contract negotiations. The union seeks to get the best contract terms in regard to pay, benefits, and working conditions. It can also handle any grievances that inspectors may have against their employers.

## Tips for Entry

1. To learn about job vacancies in local and state governments, contact your state employment office. For federal government vacancies contact a local U.S. Office of Personnel Management (OPM): or visit its Web site (http://www.usajobs.opm.gov) on the Internet.
2. Every agency has specific job qualifications that applicants must meet. For example: the Food and Drug Administration requires applicants to be U.S. citizens and possess a valid driver's license.
3. Read vacancy announcements and job descriptions thoroughly and carefully.
4. A willingness to relocate to another city or state may enhance your employability.
5. Use the Internet to learn more about consumer safety. For a list of of relevant Web sites, enter the keywords *consumer safety* or *consumer product safety* into a search engine.

# ENVIRONMENTAL HEALTH INSPECTOR

## CAREER PROFILE

**Duties:** Enforce laws and regulations that protect the public from environmental health hazards

**Alternate Title(s):** Sanitarian, Environmental Health Officer, Public Health Inspector

**Salary Range:** $34,000 to $65,000

**Employment Prospects:** Fair

**Advancement Prospects:** Limited

**Prerequisites:**

    **Education or Training**—Bachelor's degree

    **Experience**—Varies from agency to agency

    **Special Skills and Personality Traits**—Communication, writing, interpersonal, critical-thinking, and self-management skills; be detail-oriented, responsible, impartial, ethical, fair, tactful, and courteous

    **Licensure/Certification**—Professional certification

## CAREER LADDER

```
┌─────────────────────────────────────────┐
│   Senior Environmental Health Inspector   │
└─────────────────────────────────────────┘

┌─────────────────────────────────────────┐
│      Environmental Health Inspector       │
└─────────────────────────────────────────┘

┌─────────────────────────────────────────┐
│   Environmental Health Inspector Trainee  │
└─────────────────────────────────────────┘
```

## Position Description

Environmental Health Inspectors work for local, state, and federal public health departments. Their job is to enforce laws and regulations that protect the public from environmental health hazards such as unsanitary food handling, pest infestations, air pollution, and tainted water supplies. They inspect restaurants, food processing plants, schools, public buildings, apartment buildings, sewage disposal systems, waste disposal sites, recreational areas, swimming pools, refineries, factories, or other public and private establishments. These are just a few of the types of inspections they conduct:

- They examine the way food is handled, processed, and served in restaurants, hospitals, schools, and other institutions.
- They check the cleanliness and safety of food and drink as they are produced in food and beverage processing plants. In addition, they examine how sewage, refuse, and garbage are treated and disposed.
- They determine the nature and cause of air or water pollution in refineries, factories, and other facilities; and if necessary, initiate action to stop further pollution.
- They inspect private and public dwellings and buildings for insect and rodent infestation.

- They survey swimming pools and other public bathing places for unsanitary conditions.

In large public health departments, Environmental Health Inspectors usually specialize in a particular area such as waste control, institutional sanitation, or water pollution. In rural areas and small towns, Environmental Health Officers are responsible for all environmental health inspections.

Environmental Health Inspectors perform routine inspections as well as investigate consumer or employee complaints. Their inspections involve performing visual examinations, conducting field tests, and collecting samples that they send to laboratories for analysis.

Upon completing an inspection, they review their findings with owners or employers and issue citations for any violations. Environmental Health Inspectors may initiate court complaints if violations are not corrected. Some inspectors have the authority to issue citations for owners or employers to appear in court. Furthermore, Environmental Health Inspectors help in preparing evidence and testifying in court trials.

In addition, Environmental Health Inspectors perform these duties:

- evaluate license applications and construction plans to make sure owners would be in compliance with relevant environmental health codes
- provide education and training programs about public health and environmental standards
- investigate sudden epidemic outbreaks of hepatitis, tuberculosis, or other diseases within their communities
- recommend new or revised environmental health ordinances

Environmental Health Inspectors spend most of their time on field inspections and investigations that often require long hours of walking, standing, stooping, and climbing. Their work also involves accurately documenting inspections and preparing official reports and correspondence. They work a 40-hour week, and may sometimes work irregular hours.

## Salaries

Earnings for Environmental Health Inspectors vary, depending on such factors as their experience, education, employer, and geographical location. According to the Texas Health Careers Web site (http://www.texashealthcareers.org), environmental health specialists, which includes inspectors, generally earn between $34,000 to $65,000 per year.

## Employment Prospects

Most Environmental Health Inspectors work for local and state public health agencies. Some work for federal agencies that have environmental regulatory responsibilities, such as the Department of Energy and the Environmental Protection Agency.

Most job opportunities will become available as inspectors retire, resign, or become promoted. The creation of additional job openings depends on the agency's needs and budget.

## Advancement Prospects

Supervisory and management opportunities are available, but limited to lead officer, supervisor, assistant chief, and director positions. Many Environmental Health Inspectors pursue career growth by way of wage increases and complexity of new assignments.

Research work, teaching, consultation work, or employment in the private sector are other career paths that Environmental Health Inspectors might pursue.

## Education and Training

In general, applicants must have a bachelor's degree in environmental health or in the physical or biological sciences.

Some agencies accept a combination of college study and work experience. Trainees must successfully complete their agency's training program on applicable laws and inspection methods and techniques.

## Special Requirements

Applicants may be required to possess professional certification that is granted by a state agency or professional association. Entry-level candidates may be expected to obtain certification within a certain time frame.

## Experience, Skills, and Personality Traits

Experience requirements vary from agency to agency. Normally, entry-level applicants must have a practical knowledge of basic environmental health concepts, principles, methods, and techniques.

Environmental Health Inspectors must have excellent communication, writing, and interpersonal skills as well as critical thinking and self-management abilities. Being detail-oriented, responsible, impartial, ethical, fair, tactful, and courteous are some personality traits that successful Environmental Health Inspectors share.

## Unions and Associations

The National Environmental Health Association and the American Public Health Association are two national professional groups for Environmental Health Inspectors. Joining such organizations gives Environmental Health Inspectors the opportunity to network with peers and obtain professional support and services, such as certified training, continuing education programs, technical information, and job resources.

## Tips for Entry

1. High school courses that may help you prepare for a career in environmental health are math, life science, physical sciences, and English composition.
2. Network with professionals to learn more about the field and job opportunities. Attend professional conferences as well as join professional associations that allow student memberships.
3. For career information and job vacancies at the local level, contact the local Public Health Department or Office of Environmental Health.
4. Many local public health departments have Web sites on the Internet. To get a list of Web sites to browse, enter the keywords *local public health department* into a search engine.

# COMPLIANCE SAFETY AND HEALTH OFFICER

## CAREER PROFILE

**Duties:** Enforce occupational safety and health laws and regulations; inspect work sites for unsafe or unhealthy working conditions

**Alternate Title(s):** Safety Compliance Officer, OSHA Compliance Officer, Safety and Health Specialist

**Salary Range:** $26,000 to $75,000

**Employment Prospects:** Fair

**Advancement Prospects:** Limited

**Prerequisites:**

**Education or Training**—Bachelor's degree

**Experience**—Varies from agency to agency

**Special Skills**—Interpersonal, communication, writing, reading skills, observational, and problem-solving skills; be responsible, precise, detail-oriented, tactful, courteous, and fair

## CAREER LADDER

```
┌─────────────────────────────────────┐
│   Senior Compliance Safety and       │
│          Health Officer              │
└─────────────────────────────────────┘

┌─────────────────────────────────────┐
│  Compliance Safety and Health Officer │
└─────────────────────────────────────┘

┌─────────────────────────────────────┐
│     Compliance Safety and            │
│     Health Officer Trainee           │
└─────────────────────────────────────┘
```

## Position Description

Compliance Safety and Health Officers are government inspectors. They enforce federal and state laws that provide for safe and healthful working conditions in the workplace—factories, warehouse centers, medical facilities, construction sites, office buildings, stores, transportation companies, and so on. Their job is to look for hazards that may cause death or serious injury and illness to workers. They examine the work environment as well as the machinery and equipment at the work sites.

Compliance Safety and Health Officers follow routine procedures for performing inspections. They learn about the companies that they will inspect, and gather the necessary equipment and materials for testing health and safety hazards at the work sites. At the start of inspections, they meet with the employers, safety directors, or other authorized representatives. Compliance Safety and Health Officers explain the reason for their inspections. Examples are: a random inspection; an employee complaint; a recent serious accident; the company has a high rate of worker's compensation claims; or the company is in a high-hazard industry such as construction.

Usually accompanied by the employers or their representatives, inspectors walk through entire work sites or specific areas. They observe workers to determine compliance with safety precautions and the use of safety equipment. They also interview workers to learn about work practices, or, if it is the purpose of the inspection, about recent accidents. Compliance Safety and Health Officers might take photographs of the work environment. In addition, they review documents such as injury and illness records, safety training programs, and emergency action plans.

Compliance Safety and Health Officers have the authority to issue citations for any violations of safety and health standards. Upon completing their inspections, they discuss these violations with employers and may suggest ways to correct them. They give deadlines for correcting the violations as well as explain the penalties that may be imposed if violations are not corrected. They also explain to employers what their rights are.

If Compliance Safety and Health Officers find conditions that may cause imminent danger, they can ask employers to voluntarily correct the hazards immediately or remove workers from the areas. When employers are not willing to comply to the requests, they can initiate court complaints against them. Compliance Safety and Health Officers complete detailed inspection reports, which may be placed as evidence in legal proceedings. In addition, they may be asked to testify at court trials.

Their jobs are stressful; they sometimes handle employers' hostile objections to their inspections. In addition, officers are at risk of the same injuries and illnesses that workers are exposed to in hazardous work sites.

Compliance Safety and Health Officers often work irregular hours.

## Salaries

Earnings for Compliance Safety and Health Officers vary, depending on such factors as their experience, education, and geographical location. The estimated annual salary for most occupational health and safety specialists, which includes Compliance Safety and Health Officers, ranged between $26,480 and $74,520, according to the November 2003 *Occupational Employment Statistics* survey by the U.S. Bureau of Labor Statistics.

## Employment Prospects

Compliance and Safety Health Officers are employed by the Occupational Safety and Health Administration (OSHA), a bureau in the U.S. Department of Labor, as well as by OSHA programs operated by state departments of labor. In 2003, OSHA (the federal agency) employed more than 1,300 Compliance and Safety Health Officers, while more than 1,300 officers were employed by 26 state OSHA programs.

Most job opportunities will become available as officers retire, resign, or become promoted. The creation of additional job openings depends on an agency's needs and budget.

## Advancement Prospects

Supervisory and managerial prospects are rather limited. Many officers pursue career growth by way of wage increases and complexity of new assignments.

Two other career paths for Compliance Safety and Health Officers are working for private employers or becoming consultants.

## Education and Training

Education requirements vary with the different agencies. Employers prefer applicants who have a bachelor's degree with a major in safety, occupational health, industrial hygiene, or other related field.

Compliance Safety and Health Officers must successfully complete a training program that includes the study of occupational safety laws and regulations; industrial processes and hazards; and investigation and inspection techniques. Training programs usually involve both classroom and field training.

## Experience, Skills, and Personality Traits

Experience requirements vary from agency to agency. Entry-level applicants should have general experience in scientific or technical work using basic principles and concepts of the occupational safety and health field.

Compliance Safety and Health Officers must have excellent interpersonal skills along with good communication, writing, and reading skills. In addition, they need strong observational skills and problem-solving skills.

Being responsible, precise, detail-oriented, tactful, courteous, and fair are some personality traits that successful Compliance and Safety Health Officers share.

## Unions and Associations

Compliance and Safety Health Officers can join professional associations to take advantage of networking opportunities, educational programs, and other professional services and resources. One national society that serves the interests of occupational and safety professionals is the American Industrial Hygiene Association. For contact information, see Appendix IV.

## Tips for Entry

1. High school courses that are valuable for a career in occupational safety and health are chemistry, biology, math, psychology, writing, and communication. Enrolling in any of these college courses is also valuable: safety, occupational health, industrial hygiene, occupational medicine, toxicology, public health, mathematics, physics, chemistry, biological sciences, engineering, and industrial psychology.

2. To learn about job vacancies in local and state governments, contact your state employment office. For federal government vacancies, contact a local Office of Personnel Management (OPM). Or visit its Web site (http://www.usajobs.opm.gov) on the Internet.

3. To enhance your employability, you might obtain professional certification such as the Certified Safety Professional (CSP) or the Certified Industrial Hygienist (CIH) designation. (For further information about these certifications, see Appendix II.)

4. You can learn about the Occupational Safety and Health Administration on the Internet. Its Web address is http://www.osha.gov.

# AVIATION SAFETY INSPECTOR

## CAREER PROFILE

**Duties:** Enforce federal laws and regulations that govern the quality, performance, and safety of aircraft equipment and personnel

**Alternate Title(s):** A specific title such as Manufacturing Inspector or General Aviation Avionics Inspector

**Salary Range:** $36,000 to $69,000

**Employment Prospects:** Fair

**Advancement Prospects:** Limited

**Prerequisites:**

　　**Education or Training**—High school diploma

　　**Experience**—Depends on the type of inspection to be performed

　　**Special Skills and Personality Traits**—Self-management, communication, interpersonal, and report-writing skills; be reliable, dedicated, trustworthy, ethical, and impartial

　　**Licensure/Certification**—Driver's license; appropriate FAA certification

## CAREER LADDER

```
┌─────────────────────────────────┐
│           Supervisor            │
└─────────────────────────────────┘

┌─────────────────────────────────┐
│    Aviation Safety Inspector    │
└─────────────────────────────────┘

┌─────────────────────────────────┐
│ Aviation Safety Inspector Trainee │
└─────────────────────────────────┘
```

## Position Description

Aviation Safety Inspectors work for the Federal Aviation Administration (FAA), a division of the U.S. Department of Transportation. Their job is to enforce the FAA regulations that govern the quality, performance, and safety of aircraft equipment and personnel.

Aviation Safety Inspectors specialize in inspecting either commercial aircraft (such as air carriers) or general aviation aircraft (single- and multi-engine aircraft used for pleasure, air taxi, industry, and agriculture). In addition, Aviation Safety Inspectors specialize in different inspection areas, or options.

Some Aviation Safety Inspectors perform maintenance inspections. They evaluate aircraft mechanics and repair facilities as well as training programs for mechanics. In addition, these Aviation Safety Inspectors evaluate aircraft and related equipment for airworthiness. Other Aviation Safety Inspectors perform avionics (electronics systems) inspections. This includes the evaluation of avionics technicians and repair facilities as well as training programs for avionics technicians. These Aviation Safety Inspectors also

inspect aircraft and related equipment for airworthiness in regard to avionics programs.

Operations inspections is another option in which some Aviation Safety Inspectors specialize. These inspectors perform the evaluation of commercial and other aviation operations. In addition, they certify pilots, flight instructors, and other airmen. These Aviation Safety Inspectors also evaluate flight training programs along with their equipment and facilities.

Another option that some Aviation Safety Inspectors specialize in is manufacturing inspections. They evaluate any manufacturing facility that makes or modifies aircraft, aircraft equipment, and avionics equipment. They also inspect any originally built or modified aircraft, aircraft parts, and avionics equipment. Furthermore, they issue FAA certificates for all civil aircraft, such as imports, amateur-built planes, and modified planes.

Aviation Safety Inspectors have irregular work schedules, which may include weekends and holidays. They may work different hours from one day to the next, depending on the tasks that they are performing. Some inspections require traveling to other geographical locations for extended periods of time.

## Salaries

Annual earnings for Aviation Safety Inspectors vary, depending on such factors as their experience, education, and geographical location. Salaries are generally higher in metropolitan areas, such as Dallas and New York, where the cost of living is high.

Entry-level inspectors earn a salary at the FG-9 level of their pay schedule. Their salaries progress up to the FG-12 level. (Their pay schedule is equivalent to the general schedule [GS] for regular federal employees.) In 2004, the basic annual salary at FG-9 to FG-12 level ranged between $36,478 and $68,766.

## Employment Prospects

Aviation Safety Inspectors who perform air carrier, aviation avionics, maintenance, and operations inspections work out of Flight Standards division and district offices throughout the United States and Puerto Rico. Those performing manufacturing inspections work out of FAA Manufacturing Inspection division and district offices.

Competition for Aviation Safety Inspector jobs is high; and most job opportunities become available when inspectors retire, resign, or are promoted to higher positions. The creation of additional positions depends on the agency's needs, as long as funding is available.

## Advancement Prospects

Supervisory and management opportunities are available, but limited. Advancement is competitive, based on agency needs and individual merit. Many inspectors pursue career growth by way of wage increases and complexity of new assignments.

## Education and Training

Applicants must have at least a high school or general equivalency diploma.

New Aviation Safety Inspectors must successfully complete training programs which includes the study of federal air regulations, FAA policies, and inspection procedures.

## Special Requirements

Applicants must possess a valid driver's license.

Applicants seeking maintenance inspector positions must possess the FAA mechanic certificate with an airframe and powerplant (A&P) rating. Those seeking operations inspector positions must hold appropriate FAA pilot certificates and rankings as well as the first-class FAA medical certificate. Additionally, applicants may not have more than two FAA violations within the five years prior to their application.

## Experience, Skills, and Personality Traits

Applicants must be U.S. citizens, be fluent in the English language, meet physical requirements, and have no chemical dependencies or drug abuse problems.

Minimally, applicants must meet the following requirements for the different positions:

- Avionics inspector positions. Prior to applying, applicants must have completed three years of avionics work on the types of aircraft they would be inspecting. Additionally, they need three years of supervisory experience as a lead mechanic or repairman in an appropriate repair facility.
- Maintenance inspector positions. Prior to applying, applicants must have completed three years of aviation maintenance work on the types of aircraft they would be inspecting. Additionally, they need three years of supervisory experience as a lead mechanic or repairman in an appropriate repair facility.
- Operations inspector positions. Applicants must have completed a minimum of 1,500 hours of total flight time as pilots or copilots of appropriate aircraft. They must also meet flight and work experience requirements that are pertinent to the positions for which they are applying.
- Manufacturing inspector positions. Applicants must either have experience in quality control and quality assurance systems, and be knowledgeable about the manufacturing methods and techniques of aircraft, aircraft engines, and other aircraft parts, or they must have experience issuing certificates or approvals for the airworthiness of aircraft and aircraft parts, or in managing programs that lead to such issuance.

To perform their work effectively, Aviation Safety Inspectors need strong self-management skills, such as the ability to meet deadlines, work independently, handle stressful situations, and organize and prioritize tasks. They must also have excellent communication, interpersonal, and report-writing skills.

Some personality traits that successful Aviation Safety Inspectors share include being reliable, dedicated, trustworthy, ethical, and impartial.

## Unions and Associations

Aviation Safety Inspectors are members of the Professional Airways Systems Specialists, a union that represents them in contract negotiation. The union seeks the best contractual terms relating to pay, benefits, and working conditions.

## Tips for Entry

1. To obtain information about student internships, career information, job vacancies, and job applications, visit the FAA job Web site at http://jobs.faa.gov.
2. Applicants for Aviation Safety Inspector positions must apply online. If you do not have personal access

to the Internet, you can obtain access through public sources such as a library or a state employment office.

3. Eligible applicants for avionics, maintenance, operations, and manufacturing positions are placed on a national register for one year. As vacancies become available, regional offices will refer to the register for potential candidates. If you have not been selected for a position after a year, you must complete another application package if you wish to be considered an eligible applicant.

4. To learn more about aviation safety, check out the FAA Flight Standards Service Web site at http://www.faa.gov/avr/afs.

# BANK EXAMINER

## CAREER PROFILE

**Duties:** Investigate banking institutions to make sure they are safe, sound operations and are in compliance with federal or state banking laws

**Alternate Title(s):** Financial Examiner

**Salary Range:** $34,000 to $103,000

**Employment Prospects:** Limited

**Advancement Prospects:** Limited

**Prerequisites:**

**Education or Training—**Bachelor's degree

**Experience—**Varies with the different agencies

**Special Skills and Personality Traits—**Problem-solving, research, writing, computer, teamwork, interpersonal, and communication skills; be confident, tactful, articulate, persistent, analytical, creative, and self-motivated

## CAREER LADDER

```
Senior Bank Examiner
```

```
Bank Examiner
```

```
Assistant or Associate Examiner
```

## Position Description

Bank Examiners are responsible for enforcing banking laws and regulations and ensuring that banking institutions are in compliance. They conduct investigations on commercial banks, savings banks, credit unions, home financing institutions, and other banking institutions to determine whether they are safe and sound operations. These governmental inspectors are employed by state and federal banking regulatory agencies.

Bank Examiners usually work in teams of two or more. They make regularly scheduled inspections on banks within their assigned districts as well as conduct investigations of consumer complaints. Their examinations involve auditing financial records as well as reviewing bank procedures, board policies, and other relevant data. They may also interview bank officers and employees.

Upon compiling all pertinent data, Bank Examiners analyze the information to determine:

- the bank's financial condition
- how well management runs the bank
- whether there are adequate internal controls
- if there are any unsafe and unsound practices
- if the bank has violated any federal or state laws and regulations

Bank Examiners meet with bank officials after completing their assessments. The inspectors discuss their findings and make appropriate suggestions for correcting any weaknesses. In addition, Bank Examiners write a well-detailed report of their examinations and recommendations.

Bank Examiners work a 40-hour week, five days a week. Overnight travel is a frequent part of their job.

## Salaries

Earnings for Bank Examiners vary, depending on such factors as their experience, education, employer, and geographical location. According to U.S. Bureau of Labor Statistics (BLS) in its November 2003 *Occupational Employment Statistics* survey, the estimated annual salary for most financial examiners, which includes Bank Examiners, ranged between $34,040 and $102,590.

## Employment Prospects

At the state level, Bank Examiners are employed by state banking departments. At the federal level, Bank Examiners are employed by the Federal Reserve System and the Federal Deposit Insurance Corporation, two independent federal agencies. Federal examiners also work for the Office of the Comptroller of the Currency, an agency within the U.S. Department of the Treasury.

According to the BLS, job growth for financial (or bank) examiners is projected to increase by 3 to 9 percent through 2012. Most openings will become available as Bank Examiners advance to higher positions, retire, or transfer to other occupations.

## Advancement Prospects

Bank Examiners usually start in the position of assistant examiners or trainees. After a few years, assistant examiners can advance to Bank Examiners. Further advancement into supervisory and management positions is possible, but limited. Promotions are competitive, based on an agency's needs and on individual merit.

## Education and Training

In general, entry-level applicants must have a bachelor's degree in finance, accounting, business administration, economics, or other related field. In addition, applicants must have completed a minimum number of semester hours in accounting. (Many agencies allow a combination of education and experience to be substituted for the education requirement.)

Trainees must successfully complete training programs that include classroom, self-study, and on-the-job training.

Bank Examiners must undergo regular training throughout their careers to keep up with constantly changing laws and financial products and services.

## Experience, Skills, and Personality Traits

Requirements vary with the different agencies. For example, federal agencies require applicants without a bachelor's degree to have three years of work experience in a financial institution reviewing, analyzing, recommending, or approving loan applications or investment decisions. In addition, applicants must have knowledge of accounting or auditing principles.

To perform well at their job, Bank Examiners need excellent problem-solving, research, writing, and computer skills. They also need effective teamwork, interpersonal, and communication skills. Being confident, tactful, articulate, persistent, analytical, creative, and self-motivated are some personality traits that successful Bank Examiners share.

## Unions and Associations

Bank Examiners may join professional associations to take advantage of networking opportunities, educational programs, and other professional services and resources. For example, these professionals might join the Society of Financial Examiners or the Association of Certified Fraud Examiners.

Some Bank Examiners are members of a union, which represents them in contract negotiations with their employers. For example, Bank Examiners with the Federal Deposit Insurance Corporation and the Office of the Comptroller of the Currency are eligible to join the National Treasury Employees Union.

For contact information for the above organizations, see Appendix IV.

## Tips for Entry

1. To learn about internship and career opportunities, contact state banking departments and appropriate federal agencies directly.

2. Some state banking departments have Bank Examiner trainee programs for which persons who have little or no work experience may apply.

3. Applicants may be ineligible to apply at an agency if they are customers or own stock in banks that the agency regulates. In addition, they may be ineligible if they are related to any employee or paid consultant of any bank that the agency regulates.

4. To enhance your employability, you might obtain professional certification, such as the Certified Public Accountant (CPA) or Certified Fraud Examiner (CFE) designation. Talk with professionals, employers, or professional associations for advice about other certifications that you should obtain.

5. You can learn about various state and federal banking regulatory agencies on the Internet. The Web addresses for the federal agencies are: Office of the Comptroller of the Currency, http://www.occ.treas.gov; Federal Deposit Insurance Corporation, http://www.fdic.gov; and Federal Reserve System, http://www.federalreserve.gov. To find Web sites for state agencies, enter the keywords *state banking department* or *state department of commerce* into a search engine.

# REVENUE OFFICER

## CAREER PROFILE

**Duties:** Collect delinquent taxes for the federal or state governments; conduct investigations

**Alternate Title(s):** Revenue Compliance Officer, Revenue Agent (states)

**Salary Range:** $25,000 to $79,000

**Employment Prospects:** Limited

**Advancement Prospects:** Limited

**Prerequisites:**

**Education or Training**—Bachelor's degree

**Experience**—One or more years of relevant work experience

**Special Skills and Personality Traits**—Problem-solving, analytical, organizational, communication, interpersonal, report-writing, and interviewing skills; be calm, tactful, adaptable, resourceful, and persistent

## CAREER LADDER

```
┌─────────────────────────────┐
│   Senior Revenue Officer    │
└─────────────────────────────┘

┌─────────────────────────────┐
│      Revenue Officer        │
└─────────────────────────────┘

┌─────────────────────────────┐
│   Revenue Officer Trainee   │
└─────────────────────────────┘
```

## Position Description

Revenue Officers enforce tax laws and regulations. Their primary role is to collect delinquent taxes—income tax, sales tax, franchise tax, inheritance tax, estate tax, and so on—that are owed to the federal, state, and local governments. These compliance inspectors investigate cases that involve individuals, small businesses, corporations, non-profit organizations, and institutions.

Revenue Officers are usually assigned to cases involving specific types of tax collections. Their caseloads are often heavy. For example, federal Revenue Officers may be responsible for 40 to 100 cases of delinquent tax returns. With each case, Revenue Officers examine the tax return, checking the accuracy of the math as well as the taxpayer's compliance with tax laws. Upon reviewing a case, they send a collection notice to the taxpayer. They might also call or visit the taxpayer in person. If the Revenue Officers do not have current addresses, they then use professional skiptracing methods to locate taxpayers.

Revenue Officers conduct interviews with taxpayers and their representatives to gather more information for determining the amount of tax liability. They also hold meetings with taxpayers to discuss how they plan to resolve their unpaid tax debts. Revenue Officers may negotiate payment schedules (a minimum amount every month over a period of time) with taxpayers; but final approval for any payment schedule is made by their superiors.

When taxpayers do not pay, Revenue Officers conduct investigations into their financial background, learning what assets—wages, bank accounts, houses, cars, and other personal and real property—taxpayers own. Some Revenue Officers work complex or sensitive cases that involve surveillance as well as seizures of taxpayers' assets, which are done with warrants and other appropriate legal notices.

As part of their duty, Revenue Officers keep detailed, up-to-date records on all their cases. If any of their cases are brought to trial, they may help prepare documentary evidence for court officials. In addition, they may testify as witnesses in court.

Revenue Officers work independently under the supervision of a senior officer. They normally work five days a week, 40 hours per week. Some travel is required on their job.

## Salaries

Earnings for Revenue Officers vary, depending on such factors as their education, experience, employer, and geographical location. According to the November 2003 *Occupational Employment Statistics* survey by the U.S. Bureau of Labor

Statistics (BLS), the estimated annual salary for most tax collectors (or Revenue Officers) ranged between $24,910 and $78,810.

## Employment Prospects

Local and state Revenue Officers are employed by municipal and state government agencies that are responsible for tax collection. At the federal level, Revenue Officers work for the Internal Revenue Service, an agency within the U.S. Department of the Treasury.

Job seekers can expect strong competition. The BLS reports that employment for Revenue Officers is expected to grow more slowly than average (between 3 and 9 percent) through 2012. Openings generally become available as individuals advance to higher positions, retire, or transfer to other occupations. An agency may create additional positions to meet growing needs, as long as funding is available.

## Advancement Prospects

Supervisory and management opportunities are available, but limited. Many Revenue Officers pursue career growth by way of wage increases and complexity of new assignments.

With their experience and training, Revenue Officers can also become accountants, auditors, financial analysts, loan officers, or criminal investigators.

## Education and Training

In general, applicants should possess a bachelor's degree in business administration, accounting, public administration, law, police science, or other related field. (Experience or a combination of education and experience may substitute for the education requirement.)

Revenue Officer trainees must complete their agency's training program in tax laws and collection techniques. In many agencies, the program is one year long and includes both classroom and field training.

Throughout their careers, Revenue Officers enroll in workshops, seminars, and classes to update their knowledge and skills.

## Experience, Skills, and Personality Traits

Depending on the agency, applicants for entry-level positions need one or more years of relevant experience. They should be able to demonstrate business and financial practices related to the collections of delinquent accounts.

Revenue Officers must have excellent problem-solving, analytical, organizational, communication, and interpersonal skills to perform their work effectively. In addition, they need strong report-writing abilities as well as interviewing skills. Being calm, tactful, adaptable, resourceful, and persistent are some personality traits that successful Revenue Officers have in common.

## Unions and Associations

Many Revenue Officers belong to professional associations to take advantage of networking opportunities, educational programs, and other professional services and resources.

Some Revenue Officers are also members of a labor union, which represents them in contract negotiations with their employers. For example, IRS Revenue Officers are eligible to join the National Treasury Employees Union. (For contact information, see Appendix IV.)

## Tips for Entry

1. To get an idea if this is a field you would like to work in, obtain a job with the IRS or your state's revenue office. Many seasonal full-time and part-time positions as customer service representatives and tax examining clerks are available during tax periods.
2. You must be a U.S. citizen to obtain a job with the federal government.
3. Create a job "cheat" sheet to help you complete job applications easily. List all the information (such as work history, education, and job references) that you might provide on a job application. Make sure all names, addresses, and dates are accurate.
4. You can learn about career and job information with the IRS at its Web site, http://www.jobs.irs.gov.
5. Almost all state revenue departments have Web sites. To learn about a department, enter the name of the state and the keywords *department of revenue* into a search engine. (Example: *Tennessee Department of Revenue*).

# BUILDING AND CONSTRUCTION INSPECTIONS

# PLAN REVIEWER

## CAREER PROFILE

**Duties:** Review construction plans and specifications to make sure they are in compliance with building codes, regulations, and standards

**Alternate Title(s):** Plan Examiner

**Salary Range:** $27,000 to $67,000

**Employment Prospects:** Fair

**Advancement Prospects:** Limited

**Prerequisites:**

**Education or Training**—High school diploma

**Experience**—Have several years of experience in construction supervision or in building inspections

**Special Skills and Personality Traits**—Writing, communication, customer service, and problem-solving skills; the ability to interpret written materials, drawings, and other forms; be tactful, independent, ethical, honest, and dedicated

**Licensure/Certification**—Professional license or certification

## CAREER LADDER

```
┌─────────────────────────────┐
│    Senior Plan Reviewer     │
└─────────────────────────────┘

┌─────────────────────────────┐
│        Plan Reviewer        │
└─────────────────────────────┘

┌─────────────────────────────┐
│    Plan Reviewer Trainee    │
└─────────────────────────────┘
```

## Position Description

Plan Reviewers examine construction plans for residential, commercial, and industrial projects—houses, schools, churches, restaurants, banks, shopping centers, apartment buildings, high-rise office buildings, parking garages, factories, prisons, and other structures. Projects may be new constructions or renovations on existing structures. Plan Reviewers make sure that construction plans and specifications are in compliance with building codes, regulations, and standards. Building permits are issued to owners or contractors once Plan Reviewers approve their construction plans.

For every project, Plan Reviewers review all construction documents such as architectural and site plan drawings, structural design calculations, and soil reports. They also go over plans and specifications for some or all of the following installations, checking against appropriate codes:

- structural construction (foundation, walls, ceilings, doors, roofs, chimneys, and other parts of buildings)
- electrical installations (electrical wiring and fixtures for lighting systems, heating systems, and security systems)
- plumbing installations (water-supply systems, sewer systems)
- mechanical installations (heating, ventilation, air conditioning, and cooling systems)

They also make sure that construction plans are in compliance with fire protection regulations and zoning laws as well as appropriate state statutes that enforce such matters as energy conservation and access to the disabled.

Plan Reviewers do not approve plans if they find any noncompliance with codes or problems such as the wrong types of building materials being used. Plan Reviewers record the deficiencies and later meet with owners and design professionals to explain code violations or other problems. When documents are corrected, they are resubmitted to Plan Reviewers for another examination.

Plan Reviewers also have other duties, which vary from agency to agency. Some duties may include:

- keeping status reports of all construction plans under review up to date

- explaining building codes, laws, and standards to the public, contractors, architects, and other building officials
- maintaining a library of building codes and related documents
- coordinating plan reviews among various building inspectors
- conducting structural, electrical, or other type of building inspection
- helping with the training of new or inexperienced Plan Reviewers

In addition, Plan Reviewers must keep up with code and regulatory changes as well as with new construction technology.

Plan Reviewers work a regular 40-hour week, performing most of their duties in their offices.

## Salaries

Earnings for Plan Reviewers vary, depending on such factors as their experience, education, and geographical location. According to the November 2003 *Occupational Employment Statistics* survey by the U.S. Bureau of Labor Statistics (BLS), the estimated annual salary for most construction and building inspectors, which includes Plan Reviewers, ranged between $27,100 and $66,760.

## Employment Prospects

Plan Reviewers work for building departments with city, county, and state governments. Some Plan Reviewers work for private architectural and engineering services firms as well as for code-consulting businesses and model code agencies that provide plan review services.

The BLS reports that job growth for building and construction inspectors is expected to increase by 10 to 20 percent through 2012. Most job openings, however, will become available as Plan Reviewers retire or transfer to other jobs or positions.

## Advancement Prospects

Supervisory and management opportunities are available, but limited. Many Plan Reviewers pursue career growth by way of wage increases and complexity of new assignments.

Another career path is working in the private sector as consultants or as staff members of architectural and engineering firms.

## Education and Training

Minimally, applicants must have a high school or general equivalency diploma. Some employers require additional college study in architecture, engineering, the construction trades, building inspection, or a related field. Other agencies prefer associate's or bachelor's degrees.

Plan Reviewers receive on-the-job training under the supervision of senior staff members. Throughout their careers, Plan Reviewers enroll in educational programs, training seminars, conference workshops, and so on to increase their knowledge and update their skills.

## Special Requirements

Professional licensure and certification requirements for Plan Reviewers vary among different employers. Plan Reviewers may be required to possess appropriate state or local licenses. Some employers require Plan Reviewers to hold professional certification granted by a recognized professional society, such as the International Code Council. (For further information about professional certification, see Appendix II.) Newly hired Plan Reviewers are usually given a certain time frame in which to obtain proper professional licensure or certification.

## Experience, Skills, and Personality Traits

In general, applicants should have several years of experience in construction supervision or in building inspections. Applicants should be able to read construction plans and drawings and understand engineering and architectural definitions and symbols.

Plan Reviewers must have good technical-writing, communication, and customer service skills—the ability to present information effectively and answer questions from the general public, architects, contractors, and other building officials. In addition, they need problem-solving skills and the ability to interpret information from verbal instructions, written materials, diagrams, and other forms.

Some personality traits that successful Plan Reviewers share include being tactful, independent, ethical, honest, and dedicated.

## Unions and Associations

Plan Reviewers can join local, state, and national professional associations to take advantage of networking opportunities, educational programs, job banks, and other professional services and resources. At the national level, Construction Inspectors might join the International Code Council. (For contact information, see Appendix IV.)

Many Plan Reviewers belong to a union that represents them in contract negotiations with their employers. The union seeks to get the best contract terms in regard to pay, benefits, and working conditions.

## Tips for Entry

1. Many associations post vacancies—for private firms and public agencies—that are available in different parts of the country.

2. Talk with Plan Reviewers in your community to learn more about their work and what you can do to prepare for a career in their field.
3. Many building departments have Web sites on the Internet. Some describe the plan's review process.

To get a list of Web sites to browse, enter the keywords *building inspections department* into a search engine.

# BUILDING INSPECTOR

## CAREER PROFILE

**Duties:** Conduct inspections of new constructions as well as renovations and repairs to make sure that all structural installations comply with building codes, regulations, and standards

**Alternate Title(s):** None

**Salary Range:** $27,000 to $67,000

**Employment Prospects:** Fair

**Advancement Prospects:** Limited

**Prerequisites:**

**Education or Training**—High school diploma

**Experience**—Be a construction worker at the journeyman level with supervisory or management experience

**Special Skills and Personality Traits**—Teamwork, interpersonal, communication, decision-making, critical thinking, and self-management skills; be tactful, impartial, self-motivated, ethical, and alert

**Licensure/Certification**—Professional license or certification; driver's license

## CAREER LADDER

```
┌─────────────────────────────────┐
│    Senior Building Inspector     │
└─────────────────────────────────┘

┌─────────────────────────────────┐
│       Building Inspector         │
└─────────────────────────────────┘

┌─────────────────────────────────┐
│    Building Inspector Trainee    │
└─────────────────────────────────┘
```

## Position Description

Building Inspectors are code enforcement officials for local, state, or federal government agencies. They conduct on-site inspections of residential, commercial, and industrial construction projects—including homes, schools, stores, hospitals, apartment buildings, office buildings, high-rise complexes, parking garages, factories, refineries, and prisons. They make sure all structural parts (foundation, floors, walls, doors, windows, roofs, chimneys, and so forth) meet building codes, regulations, and standards.

Usually working alone, Building Inspectors examine construction projects several times until their completion. (Projects may involve new constructions as well as repairs or renovations on existing buildings.) They review the quality and safety of the work and the materials being used. They check that all work follows the pre-approved construction plans and specifications. At each visit, they examine a specific phase of construction that they must approve before builders can go on to the next phase. For example, a Building Inspector would examine and approve the framework for a building's foundation before concrete is poured.

Their inspection is mostly visual; but they also use tape measures, surveying instruments, metering devices and test equipment. In addition, they keep a running log of their inspections throughout the project. Upon completion of all construction, Building Inspectors perform a comprehensive inspection, and issue an occupancy certificate if everything is in compliance.

When Building Inspectors find problems with a construction phase, they notify owners or contractors and explain the problems—such as code violations, unacceptable materials, or noncompliance with approved preconstruction plans. Building Inspectors have the authority to issue "stop work" orders, if problems are not corrected.

As part of their duties, Building Inspectors keep up with new building codes and construction legislation as well as with changing construction technology. In addition, they perform other tasks, which vary from agency to agency. For example, they might:

- review and approve preconstruction building plans and specifications

- issue building permits
- advise building contractors and property owners about appropriate building codes and regulations
- investigate complaints of unsafe buildings or construction work being done without proper permits
- perform electrical, plumbing, mechanical, or other non-structural inspections
- make recommendations for new building codes

Building Inspectors work 40 hours a week. Most of their time is spent in the field conducting inspections.

## Salaries

Earnings for Building Inspectors vary, depending on such factors as their experience, education, job duties, and geographical location. According to the November 2003 *Occupational Employment Statistics* survey by the U.S. Bureau of Labor Statistics, the estimated annual salary for most construction and building inspectors ranged between $27,100 and $66,760.

## Employment Prospects

Most Building Inspectors work for building departments at the city and county government level. Some work for state governments or federal agencies such as the U.S. Army Corps of Engineers, the U.S. Department of Agriculture, or the U.S. Department of Housing and Urban Development. Others work in the private sector. They are employed by architectural and engineering services firms that offer building inspection services.

Job opportunities are expected to grow as fast as the average for all occupations through 2012. The concern for public safety and the quality of construction should fuel a constant demand for inspectors. Most job openings, however, will become available as inspectors retire or transfer to other jobs or positions.

## Advancement Prospects

Building Inspectors with supervisory and management ambitions can rise to such positions, but opportunities are generally limited. Advancement opportunities are usually better for those with engineering or architectural degrees.

Many Building Inspectors pursue career growth by way of wage increases and complexity of new assignments. Some choose to specialize in specific types of structural inspections, such as the inspection of reinforced concrete. Another career path is to become a consultant.

## Education and Training

Applicants need at least a high school or general equivalency diploma. More and more employers prefer applicants with a bachelor's or associate's degree—or at least two years of formal study—in construction technology, engineering, architecture, or code work.

Building Inspectors receive on-the-job training to learn local codes, ordinances, and regulations; contract specifications; inspection techniques; and recordkeeping and reporting duties.

## Special Requirements

Professional licensure and certification requirements for Building Inspectors vary among different employers. Inspectors may be required to possess appropriate state or local licenses. Some employers require inspectors to hold professional certification granted by the International Code Council. (For further information about professional certification, see Appendix II.) Newly hired inspectors are usually given a certain time frame in which to obtain proper professional licensure or certification.

Many employers also require that Building Inspectors have a valid driver's license.

## Experience, Skills, and Personality Traits

Experience requirements depend on the job duties that applicants would perform. In general, applicants should have a thorough knowledge of construction practices and skills along with an understanding of building codes and regulations. Most agencies hire applicants who are journeyman construction workers with supervisory or management experience.

Building Inspectors need to be physically fit. They must also have effective teamwork, interpersonal, and communication skills. Additionally, these inspectors need strong decision-making, critical-thinking, and self-management skills. Being tactful, impartial, self-motivated, ethical, and alert are some personality traits that successful Building Inspectors share.

## Unions and Associations

Building Inspectors can join local, state, and national professional associations to take advantage of networking opportunities, educational programs, and other professional services and resources. At the national level, the International Code Council serves the general interests of Building Inspectors. (For contact information, see Appendix IV.)

Building Inspectors in government agencies may belong to a union that represents them in contract negotiations for better pay, benefits, and working conditions.

## Tips for Entry

1. Many local governments have job hotlines—phone numbers for recorded messages of current job announcements. In the city or county government list-

ings of your phone book, look for "Job Hotline" under *Personnel* or *Human Resources Department.*

2. To prepare for a career in building inspections, take construction courses along with blueprint, algebra, geometry, and English classes in high school.

3. Many building departments have Web sites on the Internet. To get a list of Web sites to browse, enter the keywords *building inspections department* into a search engine.

# MECHANICAL INSPECTOR

## CAREER PROFILE

**Duties:** Conduct on-site inspections of heating, ventilation, air conditioning, and cooling systems to make sure they comply with mechanical codes, regulations, and standards

**Alternate Title(s):** None

**Salary Range:** $27,000 to $67,000

**Employment Prospects:** Fair

**Advancement Prospects:** Limited

**Prerequisites:**

**Education or Training**—High school diploma

**Experience**—Have several years of experience installing mechanical equipment along with supervisory experience

**Special Skills, and Personality Traits**—Math, reading, writing, communication, interpersonal, problem-solving, and management skills; be ethical, impartial, honest, accurate, and tactful

**Licensure/Certification**—Professional license or certification; driver's license

## CAREER LADDER

```
┌─────────────────────────────────┐
│   Senior Mechanical Inspector   │
└─────────────────────────────────┘

┌─────────────────────────────────┐
│      Mechanical Inspector       │
└─────────────────────────────────┘

┌─────────────────────────────────┐
│   Mechanical Inspector Trainee  │
└─────────────────────────────────┘
```

## Position Description

Mechanical Inspectors are code enforcement officials for local, state, and federal government agencies. They conduct on-site inspections of mechanical installations in residential, commercial, and industrial construction projects. Their job is to make sure that the installation of new or modified heating, ventilation, air conditioning, and cooling systems complies with mechanical codes and regulations. They inspect air distribution systems; boilers and water heaters; gas piping systems; furnaces, fireplaces, chimneys, and vents; air-conditioning components; refrigeration systems; incinerators, commercial kitchen appliances and exhaust equipment; and so on.

Inspection is mostly visual; but Mechanical Inspectors also use measuring tools, calipers, scales, gauges, testing instruments, and other tools to check the quality and safety of workmanship or equipment. They also check that air quality and energy conservation standards are met. In addition, they make sure that installations comply with pre-approved construction plans and specifications.

Mechanical Inspectors give final approval for all mechanical installations and mark appropriate records that are displayed at construction sites. When work is in noncompliance of codes or pre-approved plans, Mechanical Inspectors contact owners, contractors, or supervisors and explain what problems must be corrected before approval can be given. If problems are not corrected within a specified period of time, Mechanical Inspectors may issue a "stop work" order.

As part of their job, Mechanical Inspectors maintain well-detailed records and prepare reports and correspondence about their inspections. In addition, Mechanical Inspectors keep up with new mechanical codes and regulations as well as with changing technology.

Mechanical Inspectors perform other duties, which vary from agency to agency. For example, they might:

- review and approve pre-construction electrical plans and specifications
- issue mechanical permits
- advise the public, contractors, and other building officials regarding mechanical codes and regulations
- make recommendations for new building codes

Mechanical Inspectors work 40 hours per week, mostly in the field.

## Salaries

Earnings for Mechanical Inspectors vary, depending on such factors as their experience, education, and geographical location. The U.S. Bureau of Labor Statistics reports in its November 2003 *Occupational Employment Statistics* survey that the estimated annual salary for most construction and building inspectors ranged between $27,100 and $66,760.

## Employment Prospects

Most Mechanical Inspectors work for building departments at the city and county government level. Some work for state governments or federal agencies such as the U.S. Department of Housing and Urban Development. Some Mechanical Inspectors work for architectural and engineering services firms that offer mechanical inspection services.

Job opportunities are expected to grow as fast as the average for all occupations through 2012. Most job openings will become available as Mechanical Inspectors retire or transfer to other jobs or positions.

## Advancement Prospects

Advancement opportunities are available; but engineering or architectural degrees are usually required for supervisory and administrative positions. Many Mechanical Inspectors pursue career growth by way of wage increases and complexity of new assignments. Some Mechanical Inspectors become private consultants.

## Education and Training

Applicants need at least a high school or general equivalency diploma. In some states, to obtain a Mechanical Inspectors license, a bachelor's degree in architecture or civil or structural engineering is required.

Mechanical Inspectors receive on-the-job training to learn local codes, ordinances, and regulations; contract specifications; inspection techniques; and recordkeeping and reporting duties.

## Special Requirements

Professional licensure and certification requirements for Mechanical Inspectors vary among different employers. Mechanical Inspectors may be required to possess appropriate state or local licenses. Some employers require inspectors to hold professional certification granted by the International Code Council. (For further information about professional certification, see Appendix II.) Newly hired inspectors are usually given a certain time frame in which to obtain proper professional licensure or certification, if necessary.

Many employers also require that Mechanical Inspectors hold a valid driver's license.

## Experience, Skills, and Personality Traits

Requirements vary with the different employers. Applicants should have several years of experience installing mechanical equipment along with supervisory experience. Some agencies also accept applicants' experience of performing mechanical inspections as part of their duties as general building inspectors. In addition, applicants should be able to analyze, interpret, and accurately check heating, ventilation, and air-conditioning equipment, plans, and specifications.

Mechanical Inspectors should have good math, reading, writing, and communication skills. Furthermore, they need interpersonal skills, and problem-solving and management abilities. Some personality traits that successful Mechanical Inspectors share include being ethical, impartial, honest, accurate, and tactful.

## Unions and Associations

Many Mechanical Inspectors join professional associations to take advantage of networking opportunities, educational programs, job banks, and other professional services and resources. At the national level, inspectors can join the International Code Council or the International Association of Plumbing and Mechanical Officials. (For contact information, see Appendix IV.)

Government inspectors may belong to a union, which represents them in contract negotiations with their employers. The union seeks to get the best contract terms in regard to pay, benefits, and working conditions.

## Tips for Entry

1. Network with mechanical inspectors and other building officials to learn about current job openings or jobs that may become available soon.
2. Keep up with changes in building codes, construction practices, and technical developments by self-study, enrolling in college or correspondence courses, or attending seminars sponsored by professional organizations.
3. Many building departments have Web sites on the Internet with specific information about mechanical inspections. To get a list of Web sites, enter the keywords *building inspections department* into a search engine.

# ELECTRICAL INSPECTOR

## CAREER PROFILE

**Duties:** Conduct inspections of electrical installations in construction projects to make sure work is in compliance with electrical codes, regulations, and standards

**Alternate Title(s):** None

**Salary Range:** $27,000 to $67,000

**Employment Prospects:** Fair

**Advancement Prospects:** Limited

**Prerequisites:**

**Education or Training**—High school diploma

**Experience**—Be a journeyman electrician with supervisory experience

**Special Skills and Personality Traits**—Problem-solving, management, writing, communication, and interpersonal skills; be observant, honest, ethical, accurate, and tactful

**Licensure/Certification**—Professional license or certification; driver's license

## CAREER LADDER

```
┌─────────────────────────────────┐
│   Senior Electrical Inspector    │
└─────────────────────────────────┘

┌─────────────────────────────────┐
│       Electrical Inspector       │
└─────────────────────────────────┘

┌─────────────────────────────────┐
│   Electrical Inspector Trainee   │
└─────────────────────────────────┘
```

## Position Description

Electrical Inspectors are code enforcement officials for local, state, and federal government agencies. They review installations for electrical wiring and fixtures in residential, commercial, or industrial construction projects. These projects may be new installations or alterations to existing electrical systems such as power, lighting, heating, air-conditioning, sound, and security systems. Electrical Inspectors make sure all work is in compliance with electrical codes, regulations, and standards.

Electrical inspections are done on a visual basis along with the use of inspection tools, such as metering devices and test equipment, to check the quality and safety of materials and workmanship. For example, Electrical Inspectors verify that electrical circuits can operate without overloads. As part of their inspections, Electrical Inspectors review pre-approved electrical plans and specifications to make sure that they have been followed. They also make sure work is done by licensed electricians.

Electrical Inspectors give final approvals for all electrical installations and mark appropriate records that are displayed at construction sites. When work is in noncompliance of codes or pre-approved plans, Electrical Inspectors contact owners, contractors, or supervisors and explain what problems must be corrected before approval can be given. Electrical Inspectors may issue a "stop work" order if problems are not corrected within a specified period of time.

As part of their job, Electrical Inspectors maintain well-detailed records and prepare reports and correspondence regarding their inspections. In addition, Electrical Inspectors keep up with new electrical codes and standards as well as changing technology.

Depending on the agency, Electrical Inspectors perform other duties. For example, they might:

- review and approve pre-construction electrical plans and specifications
- issue electrical permits
- advise the public, contractors, and other building officials about electrical codes, regulations, and standards
- help train new or inexperienced inspectors
- make recommendations for new electrical codes

Electrical Inspectors work a 40-hour week. Their hours are spent at the construction work site as well as in a field office, reviewing blueprints, answering correspondence or telephone calls, writing reports, and scheduling inspections.

## Salaries

Earnings for Electrical Inspectors vary, depending on such factors as their experience, education, and geographical location. The U.S. Bureau of Labor Statistics reports in its November 2003 *Occupational Employment Statistics* survey that the estimated annual salary for most construction and building inspectors, which includes Electrical Inspectors, ranged between $27,100 and $66,760.

## Employment Prospects

Most Electrical Inspectors work for building departments at the city and county government level. Some work for state governments or federal agencies such as the U.S. Army Corps of Engineers and the U.S. Department of Housing and Urban Development. Other inspectors work for architectural and engineering services firms that offer electrical inspection services.

Job opportunities for building inspectors, including Electrical Inspectors, are expected to grow as fast as the average for all occupations through 2012. Most job openings for Electrical Inspectors will become available as inspectors retire or transfer to other jobs.

## Advancement Prospects

Electrical Inspectors with supervisory and management ambitions can rise to such positions, but opportunities are generally limited. Many Electrical Inspectors pursue career growth by way of wage increases and complexity of new assignments. Some Electrical Inspectors become private consultants.

## Education and Training

Most employers require applicants to have a high school or general equivalency diploma. More and more employers prefer applicants who have enrolled in electrical training at colleges, technical schools, or vocational schools. Some employers prefer applicants to have bachelor's degrees in electrical engineering.

Electrical Inspectors receive on-the-job training to learn local codes, ordinances, and regulations; contract specifications; inspection techniques; and recordkeeping and reporting duties.

## Special Requirements

Professional licensure and certification requirements for Electrical Inspectors vary among different employers. Electrical Inspectors may be required to hold appropriate state or local inspection licenses, as well as maintain their electrician licensure. Some employers require Electrical Inspec-

tors to possess professional certification that is granted by either the International Code Council or the International Association of Electrical Inspectors. (For further information about professional certification, see Appendix II.) Newly hired inspectors are usually given a certain time frame in which to obtain proper professional licensure or certification, if necessary.

Many employers also require that Electrical Inspectors have a valid driver's license.

## Experience, Skills, and Personality Traits

In general, applicants must be journeyman electricians with supervisory experience. They should have knowledge of electrical codes and ordinances in addition to the principles of electrical inspection.

Electrical Inspectors must have problem-solving and management skills, as well as excellent writing and effective communication abilities. In addition, they need interpersonal skills.

Some personality traits that successful Electrical Inspectors have in common are being observant, honest, ethical, accurate, and tactful.

## Unions and Associations

Professional associations at the local, state, and national levels are available for Electrical Inspectors. The International Code Council and the International Association of Electrical Inspectors serve this profession at the national level. (For contact information, see Appendix IV.) By joining professional associations, Electrical Inspectors can take advantage of networking opportunities, educational programs, technical information, and other professional services and resources.

Electrical Inspectors in government agencies may belong to a union that represents them in contract negotiations with their employers.

## Tips for Entry

1. Contact city and county building departments to learn about job openings. You can also contact city and county government personnel (human resources) offices.
2. Some employers allow applicants to substitute voluntary professional certification for one or more years of required work experience.
3. Many building departments have Web sites on the Internet with specific information about electrical inspections. Enter the keywords *building inspections department* into a search engine to get a list of Web sites.

# PLUMBING INSPECTOR

## CAREER PROFILE

**Duties:** Conduct on-site inspections of plumbing installations in construction projects to make sure they are in compliance with plumbing codes, sanitation standards, and construction specifications

**Alternate Title(s):** None

**Salary Range:** $27,000 to $67,000

**Employment Prospects:** Fair

**Advancement Prospects:** Limited

**Prerequisites:**

    **Education or Training**—High school diploma

    **Experience**—Several years of work experience in plumbing and sewer systems with supervisory experience

    **Special Skills and Personality Traits**—Communication, writing interpersonal, problem-solving, and management skills; be tactful, ethical, impartial, accurate, and honest

    **Licensure/Certification**—Professional license or certification; driver's license

## CAREER LADDER

```
┌─────────────────────────────┐
│  Senior Plumbing Inspector  │
└─────────────────────────────┘

┌─────────────────────────────┐
│     Plumbing Inspector      │
└─────────────────────────────┘

┌─────────────────────────────┐
│  Plumbing Inspector Trainee │
└─────────────────────────────┘
```

## Position Description

Plumbing Inspectors are code enforcement officials for local, state, and federal government agencies. They make sure all plumbing installations in residential, commercial, and industrial construction projects are in compliance with plumbing codes, sanitation standards, and construction specifications. They inspect new plumbing systems as well as repairs or replacements to existing plumbing systems. These include water supply systems, water distribution systems, drainage systems, sewer systems, private disposal systems, water heater installations, fire sprinkler systems, and so on.

Their site visits involve visual inspections as well as the use of inspection tools and testing equipment to check on the quality and safety of the workmanship and materials. They check for proper installation of plumbing systems and that approved materials (such as back-flow prevention devices) are being used.

In addition, Plumbing Inspectors review pre-approved plumbing plans and specifications to verify that they have been followed. They also check that the plumbers doing the work possess valid certification or licensing.

When work is in noncompliance, Plumbing Inspectors notify owners, contractors, or supervisors and explain what problems must be corrected before approval can be given. If problems are not corrected within a specified period of time, Plumbing Inspectors may issue a "stop work" order.

Maintaining detailed records of their inspections is an essential part of their duties. In addition, they keep up with new plumbing codes and standards as well as changing technology.

Plumbing Inspectors perform other duties, which vary from agency to agency. For example, they might:

- review and approve pre-construction plumbing plans and specifications
- issue plumbing permits
- advise the general public, contractors, plumbers, and other building officials about plumbing codes as well as installation and permit requirements
- investigate complaints of plumbing code violations

Plumbing Inspectors work 40 hours per week, mostly in the field. They may be full-time or part-time staff members or work for building departments on a contractual basis.

## Salaries

Earnings for Plumbing Inspectors vary, depending on such factors as their education, experience, employer, and geographical location. The estimated annual salary for most construction and building inspectors, which includes Plumbing Inspectors, ranged between $27,100 and $66,760, according to the November 2003 *Occupational Employment Statistics* survey by the U.S. Bureau of Labor Statistics.

## Employment Prospects

Plumbing Inspectors are employed by state government agencies as well as by federal agencies such as the U.S. Department of Housing and Urban Development. Some Plumbing Inspectors are hired by architectural and engineering services firms that offer plumbing inspection services.

Job opportunities for Plumbing Inspectors are expected to grow as fast as the average for all occupations through 2012. Most job openings for Plumbing Inspectors will become available as inspectors retire or transfer to other jobs.

## Advancement Prospects

Plumbing Inspectors with supervisory and management ambitions can advance to such positions, but opportunities are generally limited. Many Plumbing Inspectors pursue career growth by way of wage increases and complexity of new assignments. Some inspectors become private consultants.

## Education and Training

Minimally, applicants must possess a high school diploma or general equivalency diploma. Increasingly more employers prefer to hire applicants who have completed some college work in mechanical engineering or another related field. Many employers seek applicants who have completed a technical (or trade) school program in plumbing.

Plumbing Inspectors receive on-the-job training to learn local codes, ordinances, and regulations; contract specifications; inspection techniques; and recordkeeping and reporting duties.

## Special Requirements

Professional licensure and certification requirements for Plumbing Inspectors vary among different employers. Plumbing Inspectors may be required to possess appropriate state or local licenses, which may include a journey or master plumber's license. Some employers require inspectors to hold professional certification granted by the International

Code Council. (For further information about professional certification, see Appendix II.) Newly hired inspectors are usually given a certain time frame in which to obtain proper professional licensure or certification, if necessary.

Many employers also require that Plumbing Inspectors possess a valid driver's license.

## Experience, Skills, and Personality Traits

Applicants should have several years of work experience in plumbing and sewer systems as well as supervisory experience. In addition, they should have knowledge of codes and laws governing plumbing installations.

Plumbing Inspectors must be physically fit. They must be able to communicate clearly and effectively, both orally and in writing. Interpersonal skills are essential. Also, they have good problem-solving and management abilities to handle the various projects and tasks of their job.

Some personality traits that successful Plumbing Inspectors share include being tactful, ethical, impartial, accurate, and honest.

## Unions and Associations

Many Plumbing Inspectors join local, state, or national professional associations to take advantage of networking opportunities, educational programs, job banks, and other professional services and resources. At the national level, Plumbing Inspectors might join such organizations as the International Code Council or the International Association of Plumbing and Mechanical Officials. For contact information, see Appendix IV.

Some government inspectors are members of a union, which seeks to get the best contract terms in regard to pay, benefits, and working conditions.

## Tips for Entry

1. In high school, talk with your school counselor—as well as with local Plumbing Inspectors—about courses, job skills, and work experiences that can help you prepare for a career in the plumbing inspection field.
2. To learn more about code enforcement careers or job vacancies, contact a Plumbing Inspector or building inspector at a local building department.
3. Many building departments have Web sites on the Internet with specific information about plumbing inspections. To get a list of Web sites to browse, enter the keywords *building inspections department* into a search engine.

# CONSTRUCTION INSPECTOR

## CAREER PROFILE

**Duties:** Conduct on-site inspections of the construction or repairs of streets, highways, sewer systems, and other public works to make sure the projects are in compliance with construction codes, regulations, and standards

**Alternate Title(s):** Public Works Inspector, Transportation Construction Inspector

**Salary Range:** $27,000 to $67,000

**Employment Prospects:** Fair

**Advancement Prospects:** Limited

**Prerequisites:**

**Education or Training**—High school diploma

**Experience**—Have several years of work experience in public works, engineering inspections, or construction along with supervisory or management experience

**Special Skills and Personality Traits**—Reading, math, communication, writing, problem-solving, management, and teamwork skills; be honest, trustworthy, impartial, objective, alert, and tactful

**Licensure/Certification**—Professional license or certification; driver's license

## CAREER LADDER

```
┌─────────────────────────────────┐
│   Senior Construction Inspector  │
└─────────────────────────────────┘

┌─────────────────────────────────┐
│      Construction Inspector      │
└─────────────────────────────────┘

┌─────────────────────────────────┐
│  Construction Inspector Trainee  │
└─────────────────────────────────┘
```

## Position Description

Construction Inspectors are code enforcement officials for local, state, and federal government agencies. They make sure that the construction of streets, highways, sewer systems, and other public works is in compliance with construction codes and regulations. They also make sure that construction work follows pre-approved plans and specifications.

Local Construction Inspectors (also known as Public Works Inspectors) conduct on-site inspections of the construction or repair of streets, sidewalks, driveways, water systems, sewer systems, streetlights, and traffic signals as well as the excavations and trenches dug by private utility companies. State and federal Construction Inspectors inspect the construction and repair of roads, highways, freeways, bridges, tunnels, dams, and other structures.

Construction Inspectors check the quality and safety of the workmanship and the materials being used. For example, they may check delivery tickets to verify the quality of materials; calculate quantities of material used, such as con-

crete, to compare with bid estimates; observe materials being laid, finished, and compacted; check alignment of pipe and quality of joints; and test pavement thickness.

Construction Inspectors may reject any unsatisfactory materials. They also consult with site supervisors about any deviations from preapproved plans and specifications. When code violations and other problems occur, Construction Inspectors notify contractors and explain what must be corrected. They make follow-up inspections to see that problems are corrected. If problems are not corrected within a specified period of time, inspectors may issue "stop work" orders.

Construction Inspectors keep well-detailed records and complete all necessary correspondence and reports. In addition, they keep up with changing construction codes and regulations as well as construction materials and technology.

Construction Inspectors perform other duties as required by their particular agencies. For example, they may conduct maintenance inspections, going on patrol to look for poor conditions in streets, sidewalks, driveways, traffic control devices, and other items, and issue notices to appropriate agencies or homeowners to make necessary repairs.

Construction Inspectors typically work a 40-hour week. State and federal Construction Inspectors may be required to travel, including overnight trips, to various sites throughout their state or region.

## Salaries

Earnings for Construction Inspectors vary, depending on such factors as their experience, education, employer, and geographical location. According to the November 2003 *Occupational Employment Statistics* survey by the U.S. Bureau of Labor Statistics (BLS), the estimated annual salary for most construction and building inspectors ranged between $27,100 and $66,760.

## Employment Prospects

Most Construction Inspectors are employed by local governments, particularly as part of city and county building departments. Inspectors are also hired by transportation departments at the state government level. In addition, opportunities are available with the federal government, in such agencies as the U.S. Army Corps of Engineers and the U.S. Department of Transportation. Furthermore, Construction Inspectors are employed in the private sector by engineering and architectural services firms that offer construction inspection services.

The BLS reports that applicants who possess professional certification, have engineering or architectural training, or have some college education should have better prospects for employment.

Job opportunities are expected to grow as fast as the average for all occupations through 2012. Most job openings will become available as Construction Inspectors retire or transfer to other jobs or positions. The creation of additional positions depends on a department's needs and budget.

## Advancement Prospects

Construction Inspectors who have a combination of extensive work experience and college degrees have better chances for promotion. However, advancement opportunities are limited. Many Construction Inspectors pursue career growth by way of wage increases and complexity of new assignments. Some become private consultants.

## Education and Training

Many employers prefer hiring applicants who have one of the following qualifications:

- graduated from an apprenticeship program
- completed at least two years of study in engineering or architecture

- earned an associate's degree, with courses in construction technology, blueprint reading, mathematics, building inspection, or public administration

Some employers prefer applicants who possess a bachelor's or master's degree in construction or a related field.

Construction Inspectors receive on-the-job training to learn local codes, ordinances, and regulations; contract specifications; inspection techniques; and recordkeeping and reporting duties.

## Special Requirements

Professional licensure and certification requirements for Construction Inspectors vary among different employers. Construction Inspectors may be required to possess appropriate state or local licenses. Some employers require inspectors to hold professional certification granted by the International Code Council. (For further information about professional certification, see Appendix II.) Newly hired inspectors are usually given a certain time frame in which to obtain proper professional licensure or certification.

Many employers also require that Construction Inspectors have a valid driver's license.

## Experience, Skills, and Personality Traits

Requirements vary from employer to employer. In general, applicants should have several years of work experience in public works, engineering inspections, or construction work along with experience performing supervisory or management duties.

Construction Inspectors must have adequate reading and math skills. They also must have excellent communication and writing abilities to clearly express and describe technical information. In addition, they should have problem-solving and management skills to handle various projects and tasks, as well as good interpersonal and teamwork skills. Being honest, trustworthy, impartial, objective, alert, and tactful are some personality traits that successful Construction Inspectors share.

## Unions and Associations

Many Construction Inspectors in government agencies belong to a union that represents them in contract negotiations with their employers. In addition, many Construction Inspectors join professional associations to take advantage of networking opportunities, educational programs, job banks, and other professional services and resources. At the national level, Construction Inspectors may belong to such organizations as the International Code Council, the Association of Construction Inspectors, and the American Public Works Association. For contact information, see Appendix IV.

**Tips for Entry**

1. Contact employers directly for information about career opportunities, job vacancies, and application processes.
2. Sometimes state transportation departments hire Construction Inspectors as seasonal employees, usually from March to November.
3. Many employers allow related education, such as an associate's degree in engineering technology, to be substituted for experience, on a year-by-year basis.
4. On the Internet, check out various public works or transportation departments. Enter either *public works department* or *state transportation department* into a search engine to get a list of Web sites. To learn more about the U.S. Department of Transportation, go to http://www.dot.gov.

# WORKPLACE SAFETY
# AND SECURITY

# INDUSTRIAL HYGIENIST

## CAREER PROFILE

**Duties:** Examine work sites for occupational hazards and diseases; identify any risks and eliminate or control them

**Alternate Title(s):** Industrial Hygiene Engineer; Environment, Safety, and Health Officer

**Salary Range:** $26,000 to $75,000

**Employment Prospects:** Fair

**Advancement Prospects:** Limited

**Prerequisites:**

**Education or Training**—Bachelor's degree

**Experience**—Varies with the different employers

**Special Skills and Personality Traits**—Problem-solving, teamwork, interpersonal, communication, writing and computer skills; be ethical, logical, organized, caring, and helpful

## CAREER LADDER

```
┌─────────────────────────────────┐
│   Senior Industrial Hygienist    │
└─────────────────────────────────┘

┌─────────────────────────────────┐
│      Industrial Hygienist        │
└─────────────────────────────────┘

┌─────────────────────────────────┐
│  Industrial Hygienist Trainee    │
└─────────────────────────────────┘
```

## Position Description

Industrial Hygienists help employers comply with local, state, and federal safety, health, and environmental laws and regulations. They examine and monitor work sites for potential hazards that may affect the health, comfort, or efficiency of employees. Potential hazards may include:

- exposure to lead, asbestos, pesticides, or other hazardous agents
- poor indoor air quality
- high noise levels
- radiation discharges
- work tasks that could lead to repetitive stress injuries, carpal tunnel syndrome, or other cumulative trauma disorders

Industrial Hygienists conduct scientific research to provide data on potential harmful conditions in work sites. They use skills from the chemistry, physiology, toxicology, physics, and engineering disciplines to perform their work. They might collect samples of suspected toxic materials such as dust, gases, and vapors to analyze in the laboratory. They might take relevant measurements—noise levels or measurements of carbon monoxide in the air, for example. They might also observe and interview workers.

Upon analyzing their findings, Industrial Hygienists then look for methods to eliminate or control potential hazards.

For example, they might recommend that workers wear special protective clothing or equipment, such as goggles or respirators. When corrective measures are in effect, Industrial Hygienists monitor the programs to make sure that hazards have been eliminated or are under control.

As part of their work, Industrial Hygienists prepare comprehensive reports that include their observations, inspections, analyses of laboratory results and other findings. They are responsible for record keeping and maintaining medical monitoring programs in the workplace. They may also teach safety and health procedures to employees so as to reduce their risk of injuries and illnesses. Their job also requires that they work closely with engineers, management officers, and employees.

Some Industrial Hygienists attend to safety and environmental duties. They might, for example, develop and administer safety and/or environmental programs and policies; perform safety inspections; conduct safety awareness training classes; coordinate the disposal of company waste; and monitor compliance with environmental laws and regulations.

Industrial Hygienists work 40 hours a week.

## Salaries

Earnings for Industrial Hygienists vary, depending on such factors as their education, experience, employer, and geographical location. According to the November 2003 *Occupational Employment Statistics* survey by the U.S. Bureau of Labor Statistics, the estimated annual salary for most occupational health and safety specialists, which includes Industrial Hygienists, ranged between $26,480 and $74,520.

## Employment Prospects

Industrial Hygienists are employed by manufacturing companies, chemical companies, government agencies, public utilities, hospitals, colleges and universities, and other organizations. They also work for safety consulting firms that provide industrial hygiene services.

Jobs are expected to be readily available for experienced Industrial Hygienists, but the competition is strong. Opportunities are better for those who have a combination of industrial hygiene and safety management skills and experience. Some experts in the field think prospects for consulting Industrial Hygienists should grow as more employers hire consulting firms to perform industrial hygiene services.

## Advancement Prospects

Advancement opportunities are available for supervisory and management positions, but competition is high. Industrial Hygienists typically need extensive experience, advanced education, and professional certification (such as the certified industrial hygienist designation) for those positions.

Industrial Hygienists can pursue other options as consultants, compliance inspectors, researchers, and instructors or trainers. In addition, they may transfer their experience and skills to safety management, human resources, sales, and other areas.

## Education and Training

Requirements vary with different employers. Most employers prefer applicants with a bachelor's degree in industrial hygiene, engineering, chemistry, biology, physical science, health, or other related field.

Industrial Hygienists must complete their employers' training programs, which may include both formal instruction and on-the-job training.

Throughout their careers, Industrial Hygienists enroll in educational programs, training seminars, conference workshops, and so on to increase their knowledge and update their skills.

## Experience, Skills, and Personality Traits

Requirements vary from employer to employer; many employers hire recent college graduates. In general, applicants should have knowledge of industrial hygiene concepts, principles, and practices as well as be familiar with the industry (such as manufacturing or public utilities) in which they would work. Many employers prefer candidates who are knowledgeable of state and federal occupational safety and health regulations and who have experience in developing safety programs.

Industrial Hygienists must have excellent problem-solving skills as well as teamwork and interpersonal skills. In addition, they need communication and writing abilities to effectively explain technical terms and concepts in nontechnical language. Furthermore, candidates should be computer literate.

Some personality traits that successful Industrial Hygienists share include being ethical, logical, organized, caring, and helpful.

## Unions and Associations

Among the many professional organizations that Industrial Hygienists might belong to are the National Safety Council, the American Industrial Hygiene Association, and the American Conference of Governmental Industrial Hygienists. (For contact information, see Appendix IV.) Joining professional organizations gives Industrial Hygienists the opportunity to network with peers and obtain professional support and services, such as certified training, continuing education, technical information, and job resources.

## Tips for Entry

1. To learn about available part-time and full-time jobs or student internships, contact the human resources (or personnel) offices of companies where you would like to work.
2. To stay competitive in the job market, many professionals are earning environmental or safety degrees or both. Also, they are obtaining safety professional certification as they become eligible.
3. To learn about Industrial Hygienists on the Internet, visit the American Industrial Hygiene Association Web site at http://www.aiha.org. Or, enter the keywords *industrial hygiene* into a search engine to get a list of Web sites to browse regarding associations, equipment, consulting firms, and other aspects of this field.

# SAFETY TRAINING SPECIALIST

## CAREER PROFILE

**Duties:** Plan, develop, and implement employee safety training programs; provide instruction; may perform other duties related to safety programs

**Alternate Title(s):** Training and Development Specialist, Training Coordinator, Instructional Designer, Technical Trainer, Regulatory Compliance Trainer

**Salary Range:** $25,000 to $75,000

**Employment Prospects:** Good

**Advancement Prospects:** Fair

**Prerequisites:**

**Education or Training**—Associate's degree or bachelor's degree

**Experience**—Have been training instructors in the occupational safety and training field; have experience in or be knowledgeable of the industry in which they would be working

**Special Skills and Personality Traits**—Communication, interpersonal, leadership, analytical, problem-solving, teamwork, computer, writing, and self-management skills; be positive, self-motivated, trustworthy, punctual, patient, enthusiastic, creative, and flexible

## CAREER LADDER

```
┌─────────────────────────────┐
│  Training Coordinator or    │
│     Training Manager        │
└─────────────────────────────┘

┌─────────────────────────────┐
│     Training Specialist      │
└─────────────────────────────┘

┌─────────────────────────────┐
│   Trainer or Training and    │
│    Development Intern        │
└─────────────────────────────┘
```

## Position Description

In the United States, employers are mandated by federal and state laws to provide their employees with a safe and healthy working environment. Employers must comply with occupational safety and health standards established by governmental agencies. Employers must also provide safety training programs for their employees. In most organizations, employers hire Safety Training Specialists to coordinate, develop, and implement workplace safety education and training programs.

Safety Training Specialists create effective programs to address general safety topics as well as specific safety issues for each job and department within an organization. These specialists design training workshops, seminars, and courses on various subjects, including company safety rules and policies, governmental regulations, first aid, health and safety hazards, safety procedures, the safe use of equipment and tools, back injury prevention, ergonomics, fire safety,

disaster preparedness, workplace violence prevention, and so on.

Safety Training Specialists design instructional programs in various formats. For example, training may be provided through classes, workshops, seminars, individual coaching, on-the-job training, interactive video training, computer-based training, or intranet instruction.

In developing safety training programs, Safety Training Specialists perform a variety of duties, such as:

- working with supervisors and managers to identify the safety issues and topics to be addressed
- assessing the training needs for a particular work site, department, or job category (such as supervisors)
- planning schedules and budgets
- designing curriculum and training materials
- conducting or assisting with the facilitation of training seminars and workshops

- training the instructors, department supervisors, or other personnel who will be providing the instruction
- evaluating the effectiveness of training programs and materials
- performing administrative and clerical tasks, such as preparing reports, writing correspondence, maintaining records, and administering budgets

Safety Training Specialists also make sure that their safety training programs are in compliance with company policies and standards as well as with governmental laws and regulations. Part of their job is also staying abreast of changes in federal and state laws and regulations regarding occupational safety and health. In addition, they keep up-to-date with the latest issues and methods regarding safety, accident prevention, hazards, and other topics

Safety Training Specialists may be assigned to perform safety audits, investigate work site accidents, monitor building security systems, assist with worker's compensation claims, or develop emergency preparedness plans. In some organizations, Safety Specialists help the marketing department with the development of product safety materials for customers.

Safety Training Specialists may work alone or as part of a team when designing a new safety training program. Senior specialists usually coordinate the development of programs, which sometimes involves contracting with safety consultants or trainers who are experts in their particular subject matter.

Safety Training Specialists usually work a 40-hour week. Some Safety Training Specialists work various hours and days to provide training to employees on different shifts. Some specialists travel to various locations within a city, state, or region to conduct training at different work sites.

## Salaries

Salaries for Safety Training Specialists vary, depending on such factors as their education, experience, employer, and geographical location. Safety Training Specialists in large organizations can expect to earn higher wages. According to the November 2003 *Occupational Employment Statistics* survey by the U.S. Bureau of Labor Statistics, the estimated annual salary for most training and development specialists ranged from $25,440 to $74,660.

## Employment Prospects

Safety Training Specialists work in most, if not all, industries, such as the manufacturing, construction, transportation, agriculture, environmental, waste management, banking and finance, education, government, and nonprofit industries. Many specialists are employed by companies and organizations. Some are independent contractors, while others are employed by training and development firms that offer safety training services on a contractual basis.

The demand for Safety Training Specialists is constant, as employers are required to comply with federal and state laws which mandate specific occupational safety and health training programs for employees. In general, job opportunities become available as specialists retire, advance to higher positions, or transfer to other occupations. Employers will hire additional staff members or contractors as their organizations grow and expand.

## Advancement Prospects

Safety Training Specialists can advance to supervisory and management positions, for which they may be required to transfer to other organizations. Those with entrepreneurial ambitions can become independent consultants or owners of businesses that offer safety training and development services.

## Education and Training

Depending on the employer, applicants are usually required to hold at least an associate's or bachelor's degree, which may be in any field. Having a college degree in occupational safety and health, industrial engineering, human resources, education, or another related field may be desirable.

Throughout their careers, Safety Training Specialists enroll in educational programs, training seminars, conference workshops, and so on to increase their knowledge and update their skills.

## Experience, Skills, and Personality Traits

Experience requirements vary among different employers. In general, applicants should have previous experience as training instructors in the occupational safety and training field. Additionally, they should have experience or be knowledgeable about the industry in which they would be working. Being familiar with the state and federal safety regulations pertinent to their prospective employer's workplace is also essential.

Because they work with various groups of people who come from different backgrounds, Safety Training Specialists need effective communication and interpersonal skills. Their job also requires that they have strong leadership, analytical, problem-solving, and teamwork skills. In addition, they need adequate computer, writing, and self-management skills.

Some personality traits that successful Safety Training Specialists share include being positive, self-motivated, trustworthy, punctual, patient, enthusiastic, creative, and flexible.

## Unions and Associations

Many Safety Training Specialists join various professional associations to take advantage of networking opportunities, training programs, job resources, and other professional services. Some national professional societies that serve the interests of safety professionals include the following:

- American Society of Safety Engineers
- National Association of Safety Professionals
- National Safety Council
- System Safety Society
- American Industrial Hygiene Association

Safety Training Specialists are also eligible to join the American Society for Training and Development, a national association that serves the interests of training specialists in general.

For contact information for the above organizations, see Appendix IV.

## Tips for Entry

1. While in college, obtain an internship, summer job, or part-time job in the occupational safety and health field to gain experience.
2. Get experience teaching adults. For example, you might tutor students in community adult literacy programs or teach adult classes in a continuing education program sponsored by a community college or other organization.
3. To enhance your employability and advancement prospects, obtain certification as a Safety Training Specialist as well as a safety professional. (See Appendix II for information about professional certification programs.)
4. Being fluent in Spanish or another language can be seen as an asset by companies that hire workers with limited English proficiency.
5. Use the Internet to learn more about workplace safety standards. You might start by visiting the Web site of the Occupational Safety and Health Administration, the independent federal agency that oversees compliance of federal laws and regulations. Its URL is http://www.osha.gov.

# SAFETY MANAGER

## CAREER PROFILE

**Duties:** Oversee employer's occupational safety and health program; ensure compliance with governmental laws and regulations; develop various safety plans and programs; conduct safety inspections

**Alternate Title(s):** Environmental Health and Safety Manager, Safety Director

**Salary Range:** $50,000 to $100,000+

**Employment Prospects:** Good

**Advancement Prospects:** Limited

**Prerequisites:**

**Education or Training**—Bachelor's degree

**Experience**—Varies from employer to employer

**Special Skills and Personality Traits**—Supervisory, organizational, problem-solving, teamwork, interpersonal, communication, writing, and computer skills; be ethical, trustworthy, detail-oriented, analytical, dedicated, flexible, and innovative

## CAREER LADDER

```
┌─────────────────────────────┐
│      Safety Director        │
└─────────────────────────────┘

┌─────────────────────────────┐
│      Safety Manager         │
└─────────────────────────────┘

┌─────────────────────────────┐
│ Safety Management Trainee or│
│   Safety Assistant Manager  │
└─────────────────────────────┘
```

## Position Description

Safety Managers oversee the occupational safety and health programs in industrial plants, corporations, universities, hospitals, government agencies, and other workplaces. They are responsible for instituting safety policies and procedures that maintain safe and healthy work environments.

While consulting department managers as well as employees, Safety Managers develop various safety plans and programs. These include contingency plans for fires, gas spills, and other disasters as well as safety training programs for employees. Safety Managers are also responsible for alerting employees to the danger of working with hazardous substances such as toxic fumes or chemicals.

Another major duty is conducting safety inspections to detect existing or potential accident and health hazards. Safety Managers make sure work sites are in compliance with federal and state OSHA (Occupational Safety and Health Administration) regulations, local fire and public health regulations, and insurance industry requirements.

Upon finding actual or potential safety problems, Safety Managers take necessary action to resolve them. For example, they might direct staff Industrial Hygienists to examine the air quality at a work site to determine the potential danger to employees. In addition, Safety Managers supervise or conduct investigations of all safety accidents.

As representatives of their employers, Safety Managers are contact persons for OSHA and other regulatory agencies. Safety Managers also prepare studies of industrial accidents, causes, and hazards to health for public relation uses.

Some Safety Managers are responsible for environmental issues as well. For example, they may be in charge of disposing hazardous waste or conducting inspections to make sure the workplace is in compliance with federal, state, and local environmental laws and regulations.

Furthermore, Safety Managers attend to managerial tasks such as supervising safety staff, preparing budgets, and making purchases. They also complete and maintain paperwork, such as OSHA records, accident reports, permits, employee records and invoices.

Safety Managers usually work more than their regular 40-hour week to complete their responsibilities.

## Salaries

Annual earnings for Safety Managers vary, depending on their experience, education, job duties, employer, and geographical location. According to the Career Prospects in Virginia Web site, mid-career safety professionals, such as Safety Managers, generally earn between $50,000 to $70,000. Safety Managers in large corporations may earn up to $100,000 or more.

## Employment Prospects

Safety Managers work in many different industries such as manufacturing, construction, utilities, transportation, insurance, government, education, nonprofit agencies, and health care.

The job outlook, in general, should remain favorable for experienced Safety Managers, as employers are required to comply with governmental laws and regulations regarding safety and health in the workplace. Opportunities usually become available as managers advance to higher positions, retire, or transfer to other occupations.

## Advancement Prospects

Safety Managers can advance to administrative positions, such as safety directors. Many Safety Managers change jobs or locations to move up to Safety Manager positions with higher pay or more challenging responsibilities. Having a bachelor's or advanced degree along with professional certification (such as the Certified Safety Professional designation) is usually required to obtain senior manager and director positions.

Another career move for Safety Managers is to become private consultants or start their own businesses providing safety management services.

## Education and Training

Requirements vary from employer to employer. More and more employers prefer applicants with a bachelor's degree in safety management, industrial hygiene, engineering, physical science, or other related field. Some employers accept applicants with business degrees if they have the required experience.

Employers may require their Safety Managers to attend training seminars and continuing education classes in order to stay current with changing technologies as well as with safety and health laws and regulations.

## Experience, Skills, and Personality Traits

Requirements vary with the different employers. Applicants may need as few as two years of occupational safety and health experience or as many as eight or more years. Typi-

cally, applicants must have knowledge of the daily business operations of the industry—healthcare, transportation, construction—in which they would be working. Also, they must be knowledgeable of occupational safety and health laws and regulations.

Safety Managers must have strong supervisory, organizational, and problem-solving abilities. In addition, they need excellent teamwork and interpersonal skills along with superior communication and writing abilities. Having computer skills, including the use of word-processing, spreadsheets, and graphic presentation programs, is also essential. Being ethical, trustworthy, detail-oriented, analytical, dedicated, flexible, and innovative are some personality traits that successful Safety Managers share.

## Unions and Associations

Many Safety Managers belong to professional associations to take advantage of educational programs, professional certification, networking opportunities, and other professional services and resources. Some national societies that Safety Managers might join include the following:

- National Safety Management Society
- American Society of Safety Engineers
- National Association of Safety Professionals
- National Safety Council
- System Safety Society
- American Industrial Hygiene Association

For contact information, see Appendix IV.

## Tips for Entry

1. As a college student, develop a portfolio to document your course work, internships, work experience, and related extracurricular activities. You can then submit copies of your portfolio with your applications for employment or graduate schools.
2. Join professional organizations and network with other safety professionals to learn of jobs that are currently open or may be available soon.
3. Many employers are requiring or preferring applicants to possess professional certification, such as the Certified Safety Professional (CSP) designation. For information about certification programs for safety professionals, see Appendix II.
4. Learn more about Safety Managers and the safety field on the Internet. You might start by visiting the National Safety Management Society Web site at http://www.nsms.us.

# LOSS CONTROL REPRESENTATIVE

## CAREER PROFILE

**Duties:** Evaluate clients' workplaces and develop safety plans to minimize their loss of assets; manage caseloads; inspect clients' work sites

**Alternate Title(s):** Loss Control Specialist, Safety Engineer

**Salary Range:** $26,000 to $75,000

**Employment Prospects:** Good

**Advancement Prospects:** Limited

**Prerequisites:**

**Education or Training**—Bachelor's degree

**Experience**—One to three years of safety experience; knowledge of industries (transportation, construction, healthcare, etc.) in which an individual would be working

**Special Skills and Personality Traits**—Problem-solving, negotiation, organizational, communication, writing, computer, public speaking, and self-management skills; be self-disciplined, ethical, trustworthy, analytical, and dedicated

## CAREER LADDER

```
┌─────────────────────────────────────┐
│ Senior Loss Control Representative   │
└─────────────────────────────────────┘

┌─────────────────────────────────────┐
│    Loss Control Representative       │
└─────────────────────────────────────┘

┌─────────────────────────────────────┐
│      Loss Control Trainee            │
└─────────────────────────────────────┘
```

## Position Description

Loss Control Representatives are employees of insurance companies. Their job is to help clients develop safety plans that may minimize the risk of potential losses of their clients' property, money, lives, and other assets.

Loss Control Representatives manage a caseload of clients, which may include retailers, manufacturers, construction companies, hospitals, government agencies, academic institutions, and other businesses and organizations. They are responsible for evaluating the workplaces of their clients and identifying hazards that may lead to future losses. This involves conducting inspections of their clients' work sites on a regular basis. They must also keep up with changes in all local, state, and federal regulations and laws that affect their clients' businesses.

To determine the quality and effectiveness of their clients' safety programs, Loss Control Representatives perform various tasks. For example, during inspection visits, they might:

- review safety policies and procedures
- survey the facilities and equipment (for example, checking for fire hazards, obstructions blocking emergency exits, noncompliant storage of toxic chemicals, defective equipment, or broken electrical ground wires)
- observe the workers to evaluate their safety habits (such as using tools properly or wearing proper safety protection)
- audit past losses
- review safety inspection programs or accident investigation procedures
- examine records of state or federal Occupational Safety and Health Administration (OSHA) audits

When Loss Control Representatives find real or potential hazards, they make recommendations for reducing risks. These include mandatory recommendations that clients must correct in order to be in compliance with insurance companies' requirements or OSHA laws and regulations. Loss Control Representatives prepare reports of their findings and recommendations. They submit the reports to their clients as well as hold meetings to discuss them.

Loss Control Representatives also perform other duties. For example, they conduct investigations of any sizable losses suffered by their clients, and they gather data for insurance underwriters who use the information to determine the price of new insurance policies.

Loss Control Representatives may travel throughout their state or region to visit clients. Overnight travel is often required. Furthermore, Loss Control Representatives may be reassigned to other locations throughout their career with an employer.

## Salaries

Earnings for Loss Control Representatives vary, depending on such factors as their education, experience, job duties, employer, and geographical location. According to the November 2003 *Occupational Employment Statistics* survey by the U.S. Bureau of Labor Statistics (BLS), the estimated annual salary for most occupational health and safety specialists, which includes Loss Control Representatives, ranged between $26,480 and $74,520.

## Employment Prospects

Most Loss Control Representatives are employed by insurance companies; many are employed by manufacturers and government agencies as well. Many also work for consulting firms that offer loss control services as part of their occupational safety and health services.

In general, the BLS predicts that the job growth for safety professionals, which includes Loss Control Representatives, should increase by 10 to 20 percent through 2012. Most opportunities for Loss Control Representatives become available as individuals advance to higher positions, retire, or transfer to other occupations.

## Advancement Prospects

Loss Control Representatives can pursue managerial and administrative positions as Loss Control Managers and Loss Control Directors. Typically, the larger a company is, the greater opportunity there is for advancement.

Furthermore, Loss Control Representatives may use their loss control experiences to move into other areas of insurance such as sales, human resources, underwriting, and risk management.

## Education and Training

Requirements differ from employer to employer. Employers generally look for applicants with a bachelor's degree in occupational safety and health, fire science, industrial hygiene, engineering, physical science, business, or other related fields.

Loss Control trainees must complete training programs, which vary with different employers. Some employers provide formal training to develop technical and business skills in addition to on-the-job training under the supervision of senior Loss Control Representatives.

## Experience, Skills, and Personality Traits

Requirements vary from employer to employer. Most employers prefer candidates who have at least one to three years of safety experience that includes planning and implementing safety and loss prevention programs. Larger companies sometimes hire recent college graduates without any previous work experience in loss control.

In addition, applicants should have knowledge of the industries (transportation, food industry, security firms, construction, agriculture, healthcare) in which they would be making loss control assessments. Applicants should be familiar with the practical realities of running daily business operations.

To perform their work effectively, Loss Control Representatives need excellent problem-solving, negotiation, and organizational skills. Having strong communication, writing, computer, and public speaking skills is also essential. In addition, they need adequate self-management skills, such as the ability to work independently, meet deadlines, handle stressful situations, and understand and follow directions. Being self-disciplined, ethical, trustworthy, analytical, and dedicated are some personality traits that successful Loss Control Representatives share.

## Unions and Associations

Loss Control Representatives can join professional associations to take advantage of networking opportunities, educational programs, certification programs, and other professional services and resources. Some national societies that are available to them include the following:

- Insurance Loss Control Association
- System Safety Society
- American Society of Safety Engineers
- Risk and Insurance Management Society, Inc.
- Public Risk Management Association
- National Fire Protection Association

For contact information, see Appendix IV.

## Tips for Entry

1. Many insurance companies attend job fairs at colleges and universities to recruit applicants as well as to provide career information. Contact nearby colleges and universities to learn about upcoming job fairs.
2. To enhance their employability, Loss Control Representatives obtain professional certification such as the Certified Safety Professional (CSP) designation, which is granted by the Board of Certified Safety Professionals. (For contact information, see Appendix II.)
3. Many insurance companies have Web sites on the Internet with specific information about loss control services. To get a list of Web sites to browse, enter the keywords *loss control services* into a search engine.

# SECURITY CONSULTANT

## CAREER PROFILE

**Duties:** Provide expert advice in designing effective security programs to protect clients' assets

**Alternate Title(s):** Security Management Consultant; Security Engineer; Technical Security Consultant

**Salary Range:** $37,000 to $124,000

**Employment Prospects:** Excellent

**Advancement Prospects:** Fair

**Prerequisites:**

**Education or Training**—No standard requirements

**Experience**—Highly experienced in areas of expertise

**Special Skills and Personality Traits**—Management, organizational, interpersonal, communication, and writing skills; be analytical, detail-oriented, assertive, self-motivated, ethical, trustworthy, honest, and responsible

## CAREER LADDER

```
┌─────────────────────────────┐
│     Senior Consultant       │
└─────────────────────────────┘

┌─────────────────────────────┐
│     Security Consultant     │
└─────────────────────────────┘

┌─────────────────────────────┐
│      Junior Consultant      │
└─────────────────────────────┘
```

## Position Description

Security Consultants offer themselves as resources to clients who want to develop effective security measures for their workplaces. Their clients may be small businesses, retailers, manufacturers, financial institutions, hospitals, nonprofit organizations, government agencies, academic institutions, or other organizations. These consultants provide advice in their particular areas of expertise, such as physical security, personnel security, retail security, or computer security. Security Consultants may be independent contractors or employees of security consulting firms.

Security Consultants specialize in one or more industries such as: financial, telecommunications, retail, warehousing, hospitality, entertainment, healthcare, pharmaceutical, education, utilities, transportation, construction, or manufacturing. Clients hire them to perform specific services; for example, Security Consultants might be hired to:

- conduct security surveys and audits to evaluate existing security systems
- execute risk and threat assessments to find potential areas of loss within the business and recommend security countermeasures
- develop overall security policies and procedures

- create response plans against workplace violence and against various criminal actions such as armed robbery, extortion, kidnapping, arson, and bombings
- oversee the installation of security systems (Note: Security Consultants are not connected in any way with firms that sell security equipment or services.)
- design security awareness training programs that teach employees how to incorporate security policies and procedures on their jobs
- provide executive protection (bodyguard services to executives)
- provide expert witness testimony in lawsuits that involve security personnel, technology, or other matters

One service Security Consultants do not offer is investigation work, as that is a different activity from security consulting, according to the International Association of Professional Security Consultants.

Security Consultants gather all information that is relevant to their projects. They might observe daily operations; discuss security procedures and policies with appropriate staff members; review relevant records, documents, and other materials; test security systems; and so on. Upon studying and analyzing all information, Security Consultants design plans that fit their clients' goals and objectives as well as budgets.

The work of Security Consultants involves meeting deadlines and providing clients with both oral and written progress reports. In addition, they prepare final reports that detail their findings and recommendations. Supporting documents are also included with these reports. Security Consultants usually make oral presentations of these comprehensive reports as well.

Security Consultants usually handle several projects at the same time. While working at their own offices as well as at their clients' offices, Security Consultants create their own work schedules.

Along with their consultation work, self-employed Security Consultants oversee daily business operations. For example, they may supervise support staffs, do accounts, invoice clients, pay bills, and do routine office work.

Security Consultants often work long hours to complete tasks and meet deadlines. Their projects may involve frequent travel to their clients' workplaces. On occasion, consultants work on projects that require living away from home for several days, weeks, or months at a time.

## Salaries

Earnings for Security Consultants vary, depending on such factors as their experience, specialty, fees, and geographical location; the size of their firm and the type of services it provides; and the competition for their services. Current salary surveys for Security Consultants are unavailable, but an idea of their earnings can be gained by looking at salary information for management analysts. According to the November 2003 *Occupational Employment Statistics* survey by the U.S. Bureau of Labor Statistics (BLS), the estimated annual salary for most management analysts ranged between $36,820 and $123,760.

## Employment Prospects

Security Consultants may be independent contractors, owners, or employees of firms that offer security consulting services. Some self-employed consultants offer consulting services on a limited basis while holding part-time or full-time jobs.

Security is one of the fastest-growing fields worldwide due to the increased concern with terrorism, theft, workplace violence, white-collar crime, computer crime, and other areas. Job opportunities within all levels of the security industry, including Security Consultant positions, should be favorable through 2012, according to the BLS.

Competition for staff and contractor positions is strong because of the nature of consulting work. Opportunities are usually better for highly experienced and reputable consultants.

Job openings with security consulting firms generally become available as consultants transfer to other positions,

retire, or resign. Employers create additional positions as their firms grow.

## Advancement Prospects

Staff consultants may rise through the ranks as junior consultants, senior consultants, project managers, or partners. Consultants might seek positions with other firms to earn higher pay, receive greater responsibilities, or advance to higher positions. The top goal for some consultants is to become successful as an independent contractor or a security consulting firm owner.

## Education and Training

There are no standard education requirements for Security Consultants. However, clients prefer hiring Security Consultants who have a college degree as well as professional certifications, such as Certified Protection Professional.

Throughout their careers, Security Consultants enroll in educational programs, training seminars, conference workshops, and so on to increase their knowledge and update their skills.

## Experience, Skills, and Personality Traits

Security Consultants typically have many years of experience in their areas of expertise. Many of them have gained extensive leadership, management, and technical experience through their work as security managers and law enforcement officers.

Successful Security Consultants have excellent management skills as well as organizational and interpersonal skills. They also have superior communication and writing skills, such as the ability to present technical terms and concepts in nontechnical vocabulary. Being analytical, detail-oriented, assertive, self-motivated, ethical, trustworthy, honest, and responsible are some personality traits that successful Security Consultants share.

## Unions and Associations

Professional associations that Security Consultants might belong to are: the International Association of Professional Security Consultants and ASIS International. Joining professional organizations gives Security Consultants the opportunity to network with peers and obtain professional support and services, such as education programs, technical information, and job resources.

## Tips for Entry

1. Security Consultants often obtain new clients through recommendations from other consultants and specialists in security.
2. To enhance your employability, obtain professional certification. For example, some Security Consultants

possess the Certified Protection Professional (CPP) designation, which is granted by ASIS International. (For contact information, see Appendix II.)

3. Having published professional articles and books demonstrates to many clients a Security Consultant's expertise in current security technology and issues.

4. To learn more about the security consulting field, visit the International Association of Professional Security Consultants Web site on the Internet. Its Web address is http://www.iapsc.org. In addition, many Security Consultants have Web sites on the Internet. To get a list to browse, enter the keywords *security consultant* or *security management consulting* into a search engine.

# APPENDIXES

# APPENDIX I
# EDUCATION AND TRAINING RESOURCES

In this appendix, you will learn about Internet resources for education and training programs for some of the occupations in this book. To learn about programs for occupations not listed here, talk with professionals as well as school, career, or job counselors. You can also refer to college directories produced by Peterson's or other publishers, which may be found in your school or public library.

*Note: All Web site addresses were current when this book was being written. If a URL does not work, you may be able to find a new address by entering the name of the organization, individual, or Web site into a search engine.*

## GENERAL RESOURCES
The following Web sites provide links to various academic or training programs at postsecondary institutions throughout the United States.

- All Criminal Justice Schools (All Star Directories, Inc.), http://www.allcriminaljusticeschools.com
- Education Online Search, http://www.education-online-search.com
- Trade Schools Guide, http://www.trade-schools.net
- U.S. College Search, http://www.uscollegesearch.org
- Web U.S. Higher Education, a listing of two-year and four-year colleges (maintained by the University of Texas at Austin), http://www.utexas.edu/world/univ
- The Princeton Review, http://www.princetonreview.com
- GradSchools.com, http://www.gradschools.com
- Peterson's Graduate Schools and Programs, http://iiswinprd01.petersons.com/GradChannel

## AIR TRAFFIC CONTROL
The following Web sites provide a listing of colleges and universities that offer the Air Traffic Collegiate Training Initiative (AT-CTI) program, established by the Federal Aviation Administration (FAA). Graduates of an AT-CTI program fulfill the basic qualifications needed to apply for FAA air traffic controller positions.

- AT-CTI program (FAA Web site), http://www.faa.gov/careers/employment/AT-CTI-MAP.htm
- FAA Aviation Education and Research http://www.faa.gov/education-research

## AIRCRAFT DISPATCH
A listing of some aircraft dispatcher training programs can be found at the ThirtyThousandFeet.com Web site, http://www.thirtythousandfeet.com/training.htm.

## COMPUTER SCIENCE
A listing of academic institutions that offer computer science and information systems programs is available at the Accreditation Board for Engineering and Technology Web site, http://www.abet.org.

## CRIMINAL JUSTICE/CRIMINOLOGY/LAW ENFORCEMENT/POLICE SCIENCE
The following Web sites provide information about college programs in one or more of the following majors: criminal justice, criminology, law enforcement, and police science.

- Policetraining.net has a listing of police science and criminal justice degree programs at http://www.policetraining.net/classes-college-degrees.htm.
- The American Society of Criminology has a list of undergraduate programs in criminal justice, criminology, and related fields at http://www.asc41.com/UNDERGRAD.html.
- The American Society of Criminology has a list of graduate programs in criminal justice, criminology, and related fields at http://www.asc41.com/GRADLINKS.html.
- Dr. Tom O'Connor (Justice Studies Department, North Carolina Wesleyan College, Rocky Mount, North Carolina) posts the "Graduate Education in Criminal Justice: A State-by-State Guide" at http://faculty.ncwc.edu/toconnor/jusgrad.htm.
- The Education Network (at the Corrections Connections Web site) has a listing of criminal justice programs at http://www.corrections.com/edunetwork/cjschools.html.

## ENVIRONMENTAL HEALTH
A database of college programs in environmental studies can be found at EnviroEducation.com: The Environmental Education Directory. The URL is http://www.enviroeducation.com.

## ENVIRONMENTAL STUDIES
A database of college programs in environmental studies can be found at EnviroEducation.com: The Environmental Education Directory, http://www.enviroeducation.com.

## FIRE PROTECTION ENGINEERING
The Society of Fire Protection Engineers provides a list of college programs in fire protection engineering at http://www.sfpe.org/sfpe30/becomefpe.htm.

## FIREFIGHTING

A national database of fire academies can be found at the FireJobs Web site, http://www.firejobs.com/academies.php.

## FIRE SCIENCE/FIRE PREVENTION

The National Fire Academy provides a listing of institutions that offer two-year or four-year degree programs in fire science or fire prevention. To access the list, visit http://www.usfa.fema.gov/nfa.

## FORENSIC PATHOLOGY

The Intersociety Council for Pathology Information has a database of forensic pathology programs at http://www.pathologytraining.org.

## FORENSIC SCIENCE

The American Academy of Forensic Sciences provides a list of undergraduate and graduate programs in forensic science at its Web site, http://www.aafs.org.

## INDUSTRIAL HYGIENE

The following Web sites provide a listing of some programs in industrial hygiene.

- American Board of Industrial Hygiene, http://www.abih.org/Docs/abetmih.htm
- American Industrial Hygiene Association, http://www.aiha.org/TheAcademy/html/abet_schools.htm
- EnviroEducation.com: The Environmental Education Directory, http://www.enviroeducation.com

## LOCKSMITH

The Associated Locksmiths of America provides a list of locksmithing schools at http://www.aloa.org.

## OCCUPATIONAL SAFETY AND HEALTH

A listing of academic institutions that offer occupational safety and health programs is available at the Accreditation Board for Engineering and Technology Web site, http://www.abet.org.

## NATURAL RESOURCE MANAGEMENT

A database of college programs in natural resource management can be found at EnviroEducation.com: The Environmental Education Directory, http://www.enviroeducation.com.

## PARK RANGER—SEASONAL LAW ENFORCEMENT TRAINING

The Association of National Park Rangers provides a listing of institutions that offer the Seasonal Law Enforcement Training Pro-

gram (SLETP). Graduates of an SLETP program are eligible to apply for seasonal law enforcement ranger positions with the U.S. National Park Service. To access the list, visit http://www.anpr.org/academies.htm.

## RECREATION AND PARKS MANAGEMENT

A database of college programs in recreation and parks management can be found at EnviroEducation.com: The Environmental Education Directory, URL is http://www.enviroeducation.com.

## POLICE ACADEMIES

A listing of some police academies in the United States is available at the CopCareer.com Web site, http://www.copcareer.com/academy/policeacademy.htm.

## POLYGRAPH

The American Polygraph Association provides a listing of polygraph schools at http://www.polygraph.org/schools.htm.

## PRIVATE INVESTIGATIONS

A listing of private investigator schools and programs is available at the Private Investigators Portal Web site, http://www.infoguys.com/schools.cfm.

## RESCUE TECHNICIAN

A listing of some search-and-rescue training programs is available at the SARINFO (by SAR Technology, Inc.) Web site, http://www.sarinfo.bc.ca/Sarlinks.htm.

## SAFETY SCIENCE

The American Society of Safety Engineers provides a list of safety and related degree programs in the United States. To access the list, visit http://www.asse.org. Click on the site map link, then go to the "About ASSE" section and click on the "Careers in Safety" link.

## PAYING FOR YOUR EDUCATION

Scholarships, grants, student loans, and other financial aid programs are available to help you pay for your postsecondary education. These programs are sponsored by government agencies, professional and trade associations, private foundations, businesses, and other organizations. For example, the Association of Certified Fraud Examiners offers scholarships to full-time college students who major in accounting or criminal justice. Be sure to contact organizations that serve your particular interests. You can find contact information for many professional societies in Appendix IV and for some government agencies in Appendix V.

To learn more about available financial assistance programs, talk with your high school guidance counselor or college career counselor. You might also consult college catalogs, as they usually include financial aid information. In addition, you might visit or contact the financial aid office at the college where you plan to attend or are attending now. Lastly, check out these Web sites for financial aid information:

- Information for Parents and Students by the National Association of Student Financial Aid Administrators, http://www.studentaid.org
- Student Aid on the Web (U.S. Department of Education Federal Student Aid), http://www.studentaid.ed.gov
- The Student Guide (U.S. Department of Education), http://studentaid.ed.gov/students/publications/student_guide/index.html

# APPENDIX II
# PROFESSIONAL CERTIFICATIONS

Professional certifications are granted by professional associations on a voluntary basis. Unlike occupational licensure, professional certification is not a mandatory state or local requirement for professionals to practice in their field. Employers may require or strongly prefer that applicants possess particular professional certifications. Many individuals obtain professional certifications to enhance their employability and promotional chances.

To be eligible for professional certifications, individuals must have several years of acceptable work experience. They may need to complete certified training as well as pass rigid professional examinations.

The following are professional certification programs for some of the occupations in this book. To learn about other professional certifications, talk with professionals, employers, and professional associations in the fields that interest you.

*Note: All Web addresses were accessible while this book was being written. If a URL no longer works, you may be able to find a new one by entering the name of the certification program or professional association into a search engine.*

## AIRPORT FIRE FIGHTER

The American Association of Airport Executives offers the Aircraft Rescue and Firefighting (ARFF) Certification Program. This program grants the following professional certifications:

- Certified Firefighter (CF)
- Certified Master Firefighter (CMF)

For further information, contact:

**ARFF Certification Program**
American Association of Airport
 Executives
601 Madison Street
Suite 400
Alexandria, VA 22314
**Phone:** (703) 824-0504
http://www.aaae.org
http://www.aaae.org/government/200_
 Regulatory_Affairs/260_ARFF_
 Certification (ARFF Certification Web
 page)

## ALARM INSTALLER

The National Burglar and Fire Alarm Association offers a certification program for alarm installers through its National Training School division. For information, contact:

**National Training School**
National Burglar and Fire Alarm
 Association

8380 Colesville Road
Suite 750
Silver Spring, MD 20910
**Phone:** (301) 585-1855
**Fax:** (301) 585-1866
http://www.alarm.org
http://www.alarm.org/profdev (National
 Training School Web page)

## BANK EXAMINER

The Society of Financial Examiners offers the following certification programs for financial professionals such as bank examiners:

- Accredited Financial Examiner (AFE)
- Certified Financial Examiner (CFE)

For information, contact:

**Society of Financial Examiners**
174 Grace Boulevard
Altamonte Springs, FL 32714
**Phone:** (800) 787-SOFE or
 (407) 682-4930
**Fax:** (407) 682-3175
http://www.sofe.org

## BUILDING AND CONSTRUCTION INSPECTORS

The International Code Council offers certification programs for the different types of building and construction inspec-

tors and plans examiners. For information, contact:

**International Code Council (ICC)**
5203 Leesburg Pike
Suite 600
Falls Church, VA 22041
**Phone:** (703) 931-4533
**Fax:** (703) 379-1546
http://www.iccsafe.org
http://www.iccsafe.org/certification/
 professional.html (ICC certification
 Web page)

## COMPUTER PROFESSIONAL

The Institute for Certification of Computer Professionals offers the following certification programs for computer professionals:

- Certified Computing Professional (CCP)
- Associate Computing Professional (ACP)

For information, contact:

**Institute for Certification of Computer
 Professionals**
2350 East Devon Avenue
Suite 115
Des Plaines, IL 60018-4610
**Phone:** (800) 843-8227 or
 (847) 299-4227
**Fax:** (847) 299-4280
http://www.iccp.org

## COMPUTER SECURITY PROFESSIONAL

(ICS)2, Inc. offers the following certification programs for computer security professionals:

- Certified Information Systems Security Practitioner (CISSP)
- Systems Security Certified Practitioner (SSCP)

For information, contact:

**(ICS)2 Services**
2494 Bayshore Boulevard
Suite 201
Dunedin, FL 34698
**Phone:** (888) 333-4458
**Fax:** (727) 738-8522
http://www.isc2.org

## CRIME SCENE TECHNICIAN

The International Association for Identification offers certification programs in crime scene investigation, latent print examination, footwear and tire track examination, bloodstain pattern examination, and other areas. For information, contact:

**International Association for Identification**
2535 Pilot Knob Road
Suite 117
Mendota Heights, MN 55120-1120
**Phone:** (651) 681-8566
**Fax:** (651) 681-8443
http://www.theiai.org

## ELECTRICAL INSPECTOR

The International Association of Electrical Inspectors offers a certification program for residential and master electrical inspectors. For information, contact:

**International Association of Electrical Inspectors (IAEI)**
P.O. Box 830848
901 Waterfall Way
Suite 602
Richardson, TX 75080-0848
**Phone:** (927) 235-1455
**Fax:** (972) 235-6858
http://www.iaei.org
http://www.iaei.org/certification.htm
    (IAEI certification Web page)

## EMERGENCY MEDICAL TECHNICIAN

The National Registry of Emergency Medical Technicians offers the following certification programs for emergency medical service professionals:

- First Responder
- Emergency Medical Technician (EMT)–Basic
- Emergency Medical Technician (EMT)–Intermediate
- Emergency Medical Technician (EMT)–Paramedic

For information, contact:

**National Registry of Emergency Medical Technicians**
Rocco V. Morando Building
6610 Busch Boulevard
Columbus, Ohio 43229
**Mailing address:**
P.O. Box 29233
Columbus, OH 43229
**Phone:** (614) 888-4484
**Fax:** (614) 888-8920
http://www.nremt.org

## ENVIRONMENTAL HEALTH INSPECTOR

The National Environmental Health Association grants the Registered Environmental Health Specialist/Registered Sanitarian (REHS/RS) designation to qualifying candidates. For information, contact:

**National Environmental Health Association (NEHA)**
720 South Colorado Boulevard
South Tower, Suite 970 South
Denver, CO 80246-1925
**Phone:** (303) 756-9090
**Fax:** (303) 691-9490
http://www.neha.org
http://www.neha.org/credential
    (NEHA credentialing Web page)

## FINANCE OR INSURANCE PROFESSIONAL

The Association of Certified Fraud Examiners offers a certification program to financial investigators, bank examiners, and others who want to earn the Certified Fraud Examiner (CFE) certification. For information, contact:

**Association of Certified Fraud Examiners**
The Gregor Building
716 West Avenue
Austin, TX 78701-2724
**Phone:** (800) 245-3321 or (512) 478-9000
**Fax:** (512) 478-9297
http://www.cfenet.com

## FORENSIC SCIENTISTS

The American Board of Criminalistics offers certification programs in criminalistics, forensic biology, drug biology, fire debris analysis, and trace evidence. For information, contact:

**American Board of Criminalistics**
ABC Registrar
P.O. Box 1123
Wausau, WI 54402-1123
**Phone:** (715) 845-3684
**Fax:** (715) 845-4156
http://www.criminalistics.com

The International Association for Identification offers certification programs in bloodstain pattern examination, footwear and tire track examination, and other areas. For information, contact:

**International Association for Identification**
2535 Pilot Knob Road
Suite 117
Mendota Heights, MN 55120-1120
**Phone:** (651) 681-8566
**Fax:** (651) 681-8443
http://www.theiai.org

## INFORMATION SYSTEMS SECURITY PROFESSIONAL

The Information Systems Audit and Control Association offers the following professional certification programs:

- Certified Information Systems Auditor (CISA)
- Certified Information Security Manager (CISM)

For information, contact:

**Information Systems Audit and Control Association**
3701 Algonquin Road
Suite 1010
Rolling Meadows, IL 60008

**Phone:** (847) 253-1545
**Fax:** (847) 253-1443
http://www.isaca.org

## INDUSTRIAL HYGIENIST

The American Board of Industrial Hygiene grants the Certified Industrial Hygienist (CIH) designation to qualified Industrial Hygienists. For information, contact:

**American Board of Industrial Hygiene**
6015 West St. Joseph
Suite 102
Lansing, MI 48917-3980
**Phone:** (517) 321-2638
**Fax:** (517) 321-4624
http://www.abih.org

## LATENT PRINT EXAMINER

The International Association for Identification offers certification programs for qualifying candidates. For information, contact:

**International Association for Identification**
2535 Pilot Knob Road
Suite 117
Mendota Heights, MN 55120-1120
**Phone:** (651) 681-8566
**Fax:** (651) 681-8443
http://www.theiai.org

## LEGAL INVESTIGATOR

The National Association of Legal Investigators grants the Certified Legal Investigator (CLI) designation to qualifying private investigators. For information, contact:

**National Association of Legal Investigators**
**Phone:** (800) 266-6254
**E-mail:** info@nalionline.org
http://www.nalionline.org

## LOCKSMITH

The Associated Locksmiths of America, Inc. offers the following certification programs for qualifying locksmiths:

• Registered Locksmith (RL)
• Certified Registered Locksmith (CRL)

• Certified Professional Locksmith (CPL)
• Certified Master Locksmith (CML)

For information, contact:

**Associated Locksmiths of America, Inc.**
3003 Live Oak Street
Dallas, TX 75205
**Phone:** (214) 827-1701
http://www.aloa.org

## POLYGRAPH EXAMINER

The American Polygraph Association offers a program for advanced and specialized polygraph examination certification. For information, contact:

**American Polygraph Association**
P.O. Box 8037
Chattanooga, TN 37414-0037
**Phone:** (800) APA-8037 or
    (423) 892-3992
**Fax:** (423) 894-5435
http://www.polygraph.org

## PRIVATE INVESTIGATOR

The ASIS International grants the Professional Certified Investigator (PCI) designation to qualifying private investigators. For information, contact:

**ASIS International**
1625 Prince Street
Alexandria, VA 22314-2818
**Phone:** (703) 519-6200
**Fax:** (703) 519-6299
http://www.asisonline.org

## QUALITY ASSURANCE SPECIALIST

The American Society for Quality grants the Certified Software Quality Engineer (CSQE) designation to qualifying candidates. For information, contact:

**American Society for Quality**
P.O. Box 3005
Milwaukee, WI 53201-3005
**Phone:** (800) 248-1946 or (414) 272-8575
**Fax:** (414) 272-1734
http://www.asq.org

## QUESTIONED DOCUMENT EXAMINER

The American Board of Forensic Document Examiners, Inc. grants professional certification to qualifying questioned document examiners. For information, contact:

**American Board of Forensic Document Examiners, Inc.**
7887 San Felipe
Suite 122
Houston TX 77063
**Phone:** (713) 784-9537
http://www.asqde.org/abfde.htm

## RESCUE TECHNICIAN

The National Association for Search and Rescue offers certification programs for various types of search-and-rescue skills. For information, contact:

**National Association for Search and Rescue**
4500 Southgate Place
Suite 100
Chantilly, VA 20151-1714
**Phone:** (888) 893-7788 or
    (703) 222-6277
**Fax:** (703) 222-6283
http://www.nasar.org

## SAFETY PROFESSIONAL

The Board of Certified Safety Professionals grants the Certified Safety Professional (CSP) designation to qualifying safety professionals. For information, contact:

**Board of Certified Safety Professionals**
208 Burwash Avenue
Savoy, Illinois 61874
**Phone:** (217) 359-9263
**Fax:** (217) 359-0055
http://www.bcsp.com

## SAFETY TRAINING SPECIALIST

The National Association of Safety Professionals offers certification programs for professionals who provide occupational safety training and development in the workplace. For information, contact:

**National Association of Safety
    Professionals**
1101 30th Street NW
Suite 500
Washington, DC 20007
**Phone:** (202) 625-4325
**Fax:** (202) 318-2522
http://www.naspweb.com
http://www.naspweb.com/professional_
    safety_certifications.html
    (certification programs Web page)

## SECURITY GUARD
The International Foundation for Protection Officers offers the following certification programs for security guards:

• Certified Protection Officer (CPO)

• Certified Security Supervisor (CSS)
• Certified Protected Officer Instructor
    (CPOI)

For information contact:

**International Foundation for
    Protection Officers**
P.O. Box 771329
Naples, FL 34107-1329
**Phone:** (239) 430-0534
**Fax:** (239) 430-0533
http://www.ifpo.com

## SECURITY PROFESSIONAL
The ASIS International offers the following certification programs for different types of security professionals:

• Certified Protection Professional (CPP)
• Physical Security Professional (PSP)
• Professional Certified Investigator (PCI)

For information, contact:

**ASIS International**
1625 Prince Street
Alexandria, VA 22314-2818
**Phone:** (703) 519-6200
**Fax:** (703) 519-6299
http://www.asisonline.org

# APPENDIX III
# STATE LICENSING AGENCIES FOR PRIVATE INVESTIGATORS

This appendix provides contact information for state agencies that grant private investigator licenses. Many of these agencies have Web sites that list requirements and application procedures for becoming a private investigator.

As of November 2004, nine states did not have a private investigator licensing requirement. Regardless of whether a state requires a license, it is a good idea to check with local government authorities about any local licensing requirements.

*Note: All Web addresses were accessible while this book was being written. If a URL no longer works, you may be able to find a new one by entering the name of the state and the licensing agency into a search engine.*

## ALABAMA

A state license is not required. To check for updated information, visit the state of Alabama Web site, http://www.alabama.gov. Enter the keywords *private investigators* or *private investigator licensing* into the site's search engine.

## ALASKA

A state license is not required. To check for updated information, visit the state of Alaska Web site, http://www.alaska.gov. Enter the keywords *private investigators* or *private investigator licensing* into the site's search engine.

## ARIZONA

**Licensing and Regulatory Bureau**
Arizona Department of Public Safety
2102 West Encanto Boulevard
Phoenix, AZ 85009
**Mailing address:**
P.O. Box 6328
Phoenix, AZ 85005-6328
**Phone:** (602) 223-2361
http://www.dps.state.az.us/agency/criminaljusticesupport/licensing

## ARKANSAS

**Private Investigators and Private Security Agencies**
Arkansas State Police
1 State Police Plaza Drive
Little Rock, AR 72209

**Phone:** (501) 618-8610
http://www.asp.state.ar.us/pl/pl.html

## CALIFORNIA

**Bureau of Security and Investigative Services**
California Department of Consumer Affairs, Licensing Division
401 S Street
Suite 101
Sacramento, CA 95814
**Phone:** (800) 952-5210 or (916) 322-4000
**Fax:** (916) 323-1182
http://www.dca.ca.gov/bsis/pi.htm

## COLORADO

A state license is not required. To check for updated information, visit the state of Colorado Web site, http://www.colorado.gov. Enter the keywords *private investigators* or *private investigator licensing* into the Web site's search engine.

## CONNECTICUT

**Special License and Firearms Unit**
Connecticut Department of Public Safety
1111 Country Club Road
Middletown, CT 06450
**Phone:** (860) 685-8290
http://www.state.ct.us/dps/slfu/privatedetectiveshome.htm

## DELAWARE

**Detective Licensing Section**
Delaware State Police
P.O. Box 430
Dover, DE 19903
**Phone:** (302) 739-5901
http://www.state.de.us/dsp/detlic.htm

## DISTRICT OF COLUMBIA

**Security Officers Management Branch**
Metropolitan Police Department
2000 14th Street NW
Washington, DC 20009
**Phone:** (202) 671-0500
**Fax:** (202) 673-7418

## FLORIDA

**Division of Licensing**
Florida Department of Agriculture and Consumer Services
P.O. Box 6687
Tallahassee, FL 32314-6687
**Phone:** (850) 488-6982
**Fax:** (850) 488-2789
http://licgweb.doacs.state.fl.us/investigations

## GEORGIA

**Board of Private Detectives and Security Agencies**
Georgia Professional Licensing Boards Division
237 Coliseum Drive

Macon, GA 31217-3858
**Phone:** (478) 207-1460
http://www.sos.state.ga.us/plb/detective

## HAWAII

### Board of Private Detectives and Guards
Hawaii Division of Professional and
    Vocational Licensing
335 Merchant Street
Honolulu, HI 96813
**Mailing address:**
P.O. Box 3469
Honolulu, HI 96801
**Phone:** (808) 586-3000
http://www.hawaii.gov/dcca/pvl/areas_
    private_detective.html

## IDAHO

A state license is not required. To check
for updated information, visit the state of
Idaho Web site, http://www.accessidaho.
org. Enter the keywords *private investigators* or *private investigator licensing* into
the site's search engine.

## ILLINOIS

### Division of Professional Regulation
Illinois Department of Financial and
    Professional Regulation
320 West Washington Street
Third Floor
Springfield, IL 62786
**Phone:** (217) 785-0800
**TDD:** (217) 524-6735
**Fax:** (217) 782-7645
http://www.ildpr.com/WHO/dtct.asp

## INDIANA

### Private Detective Licensing Board
Indiana Professional Licensing Agency
302 West Washington Street
Room E034
Indianapolis, IN 46204
**Phone:** (317) 234-3040
http://www.IN.gov/pla/bandc/detective

## IOWA

### Private Investigator Licensing
Iowa Department of Public Safety
Wallace State Office Building
Des Moines, IA 50319-0045
**Phone:** (515) 281-7610
**Fax:** (515) 281-8921
http://www.dps.state.ia.us/asd/license.htm

## KANSAS

### Private Detective Licensing
Kansas Bureau of Investigation
1620 SW Tyler
Topeka, KS 66612
**Phone:** (785) 296-4436
http://www.accesskansas.org/working/
    working-resources/law-enforcement.
    html

## KENTUCKY

### Board of Licensure for Private
    Investigators
Kentucky State Division of Occupations
    and Professions
P.O. Box 1360
Frankfort, KY 40601
**Phone:** (502) 564-3296
**Fax:** (502) 564-4818
http://occupations.ky.gov/
    privateinvestigators

## LOUISIANA

### Louisiana State Board of Private
    Investigator Examiners
2501 Silverside Drive
Suite 190
Baton Rouge, LA 70808
**Phone:** (808) 299-9696 or
    (225) 763-3556
**Fax:** (225) 763-3536
http://www.lsbpie.com

## MAINE

### Administrative Licensing Unit
Maine Department of Public Safety
45 Commerce Drive
Augusta, ME 04333-0104
**Mailing Address:**
104 State House Station
Augusta, ME 04333-0104
**Phone:** (207) 624-7210
http://www.state.me.us/dps (Maine
    Department of Public Safety Web site)

## MARYLAND

### Private Investigator Licensing Division
Maryland State Police
7751 Washington Boulevard
Jessup, MD 20794
**Phone:** (800) 525-5555 or
    (410) 799-0191
http://www.mdsp.maryland.gov
    (Maryland State Police Web site)

## MASSACHUSETTS

### State Police Certification Unit
Massachusetts State Police
485 Maple Street
Danvers, MA 01923
**Phone:** (978) 538-6128
**Fax:** (978) 538-6021
http://www.mass.gov/msp
    (Massachusetts State Police
    Web site)

## MICHIGAN

### Licensing Division
Bureau of Commercial Services
Michigan Department of Labor and
    Economic Growth
P.O. Box 30018
Lansing, MI 48909
**Phone:** (517) 241-5645
http://www.michigan.gov/cis
    (Click on the "Commercial Services
    and Corporations" link, then click on
    the "Professional and Occupational
    Licenses" link)

## MINNESOTA

### Board of Private Detective and
    Protective Agent Services
Minnesota Department of Public
    Safety
1430 Maryland Avenue East
St. Paul, MN 55106
**Phone:** (651) 793-2666
**TTY:** (651) 282-6555
**Fax:** (651) 793-7065
http://www.dps.state.mn.us/pdb

## MISSISSIPPI

A state license is not required. To check for
updated information, visit the state of Mis-
sissippi Web site, http://www.mississippi.
gov. Enter the keywords *private investigators* or *private investigator licensing* into
the site's search engine.

## MISSOURI

A state license is not required. To check
for updated information, visit the state of
Missouri Web site, http://www.state.mo.
us. Enter the keywords *private investigators* or *private investigator licensing* into
the site's search engine.

## MONTANA

**Board of Private Security Patrol**
**Officers and Investigators**
Montana Department of Labor and Industry
301 South Park Avenue
4th Floor
Helena, MT 59620
**Mailing Address:**
P.O. Box 200513
Helena, MT 59620-0513
**Phone:** (406) 841-2387
**Fax:** (406) 841-2309
http://discoveringmontana.com/dli/bsd/
   license/bsd_boards/psp_board/board_
   page.asp

## NEBRASKA

**Licensing Division**
Nebraska Secretary of State
Room 1305
State Capitol
Lincoln, NE 68509
**Phone:** (402) 471-8606 or (402) 471-4094
**Fax:** (402) 471-2530
http://www.sos.state.ne.us/business/
   private_eye

## NEVADA

**Private Investigator's Licensing Board**
Nevada Department of Justice
3476 Executive Pointe Way
Suite 14
Carson City, NV 89706
**Phone:** (775) 687-3223
http://ag.state.nv.us/faqs/workingaspi.htm

## NEW HAMPSHIRE

**Detective Agencies and Security Services**
New Hampshire State Police
33 Hazen Drive
Concord, NH 03305
**Phone:** (603) 271-3575
http://www.nh.gov/safety/nhsp/pluda.html
   (New Hampshire State Police Web site)
http://www.nh.gov/safety/nhsp/plu.html
   (permits and licensing unit Web page)

## NEW JERSEY

**Private Detective Unit**
New Jersey State Police
1200 Negron Road
Hamilton, NJ 08691
**Phone:** (609) 584-5051, X 5605
http://www.state.nj.us/lps/njsp/about/srb.
   html

## NEW MEXICO

**Private Investigators and Polygraphers**
**Board**
New Mexico Regulation and Licensing
   Department
2550 Cerrillos Road
Santa Fe, NM 87505
**Phone:** (505) 476-4650
http://www.rld.state.nm.us/b&c/
   pipolygraph/index.htm

## NEW YORK

**Division of Licensing Services**
New York State Department of State
84 Holland Avenue
Albany, NY 12208
**Phone:** (518) 474-4429
http://www.dos.state.ny.us/lcns/pimain.htm

## NORTH CAROLINA

**Private Protective Services Board**
North Carolina Department of Justice
900 Mail Service Center
Raleigh, NC 27699-9001
http://www.ncdoj.com/law_enforcement/
   cle_pps.jsp

## NORTH DAKOTA

**Private Investigation and Security**
**Board**
513 Bismarck Expressway
Suite 5
Bismarck, ND 58504
**Phone:** (701) 222-3063
http://www.state.nd.us/pisb

## OHIO

**Real Estate and Professional Licensing**
**Division**
Ohio Department of Commerce
77 South High Street
20th Floor
Columbus, OH 43215-6133
**Phone:** (614) 466-4100
http://www.com.state.oh.us/odoc/real/
   pisgmain.htm

## OKLAHOMA

**Private Security Division**
Oklahoma Council on Law Enforcement
   Education and Training
3530 North Martin Luther King
   Boulevard

Oklahoma City, OK 73111
**Mailing address:**
P.O. Box 11476
Oklahoma City, OK 73136-0476
**Phone:** (405) 2775
**Fax:** (405) 425-7314
http://www.cleet.state.ok.us/Private_
   Security.htm

## OREGON

**Oregon Board of Investigators**
445 State Office Building
800 NE Oregon Street
Number 33
Portland, OR 97232
**Phone:** (503) 731-4359
**Fax:** (503) 731-4366
http://www.obi.state.or.us

## PENNSYLVANIA

A state license is not required. To check
for updated information, visit the state of
Pennsylvania Web site, http://www.state.
pa.us. Enter the keywords *private investigators* or *private investigator licensing*
into the site's search engine.

## RHODE ISLAND

A state license is not required. To check
for updated information, visit the state of
Rhode Island Web site, http://www.state.
ri.us. Enter the keywords *private investigators* or *private investigator licensing*
into the site's search engine.

## SOUTH CAROLINA

**South Carolina Law Enforcement**
**Division**
Regulatory Department
4400 Broad River Road
Columbia, SC 29210
**Mailing address:**
P.O. Box 21398
Columbus, SC 29221-1398
**Phone:** (803) 737-9000
**Fax:** (803) 896-7041
http://www.sled.state.sc.us

## SOUTH DAKOTA

A state license is not required. To check
for updated information, visit the state of
South Dakota Web site, http://www.state.
sd.us. Enter the keywords *private investigators* or *private investigator licensing*
into the site's search engine.

240 CAREER OPPORTUNITIES IN LAW ENFORCEMENT, SECURITY, AND PROTECTIVE SERVICES

## TENNESSEE

**Private Investigation and Polygraph Commission**
Tennessee Department of Commerce and Insurance
500 James Robertson Parkway
Second Floor
Nashville, TN 37243-1158
**Phone:** (615) 741-6382
**Fax:** (615) 532-2965
http://www.state.tn.us/commerce/boards/
sil/pi

## TEXAS

**Private Security Board**
Texas Department of Public Safety
5805 North Lamar Boulevard
Austin, TX 78752
**Mailing Address:**
P.O. Box 4087
Austin, TX 78773
**Phone:** (512) 424-7710
http://www.tcps.state.tx.us or
http://hera.tcps.state.tx.us

## UTAH

**Private Investigator Licensing**
Utah Bureau of Criminal Identification
3888 West 5400 South
Box 148280
Salt Lake City, UT 84114-8280
**Phone:** (801) 965-4445
http://www.bci.utah.gov/BailPI/PIHome.
html

## VERMONT

**Board of Private Investigative and Security Services**
Vermont Office of Professional Regulation
26 Terrace Street
Montpelier, VT 05609-1106
**Phone:** (802) 828-2837
**Fax:** (802) 828-2465
http://vtprofessionals.org/opr1/investigators

## VIRGINIA

**Private Security Services**
Virginia Department of Criminal Justice Services
805 East Broad Street
10th Floor
Richmond, VA 23219
**Phone:** (804) 786-4000
http://www.dcjs.virginia.gov/pss/howto/
registrations/privateInvestigator.cfm

## WASHINGTON

**Private Investigators Licensing Program**
Washington Department of Licensing
2424 Bristol Court SW
Olympia, WA 98504
**Mailing Address:**
P.O. Box 9034
Olympia, WA 98507-9034
**Phone:** (360) 664-6611
**Fax:** (360) 570-7888
http://www.dol.wa.gov/ppu/pifront.htm

## WEST VIRGINIA

**Private Investigator Licensing Division**
West Virginia Secretary of State
1900 Kanawha Boulevard East
Building 1, Suite 157-K
Charleston, WV 25305-0900
**Phone:** (304) 558-6000
**Fax:** (304) 558-0900
http://www.wvsos.com (West Virginia Secretary of State Web site)

## WISCONSIN

**Bureau of Real Estate and Direct Licensing**
Wisconsin Department of Regulation and Licensing
1400 East Washington Avenue
Room 173
Madison, WI 53703
**Mailing Address:**
P.O. Box 8935
Madison, WI 53708-8935
http://drl.wi.gov/prof/burdirect.htm

## WYOMING

A state license is not required. To check for updated information, visit the state of Wyoming Web site, http://wyoming.gov. Enter the keywords *private investigators* or *private investigator licensing* into the site's search engine.

# APPENDIX IV
# PROFESSIONAL UNIONS
# AND ASSOCIATIONS

The following headquarter offices are for the professional organizations that are mentioned in this book. You can contact these groups or visit their Web sites on the Internet to learn about careers, job opportunities, training programs, seminars, conferences, professional certification, and so on. Most of these organizations have branch offices throughout the country; contact an organization's headquarters to find out if a branch is in your area.

There are also local, regional, and state professional associations and unions that can be contacted for information. To learn about any organizations that may be in your area, talk with local professionals.

*Note: Web site addresses change from time to time. If you come across an address that no longer works, you may be able to find a new address by entering the name of the organization in a search engine.*

## POLICE WORK

**Airborne Law Enforcement**
  **Association**
P.O. Box 3683
Tulsa, OK 74101-3683
**Phone:** (918) 599-0705
**Fax:** (918) 583-2353
http://www.alea.org

**American Deputy Sheriffs' Association**
3001 Armand Street
Suite B
Monroe, LA 71201
**Phone:** (800) 937-7940
**Fax:** (318) 398-9980
http://www.deputysheriff.org

**American Federation of Police and**
  **Concerned Citizens**
3801 Biscayne Boulevard
Miami, FL 33137
**Phone:** (321) 264-0911
http://www.aphf.org/afp_cc.html

**Federal Criminal Investigators**
  **Association**
P.O. Box 23400
Washington, DC 20026
**Phone:** (800) 961-7753 or
  (630) 969-8537
**Fax:** (630) 969-1961
http://www.fedcia.org

**Federal Law Enforcement Officers**
  **Association**
Member Services
P.O. Box 326

Lewisberry, PA 17339
**Phone:** (717) 938-2300
**Fax:** (717) 932-2262
http://www.fleoa.org

**Fleet Reserve Association**
125 North West Street
Alexandria, VA 22314-2754
**Phone:** (703) 683-1400
http://www.fra.org

**Fraternal Order of Police**
Grand Lodge
1410 Donelson Pike
Suite A17
Nashville, TN 37217
**Phone:** (615) 399-0900
**Fax:** (615) 399-0400
http://www.grandlodgefop.org

**International Association of Campus**
  **Law Enforcement Administrators**
342 North Main Street
West Hartford, CT 06117-2507
**Phone:** (860) 586-7517
**Fax:** (860) 586-7550
http://www.iaclea.org

**International Association of Chiefs of**
  **Police**
515 North Washington Street
Alexandria, VA 22314
**Phone:** (800) The IACP or
  (703) 836-6767
**Fax:** (703) 836-4543
http://www.theiacp.org

**International Association of Crime**
  **Analysts**
9218 Metcalf Avenue
Overland Park, KS 66212
**Phone:** (913) 940-3883
http://www.iaca.net

**International Association of Women**
  **Police**
1417 Derby County Crescent
Oakville, Ontario L6M3N8
http://www.iawp.org

**International Homicide Investigators**
  **Association**
Membership
P.O. Box 5507
Tampa, FL 33675-5507
**Phone:** (800) 742-1007
http://www.ihia.org

**International Narcotics Interdiction**
  **Association**
7613 Brittany Parc Court
Falls Church, VA 22043
**Phone:** (888) 842-8432
**Fax:** (703) 560-7472
http://www.inia.org

**North American Wildlife Enforcement**
  **Officers Association**
http://www.naweoa.org

**National Association of Women Law**
  **Enforcement Executives**
3 Dunham Street
Carver, MA 02330
http://www.nawlee.com

**National Black Police Association**
3251 Mt. Pleasant Street NW
Second Floor
Washington, DC 20010-2103
**Phone:** (202) 986-2070
**Fax:** (202) 986-0410
http://www.blackpolice.org

**National Border Patrol Council**
http://www.nbpc.net

**National Drug Enforcement Officers Association**
Drug Enforcement Administration
Office of Training/TRDS
FBI Academy
P.O. Box 1475
Quantico, VA 22134-1475
**Phone:** (202) 28-9653
http://www.ndeoa.org

**National Organization of Black Law Executives**
4609 Pinecrest Office Park Drive
Suite F
Alexandria, VA 22312-1442
**Phone:** (703) 658-1529
**Fax:** (703) 658-9479
http://www.noblenational.org

**National Sheriffs' Association**
1450 Duke Street
Alexandria, VA 22314-3490
**Phone:** (703) 836-7827
**Fax:** (703) 683-6541
http://www.sheriffs.org

**National Troopers' Coalition**
http://www.ntctroopers.com

## SPECIAL POLICE UNITS

**Airborne Law Enforcement Association**
P.O. Box 3683
Tulsa, OK 74101-3683
**Phone:** (918) 599-0705
**Fax:** (918) 583-2353
http://www.alea.org

**American Sniper Association**
472 Lakeside Circle
Ft. Lauderdale, FL 33326
http://www.americansniper.org

**ASIS International**
1625 Prince Street
Alexandria, VA 22314-2818

**Phone:** (703) 519-6200
**Fax:** (703) 519-6299
http://www.asisonline.org

**International Association of Bomb Technicians and Investigators**
P.O. Box 160
Goldwein, VA 22720-0160
**Phone:** (540) 752-4533
**Fax:** (540) 752-2796
http://www.iabti.org

**International Police Mountain Bike Association**
583 Frederick Road
Baltimore, MD 21228
**Phone:** (410) 744-2400
**Fax:** (410) 744-5504
http://www.ipmba.org

**International Society of Crime Prevention Practitioners**
3918 Chessrown Avenue
Suite 102
Gibsonia, PA 15044
**Phone:** (724) 443-4947
http://iscpp.net

**Law Enforcement Bicycle Association**
**Phone:** (800) 849-7517
http://www.leba.org

**Law Enforcement Thermographers' Association**
P.O. Box 6485
Edmond, OK 73083-6485
**Phone:** (405) 330-6988
http://www.leta.org

**National Tactical Officers Association**
P.O. Box 797
Doylestown, PA 18901
**Phone:** (800) 279-9127
**Fax:** (215) 230-7552
http://www.ntoa.org

**North American Police Work Dog Association**
4222 Manchester Avenue
Perry, OH 44081
**Phone:** (888) 4CANINE
http://www.napwda.com

**United States Police Canine Association**
P.O. Box 80
Springboro, OH 45066
**Phone:** (800) 531-1614
http://www.uspcak9.com

## FORENSIC INVESTIGATIONS

**American Academy of Forensic Sciences**
410 North 21st Street
Colorado Springs, CO 80904-2798
**Mailing address:**
P.O. Box 669
Colorado Springs, CO 80901-0669
**Phone:** (719) 636-1100
**Fax:** (719) 636-1993
http://www.aafs.org

**American Association of Police Polygraphists**
**Phone:** (888) 743-5479
http://polygraph.org/states/aapp

**American Chemical Society**
1155 Sixteenth Street NW
Washington, DC 20036
**Phone:** (800) 227-5558 or
    (202) 872-4600
**Fax:** (202) 776-8258
http://www.chemistry.org

**American Medical Association**
515 North State Street
Chicago, IL 60610
**Phone:** (800) 621-8335
http://www.ama-assn.org

**American Polygraph Association**
P.O. Box 8037
Chattanooga, TN 37414-0037
**Phone:** (800) APA-8037 or
    (423) 892-3992
**Fax:** (423) 894-5435
http://www.polygraph.org

**American Society for Clinical Pathology**
2100 West Harrison
Chicago, IL 60612
**Phone:** (312) 738-1336
http://www.ascp.org

**American Society of Questioned Document Examiners**
P.O. Box 18298
Long Beach, CA 90807
**Phone:** (562) 907-3378
http://www.asqde.org

**The Association for Crime Scene Reconstruction**
P.O. Box 51376
Phoenix, AX 85076-1376
http://www.acsr.org

**Association of Firearm and Tool Mark
  Examiners**
http://www.afte.org

**International Association for
  Identification**
2535 Pilot Knob Road
Suite 117
Mendota Heights, MN 55120-1120
**Phone:** (651) 681-8566
**Fax:** (651) 681-8443
http://www.theiai.org

**International Crime Scene
  Investigators Association**
BMB 385
15774 South La Grange Road
Orland Park, IL 60462
**Phone:** (708) 460-8082
http://www.icsia.com

**National Association of Document
  Examiners**
**Phone:** (866) 569-0833
http://documentexaminers.org

**National Association of Medical
  Examiners**
430 Pryor Street SW
Atlanta, GA 30312
**Phone:** (404) 730-4781
**Fax:** (404) 730-4220
http://www.thename.org

## PRIVATE INVESTIGATIONS

**American Institute of Certified Public
  Accountants**
1211 Avenue of the Americas
New York, NY 10036-8775
**Phone:** (212) 596-6200
**Fax:** (212) 596-6213
http://www.aicpa.org

**ASIS International**
1625 Prince Street
Alexandria, VA 22314-2818
**Phone:** (703) 519-6200
**Fax:** (703) 519-6299
http://www.asisonline.org

**Association of Certified Fraud
  Examiners**
The Gregor Building
716 West Avenue
Austin, TX 78701-2727
**Phone:** (800) 245-3321 or
  (512) 478-9000

**Fax:** (512) 478-9297
http://www.cfenet.com

**Global Investigators Network**
P.O. Box 621
La Grange, IL 60525
**Phone:** (309) 496-3900
**Fax:** (309) 496-3910
http://www.ginetwork.com

**International Association of Arson
  Investigators**
12770 Boenker Road
Bridgeton, MO 63044
**Phone:** (314) 739-4224
**Fax:** (314) 739-4219
http://www.firearson.com

**International Association of Financial
  Crimes Investigators**
873 Embarcadero Drive
Suite 5
El Dorado Hills, CA 95762
**Phone:** (916) 939-5000
**Fax:** (916) 939-0395
http://www.iafci.org

**International Association of Personal
  Protection Specialists**
World Headquarters
5255 Stevens Creek Boulevard
Suite 308
Santa Clara, CA 95051
**Phone:** (888) 671-6803
http://www.iapps.org

**International Association of Special
  Investigation Units**
8015 Corporate Drive
Suite A
Baltimore, MD 21236
**Phone:** (410) 931-3332
**Fax:** (410) 931-2060
http://www.iasiu.org

**Loss Prevention and Security
  Association**
3135 South 48th Street
Suite 104-11
Tempe, AZ 85282
**Phone:** (888) 372-7214
**Fax:** (831) 855-1110
http://www.lpsa.net

**National Association of Investigative
  Specialists**
P.O. Box 33244
Austin, TX 78764
**Phone:** (512) 719-3595

**Fax:** (512) 719-3594
http://www.pimall.com/nais/nais.j.html

**National Association of Legal
  Investigators**
http://www.nalionline.org

**National Society of Professional
  Insurance Investigators**
National Chapter
P.O. Box 88
Delaware, OH 43015-0888
**Phone:** (888) 677-4498
**Fax:** (614) 369-7155
http://www.nspii.com

## PUBLIC SAFETY

**Association of National Park Rangers**
P.O. Box 108
Larnet, KS 67550-0108
http://www.anpr.org

**Association of Public-Safety
  Communications Officials
  International, Inc.**
351 North Williamson Boulevard
Daytona, FL 32114-1112
**Phone:** (306) 322-2500 or
  (888) APCO 9-1-1
**Fax:** (306) 322-2501
http://www.apcointl.org

**International Association of Fire
  Fighters**
1750 New York Avenue NW
Washington, DC 20006
**Phone:** (202) 737-8484
**Fax:** (202) 737-8418
http://www.iaff.org

**International Municipal Signal
  Association**
P.O. Box 539
165 East Union Street
Newark, NY 14513-0539
**Phone:** (800) 723-4672 or
  (315) 331-2182
**Fax:** (315) 331-8205
http://www.imsasafety.org

**International Rescue and Emergency
  Care Association**
P.O. Box 43100
Minneapolis, MN 55493
**Phone:** (800) 85 IRECA
http://www.ireca.org

**Mountain Rescue Association**
P.O. Box 880868
San Diego, CA 92168-0868
**Fax:** (619) 374-7072
http://www.mra.org

**National Association for Search and Rescue**
4500 Southgate Place
Suite 100
Chantilly, VA 20151-1714
**Phone:** (888) 893-7788 or
    (703) 222-6277
**Fax:** (703) 222-6283
http://www.nasar.org

**National Association of Emergency Medical Technicians**
P.O. Box 1400
Clinton, MS 39060-1400
**Phone:** (800) 34-NAEMT
http://www.naemt.org

**National Emergency Number Association**
4350 North Fairfax Drive
Suite 750
Arlington, VA 22203-1695
**Phone:** (800) 332-9311 or
    (703) 812-4600
**Fax:** (703) 812-4675
http://www.nena9-1-1.org

**National Fire Protection Association**
1 Batterymarch Park
Quincy, MA 02169-7471
**Phone:** (617) 770-3000
**Fax:** (617) 770-0700
http://www.nfpa.org

**National Recreation and Park Association**
**Phone:** (703) 858-0784
**Fax:** (703) 858-0794
http://www.nrpa.org

**National Volunteer Fire Council**
1050 17th Street NW
Suite 490
Washington, DC 20036
**Phone:** (888) ASK NVFC or
    (202) 887-5700
**Fax:** (202) 887-5291
http://nvfc.org

**Park Law Enforcement Association**
http://www.parkranger.com

**United States Lifesaving Association**
http://www.usla.org

**U.S. Park Ranger Lodge**
P.O. Box 151
Fancy Gap, VA 24238
**Phone:** (800) 407-8295
http://www.rangerfop.com

**Women in the Fire Service, Inc.**
P.O. Box 5446
Madison, WI 53705
**Phone:** (608) 233-4768
**Fax:** (608) 233-4879
http://www.wfsi.org

## PHYSICAL SECURITY

**ASIS International**
1625 Prince Street
Alexandria, VA 22314-2818
**Phone:** (703) 519-6200
**Fax:** (703) 519-6299
http://www.asisonline.org

**Associated Locksmiths of America, Inc.**
3003 Live Oak Street
Dallas, TX 75205
**Phone:** (800) 532-2562 or
    (214) 827-1701
http://www.aloa.org

**International Association of Certified Surveillance Professionals**
1000 North Green Valley Parkway
Suite 440-220
Henderson, NV 89074-6170
http://iacsp.org

**International Foundation for Protection Officers**
P.O. Box 771329
Naples, FL 34103
**Phone:** (239) 430-0534
**Fax:** (239) 430-0533
http://www.ifpo.com

**Institutional Locksmiths' Association**
**Phone:** (888) 745-5625
http://www.ilanational.org

**National Burglar and Fire Alarm Association**
8380 Colesville Road
Suite 750
Silver Spring, MD 20910
**Phone:** (301) 585-1855
**Fax:** (301) 585-1866
http://www.alarm.org

**National Fire Protection Association**
1 Batterymarch Park
Quincy, MA 02169-7471

**Phone:** (617) 770-3000
**Fax:** (617) 770-0700
http://www.nfpa.org

**National Police and Security Officers Association of America**
P.O. Box 663
South Plainfield, NJ 07080-0663
http://npoaa.tripod.com

**National Society of Professional Engineers**
1420 King Street
Alexandria, VA 22314
**Phone:** (703) 684-2800
**Fax:** (703) 836-4875
http://www.nspe.org

**Society of Fire Protection Engineers**
7315 Wisconsin Avenue
Suite 620E
Betheseda, MD 20814
**Phone:** (301) 718-2910
**Fax:** (301) 718-2242
http://www.sfpe.org

## AVIATION SAFETY AND SECURITY

**Air Traffic Control Association**
1101 King Street
Suite 300
Alexandria, VA 22314
**Phone:** 703-299-2430
**Fax:** 703-299-2437
http://www.atca.org

**Aircraft Rescue and Fire Fighting Working Group**
1701 W. Northwest Highway
Grapevine, TX 76051
**Phone:** (817) 329-5092
**Fax:** (817) 329-5094
http://www.arffwg.org

**Airline Dispatchers Federation**
2020 Pennsylvania Avenue NW
Suite 821
Washington, DC 20006
**Phone:** (800) OPN-CNTL
http://www.dispatcher.org

**American Federation of Government Employees, AFL-CIO**
80 F Street NW
Washington, DC 20001
**Phone:** (866) 392-6832
http://www.afge.org

**American Federation of Police and
Concerned Citizens**
3801 Biscayne Boulevard
Miami, FL 33137
**Phone:** (321) 264-0911
http://www.aphf.org/afp_cc.html

**Fraternal Order of Police**
Grand Lodge
1410 Donelson Pike
Suite A17
Nashville, TN 37217
**Phone:** (615) 399-0900
**Fax:** (615) 399-0400
http://www.grandlodgefop.org

**International Association of Airport
and Seaport Police**
Secretariat
111, B3-1410 Parkway Boulevard
Coquitlam, British Columbia V3E 3J7
**Phone:** (604) 782-6386
**Fax:** (604) 945-6134
http://www.iaasp.net

**International Association of Fire
Fighters**
1750 New York Avenue NW
Washington, DC 20006
**Phone:** (202) 737-8484
**Fax:** (202) 737-8418
http://www.iaff.org

**International Association of Women
Police**
1417 Derby County Crescent
Oakville, Ontario L6M3N8
http://www.iawp.org

**National Air Traffic Controllers
Association**
1325 Massachusetts Avenue NW
Washington, DC 20005
**Phone:** (202) 628-5451
**Fax:** (202) 628-5767
http://www.natca.org

**National Association of Air Traffic
Specialists**
11303 Amherst Avenue
Suite 4
Wheaton, MD 20902
**Phone:** (301) 933-6228
**Fax:** (301) 933-3902
http://www.naats.org

**National Fire Protection Association**
1 Batterymarch Park
Quincy, MA 02169-7471

**Phone:** (617) 770-3000
**Fax:** (617) 770-0700
http://www.nfpa.org

**Professional Women Controllers, Inc.**
P.O. Box 950085
Oklahoma City, OK 73195-0085
http://www.pwcinc.org

# COMPUTER SECURITY

**American Society for Quality**
P.O. Box 3005
Milwaukee, WI 53201-3005
**Phone:** (800) 248-1946 or
(414) 272-8575
**Fax:** (414) 272-1734
http://www.asq.org

**ASIS International**
1625 Prince Street
Alexandria, VA 22314-2818
**Phone:** (703) 519-6200
**Fax:** (703) 519-6299
http://www.asisonline.org

**Association for Computing
Machinery**
Headquarters Office
1515 Broadway
New York, NY 10036
**Phone:** (800) 342-6626 or
(212) 626-0500
http://www.acm.org

**Association for Computing
Machinery—Special Interest Group
on Management Of Data
(SIGMOD)**
1515 Broadway
New York, NY 10036
**Phone:** (800) 342-6626 or
(212) 626-0500
http://www.acm.org/sigmod

**Computer Security Institute**
600 Harrison Street
San Francisco, CA 94107
**Phone:** (415) 947-6330
**Fax:** (415) 947-6023
http://www.gocsi.com

**Information Systems Security
Association**
7044 South 13th Street
Oak Creek, WI 53154
**Phone:** (800) 370-ISSA or
(414) 908-4949

**Fax:** (414) 768-8001
http://www.issa.org

**High Technology Crime Investigation
Association**
1474 Freeman Drive
Amissville, VA 20106
**Phone:** (540) 937-5019
**Fax:** (540) 937-7848
http://htcia.org

**International Association of Computer
Investigative Specialists**
P.O. Box 140
Donahue, IA 52746-0140
**Phone:** (877) 890-6130
http://cops.org

# CORRECTIONS

**American Correctional Association**
4380 Forbes Boulevard
Lanham, MD 20706-4322
**Phone:** (800) 222-5646
http://www.aca.org

**American Deputy Sheriffs'
Association**
3001 Armand Street
Suite B
Monroe, LA 71201
**Phone:** (800) 937-7940
**Fax:** (318) 398-9980
http://www.deputysheriff.org

**American Jail Association**
1135 Professional Court
Hagerstown, MD 21740-5853
**Phone:** (301) 790-3930
http://www.corrections.com/aja

**American Probation and Parole
Association**
2760 Research Park Drive
Lexington KY 40511-84110
**Phone:** (859) 244-8203
**Fax:** (859) 244-8001
http://www.appa-net.org

**International Association of Court
Officers and Services, Inc.**
1450 Duke Street
Suite 206
Alexandria, VA 22314-3490
**Phone:** (703) 836-7827
**Fax:** (703) 683-6541
http://www.sheriffs.org/iacos

**National Sheriffs' Association**
1450 Duke Street
Alexandria, VA 22314-3490
**Phone:** (703) 836-7827
**Fax:** (703) 683-6541
http://www.sheriffs.org

## COMPLIANCE INSPECTIONS

**American Federation of Government Employees, AFL-CIO**
80 F Street NW
Washington, DC 20001
**Phone:** (202) 737-8700
http://www.afge.org

**American Industrial Hygiene Association**
2700 Prosperity Avenue
Suite 250
Fairfax, VA 22031
**Phone:** (703) 849-8888
**Fax:** (703) 207-3561
http://www.aiha.org

**American Public Health Association**
800 I Street NW
Washington, DC 20001-3710
**Phone:** (202) 777-2742
**Fax:** (202) 777-2534
http://www.apha.org

**Association of Certified Fraud Examiners**
The Gregor Building
716 West Avenue
Austin, TX 78701-2727
**Phone:** (800) 245-3321 or
    (512) 478-9000
**Fax:** (512) 478-9297
http://www.cfenet.com

**National Environmental Health Association**
720 South Colorado Boulevard
Suite 970 South
Denver, CO 80246-1925
**Phone:** (303) 756-9090
**Fax:** (303) 691-9490
http://www.neha.org

**National Treasury Employees Union**
1750 H Street NW
Washington, DC 20006
**Phone:** (202) 572-5500
http://www.nteu.org

**Professional Airways Systems Specialists**
1150 Seventeenth Street NW
Suite 702
Washington, DC 20036
**Phone:** (202) 293-7277
**Fax:** (202) 293-7277
http://www.passnational.org

**Society of Financial Examiners**
174 Grace Boulevard
Altamonte Springs, FL 32714
**Phone:** (800) 787-SOFE or
    (407) 682-4930
**Fax:** (407) 682-3175
http://www.sofe.org

## BUILDING AND CONSTRUCTION INSPECTIONS

**American Public Works Association**
2345 Grand Boulevard
Suite 500
Kansas City, MO 64108-2641
**Phone:** (816) 472-6100
**Fax:** (816) 472-1610
Washington, D.C. Office:
1401 K Street NW
11th Floor
Washington, DC 20005
**Phone:** (202) 408-9541
**Fax:** (202) 408-9542
http://www.pubworks.org

**Association of Construction Inspectors**
1224 North Nokomis NE
Alexandria, MN 56308
**Phone:** (320) 763-7525
**Fax:** (320) 763-9290
http://iami.org/aci

**International Association of Electrical Inspectors**
P.O. Box 830848
901 Waterfall Way
Suite 602
Richardson, TX 75080-0848
**Phone:** (927) 235-1455
**Fax:** (972) 235-6858
http://www.iaei.org

**International Association of Plumbing and Mechanical Officials**
5001 East Philadelphia Street
Ontario, CA 91761
**Phone:** (909) 472-4100
**Fax:** (909) 472-4150
http://www.iapmo.org

**International Code Council**
5203 Leesburg Pike
Suite 600
Falls Church, VA 22041
**Phone:** (703) 931-4533
**Fax:** (703) 379-1546
http://www.iccsafe.org

## WORKPLACE SAFETY AND SECURITY

**American Conference of Governmental Industrial Hygienists**
1330 Kemper Meadow Drive
Cincinnati, OH 95240
**Phone:** (513) 742-2020
http://www.acgih.org

**American Industrial Hygiene Association**
2700 Prosperity Avenue
Suite 250
Fairfax, VA 22031
**Phone:** (703) 849-8888
**Fax:** (703) 207-3561
http://www.aiha.org

**American Society for Training and Development**
1640 King Street
Box 1443
Alexandria, VA 22313-2043
**Phone:** (800) 628-2783 or
    (703) 683-8100
**Fax:** (703) 683-8103
http://www.astd.org

**American Society of Safety Engineers**
Customer Service
1800 E Oakton Street
Des Plaines, IL 60018
**Phone:** (847) 699-2929
**Fax:** (847) 768-3434
http://www.asse.org

**ASIS International**
1625 Prince Street
Alexandria, VA 22314-2818
**Phone:** (703) 519-6200
**Fax:** (703) 519-6299
http://www.asisonline.org

**Insurance Loss Control Association**
c/o National Association of Mutual Insurance Companies
3601 Vincennes Road
Indianapolis, IN 46268
**Phone:** (317) 875-5250

**Fax:** (317) 879-8408
http://www.insurancelosscontrol.org

**International Association of
   Professional Security Consultants**
525 SW 5th Street
Suite A
Des Moines, IA 50309-4501
**Phone:** (515) 282-8192
**Fax:** (515) 282-9117
http://www.iapsc.org

**National Association of Safety
   Professionals**
1101 30th Street NW
Suite 500
Washington, DC 20007
**Phone:** (800) 922-2219 or
   (202) 625-4325
**Fax:** (202) 318-2522
http://www.naspweb.com

**National Fire Protection Association**
1 Batterymarch Park
Quincy, MA 02169-7471
**Phone:** (617) 770-3000
**Fax:** (617) 770-0700
http://www.nfpa.org

**National Safety Council**
1121 Spring Lake Drive
Itasca, IL 60143-3201
**Phone:** (630) 285-1121
**Fax:** (630) 285-1315
http://www.nsc.org

**National Safety Management Society**
P.O. Box 4460
Walnut Creek, CA 94596-0460
http://www.nsms.us

**Public Risk Management Association**
500 Montgomery Street

Suite 750
Alexandria, VA 22314
**Phone:** (703) 528-7701
**Fax:** (703) 739-0200
http://www.primacentral.org

**Risk and Insurance Management
   Society, Inc.**
655 Third Avenue
2nd Floor
New York, NY 10017
**Phone:** (212) 286-9292
http://www.rims.org

**System Safety Society**
P.O. Box 70
Unionville, VA 22567-0070
**Phone:** (540) 854-8630
http://www.system-safety.org

# APPENDIX V
# FEDERAL AGENCIES

Federal agencies can be contacted directly for information about careers and job vacancies. Most agencies have Web sites on the Internet that provide information. Some agencies even allow you to apply for jobs through the Internet.

Listed below are the federal agencies that were mentioned in this book with addresses to their headquarters in Washington, D.C. along with their Web site addresses. These federal agencies also have regional or field offices throughout the country. Addresses and phone numbers for the branch offices usually can be found at the agencies' Web sites. In addition, look in the white pages of telephone books under *United States Government.*

*Note: Federal agencies may change their Web addresses from time to time. If you come across an address that no longer works, you may be able to find a new one by entering the name of the federal agency in a search engine.*

## U.S. DEPARTMENTS
The following are some of the departments in the executive branch. The head officer, or secretary, of each department is a member of the president's cabinet.

**U.S. Department of Agriculture (USDA)**
14th and Independence Avenue SW
Washington, DC 20250
http://www.usda.gov

**U.S. Department of Energy (DOE)**
1000 Independence Avenue SW
Washington, DC 20585
http://www.energy.gov

**U.S. Department of Health and Human Services (HHS)**
200 Independence Avenue SW
Washington, DC 20201
http://www.dhhs.gov

**U.S. Department of Homeland Security (DHS)**
Washington, DC 20528
http://www.dhs.gov

**U.S. Department of Housing and Urban Development (HUD)**
451 7th Street SW
Washington, DC 20410
http://www.hud.gov

**U.S. Department of Interior (DOI)**
1849 C Street NW
Washington, DC 20240
http://www.doi.gov

**U.S. Department of Justice (DOJ)**
950 Pennsylvania Avenue NW
Washington, DC 20530-0001
http://www.usdoj.gov

**U.S. Department of Labor (DOL)**
200 Constitution Avenue NW
Washington, DC 20210
http://www.dol.gov

**U.S. Department of Transportation (DOT)**
400 7th Street SW
Washington, DC 20590
http://www.dot.gov

**U.S. Department of the Treasury**
Office of Public Correspondence
1500 Pennsylvania Avenue NW
Washington, DC 20220
http://www.ustreas.gov

## FEDERAL BUREAUS, AGENCIES, AND COMMISSIONS
Some of the following organizations are part of various departments of the U.S. executive branch. Others are independent agencies or commissions.

**Agricultural Marketing Service (AMS)**
U.S. Department of Agriculture
14th and Independence Avenue SW
Washington, DC 20250
http://www.ams.usda.gov

**Army Corps of Engineers**
U.S. Department of the Army
441 G Street NW
Washington, DC 20314
http://www.hq.usace.army.mil/hqhome

**Bureau of Alcohol, Tobacco, Firearms and Explosives**
U.S. Department of Justice
650 Massachusetts Avenue NW
Washington, DC 20226
http://www.atf.gov

**Bureau of Labor Statistics (BLS)**
U.S. Department of Labor
Postal Square Building
2 Massachusetts Avenue NE
Washington, DC 20212-0001
http://www.bls.gov

**Coast Guard**
U.S. Department of Homeland Security
Mailing address for Coast Guard
    Headquarters:
Commandant
U.S. Coast Guard
2100 Second Street SW
Washington, DC 20593
http://www.uscg.mil

**Consumer Product Safety Commission (CPSC)**
Washington, DC 20207-0001
http://www.cpsc.gov

**Customs and Border Protection (CBP)**
U.S. Department of Homeland Security
1300 Pennsylvania Avenue NW

Washington, DC 20229
http://www.cbp.gov

**Drug Enforcement Administration (DEA)**
U.S. Department of Justice
Mail stop: AXS
2401 Jefferson Davis Highway
Alexandria, VA 22301
http://www.dea.gov
http://www.dea.gov/resources/
   jobapplicants.html (employment
   information Web page)

**Environmental Protection Agency (EPA)**
Ariel Rios Building
1200 Pennsylvania Avenue NW
Washington, DC 20460
http://www.epa.gov

**Federal Aviation Administration (FAA)**
U.S. Department of Transportation
800 Independence Avenue SW
Washington, DC 20591
http://www.faa.gov
http://www.faa.gov/jobs/index.cfm
   (employment information Web page)

**Federal Bureau of Investigation (FBI)**
U.S. Department of Justice
935 Pennsylvania Avenue NW
Washington, DC 20535
http://www.fbi.gov
http://www.fbijobs.com (employment
   information Web site)

**Federal Bureau of Prisons**
U.S. Department of Justice
320 First Street NW
Washington, DC 20534
http://www.bop.gov

**Federal Deposit Insurance Corporation (FDIC)**
550 17th Street NW
Washington, DC 20429
http://www.fdic.gov

**Federal Reserve System**
20th and Constitution Avenue NW
Washington, DC 20551
http://www.federalreserve.gov

**Fish and Wildlife Service (FWS)**
U.S. Department of Interior
1849 C Street NW
Washington, DC 20240-0001
http://www.fws.gov
http//www.jobs.fws.gov (employment
   information Web page)

**Food and Drug Administration (FDA)**
U.S. Department of Health and Human
   Services
5600 Fishers Lane
Rockville, MD 20857
http://www.fda.gov

**Food Safety and Inspection Service (FSIS)**
U.S. Department of Agriculture
14th and Independence Avenue SW
Washington, DC 20250
http://www.fsis.usda.gov

**Immigration and Customs Enforcement (ICE)**
U.S. Department of Homeland Security
http://www.ice.gov

**Internal Revenue Service (IRS)**
U.S. Department of the Treasury
http://www.irs.gov

**National Park Service (NPS)**
U.S. Department of Interior
1849 C Street NW
Washington, DC 20240
http:/www.nps.gov
http://www.nps.gov/personnel
   (employment information Web page)

**Occupational Safety and Health Administration (OSHA)**
U.S. Department of Labor
200 Constitution Avenue NW

Washington, DC 20210
http://www.osha.gov

**Office of the Comptroller of the Currency (OCC)**
U.S. Department of the Treasury
Administrator of National Banks
Washington, DC 20219
http://www.occ.treas.gov
http://www.occ.treas.gov/jobs/careers.htm
   (careers information Web page)

**Office of Personnel Management (OPM)**
1900 E Street NW
Washington, DC 20415
http://www.opm.gov

**Transportation Security Adminstration (TSA)**
U.S. Department of Homeland Security
601 South 12th Street
Arlington, VA 22202-4220
http://www.tsa.gov

**USDA Forest Service**
U.S. Department of Agriculture
1400 Independence Avenue SW
Washington, DC 20250
http://www.fs.fed.us

**U.S. Marshals Service**
U.S. Department of Justice
http://www.usmarshals.gov
http://www.usmarshals.gov/careers
   (careers information Web page)

**U.S. Postal Inspection Service**
U.S. Postal Service
http://www.usps.com/postalinspectors/
   welcome2.htm

**U.S. Secret Service**
U.S. Department of Homeland Security
http://www.secretservice.gov
http://www.secretservice.gov/
   opportunities.shtml (careers
   information Web page)

# APPENDIX VI
# RESOURCES ON THE WORLD WIDE WEB

Listed in this appendix are some Web sites and Web pages that can help you learn more about many of the occupations in this book. You will also learn about some Internet resources that provide information about jobs and careers.

*Note: All URLs were current when this book was being written. If you come across a Web address that no longer works, you may be able to find the new URL by entering the name of the organization, individual, or Web site into a search engine.*

## GENERAL INFORMATION

**Bureau of Justice Statistics Publications**
U.S. Department of Justice
http://www.ojp.usdoj.gov/bjs/
    pubalp2.htm#fleo

**Criminal Justice Links**
by Dr. Cecil Greek
School of Criminology and Criminal
    Justice
Florida State University
http://www.criminology.fsu.edu/cjlinks

**Criminal Justice Mega-Sites**
by Dr. Tom O'Connor
North Carolina Wesleyan College
Rocky Mount, North Carolina
http://faculty.ncwc.edu/toconnor/linklist.
    htm

**eHow**
(Click on the "Careers/Education" link)
http://www.ehow.com

**National Criminal Justice Reference Service**
U.S. Department of Justice
http://www.ncjrs.org

**Office of Justice Programs Home Page**
U.S. Department of Justice
http://www.ojp.usdoj.gov

**Open Directory Project**
http://dmoz.org

**Safety Source Online: Your Source for Public Safety Information**
http://www.safetysource.com

**World Book Online Reference Center**
http://www.aolsvc.worldbook.aol.com

## CAREER AND JOB INFORMATION

**America's Job Bank**
http://www.jobsearch.org

**California Occupational Guides**
California Employment Development
    Department
http://www.calmis.ca.gov/htmlfile/subject/
    guide.htm

**CareerPlanner.com**
http://www.careerplanner.com

**Career Prospects in Virginia**
University of Virginia
http://www.ccps.virginia.edu/
    career_prospects

**Career Voyages**
by the U.S. Department of Labor and the
    U.S. Department of Education
http://www.careervoyages.gov

**CopCareer.com**
http://www.copcareer.com

**The High School Graduate.com**
http://www.thehighschoolgraduate.com

**ISEEK**
Minnesota Internet System for Education,
    Employment and Business Information
http://www.iseek.org

**Michigan Career Portal**
State of Michigan
http://www.michigan.gov/careers

**Monster**
http://www.monster.com

**911 Jobforums.com**
http://www.911jobforums.com

**Occupational Employment Statistics**
U.S. Bureau of Labor Statistics
http://www.bls.gov/oes

**Occupational Outlook Handbook**
U.S. Bureau of Labor Statistics
http://www.bls.gov/oco

**O*NET OnLine**
Occupational Information Network
http://online.onetcenter.org

**PoliceEmployment.com**
http://www.policeemployment.com

**Security Jobs Network**
http://securityjobs.net

**USA Jobs**
U.S. Office of Personnel Management
http://www.usajobs.opm.gov

**WetFeet.com**
http://www.wetfeet.com

**Yahoo! Hot Jobs**
http://hotjobs.yahoo.com

## AIR TRAFFIC CONTROLLER

**Air Traffic Control Websites**
ThirtyThousandFeet.com Aviation
    Directory
http://www.thirtythousandfeet.com/atc.htm

**Chicago O'Hare Air Traffic Control**
http://www.thetracon.com/atcjobs.htm

## AIRPORT FIREFIGHTER

**Airport Fire ARFF**
(A listing of fire departments around the
     world)
http://www.airportfire.com

**Aviation Medical, Rescue, and
     Firefighting Links**
ThirtyThousandFeet.com Aviation
     Directory
http://www.thirtythousandfeet.com/rescue.
     htm

**International Aviation Fire and Rescue
     Information**
http://www.fire.org.uk/aviation

**International Aviation Fire Protection
     Association**
http://www.iafpa.org.uk

## ALARM INSTALLER

**Security Industry Alarm Coalition**
http://www.siacinc.org

## ARSON INVESTIGATOR

**California Conference of Arson
     Investigators**
http://www.arson.org

**The Fire and Arson Investigations
     Website**
Corporate Investigative Services, Ltd.
http://www.arson-codes.com

**InterFIRE Online**
http://www.interfire.org

## AVIATION—GENERAL
## RESOURCES

**Air Transport Association**
http://www.airlines.org

**Aviation Education Resource Library**
U.S. Federal Aviation Administration
http://www.faa.gov/education/resource.htm

**Aviation Home Page**
http://www.avhome.com

**Civil Air Patrol Online**
http://www.cap.gov

**ThirtyThousandFeet.com—Aviation
     Directory**
http://www.thirtythousandfeet.com

## AVIATION SAFETY
## INSPECTOR

**Aviation Safety Network**
http://aviation-safety.net

**Flight Safety Foundation**
http://www.flightsafety.org

**Job Series 1825**
U.S. Federal Aviation Administration
http://www.faa.gov/careers/employment/
     asi.htm

**William J. Hughes Technical Center**
http://www.tc.faa.gov

## BANK EXAMINER

**American Bankers Association**
http://www.aba.com

**Bank Examiner Cooperative Education
     Program**
Office of the Comptroller of the Currency
U.S. Department of the Treasury
http://www.occ.treas.gov/jobs/coop.htm

## BIKE PATROL OFFICER

**Bicycle Links**
Hendersonville Police Department
Hendersonville, Tennessee
http://www.hendersonville-pd.org/links/
     bicyclepatrol.html

**Frequently Asked Questions**
International Police Mountain Bike
     Association
http://www.ipmba.org/factsheet.htm

**National Mountain Bike Patrol**
International Mountain Bicycling
     Association
http://www.imba.com/nmbp

## BOMB TECHNICIAN

**Bomb Squad Links**
Hendersonville Police Department
Hendersonville, Tennessee
http://www.hendersonville-
     pd.org/links/bombsquads.html

## BORDER PATROL AGENT

**National Border Patrol Council Local
     1613**
San Diego, California
http://www.nbpc1613.org

**United States Border Patrol Unofficial
     Website**
http://www.honorfirst.com/usbp1.htm

## CAMPUS POLICE OFFICER

**Campus Police and Security Web Sites**
Security on Campus, Inc.
http://www.securityoncampus.org/schools/
     policesites.html

**Department of Public Safety**
University of Southern California
Los Angeles, California
http://capsnet.usc.edu/DPS

**Security on Campus, Inc.**
http://www.securityoncampus.org

## CANINE (K9) HANDLER

**K9 Links**
Hendersonville Police Department
Hendersonville, Tennessee
http://www.hendersonville-pd.org/links/
     dogs.html

**K9 Nation dot Net**
http://www.k9nation.net

**Police Dog Home Page**
Eden Consulting Group
http://www.policeK9.com

## COAST GUARD BOARDING
## TEAM PERSONNEL

**Jack's Joint**
An Unofficial Coast Guard Library and
     More
by Jack A. Eckert
http://www.jacksjoint.com

**Pacific Tactical Law Enforcement
     Team**
U.S. Coast Guard
http://www.taclet.com

**U.S. Coast Guard**
http://www.uscg.mil

**U.S. Coast Guard Auxiliary**
http://www.auxpa.org

## COMPLIANCE SAFETY AND HEALTH OFFICER

**National Institute for Occupational Safety and Health**
Centers for Disease Control and Prevention
U.S. Department of Health and Human Services
http://www.cdc.gov/niosh

**OSHA Compliance Online Resource Center**
Quality America
http://www.osha-compliance.com

## COMPUTER FORENSICS SPECIALIST

**Berryhill Computer Forensics**
http://www.computerforensics.com

## COMPUTER SECURITY— GENERAL RESOURCES

**Center for Education and Research in Information Assurance and Security (CERIAS)**
Purdue University
http://www.cerias.purdue.edu

**Computer and Internet Security Resources**
http://virtuallibrarian.com/legal

**Computer Security Institute**
http://www.gocsi.com

**Computer Society**
Institute of Electrical and Electronics Engineers
http://computer.org

**Information Technology Association of America**
http://www.itaa.org

**Institute for Certification of Computing Professionals**
http://www.iccp.org.

## CONSERVATION OFFICER

**Careers in the FWS**
U.S. Fish and Wildlife Service

http://personnel.fws.gov/HR/Careers_FWS.htm

**Conservation Officers of Pennsylvania**
http://www.pawco.org

**Fish and Game**
http://www.fishandgame.com

**GameWarden.Net**
by Terry Hodges
http://www.gamewarden.net

**North American Game Warden Museum**
http://www.gamewardenmuseum.org

## CORRECTIONAL OFFICER

**PrisonsandJails.com**
http://www.prisonsandjails.com

## CORRECTIONS—GENERAL RESOURCES

**The Corrections Connection**
http://www.corrections.com

**Correctional Education Association**
http://www.ceanational.org

**U.S. Courts**
The Federal Judiciary
http://www.uscourts.gov

**United States Sentencing Commission**
http://www.ussc.gov

## CRIME PREVENTION SPECIALIST

**Crime Prevention and Law Enforcement Section**
Virginia Department of Criminal Justice Services
http://www.dcjs.virginia.gov/cple

**National Crime Prevention Council**
http://www.ncpc.org

**Texas Crime Prevention Association**
http://www.tcpa.org

## CRIME SCENE TECHNICIAN

**Crime Scene Investigation**
http://www.crime-scene-investigator.net

**CSI FAQ File**
International Crime Scene Investigator's Association
http://www.icsia.com/faq.html

**Forensic Enterprises, Inc.**
by Hayden B. Baldwin
http://www.feinc.net

## CUSTOMS AND BORDER PROTECTION OFFICER

**CBP Law Enforcement Explorer Program**
http://cbp.gov/xp/cgov/careers/customs_careers/explorer_program/explorer.xml

**U.S. Customs Explorer Academy**
http://cbp.gov/xp/cgov/careers/customs_careers/explorer_program/explorer_academy.xml

## DEPUTY SHERIFF

**National Sheriffs' Association**
http://www.sheriffs.org

## EMERGENCY MEDICAL TECHNICIAN

**National Association of State EMS Directors**
http://www.nasemsd.org

**National Registry of Emergency Medical Technicians**
http://www.nremt.org

## EMERGENCY SERVICES— GENERAL RESOURCES

**American Red Cross**
http://www.redcross.org

**Emergency Services WWW Site List**
http://www.district.north-van.bc.ca/eswsl/www-911.htm

**Federal Emergency Management Agency**
U.S. Department of Homeland Security
http://www.fema.gov

**Rescue-Net.com**
http://www.rescue-net.com

## ENVIRONMENTAL HEALTH INSPECTOR

**Centers for Disease Control and Prevention**
U.S. Department of Health and Human Services
http://www.cdc.gov

**National Center for Environmental Health**
Centers for Disease Control and Prevention
http://www.cdc.gov/nceh

**National Environmental Health Association Links**
http://www.neha.org/links.html

## EPA SPECIAL AGENT

**Criminal Investigations**
U.S. Environmental Protection Agency
http://www.epa.gov/compliance/criminal/investigations

**Public Employees for Environmental Responsibility**
http://www.peer.org

## FBI SPECIAL AGENT

**FBI Academy**
http://www.fbi.gov/hq/td/academy/academy.htm

## FIRE PROTECTION ENGINEER

**Fire Protection Engineering**
Society of Fire Protection Engineers
http://www.careersinfireprotection
engineering.com

**Fire Protection Engineering Career Information**
Center for Firesafety Studies
Worcester Polytechnic Institute
Worcester, Massachusetts
http://www.wpi.edu/Academics/Depts/Fire/Careers

## FIREFIGHTER

**Fire Museum Network**
http://www.firemuseumnetwork.org

**International Association of Fire Chiefs**
http://www.iafc.org

**National Fire Academy**
U.S. Fire Administration
http://www.usfa.fema.gov/training/nfa

**U.S. Fire Administration**
U.S. Federal Emergency Management Agency
http://www.usfa.fema.gov

**World Fire Departments.com**
http://www.worldfiredepartments.com

## FORENSIC CHEMIST

**International Association of Bloodstain Pattern Analysts**
http://www.iabpa.org

**Society of Forensic Toxicologists**
http://www.soft-tox.org

## FORENSICS—GENERAL RESOURCES

**American Society of Crime Laboratory Directors**
http://www.ascld.org

**Dr. Zeno's Forensic Site**
by Dr. Zeno Geradts
http://forensic.to

**FBI Laboratory Home Page**
http://www.fbi.gov/hq/lab/labhome.htm

**Forensic Education and Consulting**
by Norah Rudin and Keith Inman
http://www.forensicdna.com

**Forensic Science Resources**
by R. Scott Carpenter
http://www.tncrimlaw.com/forensic

**Reddy's Forensic Page**
by Reddy P. Chamakura
http://www.forensicpage.com

**Young Forensic Scientists Forum**
American Academy of Forensic Sciences
http://www.aafs.org/yfsf/index.htm

## FORENSIC PATHOLOGIST

**Forensic Pathology and Medicine**
Reddy's Forensic Page
http://www.forensicpage.com/new27.htm

**So You Want to be a Medical Detective**
National Association of Medical Examiners
http://www.thename.org/medical_detective.htm

## GAMING SURVEILLANCE OFFICER

**American Gaming Association**
http://www.americangaming.org

**National Indian Gaming Association**
http://www.indiangaming.org

## INDUSTRIAL HYGIENIST

**American Board of Industrial Hygiene**
http://www.abih.org

**Environment, Safety, and Health Home Page**
by Steven Gamache
http://www.if.uidaho.edu/ehs/safety.html

**Human Factors and Ergonomics Society**
www.hfes.org

## INFORMATION SYSTEMS SECURITY (INFOSEC) PROFESSIONALS

**CISSP.com, The Web Portal for Certified Information Systems Security Professionals**
http://www.cissp.com

**Information Systems Audit and Control Association**
http://www.isaca.org

**The Security Portal for Information System Security Professionals**
http://www.infosyssec.net

## INSURANCE INVESTIGATOR

**Insurance Claims Investigation Resource Center**
Thomas Investigative Publications, Inc.
http://www.pimall.com/nais/insrec.html

## LATENT PRINT EXAMINER

**Latent Print Examination**
by Ed German
http://onin.com/fp

**Latent Print Unit**
FBI Laboratory
http://www.fbi.gov/hq/lab/org/lpu.htm

## LAW ENFORCEMENT— FEDERAL

**Federal Hispanic Law Enforcement Officers Association**
http://www.fhleoa.org

**Federal Law Enforcement Training Center**
U.S. Department of Homeland Security
http://www.fletc.gov

**WIFLE (Women in Federal Law Enforcement)**
http://www.wifle.com

## LAW ENFORCEMENT— GENERAL RESOURCES

**American Police Hall of Fame and Museum**
http://www.aphf.org

**Community Policing Consortium**
http://www.communitypolicing.org

**CopSeek.com**
http://www.copseek.com

**Exploring: Law Enforcement**
(Law Enforcement Explorers)
Learning for Life
http://www.learning-for-life.org/exploring/lawenforcement

**Law Enforcement Sites On The Web**
by Ira Wilsker
http://www.ih2000.net/ira/ira.htm (Part 1)
http://www.ih2000.net/ira/ira2.htm
(Part 2 of 8)

**National Association of Police Organizations**
http://www.napo.org

**Officer.com**
http://www.officer.com

**Police Foundation**
http://www.policefoundation.org

**Police Guide**
http://www.policeguide.com

**Policing.com**
Your Headquarters for Community Policing
http://www.policing.com

**PoliceOne.com**
http://www.policeone.com

**Police Structure of the United States**
by Dr. Tom O'Connor
North Carolina Wesleyan College
Rocky Mount, North Carolina
http://faculty.ncwc.edu/toconnor/polstruct.htm

## LIFEGUARD

**American Lifeguard Association**
http://www.americanlifeguard.com

**California Surf Livesaving Association**
http://www.cslsa.org

**Lifeguards' Homepage: Oahu's Guarded Beaches**
Hawaiian Lifeguard Association
http://www.aloha.com/lifeguards

**Ocean Lifeguarding**
by Michael "Spike" Fowler
http://www.spikefowler.com/Lifeguarding/lifeguardhome.html

## LOCKSMITH

**ClearStar Security Network**
http://www.clearstar.com

## LOSS CONTROL REPRESENTATIVE

**Public Entity Risk Institute (PERI)**
http://www.riskinstitute.org

## OBSERVER

**Air Patrol Links**
Hendersonville Police Department
Hendersonville, Tennessee
http://www.hendersonville-pd.org/links/airpatrol.html

*Unofficial* **Anderson County Sheriff's Office Aviation Division Home Page**
Anderson County, South Carolina
by Sergeant Steve Lindley
http://www.acsoaviation.com

## PARK RANGER

**National Park Service Employment Information**
http://www.nps.gov/personnel

**Ranger Links**
Park Law Enforcement Association
http://www.parkranger.com/links.htm

**Seasonal Law Enforcement Training Program**
Association of National Park Rangers
http://www.anpr.org/academies.htm

**Temporary Employment**
National Park Service
http://www.sep.nps.gov

## PERSONAL PROTECTION SPECIALIST

**Executive Protection Institute**
www.personalprotection.com

**International Bodyguard Network**
http://www.samurai-warrior.com

## POLICE CHIEF

**Major Cities Chiefs Association**
http://www.neiassociates.org/about.htm

**Major County Sheriff's Association**
http://www.neiassociates.org/about.htm

**National Executive Institute Associates**
http://www.neiassociates.org

## POLICE DETECTIVE

**Crime and Clues**
The Art of Criminal Investigation
edited by Daryl W. Clemens
http://www.crimeandclues.com

**Crime Library**
http://www.crimelibrary.com

## POLYGRAPH EXAMINER

**Frequently Asked Questions about Polygraph**
American Polygraph Association
http://www.polygraph.org/faq.htm

## PRIVATE INVESTIGATORS—GENERAL RESOURCES

**Council of International Investigators**
http://www.cii2.org

**Infoguys: The Private Investigators Portal**
http://www.infoguys.com

**PI Mall**
http://www.pimall.com

**World Association of Detectives**
http://www.wad.net

## PROBATION OFFICER/PAROLE OFFICER

**New York State Probation Officers Association**
http://www.nyspoa.com

**United States Parole Commission**
U.S. Department of Justice
http://www.usdoj.gov/uspc/parole.htm

**U.S. Probation and Pretrial Services**
U.S. Courts
http://www.uscourts.gov/misc/propretrial.html

## PUBLIC SAFETY DISPATCHER

**Links to Public Safety Sites**
(list of 9-1-1 centers)
http://www.geocities.com/Heartland/2834/links.html

**National Academies of Emergency Dispatch**
http://www.emergencydispatch.org

## QUALITY ASSURANCE SPECIALIST

**International Organization for Standardization**
http://www.iso.org

**Software Testing Institute**
http://www.softwaretestinginstitute.com

## QUESTIONED DOCUMENT EXAMINER

**Questioned Document Examination Page**
by Emily J. Will
http://www.qdewill.com

**Southwestern Association of Forensic Document Examiners**
http://www.swafde.org

## RESCUE TECHNICIAN

**Charlottesville-Albemarle Rescue Squad, Inc.**
http://warhammer.mcc.virginia.edu/cars

**International Association of Dive Rescue Specialists**
http://www.iadrs.org

**National Institute for Urban Search and Rescue**
http://www.niusr.org

**SAR Technology Inc.**
http://www.sarinfo.bc.ca

## REVENUE OFFICER

**"How Income Taxes Work"**
by Kevin Bonsor
http://people.howstuffworks.com/income-tax.htm

**State Government Tax Collections**
U.S. Census Bureau
http://www.census.gov/govs/www/statetax.html

## SAFETY PROFESSIONALS—GENERAL RESOURCES

**Career Guide to the Safety Profession**
American Society of Safety Engineers
http://www.asse.org/careerguide-contents.html

**Council on Certification of Health, Environmental and Safety Technologists**
http://www.cchest.org

**Environment, Health and Safety Online**
http://www.ehso.com

**International Association of Safety Professionals**
http://www.iaspweb.com

**OSH.net**
http://www.osh.net

**Safety Online**
www.safetyonline.com

**SafetyNet Web Resources**
U.S. Department of Interior
http://safetynet.smis.doi.gov/webresA.htm

## SECURITY—GENERAL RESOURCES

**Security Industry Association**
http://www.siaonline.org

**Security Online**
http://www.securityonline.com

**Security Resource Net**
National Security Institute
http://nsi.org

## STATE TROOPER

**Official Directory of State Patrol and State Police**
http://www.statetroopersdirectory.com

## STORE DETECTIVE

**National Retail Federation**
http://www.nrf.com

**Retail Loss Prevention Exchange**
http://www.rlpx.com

## SWAT SNIPER

**Florida SWAT Association**
http://www.floridaswat.org

**Operational Tactics**
http://www.operationaltactics.org

## TRACE EVIDENCE EXAMINER

**Criminalistics and Trace Evidence Links**
Kruglick Law Offices
http://www.kruglaw.com/f_criminalistics.
   htm

## TRANSPORTATION SECURITY SCREENER

**AirSafe.com**
http://www.airsafe.com

**"How Airport Security Works"**
by Jeff Tyson and Ed Grabianowski
http://travel.howstuffworks.com/
   airport-security.htm

# GLOSSARY

**academic**   Relating to a school or college program.

**administrative**   Relating to a person or group who oversees the daily operations of an organization.

**agency**   A governmental organization or division.

**air traffic**   The flow of aircraft as they move through the air and on the airport grounds.

**applicant**   A person who is asking for a job.

**apprehend**   To arrest.

**apprenticeship**   The period of time in which a person learns a trade.

**arson**   A crime in which a fire was intentionally set.

**assets**   Money, jewelry, buildings, stocks, intellectual property, and other property that makes up an individual's or group's wealth.

**associate's degree**   The degree earned upon fulfilling the requirements of a two-year college program.

**ATF**   Alcohol, Tobacco, Firearms and Explosives; the bureau within the U.S. Department of Justice that is responsible for enforcing the federal laws and regulations relating to alcohol, tobacco, firearms, explosives, and arson.

**autopsy**   An examination of a dead body to determine its cause of death.

**aviation safety**   The programs and procedures that are used to ensure the safety of aircraft and airports as well as pilots, passengers, and others.

**aviation security**   The programs and procedures used to prevent dangerous activities, such as terrorist acts, from occurring in airports and aboard aircraft.

**bachelor's degree**   The degree earned upon fulfilling the requirements of a four-year college program.

**background check**   A thorough examination into an individual's background, which may include such areas as his or her criminal, financial, and medical histories.

**beat**   The part of a city, county, state, or region that a law enforcement officer is assigned to patrol.

**BLS**   Bureau of Labor Statistics; the agency within the U.S. Department of Labor that is responsible for collecting, processing, analyzing, and disseminating statistical data about labor economics.

**cadet**   A student who is in training to be a law enforcement officer.

**campus**   The grounds and buildings of a college, school, or company.

**candidate**   A person whom an employer is interested in hiring.

**canine**   A dog.

**career**   An individual's profession or occupation.

**CBP**   Customs and Border Protection; the bureau within the U.S. Department of Homeland Security that is responsible for managing, controlling, and protecting the U.S. borders.

**citation**   An order to appear in court.

**civilian**   A worker in a law enforcement agency who is not a commissioned officer; also, a worker in a military service who is not a military officer or enlistee.

**client**   A customer.

**code**   A collection of city, state, or federal laws.

**commissioned officer**   A law enforcement officer; also, a military officer.

**communication skills**   The speaking and listening abilities workers need to perform their jobs.

**compliance**   Meeting the standards or conditions required by a specific law or regulation.

**compliance inspection**   An examination of something or someone to ensure that governmental laws, regulations, and codes are being followed.

**computer security**   The security measures used to safeguard computer hardware, software, and databases from theft, accidents, crashes, natural disasters, and so on.

**conservation**   The protection of air, water, soil, and other natural resources.

**consultant**   An expert in his or her field who offers the services of his or her expertise to individuals and organizations for a fee.

**contraband**   Things that are not allowed to be brought into a country.

**conveyance**   A ship, airplane, truck, or other device used to transport products between locations.

**convict**   To judge someone as guilty of committing a crime.

**correctional facility**   A jail, prison, or other institution where individuals are locked up to wait for their court trial or to fulfill a court sentence for breaking a law.

**corrections**   The program of treating and rehabilitating criminals that may involve any or all of the following: serving a sentence in a correctional facility, probation, and parole.

**court security**   The programs and procedures used in a courthouse to protect the judges, juries, defendants, witnesses, general public, and others.

**CPR**   Cardiopulmonary resuscitation; a procedure used to revive persons who have stopped breathing or whose hearts have stopped beating.

**crime lab**   A laboratory where physical evidence (such as fingerprints, bullets, and bodily fluids) is examined and analyzed.

**crime prevention**   Programs and procedures used to help prevent or lower the risk of crime in a community.

**crime scene**   A place where a theft, burglary, murder, arson, or other crime has occurred.

**criminal investigation**   An examination of a crime to learn who committed it as well as when, where, how, and why it was committed.

**criminal investigator**   A law enforcement officer whose job is to find evidence that links a suspect to a crime so that he or she can be tried in court.

**criminalist**   A forensic scientist; he or she uses scientific techniques to examine and analyze physical evidence.

**criminalistics**   The application of science to the analysis, identification, and evaluation of physical evidence that is collected at a crime scene.

**critical thinking skills**   The abilities to examine and analyze a situation and make sensible judgments on how to handle it.

**data security**   The safeguarding of all facts and figures that are stored in a computer system.

**DEA**   Drug Enforcement Administration; the bureau within the U.S. Department of Justice that is responsible for enforcing the federal laws and regulations relating to controlled substances.

**defendant**   An individual who is being accused of having committed a crime; an individual who is being sued in a civil trial.

**dispatch**   A message for a law enforcement officer, firefighter, paramedic, or other protective service professional to go to a particular location to provide emergency or nonemergency assistance.

**duties**   Tasks or aspects of a job that a worker has been hired to do.

**eligible**   Qualified for something.

**emergency communication center**   The place where telephone calls from the public for emergency and nonemergency assistance are received and transferred to the appropriate law enforcement or protective services agencies.

**emergency medical services**   A network of protective services that provides immediate attention and medical care to a community.

**EMS**   Emergency medical services; an organization that provides emergency medical care and transportation to a community.

**enforce**   To make sure people are following laws and regulations.

**enlistee**   An individual who joins the rank and file of a military service such as the U.S. Coast Guard.

**entry-level job**   A job that people can get with little or no experience.

**environmental**   Having to do with the air, water, land, and other natural resources.

**EPA**   Environmental Protection Agency; the U.S. agency that is responsible for enforcing federal laws and regulations which protect human health and the environment.

**estimated wages**   An amount that is close to the actual pay a worker earns.

**evidence**   Any type of proof that links an individual to a crime.

**experience**   Paid and volunteer work that a person has done.

**expert witness**   An individual whom a court recognizes as having the required knowledge, expertise, and credentials to address specific issues in a court trial.

**FAA**   Federal Aviation Administration; the division within the U.S. Department of Transportation that is responsible for the safety of civil aviation, as well as the enforcement of federal aviation laws and regulations.

**FBI**   Federal Bureau of Investigation; the division within the U.S. Department of Justice that is responsible for investigating violations of federal criminal laws.

**federal**   Having to do with the U.S. government.

**felony**   A serious crime such as arson, murder, rape, kidnapping, drug dealing, or counterfeiting; an individual convicted of a felony may be sentenced to a state or federal prison.

**fire protection**   The safeguarding of a building or complex with equipment, devices, and designs to control or extinguish fires.

**forensic science**   The applications of science to the study of legal and regulatory matters.

**forensic scientist**   A criminalist; he or she uses scientific techniques to examine and analyze physical evidence.

**forensics**   Having to do with criminalistics or forensic science.

**gaming industry**   The gambling industry.

**general equivalency diploma (GED)**   A certificate that is equivalent to a high school diploma; it is earned upon passing a standardized examination.

**GS**   General schedule; a pay schedule for many U.S. government employees.

**hazard**   Something that is dangerous.

**ICE**   Immigration and Customs Enforcement; the bureau within the U.S. Department of Homeland Security that is responsible for identifying vulnerabilities as well as detecting violations that threaten national security.

**illegal**   Against the law.

**information system**   All computer hardware, software, and databases that are stored in an organization's computer systems.

**information systems security**   The programs and procedures used to protect and safeguard an organization's information systems.

**inmate**   A prisoner.

**inspection**   An examination to make sure all governmental laws and regulations are being followed.

**interpersonal skills**   The abilities a worker needs to communicate and work well with others on the job.

**interrogate**   To ask a specific set of questions of a person to find out what he or she knows about a certain subject.

**investigate**   To examine something, such as a crime, in detail.

**IRS**   Internal Revenue Service; the bureau within the U.S. Department of the Treasury that is responsible for collecting federal taxes.

**jurisdiction**   The power to interpret and apply the law; also the area in which a law enforcement officer has authority to perform his or her job.

**K9**   Canine; a dog.

**latent prints**   An impression of a set of fingerprints, palm prints, or footprints that has been taken from the surface of an object.

**local government**   A city or county government.

**log**   A record of events.

**loss control**   The process used to remove or reduce the risk of losses that a business, company, or other organization might have in the future.

**maritime**   Having to do with the sea.

**master's degree**   An advanced degree; it is earned upon fulfilling the requirements of a one- or two-year college program.

**medicolegal**   Relating to both the law and medicine.

**minimum**   The least amount.

**misdemeanor**   A crime such as vandalism or disorderly conduct; an individual who is convicted of a misdemeanor may be required to pay a fine and/or serve a short sentence in a correctional facility.

**mission**   The specific task or job that a person or group has been assigned to do.

**monitor**   To keep track of something or someone.

**municipality**   A city or town that has its own government.

**networking**   Making contacts with peers in your profession and with other professionals who may provide you with resources.

**offender**   A person who has committed a crime.

**on call**   Being available for immediate duty at any time of the day or night.

**OPM**   Office of Personnel Management; the U.S. department that is responsible for recruiting qualified persons for jobs in the various federal agencies.

**ordinance**   A law established by a city or county government.

**OSHA**   Occupational Safety and Health Administration; the division within the U.S. Department of Labor that is responsible for setting and enforcing safety and health standards in the workplace.

**POST**   Peace Officer Standard and Training Program; the training program a local or state law enforcement officer completes to obtain his or her certification.

**parole**   The conditions an offender must fulfill when released early from his or her prison sentence.

**pathology**   The study of how cells and tissues are altered by disease.

**patrol**   To travel and observe an assigned area to ensure that everything and everyone is safe and secure.

**patron**   A customer.

**permanent**   Lasting a long time without changing.

**personal protection service**   The programs and procedures a professional individual or group performs to safeguard someone who is being threatened, harassed, or in any danger or risk.

**personnel**   Human resources; the department in an organization that is responsible for hiring employees; also, the staff members who work in this department.

**physical security**   The use of security guards, security systems, and security procedures to safeguard people, buildings, and property.

**plaintiff**   The individual or group who is suing or accusing another individual or group.

**port of entry**   A land port, seaport, or airport where travelers are checked as they come into a country.

**private investigation**   An examination of an event, a person's history, a situation, or a problem that private detectives perform for a client.

**probation**   A court-supervised sentence an offender must fulfill instead of a prison sentence.

**problem-solving skills**   The abilities a worker needs to analyze problems and find ways to solve them.

**prosecution**   The city, county, or federal government attorneys who are responsible for proving to a jury that a person has committed a crime.

**public safety department**   A city, county, or state agency that oversees one or more protective services such as law enforcement, fire protection, emergency services, and inspections.

**qualifications**   The skills and experience a person has to do a job.

**quality**   Degree to which something has all the required characteristics and is free of any defects or deficiencies.

**rank**   A position or set of positions in an organization.

**regulation**   A rule that a government agency establishes in order to fulfill the requirements of a law.

**requirement**   Something that is needed.

**screen**   To examine a person or object to ensure the person or object fits specific requirements.

**search and rescue**   The operation of looking for and rescuing lost, missing, stranded, or injured persons in urban and wilderness settings as well as in natural or man-made disasters.

**security system**   The procedures, manpower, equipment, and devices that are used to provide protection for an individual, home, business, organization, or institution.

**self-management skills** The abilities a worker needs to perform his or her duties without constant supervision.

**shift** A time period for which workers are hired to do their job.

**smuggle** To take something or someone in or out of the country illegally.

**surveillance** Following, observing, and collecting information about a person because he or she is suspected of committing a crime.

**suspect** An individual who is believed to have committed a crime.

**task** A duty or job that an employee must perform.

**teamwork skills** The abilities an employee needs to work effectively as part of a group on a job or work project.

**testify** To answer questions truthfully in a court of law.

**testimony** A statement a person makes and swears is true.

**trainee** An employee who is being trained to do a new job.

**undercover** Being in disguise so as to spy on a person or group that is suspected of engaging in criminal activity.

**verify** To confirm that certain information is true or not true.

**victim** An individual against whom a crime has been committed.

**violation** A breaking of a law.

**warrant** An order issued by a court judge to allow law enforcement officers to search for evidence, arrest a suspect, or perform another specific act.

**witness** A person who has direct knowledge about a suspect or a crime.

**workplace** An office, warehouse, factory, hospital, laboratory, park, or other place where work is being done.

**workplace safety** The programs and procedures used in a workplace to protect the health and safety of employees and the environment.

**workplace security** The programs and procedures used in a workplace to protect the employer's property, workers, and visitors from harm and theft.

# BIBLIOGRAPHY

## A. PERIODICALS

Print and online publications are available for the various occupations described in this book. These include magazines, journals, newspapers, newsletters, webzines, and electronic news services. Listed below are a few publications that serve the different fields in law enforcement, security, and protective services. You may be able to find some of the print publications at a public, school, or academic library. Many of the print magazines also allow limited free access to their articles on the Web. Some of the Web-based publications are free, whereas others require a subscription to access certain issues and other resources.

*Note: Web site addresses were current when this book was written. If a Web site address no longer works, you may be able to find its new address by entering the name of the publication into a search engine.*

### CORRECTIONS

*American Jails*
American Jail Association
**Phone:** (301) 790-3930
http://www.corrections.com/aja/
    publications/magazine_about.shtml

*Corrections.com*
http://www.corrections.com

*Corrections Today*
American Correctional Association
**Phone:** (301) 918-1800
http://www.aca.org/publications/
    ctmagazine.asp

*Criminal Justice*
American Bar Association Criminal
    Justice Section
ABA Publication Orders
P.O. Box 10892
Chicago, IL 60610-0892
**Phone:** (800) 285-2221
**Fax:** (312) 988-5568
http://www.abanet.org/crimjust/cjmag/
    home.html

### FORENSIC SCIENCE

*The American Journal of Forensic
    Medicine and Pathology*
http://www.amjforensicmedicine.com

*Forensic-Evidence.com*
Andre A. Moenssens (editor)
http://www.forensic-evidence.com

*Forensic Science Communications*
FBI Laboratory

http://www.fbi.gov/hq/lab/fsc/current/
    index.htm

### LAW ENFORCEMENT

*American Police Beat*
P.O. Box 382702
Cambridge, MA 02238-2702
**Phone:** (800) 234-0056
**Fax:** (617) 354-6515
http://www.apbweb.com

*Campus Law Enforcement Journal*
International Association of Campus Law
    Enforcement Administrators
342 North Main Street
West Hartford, CT 06117-2507
**Phone:** (860) 586-7517
**Fax:** (860) 586-7550
http://www.iaclea.org

*CyberSleuths.com*
http://www.cybersleuths.com

*FBI Law Enforcement Bulletin*
Federal Bureau of Investigation
935 Pennsylvania Avenue NW
Washington, DC 20535-0001
http://www.fbi.gov/publications/leb/leb.
    htm

*International Game Warden Magazine*
P.O. Box 1254
Altoona, PA 16603-1254
**Phone:** (814) 940-1155
http://www.igwmagazine.com

*Law and Order Magazine*
P.O. Box 16088
North Hollywood, CA 91615-9837

**Phone:** (888) 329-0770 or
    (818) 760-0445
http://lawandordermag.com

*Law Enforcement News*
John Jay College of Criminal Justice
899 10th Avenue
New York, NY 10102-1093
http://www.lib.jjay.cuny.edu/len

*Officer.com: The Source for Law
    Enforcement*
http://www.officer.com

*Police Chief*
International Association of Chiefs of
    Police
515 North Washington Street
Alexandria, VA 22314
**Phone:** (800) THE-IACP or
    (703) 836-6767
**Fax:** (703) 836-4543
http://policechiefmagazine.org

*Police Magazine*
http://www.policemag.com

*Women Police Magazine*
International Association of Women
    Police
P.O. Box 50365
Tulsa, OK 74150-0365
**Phone:** (918) 628-0854
http://www.iawp.org/wom_pol.htm

### PUBLIC SAFETY

*Advanced Rescue Technology*
Summer Communications Inc.
7626 Densmore Avenue

Van Nuys, CA 91406-2042
**Phone:** (800) 224-4367 or
  (818) 786-4367
**Fax:** (818) 786-9246
http://www.advancedrt.com

*American Lifeguard Magazine*
United States Lifesaving Association
http://www.usla.org/LGtoLG/mag.asp

*Aviation Fire Journal*
AFJ Multimedia
P.O. Box 976
Baldwin Place, NY 10505
http://www.aviationfirejournal.com

*Dispatch Monthly*
P.O. Box 8387
Berkeley, CA 94707-8387
**Phone:** (877) 370-3477
**Fax:** (510) 558-3109

*Emergency Medical Services
  Magazine*
Summer Communications Inc.
7626 Densmore Ave
Van Nuys, CA 91406-2042
**Phone:** (800) 224-4367 or
  (818) 786-4367
**Fax:** (818) 786-9246
http://www.emsmagazine.com

*EMS Village*
http://www.emsvillage.coms

*Firefighting.com*
http://www.firefighting.com

*Jems.com—The Online Emergency
  Services Resource*
http://www.jems.com

*National Fire and Rescue*
5808 Faringdon Place
Suite 200
Raleigh, NC 27609-3930
**Phone:** (919) 872-5040
**Fax:** (919) 876-6531
http://www.nfrmag.com

*9-1-1 Magazine*
Subscription Department
18201 Weston Place
Tustin, CA 92780
**Phone:** (800) 231-8911
**Fax:** (714) 838-9233
http://www.9-1-1magazine.com

# PRIVATE INVESTIGATIONS

*Legal Investigator*
National Association of Legal
  Investigators
For subscriptions, write to:
Rich Robertson Consulting and
  Investigation
P.O. Box 825
Gilbert, AZ 85299
**Phone:** (480) 726-3961
**Fax:** (480) 792-6642
**E-mail:** Rich@RRRobertson.com
http://www.nalionline.org/
  nalipublications.html

*PI Magazine*
**Phone:** (800) 836-3088
http://www.pi.org

# SAFETY/REGULATORY
# COMPLIANCE

*Air Traffic Control Quarterly*
Subscription Manager
Air Traffic Control Association
1101 King Street
Suite 300
Alexandria, VA 22314
**Fax:** (703) 299-2437
http://www.atca.org

*Building Safety Journal*
International Code Council
Birmingham District Office
900 Montclair Road
Birmingham, AL 35213
**Phone:** (866) 284-0235
**Fax:** (205) 599-9891
http://www.iccsafe.org/news/bsj

*Compliance Magazine*
http://www.compliancemag.com

*Environmental Health News*
Environmental Health Sciences
619 B East High Street
Charlottesville, VA 22902
http://www.environmentalhealthnews.org

*Environmental Health Perspectives*
c/o Brogan and Partners
1001 Winstead Drive
Suite 355
Cary, NC 27513-2117
**Phone:** (866) 541-3841
**Fax:** (919) 678-8696
http://ehp.niehs.nih.gov

*Flight Safety Digest*
Flight Safety Foundation
601 Madison Street
Suite 300
Alexandria, VA 22314
**Phone:** (703) 739-6700
**Fax:** (703) 739-6708
http://www.flightsafety.org./flight_safety_
  digest.html

*Food Safety Magazine*
1945 West Mountain Street
Glendale, CA 91201
**Phone:** (818) 842-4777
**Fax:** (818) 769-2939
http://www.foodsafetymagazine.com

*Industrial Hygiene News*
Rimbach Publishing Company
8650 Babcock Boulevard
Pittsburgh, PA 15237
**Phone:** (888) 746-2224 or
  (800) 245-3182
http://www.rimbach.com/home/ihnpage/
  IHN.HTM

*Industrial Safety and Hygiene Online*
BNP Media
http://www.ishn.com

*Journal of Environmental Health*
National Environmental Health
  Association
720 South Colorado Boulevard, 970-S
Denver, CO 80246-1925
**Phone:** (303) 756-9090
**Fax:** (303) 691-9490
http://www.neha.org/JEH

*The NATCA Voice*
National Air Traffic Controllers
  Association
http://www.natcavoice.org

*Occupational Health and Safety*
Stephens Publishing Corporation
http://www.ohsonline.com

*Professional Safety*
American Society of Safety Engineers
http://www.asse.org/bprofe.htm

*Risk Management Magazine*
www.rmmag.com

*Safety and Health*
National Safety Council
http://www.nsc.org/pubs/sh.htm

## SECURITY

*Casino Surveillance News*
http://www.casinosurveillancenews.com

*Cipher*
Technical Committee on Security and
    Privacy
Computer Society of the IEEE
http://www.ieee-security.org/cipher.html

*Fire Engineering*
http://fe.pennet.com

*Information Security*
http://infosecuritymag.techtarget.com

*Information Systems Security*
Auerbach Publications
http://www.auerbach-publications.com

*SDM (Security Distributing and
    Marketing) Online*
http://www.sdmmag.com

*Security Focus*
http://www.securityfocus.com

*Security Management Online*
ASIS International
http://www.securitymanagement.com

*Security News Portal*
http://www.securitynewsportal.com

## HOW TO FIND MORE PUBLICATIONS

Here are some things you might do to find publications that are specific to a profession in which you are interested.

- Talk with librarians, educators, and professionals for recommendations.
- Check out professional and trade associations. Many of them publish journals, newsletters, magazines, and other publications.
- Visit an online bookstore, such as Amazon.com, to view the listings of magazines it has for sale. Use such keywords as *law enforcement, police, criminal justice, forensic science, compliance,* or *industrial hygiene.* If the Web site does not have a particular search engine for magazines, be sure to add the word *magazines* to your keyword. (For example: *law enforcement magazines*).

# B. BOOKS

Listed below are some book titles that can help you learn more about careers in law enforcement, security, forensic science, safety, compliance inspections, emergency services, or another protective service field. To learn about other books that may be helpful, ask professionals—individuals and organizations—as well as librarians for suggestions.

## CAREER INFORMATION

Camenson, Blythe. *Real People Working in Service Businesses.* Lincolnwood, Ill.: VGM Career Horizons, 1997.

Damp, Dennis V. *The Book of U.S. Government Jobs: Where They Are, What's Available and How to Get One, Eighth Edition.* Mckees Rocks, Pa.: Brookhaven Press, 2002.

Farr, J. Michael, et al. The O*NET *Dictionary of Occupational Titles.* Indianapolis, Ind.: JIST Works, 2001.

Jakubiak, Joyce, ed. *Specialty Occupational Outlook: Trade and Technical.* Detroit: Gale Research, 1996.

Lee, Mary Price, Richard S. Lee, and Carol Beam. *100 Best Careers in Crime Fighting.* New York: Macmillan, 1998.

Quintana, Debra. *100 Jobs in the Environment.* New York: Macmillan, 1996.

Smith, Russ, ed. *Federal Careers in Law Enforcement.* Manassas Park, Va.: Impact Publications, 1996.

Stinchcomb, James. *Opportunities in Law Enforcement and Criminal Justice, Second Edition.* Chicago, Ill.: VGM Career Horizons, 2002.

Taylor, Dorothy L. *Jumpstarting Your Career: An Internship Guide for Criminal Justice, Second Edition.* Upper Saddle River, N.J.: Prentice Hall, 2004.

U.S. Bureau of Labor Statistics. *Occupational Outlook Handbook 2004–05 Edition.* Washington, D.C.: Bureau of Labor Statistics, 2004. Available online. URL: http://stats.bls.gov/oco.

U.S. Bureau of Labor Statistics. *Career Guide to Industries, 2004–05 Edition.* Washington, D.C.: Bureau of Labor Statistics, 2004. Available online. URL: http://www.bls.gov/oco/cg

## POLICE WORK

Ackerman, Thomas. *FBI Careers: The Ultimate Guide to Landing a Job as One of America's Finest.* Indianapolis, Ind.: JIST Works, 2002.

Baker, Mark. *Cops: Their Lives in Their Own Words.* New York: Pocket Books, 1995.

Burns, Ronald G., and Michael J. Lynch. *Environmental Crime: A Sourcebook.* New York: LFB Scholarly Publishing, 2004.

Butler, Daniel R., Leland Gregory, and Alan Ray. *America's Dumbest Criminals: Based on True Stories from Law Enforcement Officials Across the Country.* Nashville, Tenn.: Rutledge Hill Press, 1995.

Gaines, Ann Graham. *The Coast Guard in Action.* Berkeley Heights, N.J.: Enslow Publishers, 2001.

Hutton, Donald B., and Anna Mydlarz. *Guide to Homeland Security Careers*. Hauppauge, N.Y.: Barron's Educational Series, 2003.

Jeffreys, Diarmuid. *The Bureau: Inside the Modern FBI*. Boston: Houghton Mifflin, 1995.

Lyman, Michael D. *Criminal Investigation: The Art and the Science*. Upper Saddle, N.J.: Prentice Hall Career and Technology, 1998.

Ostrom, Thomas P. *The United States Coast Guard: 1790 to the Present*. Oakland, Ore.: Elderberry Press, 2004.

Perry, Tim. *Basic Patrol Procedures, Second Edition*. Salem, Wis.: Sheffield Publishing, 1998.

Purpura, Philip P., *Criminal Justice: An Introduction*. Boston: Butterworth-Heinemann, 1997.

Ragle, Larry. *Crime Scene*. New York: Avon Books, 1995.

Rowland, Desmond, and James Bailey. *The Law Enforcement Handbook*. New York: Facts On File, 1985.

Scarborough, Kathryn E., and Pamela A. Collins. *Women in Public and Private Law Enforcement*. Boston: Butterworth-Heinemann, 2001.

Stephens, W. Richard. *Careers in Criminal Justice, Second Edition*. Boston: Allyn and Bacon, 2002.

Stroud, Carsten. *Deadly Force: In the Streets with the U.S. Marshals*. New York: Bantam Books, 1996.

Trautman, Neal E. *How to Be a Great Cop*. Upper Saddle River, N.J.: Prentice Hall, 2002.

Weston, Paul B., Kenneth M. Wells, and Marlene Hertoghe. *Criminal Evidence for Police*. Englewood Cliffs, N.J.: Prentice Hall, 1995.

Winkleman, Katherine K. *Police Patrol*. New York: Walker, 1996.

## SPECIAL POLICE UNITS

Bryson, Sandy. *Police Dog Tactics*. New York: McGraw-Hill, 1996.

Eden, R.S. *K9 Officer's Manual*. Bellingham, Wash.: Detselig Enterprises Ltd.: Temeron Books, 1993.

Greenberg, Keith Elliot. *Bomb Squad Officer: Expert with Explosives*. Woodbridge, Conn.: Blackbirch Marketing, 1995.

Lonsdale, Mark V. *Sniper II: A Guide to Special Response Teams*. Los Angeles: Specialized Tactical Training Unit, 1992.

Snow, Robert L. *SWAT Teams: Explosive Face-Offs with America's Deadliest Criminals*. New York: Plenum Press, 1996.

## FORENSIC INVESTIGATIONS

Abrams, Stanley. *The Complete Polygraph Handbook*. Lexington, Mass.: Lexington Books, 1989.

Di Maio, Dominick J., and Vincent J. M. Di Maio. *Forensic Pathology, Second Edition*. Boca Raton, Fla.: CRC Press, 2001.

Dix, Jay. *Guide to Forensic Pathology*. Boca Raton, Fla.: CRC Press, 1998.

Ellen, David. *The Scientific Examination of Documents: Methods and Techniques*. Bristol, Pa.: Taylor and Francis, 1997.

Fisher, Barry A. J. *Techniques of Crime Scene Investigation, Seventh Edtion*. Boca Raton, Fla.: CRC Press, 2003.

Gardner, Robert. *Crime Lab 101: Experimenting with Crime Detection*. New York: Walker, 1992.

Genge, Ngaire E. *The Forensic Casebook: The Science of Crime Scene Investigation*. New York: Ballantine Books, 2002.

Hawthorne, Mark. *First Unit Responder: A Guide to Physical Evidence Collection for Patrol Officers*. Boca Raton, Fla.: CRC Press, 1998.

Heard, Brian. *Handbook of Firearms and Ballistics: Examining and Interpreting Forensic Evidence*. New York: John Wiley, 1996.

Inman, Keith and Norah Rudin. *An Introduction to Forensic DNA Analysis*. Boca Raton, Fla.: CRC Press, 1997.

Lee, Henry C. *Advances in Fingerprint Technology*. Boca Raton, Fla.: CRC Press, 2001.

Nickell, Joe. *Detecting Forgery: Forensic Investigation of Documents*. Lexington: University Press of Kentucky, 1996.

Saferstein, Richard. *Criminalistics: An Introduction to Forensic Science, Eighth Edition*. Upper Saddle, N.J.: Prentice Hall, 2003.

## PRIVATE INVESTIGATIONS

Akin, Richard H. *The Private Investigator's Basic Manual*. Springfield, Ill.: Charles C. Thomas, 1979.

Anderson, Kingdon Peter. *Undercover Operations: A Manual for the Private Investigator*. Boulder, Colo.: Paladin Press, 1998.

Dehaan, John D. *Kirk's Fire Investigation, Fifth Edition*. Upper Saddle, N.J.: Prentice Hall, 2002.

Dempsey, John S. *An Introduction to Public and Private Investigations*. Minneapolis/St. Paul, Minn.: West Publishing, 1996.

Golec, Anthony M. *Techniques of Legal Investigation*. Springfield, Ill.: Charles C. Thomas, 1995.

June, Dale L. *Introduction to Executive Protection*. Boca Raton, Fla.: CRC Press, 1998.

Lonsdale, Mark. V. *Bodyguard: A Guide to VIP Protection*. Los Angeles: Specialized Tactical Training Unit, 1995.

Redsicker, David R., and John J. O'Connor. *Practical Fire and Arson Investigation, Second Edition*. Boca Raton, Fla.: CRC Press, 1996.

Riddle, Kelly E. *Insurance Investigations from A to Z, The Investigator's Guide to Uncovering Insurance Fraud*. Austin, Tex.: Thomas Investigative Publications, 1998.

Thomas, Ralph D. *How to Investigate by Computer.* Austin, Tex.: Thomas Investigative Publications, 1999.

## PUBLIC SAFETY

American Red Cross. *Basic Water Rescue.* St. Louis, Mo.: Mosby Lifeline, 1997.

American Red Cross. *Emergency Response, Revised Edition.* St. Louis, Mo.: Mosby Lifeline, 2001.

American Rescue Dog Association. *Search and Rescue Dogs: Training Methods.* New York: Howell Books, 1991.

Braunworth, Brent, and Laurence W. Schlanger. *Street Scenarios for the EMT and Paramedic.* Englewood Cliffs, N.J.: Prentice Hall, 1994.

Brewster, B. Chris, ed. *The United States Lifesaving Association Manual of Open Water Lifesaving.* Englewood Cliffs, N.J.: Prentice Hall, 1995.

Delmar Publishers. *Firefighter's Handbook: Essentials of Firefighting and Emergency Response.* Albany, N.Y.: Delmar, 2000.

Delsohn, Steve. *The Fire Inside: Firefighters Talk About Their Lives.* New York: HarperCollins, 1996.

Farabee, Charles R. *National Park Ranger: An American Icon.* Lanham, Md.: Roberts Rinehart, 2003.

Fox, Deborah. *People at Work in Mountain Rescue.* Parsippany, N.J.: Silver Burdett, 1998.

Garter, Robert. *Exploring Careers in the National Parks.* New York: Rosen Publishing Group, 1993.

Lloyd, Joan E., and Edwin B. Herman. *EMT: Race for Life.* New York: Ivy Books, 1998.

Miller, Charly D. *Jems EMS Pocket Book,* St. Louis, Mo.: Mosby-Year Book, 1996.

Mudd-Ruth, Maria. *Firefighting: Behind the Scenes.* Boston: Houghton Mifflin, 1998.

Muleady-Mecham, Nancy Eileen. *Park Ranger True Stories from a Ranger's Career in America's National Parks.* Flagstaff, Ariz.: Vishnu Temple Press, 2004.

Paul, Caroline. *Fighting Fire.* New York: St. Martin's Press, 1998.

Ray, Slim. *Swiftwater Rescue: A Manual for the Rescue Professional.* Asheville, N.C.: CFS Press, 1997.

Walter, Andrea. *Firefighter's Handbook: Basic Essentials of Firefighting, Second Edition.* Clifton Park, N.Y.: Thomson Delmar Learning, 2004.

Zullo, Allan, Mike Santangelo, and Mara Bovsun. *The Greatest Firefighter Stories Never Told.* Kansas City, Mo.: Andrews McMeel, 2002.

## PHYSICAL SECURITY

Fischer, Robert J., and Gion Green. *Introduction to Security, Seventh Edition.* Woburn, Mass.: Butterworth-Heinemann, 2003.

Heitert, Robert D. *Security Officer's Training Manual.* Englewood Cliffs, N.J.: Prentice Hall, 1993.

Kehoe, Edward P. *The Security Officer's Handbook.* Boston: Butterworth-Heinemann, 1994.

Purpura, Philip P. *Security and Loss Prevention: An Introduction, Fourth Edition.* Boston: Butterworth-Heinemann, 2002.

Sennewald, Charles A. *Security Consulting.* Boston: Butterworth-Heinemann/Elsevier, 2004.

Wade, Leigh. *Careers in Private Security.* Boulder, Colo.: Paladin Press, 2002.

## AVIATION SAFETY AND SECURITY

Echaore-McDavid, Susan. *Career Opportunities in Aviation and the Aerospace Industry.* New York: Checkmark Books/Facts On File, 2005.

Nolan, Michael S. *Fundamentals of Air Traffic Control, Fourth Edition.* Pacific Grove, Calif.: Brooks Cole, 2003.

Sweet, Kathleen M. *Aviation and Airport Security: Terrorism and Safety Concerns.* Upper Saddle River, N.J.: Prentice Hall, 2004.

Wells, Alexander T., ed. *Commercial Aviation Safety, Third Edition.* New York: McGraw-Hill Professional, 2001.

## COMPUTER SECURITY

Bishop, Matt. *Computer Security: Art and Science.* Boston: Addison-Wesley, 2003.

Campen, Alan D., Douglas H. Dearth, and R. Thomas Gooden, eds. *Cyberwar: Security, Strategy, and Conflict in the Information Age.* Fairfax, Va.: AFCEA International Press, 1996.

Bosworth, Seymour, and M. E. Kabay, eds. *Computer Security Handbook, Fourth Edition.* New York: John Wiley, 2002.

Henderson, Harry. *Career Opportunities in Computers and Cyberspace.* New York: Checkmark Books/Facts On File, 2004.

Icove, David, Karl Seger, and William Von Storch. *Computer Crime.* Sebastopol, Calif.: O'Reilly and Associates, 1995.

Kabay, M. E. *The NCSA Guide to Enterprise Security: Protecting Information Assets.* New York: McGraw-Hill, 1996.

Kovacich, Gerald. *The Information Systems Security Officer's Guide: Establishing and Managing an Information Protection Program, Second Edition.* Boston: Butterworth-Heinemann, 2003.

Markoff, John, and Tsutomu Shimomura. *Takedown: The Pursuit and Capture of Kevin Mitnick, America's Most Wanted Computer Outlaw—By the Man Who Did It.* New York: Hyperion, 1996.

Vacca, John R. *Computer Forensics: Computer Crime Scene Investigation.* Hingham, Mass.: Charles River Media, 2002.

## CORRECTIONS

Abadinsky, Howard. *Probation and Parole: Theory and Practice.* Upper Saddle River, N.J.: Prentice Hall, 2003.

Allen, Harry E., and Clifford E. Simonsen. *Corrections in America: An Introduction.* Upper Saddle River, N.J.: Prentice Hall, 2001.

Champion, Dean J. *Probation, Parole, and Community Corrections.* Upper Saddle River, N.J.: Prentice Hall, 2002.

Goodman, Debbie J. *Enforcing Ethics: A Scenario-Based Workbook for Police and Corrections Recruits and Officers.* Upper Saddle River, N.J.: Prentice Hall, 1998.

McCleary, Richard. *Dangerous Men: The Sociology of Parole.* New York: Harrow and Heston, 1992.

Petersilia, Joan, ed. *Community Corrections: Probation, Parole and Intermediate Sanctions.* New York: Oxford University Press, 1997.

Strinchcomb, Jeanne B., and Vernon Brittain Fox. *Introduction to Corrections.* Upper Saddle River, N.J.: Prentice Hall, 1998.

## COMPLIANCE INSPECTIONS

Koren, Herman. *Illustrated Dictionary of Environmental Health and Occupational Safety, Second Edition.* Boca Raton, Fla.: CRC Press, 2004.

Moeller, Dade W. *Environmental Health, Third Edition.* Cambridge, Mass.: Harvard University Press, 1997.

Moran, Mark. *The OSHA Answer Book.* Washington, D.C.: Moran Associates, 2000.

Sparrow, Malcolm. *The Regulatory Craft: Controlling Risks, Solving Problems, and Managing Compliance.* Washington, D.C.: Brookings Institution Press, 2000.

## BUILDING AND CONSTRUCTION INSPECTIONS

Ching, Francis C. K., and Steven R. Winkel, FAIA. *Building Codes Illustrated: A Guide to Understanding the International Building Code.* Hoboken, N.J.: John Wiley, 2003.

Kardon, Redwood. *Code Check: A Field Guide to Building a Safe House.* Newton, Conn.: Taunton Press, 1998.

O'Brien, James J. *Construction Inspection Handbook: Quality Assurance and Quality Control.* New York: Von Nostrand Reinhold, 1998.

## WORKPLACE SAFETY AND SECURITY

Ashton, Indira, and Frank S. Gill. *Monitoring for Health Hazards at Work.* Malden, Mass.: Blackwell Science, 2000.

Della-Giustina, Daniel E. *Safety and Environmental Management.* New York: Von Nostrand Reinhold, 1996.

Gasana, Janvier. *Essentials of Environmental Health Management.* Hallandale Beach, Fla.: Aglob, 2003.

Geller, Scott. *The Psychology of Safety: How to Improve Behaviors and Attitudes on the Job.* Radnor, Pa.: Chilton Book, 1996.

Plog, Barbara A., and Patricia J. Quinlan. *Fundamentals of Industrial Hygiene, Fifth Edition.* Itasca, Ill.: National Safety Council Press, 2002.

Richardson, Margaret. *Managing Worker Safety and Health Excellence.* New York: John Wiley, 1997.

Scott, Ronald. *Basic Concepts of Industrial Hygiene.* Boca Raton, Fla.: Lewis, 1997.

# INDEX

Boldface page numbers denote major treatment of a topic.